Britain on the Couch

To my father, Martin, RIP
and
To CPG and Zigzag

Britain on the Couch

*Why We're Unhappier Compared With 1950
Despite Being Richer*

A Treatment for the Low-Serotonin Society

Oliver James

Century · London

Published by Century in 1997

1 3 5 7 9 10 8 6 4 2

First published in the United Kingdom in 1997 by Century
Random House UK Limited
20 Vauxhall Bridge Road, London SW1V 2SA

Random House Australia (Pty) Limited
20 Alfred Street, Milsons Point, Sydney
New South Wales 2061, Australia

Random House New Zealand Limited
18 Poland Road, Glenfield
Auckland 10, New Zealand

Random House South Africa (Pty) Limited
Endulini, 5a Jubilee Road, Parktown 2193, South Africa

Random House UK Limited Reg. No. 954009

A CIP catalogue record for this book is available
from the British Library

Papers used by Random House UK Limited
are natural, recyclable products made from wood grown in
sustainable forests. The manufacturing processes conform to
the environmental regulations of the country of origin.

ISBN 0 7126 7885 9

Typeset by SX Composing DTP, Rayleigh, Essex
Printed and bound in Great Britain by
Mackays of Chatham, plc, Chatham, Kent

To be discontented with the divine discontent, and to
be ashamed with the noble shame, is the very germ
and first upgrowth of all virtue.

Charles Kingsley, *Health and Education*, 1874

Contents

Acknowledgements

I am indebted to Paul Gilbert of the University of Derby for his enthusiastic encouragement in the early research stages and subsequently for his detailed assistance.

Thanks to all the friends, colleagues and relatives who read various parts of the manuscript and offered their helpful observations, including my mother Lydia, Clare Garner, Professor David Downes, Dr Brett Kahr and Jemima Biddulph.

I am deeply grateful to all the various anonymous individuals who are quoted or described in the book's case histories. Also to the mental health professionals who provided me with anonymous examples of the efficacy of antidepressant pills and therapies.

Many thanks to Mark Booth for taking the book on at Century and for his calming, reassuring, steady hand in the rush to complete it, and a big thank you to my agent Sara Menguc, who persuaded Mark to take it on, having patiently encouraged me over a long period of time to define more precisely what the book should be about.

Preface: What This Book Is About

This book is about the angst of normal people, of people like us. It offers an explanation of why we are so much more likely to be miserable than our grandparents, why we are so discontented and self-attacking ('I'm fat, I'm stupid, I'm ugly', when you are not), why we feel our lives are not under our control, why the moments of emotional richness and freedom of our childhood are less frequent, why so many of us feel there is 'something missing' from our life. It establishes that compared with 1950, there is an epidemic of irritability and aggression, of depression and paranoia, of obsessions, panics, addictions, compulsions, relationships that are not working, careers that dissatisfy, an outbreak of living in the future and pathological re-enactment of the past.

People with most of these problems are more likely than those without to have low levels of the neurotransmitter serotonin, the so-called 'happiness brain chemical'. Given that there is a chemistry of despair, you might suppose that it has a chemical, physical cause. Perhaps the problem is pollution. Is it something to do with the processing of the foods we eat or the methods of cultivation of the raw materials? Maybe the new technologies, such as mobile phones and computers, are interfering with our brains? Although it is not impossible that some of these things are contributing, by far the strongest contender for explaining what has gone wrong is the way we organize our society. I shall show that advanced capitalism, as currently organized, creates low-serotonin societies. Far from being the product of other chemicals, serotonin levels in animal and human brains largely reflect what is happening around them, socially and emotionally, now and in the past. If you are feeling lousy today or in urgent need of a drink or a fix or a fling or a fight, you probably have low serotonin levels caused by the way we live now.

Put crudely, advanced capitalism makes money out of misery and dissatisfaction, as if it were encouraging us to fill the psychic void with material goods. It can also profit from fostering spurious individualism by encouraging us to define ourselves through our purchases, with ever more precisely marketed products that create a fetishistic concern to have 'this' rather than 'that', even though there is often no significant practical or aesthetic difference. It can even make money from restoring the chemical imbalance in our brains which results from these false ambitions and identities, by selling pills and therapeutic services.

I am not suggesting there is a conspiracy by a secret society of top-hat-clad, black-coated bankers and blindly materialistic retailers to make us miserable. Writing of 'advanced capitalism' as if it has volition is to anthropomorphize an abstract entity which has no will of its own (it has no mind and cannot 'do' anything), just as describing genes as 'selfish' is a nonsense. But it must be acknowledged that the way advanced capitalism happens to have evolved, it does very nicely at both ends (creating and curing misery), with our inner lives footing the bill.

Nor am I suggesting that a spiritual renaissance is what is required, and that we must eschew our materialism and return to the simple agrarian life of idealized Noble Savages; rather, that we are suffering from a crucial delusion in believing that we need to be richer as a nation in order to be happier. Increased prosperity is the cornerstone of all major political parties' manifestos and yet, if studies of national well-being are to be believed, voters are mistaken in supposing that greater national wealth will be accompanied by greater happiness. It is a remarkable fact that the relative wealth of a developed nation compared with others does not correlate with its citizens' well-being. Many relatively poor developed nations, such as Ireland, are higher in the 'well-being league table' than much richer nations, such as America and Japan. Once a society passes beyond a basic level of wealth, anything beyond that makes no difference to overall contentment. Advanced capitalism has made most of us physically better off by meeting material and biological needs with unprecedented efficiency, but it has actually made us more prone to low-serotonin problems such as depression and aggression. Although most of us have enough to eat, live in warm accommodation, are able to read and write and have unprecedented choice as to how and where we live, travel and entertain ourselves, at least half of us are suffering from low-serotonin problems at any one time.

As an abstraction, advanced capitalism is currently out of fashion as an explanatory tool compared with 'The Selfish Gene', but in combination they explain a great deal of what has gone wrong since 1950. The new disciplines of evolutionary psychology and psychiatry suggest that advanced capitalism does not meet our primordial needs, evolved over millions of years, for status and for emotional attachment. Our genes were developed to cope with completely different social psychological and technological circumstances from the ones facing us today. For example, most of our adult lives most of us fight a battle against being overweight. This is a wholly new problem in the history of the world, caused in the first instance by the phenomenal success of modern technology in creating diverse and abundant foods. Unfortunately, like all animals, humans were designed to assume that food is scarce and not on the premise that there would be unlimited supplies of highly calorific food available at all times. Advanced capitalism exploits our instinctive tendency to overeat fats and sugars by dressing food products up as 'healthy' or 'nourishing' or 'energy-giving', when what most of us need is plenty of roughage and a lot fewer calories. Having overeaten, we come to hate our shape and to resent our ponderous bodies and so we can be sold diets and diet products. Alternatively, we may starve ourselves. Either way, the net result is an unceasing sense of failure, of a losing battle against over-weight. That we have beaten one of the most enduring challenges to human life – starvation – has actually become a threat to our mental health.

This is just one example (alcohol, tobacco use, the feeling of never having enough time are some others) of how the combination of advanced capitalism and our basic instincts can leave us feeling like losers, even if our status or income would seem to make us winners. The problem extends to some of the cleverest, wealthiest and most attractive people in the land – be they Princess Diana, the Duchess of York, Stephen Fry or Paul Gascoigne. A sharp rise in aspirations and individualism since 1950, necessary for continuous economic growth, has led to an all-consuming preoccupation with our status, power and wealth relative to others. We compare ourselves obsessively, enviously and self-destructively, thus corrupting the quality of our inner lives. No sooner than we achieve a goal, we move the goalposts to create a new, more difficult one, leaving ourselves permanently dissatisfied and depleted, always yearning for what we have not got, a nation of Wannabees.

At the same time, our attachments are falling apart. Despite their greatly improved opportunities, women are dissatisfied in bed and in the workplace. Men are confused and reluctant to accept the new status quo. The result is an unprecedented Gender Rancour and divorce rate, a holo-caust of broken bonds at precisely the point in history when we are demanding vastly more from our relationships than ever before. We are addicts searching for a fix of intensity and intimacy but, ironically, it is the breaking of passionate attachments that is the greatest single cause of despair – the embittered divorcees, the abandoned children, the lonely elderly relatives. We have not yet discovered a way to encourage every member of society to reach for the sky and yet to avoid selfishness and disappointment when he or she falls to earth.

It is neither a necessary condition nor an inevitable destiny of advanced capitalism that it should induce low levels of serotonin. By changing the social environment to one that is more in accord with our species' inherited tendencies we could correct the chemical imbalance. In the short term, low-serotonin individuals can do so through psychotherapy as well as by taking pills. But only changes in the way we are organized as a society will address the fundamental problem.

There is a saying that 'If it ain't part of the solution, it's part of the problem'. My analysis is part of the solution. If the reader feels the evidence presented in the first six chapters is somewhat depressing I would urge him or her to persevere to the last three. These offer unambiguous implications for treating the low-serotonin individual and society.

All chapters except 1 and 2 contain some anecdotal and clinical cases as illustration, but for the most part they consist of scientific theories and evaluation of them in the light of relevant empirical evidence. My earnest hope is that this book will be an interdisciplinary treasure trove of sources from a wide variety of literatures for my scientific peers. However, wherever possible, to make the book accessible to the general reader, detailed technical debates or literature reviews are put in footnotes or appendices.

The introduction is different from all the other chapters in that it offers no scientific evidence to support its contentions. To introduce the themes of the book, I offer some relevant snatches of subjective evidence – anecdotes to evoke some of the psychic territory and social problems – interwoven with brief summaries of each chapter's argument.

To protect anonymity, unless otherwise specified, throughout the book all names have been changed and many factual details altered.

The reader will notice that many of the cases described in the book are middle- or upper-middle-class people. This is because it is their angst which is the most puzzling and seems the hardest to explain. As a group, given their privileged status and increased breadth of opportunity, they ought in theory to be happier compared with 1950, not unhappier. Likewise, there is a high concentration of young women in the cases. Compared with their mothers they have unprecedented opportunities, yet many of them are conspicuous by their unhappiness.

Introduction:
People Like Us

JIM'S CRISIS

Jim seemed an unlikely candidate for a major emotional crisis. Aged 33, he was progressing steadily in his career as a commercial lawyer and at home was Freda, his steady girlfriend. Witty (a Cambridge First), sceptical and popular as well as a bit of a looker (tall, blond, blue-eyed), Jim had no history of 'mental problems' and came from a solid West Country family.

It was not his habit to take drugs, not even marijuana, but during a weekend in Scotland away from Freda with a mate from university days, he was persuaded to take some of the 'rave drug' ecstasy. Within minutes he was panic-stricken. He felt extremely guilty about the fact that he had betrayed Freda sexually (once) and now felt the relationship was valueless; then he worried that his job was going nowhere, that he was a failure and there was no virtue in his line of work; then he feared that at any moment he might 'do something stupid'.

Despite his friend's best efforts to reassure him, there was a steady inflation of the panic as it wore on into the next day and on through the next night to the day of their return. Sleepless for 48 hours, Jim returned to the bosom of a Freda who could scarcely believe the change that the Scottish sojourn had wrought. Twenty-four more hours passed until, after an evening out, I listened at midnight to an answerphone message from a mutual friend imploring me to call whatever the hour I got back. I had not actually met either Freda or Jim but had heard of them through a mutual friend and I roused myself to action.

We have all known people who judder through life hanging onto their sanity by a thread that periodically snaps. They bounce between psy-

1

choanalysis, pill doctors, expensive mental asylums, drug addiction, religion and their Next Big Thing (diet, yoga, homeopathy, Third World travel). It reaches a stage where nothing they can do surprises you. But when a rock-solid Jim goes off the deep end, it's quite a different matter. 'Anyone can go mad, no one is safe' is the scary implication, and unlike those for whom instability is the rule, with the Jims you somehow feel more compelled to take action to return them to their normal state. Although Jim's temporary crisis may be more extreme and acute than anything within the reader's firsthand experience, the story illustrates many of the emotional problems analysed in this book, albeit that they are generally more chronic – a psychic drip, drip, drip, rather than a torrent.

Those with little or no experience of acute psychiatric distress feel ill-equipped to deal with it. Nothing has prepared them for this moment: do you just leave it up to the doctors, or do you try to take a view on the very conflicting ways of looking at the problem that are propounded by all and sundry? How much should you take over the afflicted person's life and how much should you leave them be? The chances are that at some point in your life you will find yourself responsible for a close friend, a relative or a lover who has suddenly stopped being able to be the person they normally are, and if that moment comes, that you will be at a complete loss.

Such was the urgency of the voice on the answering machine that I rang back immediately. Jim's voice was querulous. 'Ummm, I seem to have sort of been having a problem. I'm not sure what it is really, it's, umm, hard to describe. Can you come round now?'

He looked haggard and extremely thin. He had not eaten or slept for three days and had an ethereal, ghostly aspect. He met my eyes more than usually, a gaze that was both beseeching and challenging. You sensed that at any moment he might run out of the room if the emotional climate changed. With Freda's help, he filled me in on the Scottish misadventure and its sequelae.

My first reaction was of relief. Being a clinical psychologist (although I was there not as a professional but as a friend of a friend), I knew that ecstasy can sometimes provoke panic attacks which respond well to tranquillizers and usually soon pass. Clearly it was best to blame it all on dodgy drugs, although I was aware that his friend had consumed the same drug and not been deranged by it. Most of us manage to keep the lid on our inner lives but recreational drugs at the wrong moment can prise it open.

I pushed the dodgy dope theory as strongly as possible. Levels of certain brain chemicals had probably been affected and the first step was to correct the balance with other chemicals. Had they visited a doctor? Jim had already taken the three very weak antianxiety pills (Ativan) that his GP had prescribed that morning, to no effect. I assumed the GP had been anxious about an overdose and given neither strong drugs nor many weak ones for that reason.

Jim had indeed been thinking and talking not only about suicide in general but about specific methods, a strong predictor that a real attempt is on the cards. Whenever I asked him to fill me in on exactly what he had felt in Scotland he shuddered and his face went down on his chest. He was still too frightened to describe it because the words might make it all happen again, he said. From time to time he leapt to his feet, looking extremely agitated. It was now 1.30 a.m. and I could see only one solution.

There were a couple of patients ahead of us in the queue at the hospital Accident and Emergency department. A male nurse took Jim's details and we sat down to wait our turn with the duty doctor. LBC talk radio dribbled on in the background. Every half hour we heard the same news round-up, including (amazingly enough) an item about a man who had thrown himself off Beachy Head. Four round-ups later, the nurse took Jim off for a preliminary examination and I insisted on coming along as moral support. I explained that I imagined what was needed was a stronger antianxiety drug than Ativan. The nurse did not agree. He seemed to be from the New Age school of psychiatry (gold earring, shock of bleached white hair, crystals, reading *The Big Issue*): drugs would only interfere with 'the natural healing process' that he believed was occurring in Jim's mind.

We returned to the half-hourly news summaries. Jim was convinced he would never recover. He told me he was riddled with guilt, that since the crisis had begun he had been masturbating constantly (a common way of trying to create a reliable, pleasant sensation amidst psychic chaos and fear; small children often do it when they are feeling stressed). When the man had thrown himself twice more off Beachy Head, the duty doctor got around to us.

She cannot have been aged more than 24 and was accompanied by a carbuncular youth, a student doctor who looked as if he might pull a girl's pigtails. The duty doctor asked the standard psychiatric questions: 'Do you think anyone is trying to control your thoughts? Have you considered ways of killing yourself? Are there any forces at work in this room that I might not know about?' Jim struggled to answer, requested that the spotty youth leave, and struggled some more.

Eventually, I asked the doctor if it might not be possible to prescribe something like Largactyl, a standard antipsychotic which usually shuts off the flow of grim and crazy thoughts within hours. Oh no, she would have to call in the duty psychiatrist for something like that, she had little experience of this kind of thing and would need a specialist opinion before letting Jim home.

Jim sighed and wondered out loud how long he could stand it. He had been awake for 90 hours and was oppressed by the interminability of his plight. Waiting to feel better was becoming intolerable because he was convinced it would not happen. An hour later we were out, clutching three tablets of 5mg Valium prescribed by the duty psychiatrist down the phone, a pitifully inadequate chemical rejoinder to the ecstasy.

Despite popping all the pills, Jim got only two hours of intermittent sleep and the next day Freda stayed at home from work, at her wits' end that Jim would not recover, despite my repeated assurances to the contrary. At last, through a private GP of my acquaintance, we managed to score some Largactyl and there was a new sense of hope when I left Jim's flat at midnight.

My phone rang at 3 a.m. 'Jim has only slept two hours and he is no better despite the new pills,' said Freda, who had placed all her faith in them.

Jim was sitting hunched up with his arms around his knees in a semi-foetal position. 'It hasn't worked,' he said angrily. 'Nothing works and nothing ever will.' For the first time I began to consider the possibility that he might actually not recover. He was as thin as a parking meter and his eyes were black with exhaustion.

I asked what happened when he tried to sleep or eat and he described a process that sounded very like picking the scab off an infected wound. Whenever he felt drowsy, an interrogative, sneering internal voice would interrupt and keep him awake. The Voice was refusing to eat as well. 'Are you angry?' I said. 'I'm very angry,' he replied.

The obvious way to look at Jim's predicament *is* chemistry. He is a physical system and at that point, a malfunctioning one. The neurotransmitters which make up our thoughts vary from person to person. Most of the chemicals cannot be measured but in a few cases, it has been proven that when levels of one chemical are low, there are predictable mental consequences. Thus, people with low serotonin levels are more likely to be depressed than those with normal ones. When they are given antidepressants, the serotonin level rises and the depression lifts, *quod erat demonstrandum*.

Many psychiatrists believe that the basic levels of our neurotransmitters are regulated by genes. However, it very much 'ain't necessarily so'. The fact that our thoughts and feelings are electro-chemical events tells us nothing in itself about what causes the particular levels; it could be experiences that control them every bit as much as genes.

Studies of rats and monkeys show that levels of neurotransmitters rise and fall predictably according to environmental influences. Levels of serotonin in rats plummet if they have just been beaten up by another rat, whilst the winners' levels soar. If you carry this across to humans, a child that has been abused consistently over many years could easily end up with low serotonin levels, set by that environment rather than genes.

In Jim's case, the ecstasy had clearly been the initial, unambiguously chemical stimulus for his adverse mental state. However, his friend had also chewed the same pills and had no problems. The drugs had brought out something which was already there in Jim, something from his present or past life.

Knowing nothing about Jim's family history, I asked some simple questions, such as 'What sort of people are your parents?' and 'Did you get on better with one than the other as a child?'

His parents had had difficult childhoods. Although it was never discussed, he had somehow found out that both of them had lost one of their parents at a young age and both had mentally ill uncles and aunts. They very much played down the significance of these problems although his father had grown into a heavy drinker (nonetheless successful in his career) and his mother was a rather remote figure. There were plenty of skeletons in their cupboards, the most obviously relevant of which was a fear of mental (and social) abnormality. Jim's current fear of being permanently mad had been in his parents all his life; now it was in him.

Perhaps even more significantly, Jim had been accorded the role of the successful, normal, responsible child among his three siblings, none of whom had achieved much by comparison. Jim was their embodiment of health and the idea of telling his parents about his current problems made him visibly shudder. They would be devastated to see their model child broken.

As we talked, Jim's lucidity returned in snatches. He became able for the first time to really feel angry with his parents for having made him be such a goody-goody. He wondered if his current refusal to let the Largactyl settle him down – the inner voice picking at the scab – might not partly be a wish not to return to his pre-morbid state. Maybe the New Age nurse had not been so far off the mark after all: the ecstasy had set off a process of revolution that Jim was not prepared to quash. As he talked about his career he realized it had been less meaningful to him than he had always believed, that pleasing others was a central preoccupation.

He had spent his life comparing himself with others and had never had much opportunity to ask what he himself actually wanted. If he allowed the pills to work he would, in a sense, be no longer acknowledging his distress at a status quo which he desperately needed to challenge, however frightening the experience.

Not a very therapy-minded person at the best of times, Freda displayed understandable alarm at my line of questioning. It did not seem the right moment for Jim to be having blinding realizations about his childhood. In general, this intuition was correct – when people lose the plot it is often a bad idea to start debating the finer points of their psychic script; it can be confusing, distressing and make matters even worse. But in this case it seemed as if Jim was forcing us to engage with him about these matters. Before I had arrived he had been fragile, his confidence all shot away, and I have no doubt that the conversation was crucial in giving recognition to real, deep-seated problems which the ecstasy had brought to the surface. Jim was insisting that these be acknowledged and not just drugged away.

The proof of this pudding was that after our talk Jim slept for six consecutive hours. Over the next four days there were daily crises when Jim would fear that he was slipping back into the panic. 'I am feeling okay except that I keep worrying that I will never be better' – the fear of fear and of permanent insanity. He was also bored stiff and we watched supposedly soothing, amusing films such as *Groundhog Day*, only to find something apocalyptic in the most innocent scenes and storylines.

As the days passed, Freda began to get a bit fed up with Jim. She wondered if he might not be putting on an act to get attention sometimes, just as mothers may wonder if their babies are crying to manipulate them. Jim had become very like a toddler, insecure if there was no one familiar around, so we had to make sure one of us (usually Freda) was with him at all times. Once we talked it over, Freda realized that Jim had regressed into a child and that she must mother him; I repeated again and again that it would not be for ever.

During the succeeding week Jim was more depressed than panicky but the depression was suicidal. Freda took him to an NHS doctor who prescribed the antidepressant Prozac. Luckily his employers were extremely sympathetic, one of his bosses having had a 'bad trip' when a student, so there was no pressure from that quarter. For another three days I would see Jim or speak to him twice a day but then the frequency gradually dropped off. The Prozac kicked in after two weeks and from then on, Jim stopped being depressed.

However, he did not simply blank out the whole episode and return to being a machine for pleasing his parents. He began therapy in order to build on what he had learnt about himself. First he went to a cognitive therapist (see Appendix III for definitions of mental health professionals) who tried to help him identify the irrational thoughts that passed through his mind and to develop mental strategems as an antidote. However, being highly educated and intelligent, Jim felt these were too crude and simplistic. Whilst cognitive treatments are often very helpful, Jim felt it was not really addressing his 'deeper problems'. He stopped going and switched antidepressants, to Lustral, a similar drug to Prozac but one which can be taken in small doses. After 18 months he still had the feeling that there was something he needed to get to the bottom of and Freda was getting a bit fed up with having to listen to him banging on about himself. So he went to a psychoanalyst for twice-weekly psychotherapy (see Appendix III) to talk about the childhood origins of his problems, still continuing to take the smallest dose of Lustral. The new therapy was a great success. Indeed, Jim's story had such a happy ending that he feels now that he is glad he had his crisis; without it he would 'still be in the grip of my past'. Today he has a much more balanced view of his life, less concerned with what everyone else wants for him, more concerned to find what is important for him . . . and his chemical balance is better as a result.

WHAT JIM'S STORY ILLUSTRATES

There have always been low-serotonin individuals and doubtless, there always will be. But compared with a Jim in 1950, a great many fundamental changes have occurred which place 1990s Jim at higher risk of having low serotonin. From a very young age he was under constant pressure to compare his performance in all spheres of his life with that of others, so much so that his self-confidence was extremely brittle. Even though he was doing well and had always done so, Jim felt subordinated by these comparisons. He was constantly under the impression that he was not doing well compared with the impossibly high standards he was set. Since 1950, expectations have risen dramatically for personal and professional fulfilment (especially among young women as well as men, as we shall see). Likewise, demands for individualism have inflated. The media (particularly television), increased hours spent at school and competitiveness there and increased pressure to compete at work make us obsessively preoccupied with how we are doing compared to others and whether we are individual enough. Filled with these new needs, Jim was exhausted and dispirited before he took any ecstasy. Until then, the only drugs he had used for solace were alcohol and cigarettes, but like most

7

people of his generation, he was prescribing these for himself to keep his spirits up, stave off discontent and stifle a nagging unease. That ecstasy should have provoked his crisis is fitting since it is the drug of choice for today's youth: it raises serotonin levels soon after ingestion, but in many cases, levels crash when the drug wears off.

Equally typical were the solutions to Jim's individual crisis. Pills which raise serotonin levels are already widely prescribed. There were 5.6 million prescriptions for antidepressants in Britain in 1995 and as these drugs become increasingly side-effect free, it is possible (probable, I believe) that they will become endemic among members of low-serotonin societies. Likewise, therapy is increasingly popular (and will continue to be so). That the combination of the two eventually helped Jim out of his pit of despair is a common experience. They are not the solution to the low-serotonin society but for the low-serotonin individual, they are the best we have.

PEOPLE LIKE US: AN ANECDOTAL INTRODUCTION TO THE BOOK'S CONTENTS

A combination of our individual genes and upbringing leave all of us more or less vulnerable to developing low-serotonin problems in later life – let us say, at high, medium or low risk. But whether the risk is realized depends on the kind of society that the fledgeling adult emerges into. In this model, high-risk people would develop problems unless the society they were in was extremely benign. Medium-risk people could survive in more malign conditions and low-risk people would have to be in an extremely toxic society to succumb.

In addition, the proportion of people emerging from childhood with varying risks varies from society to society. In some societies, childcare practices and genes might mean that, for example, only 10% of the population emerged into adulthood at high risk, 20% at medium risk and 70% at low risk, whereas other societies might have the opposite proportions (70% high, 20% medium, 10% low).

Thus, the number of low-serotonin people in a society depends on two issues: how many have low-serotonin-inducing childhoods and genes; and how emotionally toxic the society is once they become adults. This reasoning creates several conceptual possibilities in explaining the rise in the proportion of low-serotonin adults since 1950.

Firstly, as an explanation of what has changed since 1950, changes in our collective genes (as opposed to the individual genetic differences between us) can be ruled out. It takes many centuries for a gene pool – genetic stock – to change, so a change in any human trait over a 50-year period could not be due to changes in genes.

However, secondly, it could be that more of us have had low-serotonin-inducing upbringings. Upbringing changes considerably from generation to generation and has done so between 1950 and today. Jim's childhood and that of his peers was considerably different in many important respects from that of his parents. These patterns are themselves determined by the wider society. New patterns of parental behaviour, such as the increased divorce rate or pressure to succeed at school, have almost certainly increased the proportion of people emerging from childhood with high and medium risk of low serotonin compared with 1950.

Thirdly, the society could have become more emotionally toxic for adult members, increasing the proportions of at-risk people who actually go on to fulfil their low-serotonin potential. For example, social class and gender have an enormous influence both on the kind of upbringing you have and on the role you occupy in society, and they influence rates of low-serotonin. Women are twice as likely to say they are depressed as men and people from low, compared with high, social classes are generally much more likely to be both depressive and aggressive. Changes in our class structure and gender roles could lead to changes in rates of low-serotonin people – as they have. Likewise, as we shall see, the introduction of television and changing values have profoundly affected our expectations and contentment.

Thus the object of this book is to explain the shift from a relatively benign to a relatively toxic society, creating a higher proportion of people that emerge from childhood at risk of low serotonin and increasing the likelihood that vulnerable individuals will express their low-serotonin potential.

A reasonably straightforward example of the differences between vulnerable individuals is the Money family (this is their real name). I interviewed them for a *Horizon* BBC2 television programme in 1995.

Michael Money, then aged 29, had a history of violence and minor criminality in his teenage and early twenties. He works in casual jobs and is single. By contrast, his brother David, aged 30, is law-abiding, has had a steady job as a warehouseman for 13 years driving fork-lift trucks and has been happily married for two years. Their parents, Maureen and Terry, separated when Michael was aged 11.

What accounts for the difference between these two brothers? Here is the rebellious Michael's account of himself and his family:

'David's a total opposite. He took lots of exams at school, he stuck it out. He got himself married, stayed with the same girl, never strayed, I see him as responsible and reliable, all the things that I would like. I wish I could swap places with him.

'I never used to like him and he didn't like me. We get on better now that we don't see each other so much, he's an OK geezer.

'When my dad left, David stuck by my mum more than I did. He took on the father role and me and him used to fight nonstop then. He gets on better with my father than me.

'I've no time for my dad. He was a joke really. He'd put about four or five pints of strong beer down his neck really quickly, climb into his 3-litre Monza motor, piss off to Dorking and wonder why he pranged the motor! When he started seeing his bird in our house during the day when my mum was at work I'd think, He's upstairs shagging some old bird, and my mum is the most attractive woman on the planet. Even at a young age I found it hard to understand.

'When my mum sold the house she got me brother sorted out, and this is what hurt: all she said to me was, "You've got to find somewhere else to live for yourself", about two weeks before we had to leave.'

David's account was as follows:

'Mike hangs around with a very different sort of crowd: wide boys, likes flash cars, booze, girls. I like the intellectual side of life, books, films, that sort of thing. I save every penny and I enjoy my life with Linda.

'Mike says to me, "At least I'm not boring like you, sitting indoors all the time, doing nothing." I say, "But you'll be nothing if you carry on like this." But he's like the Trotters from *Only Fools and Horses* [a BBC television series about a pair of 'wide-boy' brothers] – "Ooh, I'll have made my fortune by the time I'm old" – it's always just around the corner.

'He idealizes people he meets. Everyone's a "Diamond Bloke" until he meets the next one, he loves all that cockney spiel. He sees a lot of people, drifts in and out of friendships and relationships.

'I wouldn't say he is a violent man. During that skinhead craze in the Eighties he used to go round beating up language-school kids, foreigners, but that was just letting off steam. I went through some trouble at school as well as Mike, but I was more devious.

'The divorce happened at the wrong time for both of us. I took on board what my grandpa said to me at the time: "You've got to look after your ma now, be the head of the family."

'Basically Mike looked for role models outside the family after the divorce and got in with a bad set. I was very lucky in the people I took as my models.

'Mike is like my parents in all the wrong ways. He bottles things up and needs a drink to open up, like my dad. He's like my mum in that he's very highly strung.'

Michael and David recognize that they were very different and both agree that their relationship with their parents was also different. Some of the explanation for these differences emerges when we hear from their mother, Maureen:

'I suffered postnatal depression after Michael was born. He wasn't a very good sleeper so I was really down in the dumps a lot. When he was one I had to go out to work and I left him with a childminder. She kept Michael in a wet nappy all day so that he was red raw when I got him home – I suppose nothing like that happened to David.

'As a boy he was very mischievous. I had a job getting him to school and he didn't concentrate very much there, he liked to clown about. Punishing him was like banging your head against a brick wall. He played truant, I forever had the school inspector up and he was involved with the police. I had to get him from the police station.

'David was more serious. He thought he ought to be the man of the house after Terry [Maureen's husband] had gone but Michael thought otherwise and there was a lot of fighting between them.

'When Terry left, Michael really did want to go with him, I don't know why. Terry said, "No, you'd better stay with your mum" and that did turn Michael against his dad.

'Terry had a different relationship with Michael than with David, and so did I. We always seemed to rub each other up the wrong way, we really clashed, I don't know why. Even now I'm afraid of what I say to Michael just in case we row. To me he's always been the baby, most vulnerable.'

Obviously these fragments leave a lot of unanswered questions, but they illustrate that siblings are mostly as different from each other as people who are not related by blood and the main reason is that they have very different relationships with their parents and subsequently, search out different environments for themselves. Differences between individuals in some aspects of personality, intelligence and mental health are undoubtedly affected by genetics but it is the way parents relate to their children and the position the child occupies in the family system that is most important in most cases. This provides the starting point for my analysis: if patterns of childcare are so influential on individual personality, then if they changed society-wide, it could increase the proportion of subsequent adults at risk of low-serotonin problems.

WHY WE FEEL LIKE LOSERS: STATUS AND THE WAY WE LIVE NOW

On first meeting Juliet I doubt you would consider her anything other than an attractive, intelligent, well-adjusted, confident, thriving individual. But as with most people, when you get to know her better you find all sorts of hitherto invisible complexities and problems. In her case, for much of the time she is plagued by doubts and confusion and is mildly depressed. Aged 25, her present and past life illustrate many of the low-serotonin problems with which this book is concerned and I shall be using her case to illustrate several other chapters as well.

She attended 'St Luke's', one of the most competitive girls' schools in the world, progressed to Oxford and today works in an exacting, high powered profession. In terms of her education and career, she is representative of the privileged British upper-middle-class élite. If wealth, social status and education increase happiness, then she and her peers more than almost any other group in our society should be happy, yet that is hardly the adjective which springs to mind when describing her prevailing mood, nor is it applicable to many, perhaps most, of her peers.

An only child, Juliet's parents divorced when she was aged ten but she recalls already showing signs of emotional distress before then. 'I became aware of my brain when I was seven and started to "do patterns": walking in sevens and thinking in sevens, I remember learning my seven times table, which started it. I had a notebook where you wrote down "2 times 7 = 14, 3 times 7 = 21" and so on and I spent a lot of time looking through that, for some reason. I was quite introspective. There are loads of pictures of the "lone figure on a beach" variety.' Her obsessionalism was funnelled into her academic work – 'I was doing well at school, I always have' – but despite this success, as she entered puberty she was already suffering from low-serotonin problems. She had a lack of self-confidence and was depressed. She felt very lonely and sometimes unreal, so much so that she would cut her wrists lightly with a razor blade. 'At least I felt something when I did that. Obviously it was also a pathetic "plea for help" kind of thing, as well.' She averagely smoked, drank and drugged at Oxford and felt desperately unhappy. During her early twenties she developed Chronic Fatigue Syndrome, which required her to alter her behaviour.

'Illness totally changes your approach to drugs and alcohol and things like keeping fit. I know that there's a big conflict going on between being self-destructive and having a chance to be happy. There's something so convenient about Chronic Fatigue: it forces you not to drink massive amounts, to eat regularly and well, to sleep, and all the rest of it, which just happens to be a sensible way of going on, whether ill or not. I've always had this tension between keeping myself well and resisting doing so, this incredible compulsion to do the wrong fucking thing. I used to lose my brace from my orthodontist and I would be so fucking bewildered and upset and depressed, and then I'd do the same thing the next week. I used to get my friends to help me climb through the bins at school to find the brace among the leftovers from the dinners. The same sort of thing happens with any kind of illness I have (which are always chronic and stress-related – surprise, surprise): I don't deal with them.'

Juliet qualified for a diagnosis of minor depression on her only visit to a psychiatrist, like millions of other women of her generation: a 25-year-old woman today is between three and ten times (depending on which study you read) more likely to be depressed than her grandmother was at the same age. Few of us are free from the unending conflict between living healthy lives and the short-term gratification of drugs of solace (including food as well as tobacco, alcohol and illegal drugs) and other compulsions (such as overwork and gambling). Many of us feel permanently run down, below par emotionally, highly irritable (e.g. prone to 'road rage'), and we seek these temporary reliefs for our low serotonin, even though many of them only serve to make matters worse in the longer term.

The starting point for my explanation is the research showing that serotonin levels correlate with relative social status in male vervet monkeys. High-status vervets have high levels of serotonin, low-status ones, low levels. If the status changes, the level follows suit. When vervets are given serotonin-raising drugs their status rises as a result, but in natural conditions it is the status which causes the serotonin levels: when vervets rise up the hierarchy their levels go up after the rise has occurred. Applied to humans, this makes sense. Overall, the groups most at risk of low-serotonin problems such as depression and violence are also most likely to be of low status: women and people of low income. But if this were all there was to be said, it would merely be to add low serotonin to the long list of nasty things that happen to women and the lower classes in developed nations. The interesting thing is that modern life has achieved the feat of making even high-status people – even upper-middle-class people like Juliet and Jim – feel subordinate and inferior and therefore develop low serotonin levels. Maladjusted and excessive 'social comparison' are the first means by which this occurs.

Modern life fails to meet a fundamental human need that evolved millions of years ago – for rank, for a status in relation to others. It has a remarkable facility for inducing a feeling of subordination in us, of making us feel like losers even if we are winners. Originally, during our evolution, the low self-esteem, shame, guilt, humiliation, hopelessness and helplessness (feelings of depression) that resulted from subordination served a useful function and they still do so amongst primates such as monkeys. By behaving in a depressed way, low-status monkeys indicate their recognition of their inferiority to stronger, more powerful ones and thereby avoid the potentially life-threatening physical attacks which posing a threat could provoke. But we have moved on a long way since then and today depression no longer serves any useful purpose for humans. It is a redundant inheritance from our primeval ancestry.

Although it is true that in general, people with objectively low status, power and wealth are more at risk of suffering low-serotonin problems, it is also true that the higher echelons are now very much at risk as well. Even 'the most beautiful woman in the world' who married 'the most eligible bachelor' has been touched by the epidemic of depression and eating disorders which has plagued young women for the second half of the twentieth century. But why on earth should Princess Diana, a raving beauty of the highest imaginable status, have these problems?

One answer may be that she compares herself too often with too many people in ways that leave her feeling inadequate and insecure. Almost certainly, she wishes she could have the happy marriage of her friends X and Y, wishes she had obtained the O and A levels and university degrees of her female peers, and most astonishing of all, feels fat or ugly compared with the models or actresses who are her competitors in the beauty stakes. In this she is truly iconic of a generation of wannabees, who feel much the same as her about themselves.

Depressed people have a disastrous tendency to compare themselves to an excessive extent with others. Just doing that increases their risk of feeling they fall short of the standard; but even worse, they do not use comparison with admired others to improve themselves because they do not make appropriate allowances when doing so. If I compare myself upwards to the golfer Tiger Woods without taking into account the fact that he was born with an extraordinary talent which he has devoted his whole life to nurturing, my confidence will suffer. It is crazy if I say to myself, 'You're not much cop at golf, look how much better Tiger Woods hits the ball', yet too many of us are constantly doing something equivalent to just that.

Equally destructive is to make 'discounts' when comparing downwards. If (as is usually the case) I thrash my friend Hugo on the golf course and if I say to myself, 'I should have beaten him by even more, *given that he hardly ever plays and has had no lessons*', then I gain no solace from the experience. No wonder if I reach for the first drugs of solace that come to hand on reaching the club house. Not only have I humiliated myself by my comparison with Tiger Woods, I have done nothing to repair the damage by beating Hugo. If I compare myself in these ways persistently, it will do nothing to help me feel good and go a long way to making me feel bad.

These problems start early. Aged seven to nine, children begin to make plentiful social comparisons and this is often accompanied by a significant dousing of their mood at school and a dislike thereof.

Juliet can recall that from a young age: 'I tried to do well. You had to do writing and you had to copy out poems by that awful Walter De la Mare or draw patterns through tracing paper. I used to try hard.' Around the age of nine she can remember becoming highly competitive with peers. 'There was an occasion when we had to do a project and I got the same number of points as my friend Jessy and she got a higher mark than me and I remember thinking, This is really out of order. The head bully at the school was Adam (who's now a stand-up comic – bastard), he did very well as well, it was the three of us. He came from a very mixed-up background and I remember thinking it was odd that he spent all his time being a bastard and didn't come across as a hard worker or anything, and although I usually beat him he still did well. I had to compete for friends there. Jess was in with the trendy girls, and I had to compete for her.'

Note how detailed and complex were Juliet's comparison criteria even at age nine. She was already taking Adam's disturbed background into account, feeling put down by the fact that he could succeed despite it and despite his lack of application. Instead of feeling good by concentrating on the fact that she was one of the top three, she made comparisons with his success which made her feel inadequate.

Aged 11 Juliet had to take common entrance exams to gain access to the highly competitive St Luke's. 'I wasn't particularly interested. I wanted to go to the local school where all my friends were going and where my siblings had gone. I was developing a nostalgia for things my family had done because it was pretty fractured. I think it was Mum's idea that I go in for St Luke's but she was already going out with Steven [her stepfather] and he exerted quite an influence in that direction: it was really "not on" for me to go to a comprehensive; his kids from his first marriage were all at boarding school and he expected everybody to go to Oxbridge. He went to Oxford, he thinks it's important. I didn't have a clue.

'I sat exams for four different places. I got into all of them and was offered a scholarship at one. I was quite excited about that because I'd been really precocious and everyone was making jokes about it because it was a bit of a scam. I'd just been to a Lowry exhibition with Mum and that was the artist that I was asked about in the interview and was able to talk all about it. I remember getting quite shirty when I got something wrong, some Gerald Durrell book, *Beasts in My Belfry*, and the interviewer asked me what a belfry was and I got it wrong. I thought it was a basement and a place where you have bells is just not generally a basement! I was quite cross about having got it wrong. Anyway, I hated that school because they all wore purple or yellow or something. I wanted to go to another one because they had flowers, but in the end I said I didn't care and they could make the decision, so they sent me to St Luke's.

'The first day was pretty scary, the first year pretty horrible. It was extremely competitive and pressuring. I felt completely out of place, a lot of them had been to the same prep school and knew each other. They'd done a lot more of the work before, a lot more. I'd only done English, Maths, Art, Games and Weather, never done any History, Geography or Science; but I suppose I coped with the work OK, although I started to not do work when I got there. I managed to get away with doing very little. I was in the top class for English and I thought I could be really good at that. Science I was fucking dreadful at, didn't understand and wasn't interested in at all. History I hated, felt as if nothing would ever sink in. I was depressed, I think, I felt very lonely. I did feel sort of bullied when other people blanked you or didn't speak to you. I made some friends who were oddbods on the fringes.'

Thus it was that after entering the subordinating environment of St Luke's Juliet began to show persistent signs of low serotonin.

One of the most dramatic changes compared with 1950 is the increased aspirations of women and people of low incomes. Where once they were required to live subordinate lives with no expectation of significant improvement in their material and psychosocial circumstances, today they are encouraged to have sky-high expectations and to believe they are entitled to fulfil them. Unfortunately, aspirations and sense of entitlement far outstrip opportunity in the great majority of cases. This creates a state of 'Relative Deprivation', a feeling that compared with the deserved outcome, the current reward is inadequate.

St Luke's has existed from long before 1950 and it has always been extremely exacting. It has not changed much but there have been several crucial changes in the families from which its girls come, reflecting the society in which they live. Increased aspirations and individualism, the media, and increased levels of educational and career competition have made its alumni and their peers of both sexes at greater risk of low-serotonin problems. At St Luke's in the 1980s, not only were the girls competing in the classroom, they were competing to be individuals and to be physically attractive. The intensity of this competition is what was different from the 1950s.

Until her last year at St Luke's, Juliet felt she was a social failure but eventually she found a way to make a mark. 'When I was 17 I bumped into a friend who had been expelled and she was at a Further Education college where all the cool people were and that rang bells because my brother had been there and I started going to gigs [performances by rock groups] which was very nerve-racking because I didn't know how to socialize with those sorts of people, but it really helped because I started to wear their sorts of clothes and to express myself with clothes. I'd come into school and at first people just thought it was ridiculous because I looked like a Goth or a Grunge Kid, but after a bit they started coming up to say I looked cool and it was most peculiar. I realized I was getting a completely different reaction off people because nobody else looked like that at school. Once I'd been doing it for a while they'd see the style on a poster and I began to feel – or at least look – more confident.

'I never worked out before how you got to know people, what you said, I never felt I asked the right questions, felt that what I asked was really obvious. So I concentrated on learning to ask the right questions which didn't give away what you didn't know and sounded like you were making quite an interesting point, when actually all you wanted was to know where the bloody toilets were.'

But having discovered how to be perceived as an individual, there remained one area in which Juliet still felt like a failure. 'The key criterion for success at that age was being trendy. At one stage it was having a matching dress and socks, another year it was ankle boots, the next it was something else – clothing, bag, hair, shoes – always appearance. There was no uniform, whereas at my previous school they had been very strict on uniform and you had to clean your plimsolls yourself. If they came in too clean they would say, "Your mum's put them through the washing machine, do them again." I quite got along with that.

'As a system for creating low self-esteem St Luke's certainly succeeded in my case. The Full House of things you needed were to be brilliant at work, really sexy and very individual, which do not usually go together – although there were about ten a year who managed it. X has done well as an actress, Y went to an American university and then to Cambridge and I think she's an up-and-coming pop star now. Z did all those things although she's miserable. Very individual and beautiful, she did some modelling, none of them did academia.

'I think physical appearance is important to all teenagers. I don't think anybody at that age believes you're going to be happy and have a good life through doing well in your work or career but appearance would be greater for girls. Girls have always been evaluated by how they look, it's what you know about girls. Girls are famous for what they look like a lot of the time, as models and actresses, celebrities. A lot of girls who were bright and more popular than me, they were also more attractive. Quite a lot of girls in my year actually were real paid-up models or are actresses and really were just perfect physically and in appearance. They had things like perfect skin and they knew what to do about make-up and what to wear – it was a mixture of Gaultier and Oxfam – and they were the ones who didn't give a toss about boyfriends! It was just so confusing, but it was such a high standard. St Luke's really did seem to have lot of very beautiful people in it and I did not feel much cop by comparison.

'So perhaps I've got a warped sense of what I look like but I've never thought of myself as beautiful. I've always thought of myself as somebody who looks OK, not really ugly not really beautiful, can look quite good if I really make an effort. I think I've got a nice figure but I've really always wanted to be pretty. I really have, and it's been a really important thing that's gone through and it's been quite difficult to cope with, being bright and knowing why I want to be pretty and that there are lots of horrendous reasons (feminist conspiracy ones or otherwise) why this is the case, and having been taught by a very feminist woman teacher and all that sort of thing. I find it very problematic that I do, but I would love to look different from how I look, not necessarily more stupid but more glamorous, and that's a product of what I've seen around me.

'Many of us had eating disorders – mostly anorexia – although I didn't; but I was definitely funny about food, I had Food Phobia.'

Of course, women have always been evaluated by their looks but the bombardment of Juliet's generation with media images of beautiful women and girls is a completely new phenomenon, and although Juliet's school was exceptional, it shows how subordinated a woman can feel if constantly surrounded by more attractive ones. Experimental studies show that young women feel worse about themselves after being shown pictures of beautiful women compared with women shown average ones. Young men have higher standards for what they would regard as attractive after seeing beauties rather than average women. Given the pressure to be clever and individual, the demand to be beautiful as well led Juliet to have an enduringly negative self-image.

Some of these changes compared with 1950 are particularly applicable to women, but the greater amount of time spent at school *per se* and the hugely increased competitiveness when there applies as much to boys.

Frank was tall, well built and every inch the perfect schoolboy at his major public school. He was head of everything there was to be head of, sporting, prefecture and academic. The teachers in charge of the different activities vied for his services, like soccer managers head-hunting an especially promising young star. Just as some of his contemporaries attracted punishment for smoking and other crimes, he attracted responsibility, yet apart from in cross-country running, he never showed any exceptional skills on the playing fields. He seemed an uncreative, even an empty vessel but he was extremely successful.

A scholarship to Oxbridge and a Blue for rowing in the Boat Race in his first year followed. On the first morning of his second-year university exams he set off from the house he shared with friends. When he had not returned at 2 a.m. they became worried. He appeared 48 hours later with little memory of the intervening time. Forced to drop back a year, 12 months later he set off again to attempt the fence of these exams which, to a man of his calibre, should have been like jumping a row of matchboxes. But exactly the same happened as before. This time he took a year out before finally graduating with a Third Class degree.

During his year out he had travelled and on graduation he took off again, ending up in a southern European city. He is still there today, 18 years later, teaching English as a foreign language to support a regime of remarkable sexual promiscuity. Aged 42, he truly does seek a new sexual conquest every single day, despite being recently married, and just as he excelled at school, now he excels in promiscuous sex.

Frank's obsession with high achievement consumed his self. He had learnt to define himself so utterly through comparing his performance to others that he had completely lost sight of any purpose it might serve for him. Frank's self-definition was almost indivisible from external success, and when he left the little society that was his school and had choice, he quickly discovered there was no 'him' to make the choices. He had become wholly subordinated to the system of winning and losing. Only by escaping to a foreign land where he had no history could he begin the process of finding out what he wanted. But unlike Jim, he has received no treatment to help him and he languishes in a repetitive, compulsive loop of pointless achievement, with sex merely having replaced academia and sport as the challenge.

This is the death that so many people suffer today: death by social comparison. If we make all our self-esteem so contingent on external standards, we run a huge risk of feeling like failures. Even if we succeed in these terms there will always be someone better than us.

HOW BROKEN ATTACHMENTS AND GENDER RANCOUR MAKE US FEEL LIKE LOSERS

The impulse to form emotional bonds with others is found in almost all humans at all times and places in history, and in evolutionary terms, it makes a great deal of sense. If a woman was to reproduce her 'selfish genes' back in the primordial swamp it was advisable to have a man to protect and provide for her whilst she was caring for the children, and if he wanted his offspring to thrive, it was advantageous to the man to perform this role. The bonds between children and parents made similar sense, as did a genetic tendency to form groups and to make alliances and friendships. In short, there is a clear logic to the idea that we have inherited a tendency to develop warm feelings and intimate relationships and that if we do not, we are penalized by loneliness and ill health.

Unfortunately, advanced capitalism has not evolved to meet these needs very well. We are increasingly likely to live alone, the care of children has become increasingly erratic and the elderly are liable to be left to fend for themselves in unnaturally lonely, estranged circumstances. But above all these things, like an infected wound that keeps being reinfected, we divorce and separate from our partners vastly more than in 1950.

There are two main damaging effects of the divorce epidemic. The first is upon the adult participants themselves. Divorcees are much more likely to suffer almost every imaginable low-serotonin problem than people in intact relationships. The cry of their anguish is to be heard throughout popular culture, a sad refrain in pop songs, soap operas, feature films and magazines.

The second damage is to the offspring. Increased aggression and delinquency in the boys is accompanied by increased risk of educational underperformance, depression and of being divorcees themselves, in their sisters. For once the more or less insincere adoption of an issue by politicians is correct: the rusting of The Family corrodes social cohesion and mental health.

Had Juliet been aged ten in 1900 it is extremely unlikely that her parents would have divorced. In that year the total number of divorces in England and Wales was 590, whereas in 1993, the number was 165,000. The divorce of Juliet's parents undoubtedly had a significant effect on her serotonin levels at the time and continues to do so today.

'When I was ten we moved to a new home without my father. Eventually I asked my sister, a year later maybe, when Dad was going to be joining us and she said, "Oh, he's not. Hasn't Mum told you?" and I said, "No," and she said, "Oh they're getting a divorce." In fact they might have already got one. Apparently he contested custody for me and there was a hearing.

'I don't think I realized there were problems in their marriage beforehand but Mum says I must have. I certainly remember being completely bloody miserable at the time. There were occasional fights, there were arguments, I didn't really know any different. Apparently my dad had been having affairs and he was an alcoholic and still is. I don't think he was drunk very often but he was very aggressive sometimes, not physically to any of us, but he was really hard on people.'

Juliet has no doubt that her difficult father and her parents' unhappy relationship has affected her feelings about men. 'Oh God no, I don't trust men to look after me. I feel phenomenally uncomfortable about being looked after by anyone. I really want it and think I would like it, but it's like people giving you massages, you just know they're going to stop too early.'

The collapse of marriage and of the close social networks that characterized our ancestors is a major cause of low-serotonin problems: depression, aggression, compulsions. It is particularly visible among young women today, who seem to be caught in a viciously confusing and destabilizing stage in the evolution of a new order in relations between the genders. As their rates of smoking, drinking and other signs of distress rocket, they seem torn between the goals of pursuing a career and forming stable attachments. But men are also deranged by the emerging new status quo. They often loathe the bold assertiveness of younger women and feel cheated when their partners become working mothers. I believe there has never been a time in history when the battle of the sexes has been more bloody.

Evolutionary theory predicts that women have an instinct to care for children and that men are born breadwinners. When confronted by the scientific evidence, this theory emerges as highly debatable.

On the one hand, it is far too early to come to any firm conclusions about inborn tendencies in regard to work and gender. As children, today's adults were subject to persistent, well-proven gender biases in childcare and at school, before emerging into a society which still has a long way to go before it offers genuine equality of opportunity.

On the other hand, it must be admitted that women have not raced into the workplace with as much enthusiasm as might have been expected. According to one researcher, full-time work by women has not increased at all in Britain for 150 years, despite the much greater opportunities: all the increase in work by women since 1950 has been in part-time jobs. The main reason seems to be that when women have children they either drop out of the workforce altogether during their offspring's earliest years or they work part-time. Thus, in 87% of families where the youngest child is aged three, the mother does not work full-time – only 13% of under three-year-olds have a full-time working mother.

There have been some dramatic changes in the options open to women and although they have been clearly beneficial in many cases, there also seems to be considerable confusion and anxiety provoked by the difficult choices that result. Overall, the evidence shows that the best thing for both mother and child is if the mother does what she really wants. Mothers who stay at home to care for the child full-time but who would prefer to be working are at grave risk of depression. But mothers who work full-time and wish they were not doing so are equally at risk. So much choice, combined with very mixed messages from their childhood socialization, the wider society and from their menfolk, places a considerable 'role strain' on women and can provoke depression.

Juliet has the typically mixed feelings of a woman of her age and background. Part of her would like to give up her extremely exhausting career, have babies and concentrate on writing fiction. Another part feels nervous about relying on a man for her subsistence and would like to hang on to the control that her present profession gives her. 'It's not really heading towards caring for a baby and writing is it? I can't risk being an artist because I know many, many of them and none are a success financially or recognized in other ways, even though they're good. I do what I do well and that should satisfy me, although I expect that I will then want a more senior role. But I am more comfortable with a structure. I feel too unstable when I'm doing something unstructured. I want a timetable and to stick to it.

'I just don't know where to go from here at all. Like, if this was a board game, I always assume it's my go for a start: "Oh yeah, sorry it's my go," I'll go, "Umm, I don't know, what's the point, so who's winning? So I'm here, right, is that the beginning or the end? Is that a good place for me to be at this particular stage?" And I've just got no idea what's right or wrong. I don't know if when I'm 50 or 80 or 90 I will be valuing what I believe or whether I will be worrying what other people think too much. It would help if I valued what I believe.

'It might be me who wants to look after the baby, but it might not. I can quite picture – it might be unrealistic – but going out with a bloke who's a house-husband and looks after the kids. I can quite easily visualize that, until I have had enough of my career. But all those ideas which adapt conventional ways are fraught with difficulty, as you know.

'I do not feel confident, the one thing I do not feel confident about is making up the rules. What I'm doing now in my job is learning what the rules are and then you tell people what they must do, because the rules say this is what you must do. Looking after a baby would be unstructured. Yet I cannot really see myself wanting to work this hard and slogging on like this at work forever.

'I'd like to find the right man but I just don't believe it's going to happen at the moment. I suppose in the Fifties he would have been the one to earn the money and my status would have depended on him, which is crap. But it's funny because I do still care what other people think a bit, because there's this bloke I've been considering having an affair with and he's obsessed with me, but I realized with horror that one of the reasons I couldn't have an affair with him is because I couldn't bear to introduce him to my family because of what they'd say: "What are you doing, you're with a loser again, why is it? You could have somebody really interesting" – he works in a shop – "what exactly are you doing?" They would be shocked and I was really amazed to notice that I cared what they thought.'

Thus, Juliet is torn between her socialized impulse to find a breadwinner (and any genetically evolved tendencies in this direction, if any such exist) and her New Woman desire for independence.

At the same time, men are no clearer about their role in all this. Jim realizes that Freda is ambitious and wants a career but he also fears their offspring will suffer if she works throughout their early childhood. He does not want to inhibit Freda or make her unhappy but he would prefer it if she cared for their children, if they have some. He dare not say this to her for fear of being screamed at, yet it is an important confusion to him. He has even considered giving up his job to be a house-husband, except that when he raised this with Freda, she said she would not even contemplate it. Many women impose traditional sex roles on men as much as vice versa. The evidence shows that men who accept and support their partner's aspirations are much less prone to depression than men who do not. But since most adult men today were raised to be breadwinners with a view to supporting a full-time mother of their children, true acceptance of working motherhood by men (as opposed to lip service) remains relatively rare.

Attraction and sexual relationships have emerged as the other great battlefield of the sexes, apart from work. Again, evolutionary theory makes some highly contentious (and typically politically incorrect) predictions. Given that women wish to maximize the continuation of their selfish genes, they will seek out a mate who will be as reliable and capable as possible of protection and support whilst they care for offspring. In the primordial swamp this meant an intelligent yet hunky fighter, but in the modern context it means an ambitious and industrious breadwinner first, a hunk second. The theory further predicts that women will be more cautious than men about engaging in sexual intercourse. This is partly because, before the advent of the contraceptive pill, a single sexual act was liable to put them out of the reproductive rat race for a minimum of nine months. If they allow any old man to impregnate them, not only might the man's genes be of inferior quality but also, if the relationship is only casual, there would be a risk that he would not hang around after the sex. Thus, women will be less preoccupied with sexual pleasure and with multiple partners than men and more concerned to establish a lasting relationship in association with the sex.

Regarding men, by contrast, evolutionary theory predicts that they will develop traits that attract women (ambition-industriousness) and enable them to beat off competition (using physical strength in the primordial swamp, the capacity to accrue power, status and wealth in modern societies). In selecting a mate, men's primary criterion will be fertility and the surest sign thereof is held to be nubility and pubescent youth. Indeed, the beauty of young women and the preoccupation of women with appearance, according to this theory, have evolved to indicate to men which women are most likely to be capable of reproducing their selfish genes. On top of this, whereas women are supposedly cautious about casual sex, men are predicted to seek it out avidly since the more women they can impregnate, the more their selfish genes will be reproduced.

When these theories are tested against the scientific evidence the results seem on first sight to support it. There is little doubt that worldwide and historically, women are more likely than men to value ambition-industriousness in a partner and to prefer a partner who is older than them. This seems to apply even to wealthy, high-status and powerful women who could afford to choose 'toy boys' and lower-status men. Physical appearance is higher on men's list of priorities than women's: men want attractive partners who are younger than them and emphasize nubile physical features as the most desirable attributes. On top of all this, studies of male and female sexual fantasies seem to support evolutionary predictions: men fantasize more, about physical parts of the body more, with more partners in more positions and detail than women, who tend to picture settings and moods relevant to their relationship with one particular man, rather than detailed sexual acts. This is taken by evolutionists as proof that men are more instinctively preoccupied with the sexual act and variations thereof, whereas women are concerned more with the emotional attachment associated with sex.

However, there are alternatives to the evolutionary interpretation of these findings. The most convincing points out that all or most of them could be due to the differing social and economic roles of men and women. For women in almost all societies at all times, men have been the only route to a measure of power, wealth and status. If they seek such men it is hardly surprising: it is their only hope of having a less than total subordination. Added to this, if men prefer nubility then is it any surprise that women work hard to approximate as closely as possible to this ideal, especially in modern societies where there is an unceasing diet of such images to live up to. Furthermore, since the reproductive period available to women is very much shorter than that for men, women are under even greater pressure to supply what men want if they are to maximize their selfish gene chances.

Whatever the causes of these enduring differences in what attracts men and women and in their sexual proclivities, they do still exist. Men are made to feel guilty for desiring nubile women and women suffer for seeking out ambitious-industrious men. Both may feel resentful and betrayed: when the man leaves his wife or lover for a 'younger model' he is castigated, when the woman dumps her low-achieving estate agent for the merchant banker, their victims cry out, 'He/She was only after one thing.' That new notions of what men and women should want so contradict what happens in practice is a major cause of gender rancour.

Juliet neatly illustrates this problem. Remember that she is the acme of modern woman: independent, successful, intelligent, assertive. 'My main sexual fantasy at the moment is of this bloke who I don't actually want to have an affair with because I don't actually fancy him really. I'm lying there and being completely sprinkled with a million rose petals, and just being told that I'm the most heavenly creature on earth. And then there's some involvement with croissants and honey, and there's lots of sunlight, and choirs. That's what I want! That's what I want! I just want to be treated like the most precious thing on earth and it's all very fragile. I would let him do that in reality. I've never been given flowers in my whole fucking life by a bloke, never ever, I can't believe it, I feel so affronted.

'But I want someone I'm going to have fun with, an express route to fun and I want him to make me laugh. Oh yeah, don't laugh at me. If that's all men want to do with women, buy them flowers and have a fuck, well, that's all I want from a man. Go on, get me one but also who's really bright and stimulating. It's not easy to find that. My colleagues all work too hard and won't buy me the right kind of flowers.'

Of course, not all young women share Juliet's fantasies; but many do. The fascinating and wholly unresolved question is the extent to which they derive from 25 years of being socialized into this way of thinking because even the most gung-ho evolutionist must accept that our culture is still placing enormous pressure on women to think like this. If the evolutionists are to be believed, this form of this fantasy (her in a passive role being admired) is a species inheritance.

Although the effects of the low-serotonin society on men have been touched on here and there, until this point a major consequence for men has not been addressed: increased violence. When women feel subordinated, frustrated and angry, they tend to direct the aggression against the self, and given that women are twice as likely as men to say they are depressed, much of the rise in depression since 1950 has been among females. Men, by contrast, are much more likely to medicate frustration and anger with alcohol and to go on the offensive – on average, worldwide, 85% of violence is by men.

With the exceptions of Switzerland and Japan, throughout the developed world violence has increased at an astonishing rate since 1950. Astonishing, because most recorded violence is committed by people of low income and yet during that time, these countries became considerably more affluent. If anything, logic would dictate that violence should have fallen during that time, but in England and Wales, for example, 6,000 crimes of violence against the person recorded by the police in 1950 became 239,000 in 1996. Since three-quarters of convicted violent men are depressed and since impulsively violent men have low serotonin levels, this represents a large increase in low-serotonin men.

The failure of modern life to meet our evolved needs for status and attachment described in earlier chapters explain the rise in violence as well as in depression. Even though the majority of people are considerably richer than in 1950, the men at the bottom of society experience their position as considerably more deprived than then, because of relative deprivation. They contrast the consumer goods, the permissive lifestyle and the self-focused opportunism of the media role models offered on film and television with the reality of their own lives. They listen to politicians telling them that opportunities have never been greater, yet find themselves pressing against the window of affluence with no legal means of entry: no wonder they throw a brick through it from time to time. The solution is often to create alternative subcultures in which their attributes – impulsiveness, aggression, nothing to lose – are valuable. By forming gangs which offer competitions in which they can be winners, they can temporarily raise their low serotonin. In the wider society's terms they may be losers but in their subculture, they can be on top of the world.

Alongside all this, the young men who do the violence have been raised in homes where gender rancour was more rife than ever before, resulting in unprecedented divorce rates. This creates profound distress and anger. Such homes are more likely to result in the kind of childcare which is violence-inducing: severe and frequent physical punishment amounting to abuse. These are out of control, chaotic families where what was punished last time may be rewarded the next. Such erratic schedules of disciplining create a boy who expects at any moment to be thumped for no good reason, and a paranoid man. It is no coincidence that the most common comment preceding a city-centre violent crime is 'What are you looking at?' In most cases, the assailant has imagined a slight because psychically, he is still living in a place (his original family) where the next unprovoked assault is just a look or a movement away.

There is another development which has greatly exacerbated these trends: the large increase in inequality in Britain since 1979. If the rise in violence since 1950 has been a bush fire, steadily smouldering, the increase in inequality has been like pouring paraffin on the flames. It has greatly increased the proportion of boys raised in the low-income homes which are most likely to provide violence-inducing childcare. But it has also created a greed-is-good, winner-loser, there's-no-such-thing-as-a-society culture. By importing this ethos from the most violent developed nation on earth – America – Britain has created a violent conflagration which it will take several generations to douse.

SOLUTIONS FOR THE LOW-SEROTONIN INDIVIDUAL AND SOCIETY

The cause of the low-serotonin society is at a collective rather than individual level but for the afflicted individual, this is of little practical help. Chapters 7 and 8 offer the best that is available for a person with specific low-serotonin problems: pills and therapy.

There is a tendency for people to fall into one or other camp, for the personal choice to be posed as Prozac versus Therapy. My view is that both approaches can be helpful and that a low-serotonin individual must work hard to overcome their prejudice either way. Modern antidepressants raise serotonin levels and so long as there are few or no side effects, it would be foolish to rule them out just because they entail taking a pill. There is a lack of logic in this position. Nearly all of us are happy to take prescription drugs for physical ailments, such as penicillin for a serious bacterial infection, but much less happy about the idea of pills for our emotional states. Most of us drink, many young people take illegal stimulants and smoke cigarettes, but baulk at the thought of a carefully tested legal remedy for depression or anxiety.

Of course, such pills are not a long-term solution in the sense that they do not address the causes of an individual's low serotonin. Therapy can do this, sometimes. At the first level, cognitive therapies use thoughts to change emotions and can be highly effective, especially where there are easily identifiable cycles of thought and specific problems. If this does not work, the dynamic therapies offer a range of treatments which at one extreme, entail relatively little expense and commitment and help to manage problems, and at the other, aim to bring about a profound and permanent change as a result of considerable outlay of time and money.

Using cases extensively, chapters 7 and 8 offer a detailed account of the pitfalls of the various pills and therapies and make concrete suggestions for what combination will suit which low-serotonin problems.

The final chapter examines solutions for the low-serotonin society. To propose specific legislative measures for creating an advanced capitalism which works in favour of our well-being rather than against it is beyond my capacities or the ambition of this book. However, there are some practical implications of my thesis. For example, the Government could be more effective in ensuring that low-serotonin people who feel in need of therapy or drug treatment can obtain them. On a broader scale, I discuss the tension between individualism and collectivism in advanced capitalist societies and explore models which provide a better balance than our existing one. My conclusion is that calls for a new moral order are inappropriate. The core problem lies in the way advanced capitalism has evolved since 1950.

One ray of hope is that we may already have begun to realize that our aspirations exceed what is realistic and that increased national wealth will not solve our problems. The election of the Labour Government in May 1997 may be a sign that our values are changing. Given that the Conservative Government had created a successful economy, it was suprising to some political commentators that they were not re-elected – normally electors vote with their wallets. Furthermore, the incoming Prime Minister was at pains to emphasize that expectations of what he could achieve should not be exaggerated.

If we are about to enter a phase of reassessment of what our massively successful economic system can do for us emotionally and of reappraising our material, personal and professional ambitions, it is possible that we have already taken the first steps down the road that leads away from the low-serotonin society.

Chapter 1

The Low–Serotonin Society

The premise of this book is that we are unhappier compared with 1950. This chapter presents the scientific evidence for the claims that we are unhappier, that people who are unhappy tend to have low levels of serotonin and that levels thereof are largely caused by our social psychological environment.

THE RISE IN ANGST: THE OVERALL PICTURE

There is a growing consensus amongst psychiatric researchers that rates of depression have increased since the Second World War (see Appendix I: A Brief Review Of The Scientific Evidence That Rates Of Depression Have Increased Since 1950). Across the developed world the increases are of varying magnitude but in almost all nations there was a significant rise. This was so in a comprehensive review of studies which asked large samples of the general population of all age groups about their mental health in 39 different countries. In America, a survey of over 18,000 adults found that a person born between 1945 and 1955 was between three and ten times more likely to suffer major (i.e. severe, life-threatening) depression before the age of 34 than a person born between 1905 and 1914. Likewise, when surveys have been done prospectively, with samples being questioned at different times using the same questions, rates of depression are found to be significantly greater today compared with 20 to 40 years ago (see Appendix I).

Rates of suicide have increased since 1950. The average number of people who committed suicide in European nations increased and in the last decade, rates among young men have rocketed (and especially in Britain, where they have trebled since 1970).[1] Violence and substance

29

use have dramatically increased since 1950 as well. Violence against the person has risen in all developed nations (except Japan). In the USA it has increased fivefold and in England and Wales by an average of 10% a year since 1950, accelerating particularly sharply since 1987.[2] There is more angry incivility, as seen in increased 'road rage'[3] and violence towards staff in retail outlets, to teachers, General Practitioners and welfare officials.[4] Given that three-quarters of convicted violent men suffer from depression and that there is a strong association between drug and alcohol use and depression,[2] these are also clear indicators of a rise in angst.

Alcohol consumption has increased in all European nations except France (which started at a very high level), as has cirrhosis of the liver.[5] The use of such illegal drugs as marijuana, cocaine and heroin has increased exponentially, most dramatically among the young.[6] In the USA, 60% of 18- to 29-year-olds will use an illegal drug in their lifetime (compared with 36% of 30- to 44-year-olds) and 13% will become fully-fledged abusers. 15% of American 12- to 34-year-olds have taken cocaine. The USA is virtually the only developed nation not to have had an increase in heroin addicts in the last 20 years, because it was already widespread there – over half a million addicts in 1976, the same today. By contrast, Italy went from 343 addicts in 1976 to 183,386 in 1991 and Britain from 79 registered addicts in 1979 (2,800 methadone users in 1980) to 50,740 registered heroin abusers in 1990. Other compulsive behaviours indicative of emotional problems have also increased, including gambling,[7] eating disorders[8] and gender rancour (as seen in the rise in the divorce rate from 10% to 40% in Britain[9] – see Chapters 4 to 6).

What, then, is the probable overall extent of actual mental illness as defined by official psychiatric (medical) criteria in developed nations today? The best guess comes from a huge survey of the American population done in the early 1980s.[10] Over 19,000 people were interviewed in five different sites around the country. The conclusion was that 20% of the total American population suffer from a mental illness (as defined by the psychiatric bible, the *DSM* – the *Diagnostic and Statistical Manual of Mental Disorders*) during any given 12 months and 32% will suffer at some point during their lifetime. Because the definitions used are so strict, the real incidence of unhappiness is almost certainly much higher than this. One of the most respected authorities in this field estimated that for every one person fitting the rigorous criteria employed by the *DSM* there are two to three who are close to fitting them.[11] In other words, the proportion of Americans suffering serious problems in any one year was between 40% and 60% in the early 1980s. This is supported by studies which take a broader view of what is meant by angst, such as the one[12] which found that three-quarters of the population suffer from one or more unreasonable fears, spells of panic or general nervousness. Given the likelihood that rates of psychiatric morbidity have increased since these studies were done in the early 1980s, the proportions are likely to be even greater today. For once, it is no exaggeration to use the word 'epidemic' in describing a social trend.

SEROTONIN AND ANGST

If angst in general and depression in particular have increased since the Second World War, then it is highly probable that more of us suffer from low levels of serotonin because there is now a large body of evidence that people who suffer from these problems have lower levels of serotonin than people who do not.

SEROTONIN

First identified in the 1940s, serotonin is found widely in plants and mammals as well as humans. Only 1–2% is actually in the brain and nervous system, the rest is in the blood and in cells in the gut.[13] It was serotonin's role in regulating the tone of blood vessels that first interested scientists and gave rise to its name: the 'sero' refers to blood and 'tonin' to its effect on tone. If you have heard of the chemical it is probably because you have read articles about the new antidepressant Prozac, which increases levels of serotonin in the brain. In fact, serotonin is crucial in many other parts of the body. The smooth muscle contraction of the gut depends on it (which is why antidepressant drugs such as Prozac can have temporary indigestion as a side effect). It is also important in concentrating blood platelets.

It was not until the late 1950s that a Swedish scientist began to map out the brain pathways containing serotonin and that it began to be realized how important the chemical is for our mental health. In the early 1960s it was accidentally discovered that drugs which raised levels of serotonin eased depression (the old generation of antidepressants, known as Tricyclics, with such brand names as Imipramine).[13] Serotonin is just one of thousands of chemicals found at the place in the brain where physics and chemistry meet, the synapse. The synapse is a gap between the neurones which electrical impulses pass down. When the current reaches the end of a neurone it causes a chemical reaction in the synapse. Chemical messengers – including serotonin – are dispatched and pass a message to the next neurone, which fires off the next electrical impulse, and so on. Serotonin is crucial in carrying messages that damp down and inhibit our animal selves. Antidepressants work by preventing the serotonin from leaving the synapse, locking the door through which it normally passes out. The active ingredient in Prozac (called Fluoxetine), for example, fits like a key into the receptors at the end of the neurone so that the serotonin cannot escape.

In what follows, I shall give a brief summary of the evidence that low levels of serotonin are associated with the increase in depression, aggression and compulsion since 1950. Detailed evidence and references are provided in Appendix II: 'Psychological And Psychiatric Correlates Of Low Levels Of Serotonin'.

LOW SEROTONIN: DEPRESSION, AGGRESSION AND COMPULSION

In innumerable studies, animals who display depression-like symptoms, such as withdrawn and fearful behaviour, have been found to have lower serotonin levels than normal animals. In humans, all the techniques for measuring serotonin have shown that people diagnosed as depressed are more likely to have lower levels than normal people. When depressed people are administered drugs which raise serotonin levels, at least half become less depressed. People who attempt suicide or complete a suicide also have low levels.

Very similar results have been found for aggression. Animals with low serotonin levels are consistently more aggressive and so are humans. Low serotonin levels predict which convicted violent men will reoffend. Impulsively violent men and firesetters, antisocial men and antisocial teenagers have all been similarly found to have low levels, as have irritable people, liable to sudden outbursts of rage (known as anger attacks). In animals, raising serotonin levels with antidepressants reduces violent aggression and it is highly probable that the same would be true of humans if the studies were conducted (see Appendix II).

People with a variety of compulsions have also been shown to suffer from low levels. It has been suggested that people abuse 'drugs of solace' because they are feeling depressed. Thus, alcohol raises serotonin levels in the short term but alcoholics have lower levels than normal because in the longer run, alcohol reduces them. Likewise, the drug ecstasy (MDMA) provides short-term increases and longer-term depletion and studies of animals suggest that ecstasy destroys serotonin receptors. Cigarette smokers are twice as likely to suffer from depression as non-smokers and it may be that smoking provides temporary relief from the depressed mood associated with low serotonin.

The eating disorder bulimia (bingeing and vomiting) is also associated with depression and bulimics have lower serotonin than nonbulimics.

Starvation reduces serotonin levels, so it is not surprising that anorexics have low levels whilst fasting. Sufferers from Obsessive Compulsive Disorder (OCD) have low levels and some kinds of sex addicts may also do so. It is likely that gamblers have low levels because they tend to have impulsive personalities – who tend to have low serotonin. Finally, sufferers from ME (Myalgic Encephalomyelitis) and Chronic Fatigue probably have low levels because both of these conditions often are accompanied by depression.

With the exception of cigarette smoking, the prevalence of all of the problems listed above as correlating with low serotonin levels has increased substantially since 1950: depression, suicide, aggression and impulsive violence, alcohol use and abuse, ecstasy use, bulimia, anorexia, OCD, gambling, and ME and chronic fatigue. It is reasonable to assume, therefore, that the proportion of the population with low serotonin levels has also increased substantially. The key question of this book is: why? The first step in answering it is to present what is known about the fundamental causes of differing serotonin levels.

It must be admitted at the outset that very little is known in hard scientific terms about what causes levels of any brain chemicals to vary between individuals or groups, whether it be serotonin or anything else. Most of the evidence is inferential and therefore, we can only be in the business of building an argument. Another person, armed with the same data, might come to different conclusions. Nonetheless, there are some areas of agreement in this field and although nothing in what follows is certain, it is based on carefully constructed scientific studies rather than mere speculation.

It seems highly probable that, to some extent, differences in genes explain why individuals vary in their serotonin levels but it is unclear how much of the difference is so explained. Studies of identical twins and adoptees prove that major depressive illnesses (i.e. the sustained, life-threatening states called either 'manic' or 'unipolar' depression, which are far in excess of simply having a depressed mood) are partly caused by genes.[39] These studies suggest that as much as 60% of the difference between normal and depressed people may be caused by genes. Yet the extent to which genes actually have a direct influence on serotonin levels is less clear. Twin studies suggest that genes play a much smaller role in causing minor depression (as opposed to major depression – see footnote 14 for definition). At present, the best guess is that they affect only about 10% of minor depression, possibly less in other low-serotonin problems (see footnote 15 for a brief summary of the genetic evidence).

It must be the case that genes play some part, but there is good reason to suppose that environmental factors are critical in most cases.

SOCIAL STATUS AND LEVELS OF SEROTONIN

Since serotonin levels correlate with problems such as aggression and depression, in the sense that high levels have one consequence and low levels another, they are causal. However, they can also be seen as effects rather than causes depending at what point you are inspecting the causal chain. They could be 'markers' of other processes, the true causes. For example, there is considerable evidence that consuming ecstasy is associated with low levels and that people who take the drug may suffer various emotional problems as a result (see Appendix II). If you only inspect the last two links in the chain, you can say that low serotonin causes these emotional problems. But if you go a step further back, you would say that ecstasy causes the problems because it causes the low serotonin levels. If you wanted to go further back still, you would say that whatever causes people to take ecstasy is the 'true' cause of the low levels and emotional problems.

In this sense, the evidence presented below suggests that serotonin levels are an effect – an effect of social status. More than anything, serotonin levels seem to reflect our ranking in social hierarchies, or our perception of our ranking.

SOCIAL STATUS AND SEROTONIN LEVELS IN HUMANS

Studies of vervet monkeys – a species with many similarities to humans – over the last 20 years by Michael McGuire and colleagues at the University of California in Los Angeles do more to explain why serotonin levels vary than any other single body of research.

After humans, vervets are the most successful primate species, found throughout most of sub-Saharan Africa. The vervets that McGuire's group study are kept in large open-air enclosures which are designed to avoid crowding and the other damaging effects of captivity. They live in groups of three or so adults of each gender, plus offspring. When males reach adulthood they leave the family and join another group, whereas the females stay put. Females tend to do most of the childcare and display more 'affiliative' behaviours, such as grooming and stroking others, than males. The kind of care the mothers provide and the conditions thereof have been shown to profoundly influence the subsequent personalities of offspring. Offspring whose mothers were very protective and restrictive are more timid and cautious in later life when faced with novel circumstances.[16] The amount and kind of contact between mothers and their infants during the first six months predicts strongly how daughters, in turn, care for their infants – little contact in your own infancy means you provide little contact for your offspring, likewise extensive contact.[17]

Within each group there are well-defined hierarchies, separate for each gender, and offspring are accorded the status of their parents. Dominance and subordination is a key issue for vervets and the status of males is established partly by their fighting ability but also by their capacity to gain backing from females, who join in coalitions to constrain aggression and to favour particular males. Males who are confident and unaggressive in approaching females win their support more than thuggish, socially unresponsive ones. Fights rarely last more than a few seconds or result in injuries, are more about the display of potential destructiveness than about inflicting actual damage. Unprovoked, impulsive aggression in males is not supported by females and is less successful in promoting dominance than the effective use of threats.

McGuire's first and fundamental finding is that males which are dominant in the group have higher levels of serotonin than subordinate ones (on average, dominants have 1000 ng/ml versus subordinates who have 600 ng/ml). This result has been replicated by McGuire in dozens of groups of vervets. Those with high serotonin levels affiliate more (e.g. chummy grooming), are more tolerant of other animals, eat and sleep more, and defend the group from threat more. They are less prone to launch attacks on other group members. All these behaviours promote their dominant status. But which comes first, the high status or the high serotonin levels?

In a series of experiments, changes were made to the status of male vervets, so that previously subordinate ones became dominant and the previously dominant became subordinate.[18] Sure enough, these status changes caused predictable changes in serotonin levels. If dominant vervets were removed from their group, after a couple of weeks a battle for dominance would ensue among the remaining, previously subordinate males. The winner would have a higher level of serotonin once he had established his new status than beforehand: *becoming dominant caused the increase*. Likewise, when the dominant males were placed in situations (such as total isolation) which removed this status, their serotonin levels fell. The crucial role of the submissive responses of subordinates in keeping dominants' serotonin levels high was shown in a further experiment. Dominants were put behind a one-way screen to observe their subordinates, who could neither see nor hear them. On seeing the subordinates, the dominant would offer threats and other displays but because they could neither see nor hear him, he would receive no submissive responses to his dominating behaviour. Under these conditions, the dominant's serotonin levels plummeted dramatically, proving that the receipt of submissive displays from subordinate males was crucial in sustaining high serotonin levels.

Other studies have proved the status-serotonin relationship by altering serotonin levels upwards or downwards using drugs.[17] Twelve groups of three males were observed over a three-week period and the dominants were identified (they won an average of 88% of conflict exchanges with other males) and removed. In each group, one of the remaining vervets was randomly selected and for four weeks, given a drug which increases serotonin levels. At the end of this time, in all of the 12 groups the drugged vervet was the one who became the new dominant, showing a three-step progression: an initial increase in affiliative behaviour towards the females, increased female support in coalitions against the other male as a result and regular defeats of the other male. Drug administration then ceased and three drug-free months elapsed after which a new drug was given to the same (previously drugged) vervets, but this time one that *reduced* serotonin levels. Sure enough, whereas they had all been dominant on the serotonin-enhancing drugs, on the serotonin-reducing drug the self-same monkeys all became the subordinate. Under the influence of the serotonin-reducing drug, the once charming and socially charismatic vervets became antisocial louts, liable to ignore the females and to mount futile and over-aggressive attacks on the other males.

That serotonin-raising drugs cause a rise in status might suggest that serotonin is causal. But the overall conclusion of McGuire's research is unambiguous: serotonin levels in male vervets are an effect, not a cause, of rank-status[19] because levels rise and fall in response to changes in status; high status vervets do not start out with high levels of serotonin, these are the consequence of moving from a low status. Studies of other animals support the idea that winners are liable to have high levels compared with losers.[20] One study of rats showed that levels fell if they lost a fight and rose if they won. If the winner was then put into a fight which he lost, his levels fell again. Studies of crayfish have also shown that dominants have high serotonin and subordinates, low.[21] Overall, it seems likely that serotonin is highly sensitive to changes in status in those species where hierachy is a key organizing principle – such as humans.

DIRECT EVIDENCE LINKING SOCIAL STATUS AND SEROTONIN LEVELS IN HUMANS

What is true of animals is by no means necessarily true of humans and over the years there has been a lamentable tendency for some scientists to make the leap from ape to man with rash and gay abandon, with highly selective use made of animal studies to find support for a particular argument, ignoring counter-evidence or the fact that many seeming similarities between humans and primates can be illusionary. However, in the case of serotonin and status there are a number of reasons to suppose that what is true of vervet monkeys is probably true of humans as well.

McGuire has only attempted to replicate his vervet findings with humans in one study.[20] He measured levels of students' serotonin and found that leaders of campus social organizations tended to have higher levels than nonleaders. This small study is less important than the three studies by Douglas Madsen, an American political scientist who set out specifically to test the applicability of McGuire's findings to humans. In the first study,[21] serotonin levels were measured from blood samples in 72 healthy male undergraduates, finding a normal range of levels (from 40 ng/ml to 295 ng/ml). The students were also given a questionnaire to measure how ambitious and competitive they were, specifically concentrating on how 'hard-driving' and 'impatient', and the results were correlated with serotonin levels. Madsen found that the more driven the student, the higher the serotonin level. Statistically significant relationships were found between serotonin levels and self-rating on a variety of items, including 'I probably eat faster than I should', 'I lose patience with speakers who don't get to the point', 'I have more will power than most people seem to have' and 'I plan to find a career which is difficult and challenging'. The clear implication of this work was that male students with dominant tendencies have higher serotonin levels.

Madsen's second study[22] was a reanalysis of the data from the first. He presented a list of Machiavellian attributes which various authors regarded as likely to be strongly represented in successful power seekers, including a great desire to win, little concern with conventional morality, manipulativeness, low ideological commitment and suspicion of others – but none present to the extent that they were actually pathological. Turned into a psychological scale, Madsen cited a study showing that Machiavels lied more plausibly and effectively, were more inclined to engage in and to enjoy the manipulation of others, were likely to initiate and control bargaining situations and be successful in them, were much stronger and more forceful in social relations, persuading others more often and being persuaded by others less often, and finally, perceived more manipulativeness in those around them. Madsen then reanalysed the data from his earlier study to see if high serotonin levels also correlated with Machiavellianism. They did, for all the variables except manipulativeness. Thus the higher the serotonin level, the more likely the student was to be hard-charging, competitive, impatient, aggressive, distrustful and confident. Madsen concluded that these finding were 'a clear connection with the UCLA [i.e. McGuire] group's results with male vervets'. He further concluded that McGuire's animal studies are an important guide for human studies.

A weakness of the first two studies was that they relied only on questionnaire evidence: what about the serotonin levels when the students were placed in actual competition with each other? Madsen asked his 72 students to do a series of logic tests and took blood samples at regular intervals during the competition, measuring fluctuations in levels of hormones associated with serotonin levels.[25] He found that the six students with the highest serotonin levels (an average of 251 ng/ml compared with an average of 141 ng/ml for the group as a whole) were also the most strongly competitive, dominance-seeking individuals. The fluctuations of the chemicals of this group were also significantly different to the other 66 during the course of the logic test. Again, the link between dominance and serotonin was supported.

Important though Madsen's studies are, they are far from conclusive proof that the serotonin–status relationship found by McGuire in vervets applies to humans as well. Because there are all sorts of practical and ethical difficulties associated with testing this theory which do not arise in the study of monkeys, the studies have yet to be done. Nonetheless, there is abundant indirect evidence to suggest that serotonin levels in humans are closely linked to status in similar ways to vervets. Since depressed, violent and paranoid people are more likely to have low serotonin levels, if they are also more likely to be of low status – as they are – then it is likely that low status is linked to low serotonin.

INDIRECT EVIDENCE LINKING LOW STATUS AND SEROTONIN LEVELS

Almost everything nasty that can happen to you is more likely to do so if you are at the bottom rather than the top of society, so it should hardly come as a surprise if low-status people are more depressed than high-status ones. Nonetheless, it is only recently that this has been proven. As recently as 1964, psychologist Ernest Becker[26] asserted that depression was most common in middle class women: 'High expectations leave a middle-class woman particularly vulnerable to feelings of disappointment with attendant feelings of guilt, low self-esteem and depression. Since she is less able than a working-class woman to explain her disappointment in terms of social deprivation she does so in terms of personal failure.' A number of other authorities shared this view but within a decade the empirical evidence supplied a very different picture. In 8 out of 11 studies in a 1974 review of surveys that had been conducted of randomly selected women in the community, depressive symptoms were found to be more common in the lower classes.[27] In the second half of the 1970s three large surveys found the same,[28] culminating in the publication of the highly influential 1978 study by Brown of 458 women in Camberwell, London.[29] 23% of the working-class women were seriously depressed compared to only 6% of the middle-class ones. Since then there have been at least nine further studies, from America and the Continent as well as Britain, which replicate Brown's findings.[30] The link applies across the class spectrum, not just in comparing highest and lowest statuses. Thus, a Canadian survey over a 16-year period showed that 1.9% of the highest-status people suffered a major depression, compared with 4.5% for the middle class and 12.4% for the lowest[31] and another study had similar findings.[32] Psychiatric morbidity among 17,000 civil servants working in London offices also tracked status closely – the lower the status, the greater the likelihood of psychiatric problems, of which minor depression is by far the most common.[33] Another obvious indicator of the depression–low status relationship is the simple fact that women are twice as likely as men to be depressed.[34] Since women are far more likely than men to occupy servile, low-paid or unpaid jobs and to have social roles which subordinate them – whether down the pub, where they are interrupted more than men, speak less often and act as an audience if there are men present, or whether taking low-status roles such as that of housewife – it is not surprising that they are also more likely to be depressed. Whilst there is some debate as to whether the relationship is as strong for major depressions – manic and unipolar – as opposed to minor depressions, it is one of the best-established and least-disputed data of Social Psychiatry that being in a low class is a major predictor of depressive symptoms in technologically developed nations.

Depression is also linked with the aftermath of losses of status, many of which are themselves linked to low income. Recent divorcees suffer more than those from intact marriages as do the recently and long-term unemployed. Those with few friends and intimates are also more at risk.[2]

Taken as a whole, the close link between depression and low status or loss thereof strongly suggests that humans of low status are also more likely to have low serotonin levels. As with depression, so with violent aggression. Many studies have revealed that convictions for violence are far more common among low-status males. Marvin Wolfgang's study of the criminal records of 10,000 boys born in Philadelphia in 1945 found that the lower the boy's class, the greater his chance of being convicted of a violent crime.[35] In England, David Farrington followed 411 boys from age 8 to age 32. 42% of the 93 boys from the lowest-income families had become seriously violent by age 32, a significantly greater proportion than those from higher classes.[36] These surveys are strongly supported by the evidence of what causes violence.[2] The key differences between violent and nonviolent men are threefold: being the object of severe and frequent physical punishment, amounting to abuse; witnessing parental disharmony (usually the dad thumping the mum); and parental irritability (especially in the mother, because she is depressed). All three of these patterns of childcare are more common in low-income homes,[2] which helps to explain why low-class boys are more likely to be convicted of violence in later life.

Most convictions for violence result from incidents in public places such as pubs and clubs and since these are frequented more by low-class men, that may explain why they are more often convicted. It may well be that high-class men engage in domestic violence as much as low-class ones but unfortunately, there is no reliable method for establishing this. What seems beyond reasonable doubt is that the kinds of childhood experiences which create violent men are more common in low-class homes and that low-income men do more violence in public. Taken together, these facts make it likely that more low-status men are violent and therefore, have low serotonin levels.

The tendency to feel that you are being got at when you are not (paranoia) is much more common in depressed and violent people and therefore, should be more common in low-status people. If, as is the case in many depressed people and most violent ones, you spent much of your childhood being neglected, criticized and abused it would not be surprising if you grew up tending to expect others to attack you. If, further to these childhood experiences, little monetary value is placed on your labour, you live in a cramped home in an unpleasant environment and your life is a constant struggle to make ends meet, we might expect you to feel the world is against you.

One index of paranoia is the amount of hostility people express to others – they are more likely to feel under attack and therefore, to be hostile. Several studies have shown that low-status people are more prone to be hostile than high-status ones.[37] Given the evidence that low serotonin and paranoia are linked, this is another reason for supposing that low-status people are more likely to have low-serotonin levels.

Deaths from cirrhosis of the liver – often seen as an index of the amount of alcoholism in a society – are closely linked to social status.[38] Likewise, there is evidence that people of low status are more likely to abuse drugs and to gamble.[38] Although no official statistics are available, it seems highly probable that more low- than high-status people are prescribed drugs treating low-serotonin disorders – far more low-income people present themselves to General Practitioners asking for treatment of these problems. All these are signs that more low-status people have low serotonin levels.

SUMMARY

Depression, violence and compulsive behaviour have increased considerably since 1950 and all these are linked to low levels of serotonin. Genes appear to account for only a small part of the difference between high- and low-serotonin individuals. In many primates, most clearly in vervet monkeys, they are directly caused by social status and the direct and indirect evidence suggests that the same may be true of humans.

Chapter 2

Death By A Thousand Social Comparisons

The Evolution Of Subordination And Depression

How does the status-serotonin link help us in answering our key question, namely, why are there more low-serotonin people compared with 1950?

Thus far, you may feel that the cause of low serotonin levels is not particularly surprising: it happens more to low-status groups. Everyone knows that rotten things tend to happen more to the least powerful and most oppressed members of a society, this is merely adding low serotonin levels to the list. But the explanation offered so far is the beginning, not the end of my argument. The questions that need to be addressed now are as follows. If status is the root cause of serotonin levels, then how come more people have lower levels today compared with 1950 when, in almost every way that status is measured (education, wealth, health, middle-class white collar occupation and so on), more people are better off? Of those (admittedly, still many in number and increasing since the 1980s) people who do have low status – the poor, the uneducated – why do only some suffer from symptoms of low serotonin? Finally, how come so many high-status people suffer – what have the likes of Diana, the Princess of Wales, or Sarah, the Duchess of York, to be depressed about?

The obvious reply to the latter two questions is that the happy poor and the miserable rich suffered serotonin-lowering childhoods, have had traumatizing subsequent experiences or have genes that predispose them in that direction. All of these are probably true to some extent. If her account is to be believed, for example, Princess Diana suffered a traumatic and neglectful childhood and her marriage was depressing enough. Conversely, many people from poor homes have happy childhoods and satisfying marriages. But that does not explain the first question – the overall tendency for both rich and poor to be unhappier since 1950. In fact, the serotonin-low-status relationship does help to answer this and the other two questions.

RELATIVE DEPRIVATION

A large study of American military personnel published in 1949 produced some puzzlingly counter-intuitive findings:[1] it identified many examples of people for whom subjective satisfaction did not accord with their objective circumstances. For example, Military Police reported greater satisfaction with their promotion opportunities than members of the Air Corps. This was surprising because the Air Corps personnel were twice as likely to be promoted and logically, therefore, one might have expected them to be more, not less satisfied with their promotion prospects. Another example was that black personnel stationed in the North of the country expressed more dissatisfaction than those in the South, yet racist attitudes and behaviour are more common in the South. The explanation offered for these and many other similar findings is known as Relative Deprivation. The higher rates of Air Corps personnel promotion meant that their hopes and expectations had risen accordingly. Since promotion was relatively rare in the Military Police, most did not expect it as much and it came as a pleasant suprise rather than as something expected, a hope to be dashed. Likewise, it was found that the Blacks in the North were comparing themselves with civilian Blacks who were better off than the civilians in the racist South. The comparison increased their dissatisfaction with army life.

These kinds of findings have been repeated many times across a wide variety of settings. Interviews with 2,000 American managers,[2] to take just one example, revealed that company presidents earning over $40,000 (in 1963) were more dissatisfied with their rates of pay than mere supervisors on less than $15,000. Of course, not all relatively well-to-do groups feel more dissatisfied with their lot than relatively worse-off comparison groups, but it is common. Although there have been countless papers and books published debating the details of the theory, the consensus is that this kind of finding is the result of relative deprivation, a gap between what people want and feel entitled to and what they actually get.

Such relative deprivations can lead to self-blame and depression or angry resentment. Five necessary and sufficient conditions have been proposed for creating the resentful variant:[3] wanting something (such as a pay rise or promotion); seeing that someone else possesses it; feeling entitled to it; feasibility that you could obtain it; and the absence of a sense that it was your fault that you did not get it. If a person passes through the first four stages but not the last, they are liable to self-blame rather than resentment, concluding that it was due to their inadequacy that they did not obtain what they wanted. For example, a study of 405 25- to 40-year-olds found that[4] 'participants who felt there was a gap between what they obtained from their job and what they wanted . . . expressed significantly more self-reported depression than did other respondents'. The depressed were more likely to feel that they were not getting what they deserved (i.e. were entitled to), liable to regard themselves as doing worse compared with similar others and to feel it was their fault. In line with this theory, Relative Deprivation studies have shown many times that improvements in conditions (such as pay or promotion prospects) may actually increase dissatisfaction, a principle entitled 'progressive deprivation'.[5] Studies of protest movements and civil revolts suggest that it is often precisely when people begin to get what they want that there is an inflation in feelings of what they are entitled to. Thus, although an individual or group may be objectively better off, such as after obtaining some (but not all) demands for new freedom or improved living conditions, they may feel subjectively worse off because expectations keep being adjusted upwards, beyond whatever is the present level, and the conviction that this is their entitlement endures, however high the expectations go.[6]

This theory has been used to explain another puzzling body of evidence. It is almost a tenet of modern life that as a nation becomes wealthier, the satisfaction and well-being levels of its citizens will rise accordingly – affluence should breed happiness and this is the ultimate justification offered by politicians for placing increased prosperity at the heart of their politics. Yet this principle seems to apply only up to a certain basic level and not beyond. Large surveys of national well-being and satisfaction levels show that when a nation moves from developing ('Third World') to developed status, there is a significant increase in well-being. But once nations reach the level where most or all of their citizens' basic needs for food, shelter and so on are being met, relative affluence beyond that does not make a difference. Although there are large variations between developed nations in how happy they say they are, the explanation is not differences in wealth.[7] The well-being of three of the richest, Germany, Japan and the USA, is less than that of many poorer developed nations, such as Ireland, Finland and Australia. Furthermore, the surveys have consistently found little change over time, despite increases in wealth. The USA, for example, is much richer than in the 1950s yet about the same numbers say they are happy today as compared with then. Even more dramatically, the Japanese real per capita income increased fivefold between 1958 and 1987 without any change in the amount of reported well-being.[7] Thus, within developed nations, it appears that raising the incomes of all does not increase the happiness of all.

The reason most (although not all)[8] students in this field give for this surprising finding is that as the nation gets richer, so the expectations and desired standard of living rise to match. This is neatly illustrated by the fact that when citizens in developed nations are asked what they would need as a basic subsistence income, the amount they suggest consistently rises at the same rate as the national average income for that time. As one author explains,[7] 'Imagine that your income increased substantially while everyone else's stays the same. Would you feel better off? The answer most people would give is "yes". Now suppose that your income stays the same while everyone else's increases substantially. How would you feel? Most people would say that they feel less well off. This is because judgements of personal well-being are made by comparing one's objective status with a subjective living level norm, which is significantly influenced by the average level of living of the society as a whole . . . Raising the incomes of all does not increase the happiness of all because the positive effect of higher income on subjective well-being is offset by the negative effect of higher living level norms brought about by the growth in incomes generally.'

This is not to say that money makes no difference at all to the happiness of citizens in the developed world. In general, richer people tend to say they are happier than poorer people within a given society. However, the relationship is surprisingly weak and there are large swathes of the rich who say they are unhappy, and of the poor who say they are happy. A study of 49 super-rich people from the American *Forbes* magazine's 'top 400 wealthiest people' (with a net worth of $125,000,000 or more) found that 37% were less happy than the nationwide average.[9] By contrast, 45% of a non-wealthy comparison group were considerably happier than average.

Of course, well-being studies are very superficial and open to all sorts of criticisms (see footnote 10). But they probably do tell us something, if only about the differences between how nations and groups answer immensely crude questions such as 'Generally speaking, how satisfied are you with your life as a whole? Would you say that you are very satisfied, fairly satisfied, not very satisfied, or not at all satisfied?' If nothing else, the huge numbers in the samples (e.g. 169,776 people from 16 different nations in one case)[7] are a reason to believe that the studies have some significance.

Despite its critics,[8] relative deprivation remains the most likely explanation of these various unexpected findings. As we shall see, whether applied to Princess Diana (see the next chapter), a poor but happy person or the increase in angst since 1950, the idea that as people get richer they raise their expectations partly explains the drop in serotonin levels. At the heart of this theory is the amount and way that we compare ourselves, and it is to this basic process that we turn after a brief exposition of the connections between depression and social status.

SOCIAL COMPARISON, STATUS AND DEPRESSION

The genes we have today began to evolve over 5 million years ago to deal with a completely different set of circumstances from those found in the modern world. What made sense in 5 million BC is often, no longer appropriate. Just as Freud discovered that symptoms of neurosis in an individual may have been appropriate responses in childhood but when continued into adulthood become pathological, so with modern society: our genes mean we are evolved to deal with a situation which no longer exists, just as a fear of sexual desires resulting from repressive parents in childhood may make no sense in an adult. Although we are by far the most flexible creatures on earth, able to survive equally well in deserts and sub-zero arctic conditions, even our immense adaptability cannot encompass what is now demanded of us. As Anthony Stevens and John Price put it,[11] 'It seems likely that the various neuroses, psychopathies, drug dependencies, the occurrence of child and spouse abuse, to say nothing of the ever rising crime statistics, are not unconnected with Western society's inability to satisfy the archetypal needs of our kind . . . the number of people in whom these basic needs are not met is large and growing, as indeed is the psychiatric problems which they represent.' What, then, are these 'archetypal needs'?

They are twofold: **the need for status**, related to positioning on rank hierarchies, law and order, territory and possessions; and **the need for emotional attachments**, including care giving and receiving, affiliation (the desire for emotional and physical contact) and altruism. Such momentous claims about human nature need to be treated with grave scepticism (see footnote 12) but there is little doubt that positing status and attachment as inherent helps us to make sense of our present predicament. The failure to satisfy these drives can be related to two basic pathways to depression which have been established by psychologists over the last 30 years. The authors of a survey of 21 studies of these two paths described them as follows:[13] 'Along one path we find persons whose intense need to be loved, highly esteemed and prized by others leaves them precariously sensitive to real or perceived slights, abandonments or withheld esteem by significant people in their lives . . . the second path is marked by excessive personal demands for accomplishment and control accompanied by relentless self-criticism, guilt and sensed inferiority when one fails to satisfy personal standards.' This chapter is concerned with the second path, the role of status and social comparison, and the next chapter examines how four key changes in these since 1950 have increased the amount of achievement-related depression. The attachment pathway to depression, and changes therein since 1950 are the subject of the succeeding chapter.

DEPRESSION AND SUPERIOR-SUBORDINATE STATUS
The status (or 'Rank') theory of depression argues that depression once served an extremely important and useful purpose but that it no longer does so. Stevens and Price sum this up, as follows:[11] 'Depressed mood evolved as a strategy for inhibiting challenge so that stable social hierarchies could be sustained. Depression is adaptive because it induces the sufferer to accommodate to low social rank when it has been forced upon him.' Put simply, the low self-esteem, reluctance to put yourself forward, self-attacking thoughts, loss of energy and social withdrawal of depression evolved in primates as a way of signalling to superior-status animals that you pose no threat. It oiled the primordial social wheels but such an extreme, pervasive subordination is just pathological in humans today. To understand this better we need to examine the evolution of social status.

The starting point is Charles Darwin's central proposition that genes which favour the survival of a species and its greater propagation are more likely to endure than those which do not.[14] **Natural selection** favoured the inheritance of traits that confer advantages in the struggle with the physical environment, such as camouflage skills in a chameleon or extra body fat in cold climates. Animals with these traits would survive longer than those without them. **Intrasexual selection** favoured traits that increased the chances of winning in battles for resources with animals of the same sex, traits such as strong muscles or large teeth. Animals with these genes would better able to beat off competition for resources from others. **Intersexual selection** favoured traits that would attract the opposite gender to have sex, such as bright plumage or in humans, good looks. Animals with these traits would have greater 'pulling power' leading to more sex and therefore, to more reproduction.

As primates evolved they developed increasingly sophisticated ways of furthering their species survival, of which social cooperation was the most important. It enabled them to be more effective predators and to protect themselves from attacks. But it also required organization, hence the need for hierarchy. As McGuire's vervet monkeys show, where three or four males are gathered together, a battle will ensue for dominance. This innately motivated ranking emerges as the basis for distributing resources, such as sexual access to females, and for establishing law and order within the group. It harnesses competition for resources to the greater good. Without ranking, every time there was a simple conflict of interest there would be a potentially violent and socially destructive battle. It provides a guide to who gets what without bloodshed or social rancour.

Humans inherited this tendency. As Paul Gilbert puts it,[15] in humans 'there is a natural tendency to understand, think about or construe relationships, between things, people and objects in terms of some ranked relationship, and these constructions influence our attention and behaviour towards them'. Small children illustrate this theory. Left to their own devices, there is a battle for dominance, and without any supervision, they can be very cruel (as evoked in William Golding's novel *Lord of the Flies*). When a younger sibling is born, small children exhibit 'sibling rivalry' and studies of birth rank order (position in the family)[16] suggest it can have profound and lasting effects. Eldest children tend to identify with parents' values and the adult status quo, the youngest are more likely to rebel and to challenge orthodoxy. Studies of group processes strongly suggest that there is a tendency for leaders to emerge when strangers are thrown together.[17] Whilst families, businesses and societies vary in the kinds of hierarchy they have, sooner or later a status system seems to arise in all human groups, everywhere, at all times, strongly suggesting that it is an innate tendency.

What has this to do with the evolution of depression?

In order for the status system to work, animals must have a way of recognizing their own and others' rank and of signalling their recognition of their subordinate status when faced by those of higher rank. According to evolutionary psychiatrists, patterns of emotions evolved to enable members to recognize their position in the group. Positive emotions are experienced on increasing one's rank (e.g. pride) and negative emotions (e.g. shame and self-criticism) accompany low status. Compared with high-status ones, low-status primates (and humans; as we saw in the study of 17,000 civil servants, their degree of psychiatric and physical morbidity directly tracked their status; also, low-income women are more likely to be depressed than high-income women, many times more so than high-income men) are characteristically more tense and show signs of biological stress.

In primates, the negative emotions served an important purpose: they signalled to lower-status animals that they were at risk of attack from higher-status ones unless they inhibited their behaviour and avoided posing a threat. Gilbert[15] cites the example of a farmyard fowl which has just lost dominance and has no escape (the account comes from the man who invented the term 'pecking order', Schjelderup-Ebbe). Following defeat the fowl's 'behaviour becomes entirely changed. Deeply depressed in spirit, humble with dropping wings and head in the dust it is – at any rate, directly upon being vanquished – overcome with paralysis, although one cannot detect any physical injury. The bird's resistance now seems broken, and in some cases the effects of the psychological condition are so strong that the bird will sooner or later come to grief.' In many other species, where escape from a dominant other is blocked – if escape is possible, the animal will normally do so – very similar patterns are seen.[15] Examples of submissive behaviours include lowering of the eyes, repetitive looking at and then away, sideways glances, a preparedness to give way under challenge, the fear grin (a grimace indicating both friendliness and fear), crouching the body to make it look smaller rather than threatening, retreating or backing off or down, lowering the chin and presenting the rear. Initiatory and confident behaviours cease and the animal becomes inhibited, tense, withdrawn and passive. These behaviours are only activated if the subordination is involuntary, if there is no escape or after being vanquished in a fight. They enable the subordinate to indicate to superiors that they are not competing with them for resources or mates and not to attack. It shows that they are no longer competing in the struggle for the survival of the fittest, are unfit. The submissive behaviours become ritualized and symbolic, so that real fights are rare. Just by displaying them the subordinated animal can symbolically indicate that they pose as little threat as if they had been killed or severely wounded. Through repeated encounters the relative status of each is established and the status hierarchy established. Thus do behaviours in primates which are very similar to depression in humans serve an essential social function.

HUMAN DEPRESSION AND HELPLESSNESS

Now let us consider depressed humans. In general, their reasoning is focused on negative data and inferences about the self and the world, accentuating the negative and eliminating the positive. They judge themselves negatively compared with others. Their attention and memory shifts towards the negative, with reduced mental agility and imagination. They lack energy, becoming hopeless and pessimistic.[15] In terms of

Darwin's theory, like the subordinated primate, they are in bad shape to compete for resources or to attract mates. But unlike primates, there are very few occasions in developed societies in which there is an actual danger of being physically attacked for posing a competitive threat. Indeed, developed nations encourage the belief that all their citizens, including low-status groups such as the poor, women and racial minorities, can rise up the hierarchy, however much the reality may contradict this ideology. In the USA, they even go so far as to boast that 'anyone can be president'.

Following the work of Martin Seligman, many psychologists now characterize depressed people as suffering from Learned Helplessness. Seligman's theory arose from the observation that dogs which were repeatedly given electric shocks over which they could excercise no control became listless and helpless – in many ways like depressed humans. Studies of normal humans revealed that they also became helpless if given no control in experimental situations and he hypothesized that people become depressed as a result of being placed in situations where whatever they do makes no difference to what happens.[18]

Seligman has listed eight of the nine symptoms used for diagnosing 'unipolar' depression (as opposed to manic depression, where there are periods of hyperactivity and feeling euphoric) and based on the results of over 300 studies of animals and humans rendered helpless by various experimental manoeuvres, he summarized the evidence of Helplessness research pertaining to these symptoms:[18]

Symptom 1. Depressed mood: Helplessness research showed that people given inescapable noise or insoluble problems reported that a depressed mood descended on them.

Symptom 2. Loss of interest in usual activities: Animals that suffered inescapable shock no longer competed with each other, fought back when attacked or cared for their young.

Symptom 3. Loss of appetite: Inescapably shocked animals ate less, drank less water (and more alcohol when offered it) and lost weight. They lost interest in copulation.

Symptom 4. Insomnia: Helpless animals became insomniacs, particularly the early-morning waking that depressed people have.

Symptom 5. Slow thought or movement; and *Symptom 6.* Loss of energy: Helpless people and animals did not try to escape shock, to seek food or to solve problems. They did not fight back when attacked or insulted. They readily gave up on new tasks. They would not explore new environments.

Symptom 7. Feelings of worthlessness and guilt: Helpless people blamed their failure to solve problems on their lack of ability and uselessness.

The more depressed they got, the more pessimistic and self-critical they became about their performance.

Symptom 8. Diminished ability to think and poor concentration: Helpless people and animals did not think well and were inattentive. They had extraordinary difficulty learning anything new and had trouble paying attention to crucial cues signalling that rewards or safety might be about to happen.

Seligman's conclusion was that the symptoms of experimentally helpless humans and animals were almost identical to those of depressed people. However, whilst having no argument with Seligman's basic tenets, subscribers to the rank theory of depression take them further by emphasizing the role of social status in causing helplessness. If depressed and helpless people seem similar, they are also similar to the description (given above) of involuntarily subordinated, trapped animals. The additional proposition is that a key cause of depression and learned helplessness in humans and primates is suffering a compulsory demotion in status or feeling oneself to have done so. But whereas the depression in primates serves a useful purpose, avoiding destructive fights, in humans it is a pathological hangover from our primordial past – rarely, for most people living in developed nations, is real physical danger a likely outcome of not displaying subordination. As Stevens and Price put it:[11] 'Depressed mood evolved as a strategy for inhibiting challenge so that stable social hierarchies could be sustained. Depression is adaptive because it induces the sufferer to accommodate to low social rank when it has been forced upon him . . . Psychological states of anxiety and depression are natural and universal experiences which human beings share with all mammalian species . . . [but in humans] both are pathological exaggerations of biological conditions which contributed to survival.' In short, depression is an unfortunate by-product of evolution. It worked fine as a way of preventing vervet monkeys from being at each other's throats all day long, but in humans it is maladaptive.

The different role of depression in humans compared with primates is shown when we consider a further central feature of rank theory – social comparison. For reasons that will become apparent, changes in patterns of social comparison may be a key cause of our low serotonin levels and the angst epidemic so I shall present them in some detail.

SOCIAL COMPARISON THEORY
The most fundamental reason that social comparison evolved was as a way of evaluating one's own opinions and abilities.[19] If these are badly at

variance with others' the consequences can be dire. To be a successful vervet monkey, for example, it is important not to continually compete with and challenge those who will always defeat you, for this would risk injury and waste energy. Equally, the animal needs to recognize those it can beat not to miss out on opportunities. To this end, it develops a concept of its own and others' fighting capacity (known as Resource Holding Power – RHP). The nearest equivalent to this in humans is the concept of self-esteem.

Personal estimates of capacity to challenge for and defend resources undoubtedly still play an important role in human self-esteem. It tends to rise when accompanied by success at work and to fall on being made unemployed, for example. But among humans there has been a steady tendency for aggression and physical threat to be replaced by attractiveness as the means for acquiring status (Gilbert called this Social Attraction Holding Power – SAHP).[15] To be valued, chosen, invited, desired and sought out are all now seen as key ingredients in self-esteem and attaining status in the eyes of others. Being downright aggressive in order to provoke naked submission in one-to-one encounters is less and less likely to achieve esteem. Increasingly, humans must concern themselves with seeming attractive in all manner of domains and to a wide variety of audiences. As Gilbert put it,[15] increasingly it is less a matter of ' "I am stronger than you," more "pay attention to/invest in me and I will be useful to you" '.

The comparison with others is done in order to estimate what will be regarded as attractive and to discover how to change your behaviour in order to succeed. We have to make a series of assessments of our own and others' status and to do this, we must have a notion of our own worth. Some comparisons are straightforward. If you are a civil servant, the employer assigns you a title with accompanying rates of pay, powers, privileges and so on, many of them written down in the conditions of employment and legal contracts between employer and employee. But many social comparisons, such as our sexual status, are less easily made or self-evident. All of us have a rough idea of how attractive we are in the marketplace of sexual desirability and many studies have shown that we tend to assign ourselves a particular 'pulling power' and then seek out people who are roughly similar, in terms of looks. People tend to be nervous about getting involved with someone who is grotesquely more attractive than them for fear that a more attractive competitor will come along and steal the lover away. On the other hand, stepping out with someone who seems like a gargoyle compared with you tends not to happen because you feel you are not reaping the full reward of nature's bounty towards you (see Chapter 6). However, not only looks are included in our calculations – humour, wealth, power, social esteem and countless other attributes are added to the equation both in terms of how attractive we believe ourselves to be and in our evaluation of others. Stunning men and women are sometimes prepared to trade a lack of looks in a partner for some other quality which compensates for it.[20] Although politically incorrect, there is substantial evidence that even today, men are more concerned with the physical beauty of women, who in turn rate power and status in men as more important than men do in women.[21] This may cause women to tend to be more concerned with their looks than men, who may be more concerned with their careers (see Chapter 6).

There is also evidence that women may be more influenced than men by negative assessments of partners by their female peers.[22] We do not only compare ourselves with others, we invite audiences to compare us directly against specific others (as in beauty or political contests) or against a general standard, such as in an exam or when applying for a job. In attempting to be selected for membership of a group we not only compare ourselves to that group but we are also sensitive to the criteria the group uses in making selections. Thus, selection becomes less a case of being able to kill off an individual opponent or threatening to do so, and more a case of being able to entice the audience to choose in one's favour.

Unlike in animals, there is huge potential for mismatches between self-assessment and reality in humans, especially when 'reality' is so relative for many attributes. In some domains (e.g. attractiveness), if you believe yourself to be higher than others might rate you (e.g. purely on looks), it is always possible that just by believing your own estimate it comes to pass. That ugly man or not especially pretty woman who keeps on attracting partners way above their apparent station may succeed by believing their own publicity. Likewise that apparently untalented success story in your work-place whose rapid ascent seems incomprehensible. Equally, though – and crucially in human rather than animal depression – the reverse can be true: humans can convince themselves they are stupid or fat or ugly when they are not. You might be stunningly attractive and believe yourself to be hideous. You might be very intelligent but believe yourself dim. You might be highly talented but convinced of your inadequacy. In some of these cases, you may become a high achiever in the domain where you believe yourself to be lacking precisely because no amount of objective evidence convinces you to the contrary, so you constantly strive to do better even though apparently doing very well when observed from the outside. But for the most part, people with irrationally low self-esteem simply underachieve and feel down.

According to Gilbert,[15] 'social comparison is one of the pillars of self-esteem'. As we shall see, a large increase in the amount that we make social comparisons and self-damaging ways of making them play a central role in triggering and maintaining depression and changes in our patterns thereof since 1950 helps to explain the angst epidemic. But before providing more detail of the distorted comparisons made by the depressed, we need to know how comparison operates in the undepressed.

SOCIAL COMPARISON IN UNDEPRESSED PEOPLE

Social comparison is a pervasive feature of all human societies. It is almost inevitable whether by means of competition, cooperation, discussion or observation. The media (television, films, newspapers, magazines) provide many opportunities for it and you would have to withdraw almost completely from society in order to avoid it. It begins in early childhood in the struggle to make sense of differences from siblings and other children. There is an atavistic tendency for all children to evaluate whether they are better/worse, more loved/less loved, more attractive/less attractive and so on, than peers. When its older sibling is allowed to stay up later or is given larger, more exciting presents, for example, the child grasps that age is one criterion used to rank people and that its age is different from its sibling's. As we shall see in more detail in the next chapter, its parents and teachers will use comparisons extensively to help build the child's identity. A sibling or friend's behaviour may be held up as exemplifying right and wrong behaviour, as in 'Why can't you be more like . . .' or 'Thank goodness you don't fight like Little Jimmy . . .'. The child may bring a drawing to its parent for evaluation compared with past drawings or those of other children and the responses of parents will profoundly affect how the child views itself. As one author put it.[23] 'A child may be told by her mother that she is a fine pianist, indeed finer than most children of her age. If the child believes this, then being a skilled pianist may become a salient aspect of her self-concept, even if, in fact, she is not better a pianist than anyone else.'

Social comparison theory was invented in the early 1950s by the psychologist Leonard Festinger[19] and numerous research studies testing his claims have established some of the most common processes, serving three basic purposes: self-evaluation, self-improvement and self-enhancement. We compare to evaluate our standing in relation to others, to improve our performance and to enhance our feelings of well-being.

For self-evaluation we tend to choose comparative targets of roughly similar competence in the domain being considered. If we want to work out our status as a golfer, for example, if we are already quite experienced then a beginner or Jack Nicklaus will give us little information because they are respectively so much worse and better that we cannot find much basis for comparison. Someone who shares our precise difficulties with putting or driving will tell us much more.

However, if we are seeking to improve our game rather than merely establish our precise status, we are more likely to make an upward comparison – observing Nicklaus will tell us more about better putting or driving than observing a beginner. However, observing Nicklaus carries with it a risk. Comparison with him could inspire a sense of our own pathetic inadequacy on the putting green or tee, lowering confidence and making us perform worse rather than better. To avoid this miserable feeling we engage in 'discounting'. We say to ourselves, 'beside Nicklaus I am useless **but he is a professional and he plays all the time so it is only to be expected**'. We use other domains than the direct comparative one to take the sting out of the comparison although the other dimensions can prove as galling – a peer might not only beat you to the school essay prize but she may also be stunningly attractive.

The closer to the comparative bone, the more painful it becomes: a surgeon might take pride in her brother the musician's success but be disturbed by her other brother's more successful career if he is also a surgeon. Discounting gets harder the closer the other person is to our own status because it is harder to persuade oneself that the other's superiority can be discounted by factors that do not point the finger of failure at ourselves.

Last summer I played a series of golf matches against my friend Paul. My handicap is 16 – on average, I will take 16 more shots than the ideal number (usually 72, known as 'par' for the golf course) that a really good player would take. Paul is better than me, with a handicap of five – i.e., he should take five more shots than 'par' for the course: a 'low' handicap means you are better than someone with a 'high' one. Although I played appallingly against him, I was able to keep my pecker up by discounting – I told myself, 'he has played all his life', 'he plays a lot', 'he takes it more seriously than me', and so on. If I played equally badly against my chum Hugo (he is so bad he has no handicap) I would be considerably more wounded because discounting would be much harder to do – there are no excuses for me to lose to Hugo. Many studies have demonstrated this point. For example,[24] when women were asked to compare themselves with pictures of extremely attractive beauties, they reported feeling demoralized afterwards. However, when they were shown similar pictures of equally beautiful women and told they were professional models they were less upset. They were able to use the professional status to discount.

By contrast, the enhancement of self-esteem operates through looking **downward** – choosing inferior comparison targets – and by **not** discounting the difference. So long as you do not take the reasons for their lesser ability into account, it boosts esteem. In the 'beautiful women' study, for example, the subjects may have cheered themselves up by picturing ugly or fat peers of their acquaintance, ignoring any unavoidable disadvantages with which these unfortunate competitors may have started (e.g. a genetically inherited large nose or other blemish). In golfing terms, I only have to think of the blundering incompetence of my friend Hugo on a golf tee or green to feel better. But this only works if I do not discount whilst making the comparison. So long as I conveniently ignore the fact that he hardly ever plays when reminding myself of his lamentable putting and disastrous driving, I will boost my self-esteem.

There is a large body of evidence[25] that when people suffer misfortune, threat or failure they use downward comparison to cheer themselves up. People who have been made unemployed, who are ill and who are under substantial stress have been shown to be more likely to do so.[26] Cancer patients, for example, go to great lengths to convince themselves that there are others worse off than themselves. A woman with breast cancer illustrates this:[26] 'I had just a comparatively small amount of surgery on the breast and I was so miserable because it was so painful. How awful it must be for women who have had a mastectomy.' Experiments demonstrate the same principle. When business students were told by authority figures that their 'business acumen' was 'surprisingly low' they were likely to disparage others and to feel anxious and depressed.[27] If, after filling in a questionnaire, students are told they have been the object of exceptional hostility from their parents in childhood, then when given the chance they will compare themselves with others who suffered even more. They are less likely to compare downwards if told they had good relations with parents.[28]

Among animals the ranking in one's group is unavoidable because the potentially fatal extreme of a one-to-one fight is imminent, but the threat of force is rare between humans from most sectors of society in most developed nations. In addition, unlike animals, humans have a wide variety of mental tools for evading the reality of their comparative environment. In the absense of a suitably badly off real person, one method is to simply invent an imaginary, vaguely specified comparison group against whom you come off well, rather than a real, specific person. Prejudice towards Jews, Gays, Blacks or other groups can be seen as a form of imaginary downward comparison. All your most negative feelings about yourself are attributed to a whole group and then you compare yourself with them, ignoring the fact that you have no evidence for your prejudice and that much of what you say about Them is true of you. Women with cancer often fabricated comparison with others or generalized from secondhand information about one or two people they had heard of who had had particular problems adjusting. In comparison with these hypothetical others, they could feel they were adjusting well. One woman said,[29] 'You read about a few who handle it well but it still seems like the majority really feel sorry for themselves. And I really don't think they cope with it that well. I don't understand it because it doesn't bother me at all.' On undesirable characteristics, we tend to see ourselves as typical, thereby watering down the undesirability. On desirable characteristics, we see ourselves as unique exceptions, to boost our value.[30]

Another simple method is to avoid making a comparison at all, even when it seems to be staring us in the face. When individuals believe their ability is low or they are under threat, they avoid upward comparison altogether to minimize risk to self-esteem,[26] forgoing the potential self-improvement. This is at its most obvious in the case of flagrantly oppressed or very poor people who are reminded every time they switch on the television or walk down the street that theirs is a worse material lot than most of their fellow citizens. By restricting themselves to similarly placed folk and ignoring the well off, they keep their spirits up, as in the case of this poverty-stricken American woman who said,[31] 'I am very content; I have more than my neighbours.' Asked about the wealthy residential area on the nearby hill clearly visible from her front yard she commented, 'My life is here. I don't think about them.' This, and all the other strategies described here, are a fine example of T.S. Eliot's memorable dictum from his poem 'East Coker':

> 'Humankind
> Cannot bear much reality'

Yet another tactic is to move the goalposts of comparison, so that although someone may be superior in one respect you find or invent another in which they are inferior. Cancer patients at death's door sometimes deal with comparatively less ill patients by switching to another dimension in which they might be worse off. Older women, for example, would use age as the means when talking about younger, healthier cancer victims. Said one,[26] 'that's a terrible, terrible thing for a young girl to face. It's different if you're an older woman like me.' Women on the brink of death would still find some solace by switching dimensions, such as 'I am surrounded by loved ones whereas many others are not.' In another study,[32] groups of boys at summer camps given the task of building a hut simply redefined the task to avoid adverse comparison when they realized their hut would not stand up. The experimenters deliberately handicapped the boys by giving them inferior materials, so when the hut proved impossible they started making a garden instead and attempted to persuade the researchers that this was just as satisfactory a basis for evaluation. Such manipulations can also be done in retrospect, using mental chicanery. A female medical student who had done worse than another said afterwards,[26] 'I couldn't help but think, If he's such a hotshot and does so well in classes, I bet he's really just a nerd; I bet he's one of those unfriendly, antisocial weenies that hang out in the library 20 hours a day; he probably couldn't have an interesting conversation with anyone.' Represented like this, he may have beaten her in the exam but he was not 'really' better.

The boundless ingenuity we display in dealing with uncomfortable social comparisons and turning them to our advantage is supported by the fascinating finding that most people manage to paint themselves a far rosier picture of their circumstances than is actually the case. At least 121 separate studies[33] have shown that in general, we view ourselves in unrealistically positive terms, that we believe ourselves to have far more control over the external events which dominate our lives than is truly the case and that we hold views of the future which are far more optimistic than is warranted by statistical probability. Furthermore, the evidence shows that these 'positive illusions' are crucial in sustaining mental health. To give just one (extraordinary) example from the many,[34] a study found that men who had tested positive for HIV (Human Immunodeficiency Virus) were significantly more optimistic that they would not go on to develop the AIDS illness than men who had tested negative! What is more, men with HIV who Think Positive about their prospects may take longer to develop AIDS than men who do not. (It is worth mentioning in passing that the 'positive illusions' body of evidence is perhaps the strongest single empirical basis for accepting the Freudian, psychoanalytically founded view of humans as highly defended against the truth about themselves and their world – i.e. that 'humankind cannot bear much reality' – and that these psychic defences against reality are essential to mental health, a point which, to my knowledge, has never been made by the academic psychologists who did this research, perhaps because most of them are hostile to psychoanalytic theory.) The positive illusions evidence does not suggest that we are living in a deluded Cloud

Cuckoo Land and it clearly distinguishes normal positive illusions from the full-scale delusions of the psychotically depressed and schizophrenic (e.g. believing you are someone other than the person named on your birth certificate, or hearing voices). The authors of the theory recently concluded that 'We maintain that self-aggrandizing self-perceptions, an illusion of control and unrealistic optimism are widespread in normal human thought. We further maintain that these "illusions" foster the criteria normally associated with mental health.'[35] Although attempts have been made to criticize the theory,[36] these have been successfully rebutted[36] and the consensus among cognitive psychologists is that we really do live in this illusory state.

The active mental manipulations used to evaluate, enhance and improve ourselves when making social comparisons play a crucial role in the construction of these illusions. By avoiding upward comparison altogether when it suits us, by moving the dimensional goalposts, by the discerning use of discounting when comparing upwards and not discounting when comparing with inferiors and so on, we build our edifice of well-being. Cancer patients can deceive themselves that they are well off, poor people can avoid feeling angry or oppressed, HIV-positive men can avoid negativity and I can even stop myself from wanting to commit hara-kiri after being drubbed on St Enodoc golf course by my friend Paul (three times in a week), if we tamper and juggle with the evidence to suit our needs. But the crucial corollary is that failure to make these adjustments to inner reality could contribute to ill-being, and so it does.

MALADAPTIVE SOCIAL COMPARISON IN DEPRESSED PEOPLE
There is now little doubt that the amount and kind of social comparisons made by depressed people significantly differs from those of the undepressed. Maladaptive social comparison both triggers and maintains depression. Depressives compare more, in ways that increase hopelessness and helplessness and that foster a negative mood. Far from living through positive illusion, at best they suffer from 'depressive realism' and at worst, have an irrational negativity which sours any good that may come their way. To adapt a famous adage, they believe that 'I'm not OK, nor are you, nor is the future'. Faced by cancer, poverty or a drubbing on the golf course they are inept at convincing themselves that 'things could be worse' or avoiding the negative impact in some other way. Given that depression has increased since 1950, it follows that – as we shall be seeing – more people are engaging in these maladaptive patterns of social comparison and that this has contributed significantly to the modern malaise.

Fundamental is that depressed people make more comparisons than the undepressed. This comes about in several different ways. They are more emotionally affected by negative feedback than normal people,[37] dwelling excessively on the emotional implications. They are also more likely to generalize from a single unfavourable comparison to a pervasive negative view of the self, often on the basis of a seemingly insignificant comparison[38] – 'when I look at my pretty friend's pert, snub nose I feel fat and stupid (as well as uglier) and there is nothing I can do to change this'. As a result, when they suffer a reverse or failure they become more self-preoccupied than normal people.[39] This makes them likely to engage in further social comparisons because, although people who are very self-preoccupied can be more independent thinking in some ways, in others they become more reliant on external, social standards for evaluating their performance[40] (perhaps because repeated introspection can lead to self-doubt). The increased amount of comparing then results in further negative emotion, and the cycle starts again.

Another reason depressives compare more is their uncertainty.[41] They are less clear than normal about what sort of person they are, who their friends are, whether they are accepted by groups they belong to and so on.[42] This uncertainty is uncomfortable, so they are constantly seeking external reassurance to relieve it – by comparing themselves with others. The insecurity about themselves also promotes a disastrous tendency to talk to others about deeply personal and threatening issues. Undepressed people are cautious in seeking information about highly valued aspects of the self because more is at stake. If you suffer from a nagging fear that your weight makes you unattractive or that your penis is unusually small, you are wary about initiating discussion of such matters[43] lest it confirms your inferiority. There are social taboos against discussion of subjects liable to be potentially explosive in most settings, such as the dictum that sex, religion and politics should not be raised at a dinner party. It is safer to read about them in magazines – although this is not without its hazards – but to discuss them face-to-face, even with intimates, is very risky.

Depressed people are abnormally eager to bring such potentially humiliating issues up, causing many a bruising encounter. They are liable to be self-obsessed ruminators about depressing topics – not a recipe for popularity (except in a Woody Allen or Ingmar Bergman film). Because all people tend to seek out others similar to themselves for comparison,[44] the depressed find like-minded people. They are more prone to negative self-disclosures about themselves (presumably as a necessary preliminary to finding soulmates) but this merely invites unfavourable comparisons from people who do not share their angst. They are also more liable to raise overly personal or otherwise inappropriate subjects[45] which produce negative responses.[46] Not surprisingly, people who do this tend not to be liked and to be rejected[47] and this has been shown to maintain or trigger depressive feelings,[48] since it increases the sense of isolation and encourages withdrawal from social situations altogether. Sadly, the depressed person's very eagerness to share their misery with others actually increases its likelihood. Taken together, all these grim mental operations increase the depressed person's social insecurity and make them ever more desperate to attempt reassuring comparison. Yet the more they compare, the worse they feel. No wonder that so many depressed people do not want to get up in the morning and withdraw from the world – at its most extreme, by suicide.

All of this may be exacerbated by an instinct for group membership and to avoid ostracization. Five million years ago, to be cast out of the group spelt death. In evolutionary terms, severe, clinical depression may have been an acceptance that one was no longer of value to the group, so total a devaluation of self-worth that one was prepared to die. Potentially fatal low self-esteem, as Stevens and Price put it[11] 'reaches a critical point when one begins to see oneself as such a hopeless liability that the group would be better off without one'. Whilst this made sense in the primordial swamp, it has little relevance to humans today but the intense pain caused by ostracization remains. Gilbert writes,[15] 'The belief in their inferiority is related to being an outsider. Depressed people often see themselves as different to others and are fearful of this difference being revealed. In our society people can often find themselves in groups which they did not select.' This can be at its most poignantly visible among elderly men who have been forced to join the ranks of the retired, a group at high risk of depression. As one suicidal elderly man put it, 'I feel I have served my purpose – raised the children, kept the money coming in – and now I am not any use to any fucking body. There is no doubt that the world would be better off without me now and if I could, I would curl up and die.' This fits closely with Gilbert's formulation that[15] 'depression is about not being able to control one's social place . . . unfavourable changes in one's relative social place or [having a perception of] occupying a low social place'.

Not only do the depressed compare too much, they do not do so in self-enhancing ways. Initially, depressed people are more liable to see others as similar to themselves, regardless of reality. This puts them at risk of unfavourable comparison with people who turn out to be unmistakably superior. Crucially, they are liable not to discount when comparing upwards. In one study,[49] undepressed students were negatively affected when comparing themselves with similar others who outperformed them but were unconcerned about older students who did better – they discounted on grounds of age and experience. By contrast, depressed students felt bad about both categories because they failed to discount. In another study, depression-prone adults saw themselves as in competition with both similar and advantaged competitor others, showing that they had failed to discount.[23] But equally disastrous, there is some evidence that depressives **do** discount when comparing downwards, thus depriving themselves of the esteem-enhancing benefit.[50] Given a worse-off person as the target for downward comparison, undepressed students found that it elevated their mood. Given the same opportunity, depressed students felt just as bad afterwards.[51] What may be happening here is that, whereas I am able to gain succour from my friend Hugo's golfing inadequacy because I ignore the fact that he hardly ever plays, the depressive rubbishes his own moment of glory with realism, by pointing out to himself that it was a hollow victory of practised like over unpractised unlike, or even worse, the depressive may go on to say, 'he'd probably beat me if he practised a bit'. The depressed compare downwards more than the undepressed,[52] probably in order to boost self-esteem ('there's always someone worse off than you'). However, insofar as they discount when making these comparisons, it will not make them feel better. Downward comparison actually increases negativity where the person feels there is little they can do to improve their conditions. Cancer patients who felt they had little control over the outcome of their illness who were told about others worse off than they, felt worse afterwards.[53] Whereas those who felt they could control the outcome felt better after the same comparison, the helpless ones may have simply interpreted the tales of greater suffering as a disturbing insight into what was going to happen to them in the future.

Although the depressed do more comparing than the undepressed, their basic strategies are aimed at self-protection.[54] They miss out on self-improvement because they fail to discount upwards and on self-enhancement because they do discount when comparing downwards. Often what they are protecting against is the blame, humiliation, guilt and shame which showers down upon them during and after their disastrous forays into the social world. They come to think of themselves as subordinate within their own mind, developing an inner voice which rubbishes them regardless of outer reality. If the evolutionary origin of depression is ritualized submission, it corresponds closely to the modern internalized experience of death by a thousand social comparisons, a repetitive mantra intoning, 'You have lost. Behave like a loser', whatever the evidence and options to the contrary. Thus may maladaptive social comparison create human losers with the low levels of serotonin that accompany low status. By these mental processes, even someone as high-status and objectively-seeming a winner as Princess Diana can feel sub-jectively like a loser.

Childhood Origins Of Maladaptive Social Comparison

Social comparison is inevitably and naturally found in all humans but as we have seen, not everyone goes about it to the same extent or in the same way. The kind of society you live in, your position in it and the kind of family you come from all make a big difference. As we have seen, mal-adaptive patterns are directly caused, in part, by subordinate social status. Since subordinate groups, like low-status civil servants and low-income women, are more likely to suffer from depression than superior groups, it is likely that they have maladaptive paterns of social compar-ing. However, not all adults of low status are depressed and many higher-status adults are. What makes some people particularly vulnerable to maladaptive comparing and not others?

Although genetic inheritances, such as a tendency to low levels of serotonin, almost certainly play a part in some cases, much of the differ-ence between individuals is probably caused by childhood experiences. Quite simply, you can be taught to subordinate yourself by neglect or humiliating abuse. Three-quarters of convicted violent men are depres-sive and most of them suffered severe abuse and from parental dishar-mony and irritability in childhood.[55] More generally, there is a large body of evidence showing that depressed people suffered specific kinds of damaging childcare. At least seven studies[56] have shown that highly self-critical depressed adults tend to have had strict, emotionally inconsistent parents who demand high achievement and performance – an experience likely to increase the quantity of social comparing in a child and to foster self-destructive patterns thereof. A torrent of labels presenting children in a comparatively negative light – such words as 'bad', 'stupid', 'inade-quate', 'useless', 'unwanted' – locate the child as unattractive and in a low-status position and they carry this subordination into later life. If parents also grab control from all aspects of the child it also subordinates them. Depressed adults are more likely to agree with questionnaire items such as 'my parents tried to control everything I did; tended to baby me; invaded my privacy'. Such over-control gives messages that the child is comparatively incapable of looking after itself, subordinating it.[57] Interestingly, studies which have compared what anxious only, depressed only and anxious and depressed people say about their childhoods find that there are significant differences. This suggests that quite specific kinds of childhood experience have different outcomes.[58]

The objection to these studies is that if you interview a person when they are depressed, they are likely to be irrationally and inaccurately negative about most things, including the way their parents treated them in childhood. However, studies which asked about this when the subjects had recovered – as well as while they were depressed – find that they recall the same childhood regardless of their emotional state.[59]

Arieti and Bemporad's study of 40 depressed psychotherapy patients is particularly revealing, despite its essentially anecdotal status.[60] They identified three patterns of adult personality predisposing a person to depression in the face of adverse life dramas (such as divorce or bereavement), each associated with a specific pattern of childhood care. As adults, the first vulnerable group relied heavily on a **Dominant Other** (usually the spouse) to bestow meaning and self-esteem. They formed an imaginary bargain, relinquishing autonomy in return for rewards and nurturance. This pattern originated with domineering parents, transferred onto sexual partners in adulthood. Arieti suggests it was more common among women because 'in our culture women are trained to suppress autonomy . . . and to gain their sense of self-worth from reflected praise from others rather than directly by independent effort'. In terms of social comparison theory, the parental care in this pattern demanded that the child look outwards for definition and place a low value on its own judgement compared with its parents' (and subsequently, its partners').

The second **Dominant Goal** type, described by Arieti, was thought to be more common in men. Arieti writes: 'These individuals invest their self-esteem in the achievement of some lofty goal and shun any other activities as possibly diverting them from this quest. Originally, achievement was rewarded by the parents and so high marks or some outstanding performance was sought as a way to ensure support and acceptance. In time the individual selects some fantastic goal for himself which he then pursues fanatically, apparently for its own sake . . . The individual believes that the goal will transform his life and, possibly, himself. Attaining his desired object will mean that others treat him in a special way or that he will finally be valued by others. Just as the "Dominant Other" type of depressive individual uses fantasies of the relationship to derive feelings of worth, the 'Dominant Goal' type obtains meaning and esteem from fantasies about obtaining his objective.' Arieti provides a detailed clinical example which is most illuminating of how parental care can create pathological patterns of social comparison.

'Mr B was a middle-aged research scientist who came for treatment complaining of a lack of interest in his work, a sense of futility in all of his activities, difficulty sleeping, fatigue, various psychosomatic complaints of recent origin, and a subjective feeling of depression. The various symptoms had developed over the previous two years after he had not received a specific position that he had greatly desired. It became clear that his depressive episode was not simply a response to missing out on the coveted job but that his failure to obtain the position signalled to him that his career plans, which were meticulous, had been thwarted forever. He spoke of great aspirations of being awarded spectacular prizes and becoming director of a prestigious research institution. His being passed over for the job forced him to realize that he might never achieve his goals.

'This man was obsessed with his work, putting in extraordinarily long hours (although he did not particularly enjoy what he did) and being so driven that some colleagues refused to collaborate with him. His marriage was a disaster. He expected his wife to plan her life around his work and expected special treatment from her because of the alleged importance of his work. He had no hobbies or interests but was consumed with fantasies of his glorious future, when everyone would respect him.

'He was raised by parents who were poor and centred their hopes for upward mobility on their children. The patient's two siblings were also driven professionals. In his childhood, he had been made to understand that he had a special mission in life and that the pursuit of excellence (and prestige) was his way of repaying his parents for the sacrifices they had endured to send him to the best schools, etc. Pursuits that were not "productive" were forbidden. The belief in this messianic role was further fostered by the local minister who took the patient under his tutelage and, impressed by the boy's willingness to work and learn, also painted a glorious picture of his future if he applied himself. Eventually, Mr B lived only for this great goal that, once obtained, would bring all sorts of gratification and meaning. The remote possibility that he might simply remain a respected but not extraordinary scientist so discouraged him that he no longer found meaning in his activities. The goal and the quest were his motivation for being.'

This is an extreme case of pathological social comparison, in which a person has been trained up to regard a single external comparative standard as the only reason for living. It is easy to see how victims of less extreme pressure to define their life by a comparative standard could also feel a sense of hopelessness and emptiness.

Arieti's third category of depressive was dogged by black moods from early childhood. Unlike the other two types, they are unable to invent an external guide or standard with which to ward off a sense of their use-lessness instilled by undermining, over-strict parental demands.

All three types share distorted beliefs about themselves and others, fearing criticism and rejection, overvaluing the opinion of others. After a stable early infancy, all the patients were subjected to a form of emotional blackmail as toddlers. Their mothers' love became conditional on exhibiting behaviour that achieved parental goals. Where passivity and submission were required by parents the 'Dominant Other' type of adult depression followed. Where worldly success became the means of obtaining parental approval, the 'Dominant Goal' type occurred. All of the families were excessively critical and moralistic and the child was made to feel essentially worthless unless he fitted the parental notion of good.

Several other studies suggest that some kinds of depressive come from domineering parents who overstimulate social comparison.[61] One study of 86 female undergraduates identified an abnormally self-critical subgroup whose parents had been very strictly controlling and inconsistent in their supplies of love, making it contingent on high achievement.[62] It concluded that 'Such parental child-rearing practices could be expected to hinder the development of normal self-esteem in children, resulting in an increased vulnerability to generalized feelings of helplessness and failure.'

All these studies are consistent with the idea that excessive parental pressure to succeed and strictness in childhood create maladapted social comparing, but the study that pulls all this together is by Gilbert.[63] He stresses the role of parental favouritism. 'The idea that siblings are getting preferential treatment from a desired other can lead to a sense of inferiority and reduce self-esteem because it sends a negative message about one's *relative sense* of attractiveness and/or desirability for others. Clinical experience suggests typical perceptions of favouritism are due to: gender (e.g. 'my brother was the favourite because my parents wanted/preferred a boy'); age (e.g. 'I had it more difficult because I was the oldest'); physical attributes (e.g. 'my sister was more attractive than me and got more attention'); intelligence (e.g. 'my sister got more attention because she was brighter'); need (e.g. 'my brother got more attention because he was sickly'); and personality (e.g. 'my parents preferred my sister because she fitted in with the family and its values better than me'). In free interviews with sisters, McConville (1985)[64] found these kinds of comparisons were common. Moreover, parents may use social comparison (between siblings) directly to shape a child's behaviour. He adds that comparison others from beyond the family are often held up as models too, such as successful public figures from sport or the arts, religious icons and so on.

To test these ideas further, Gilbert interviewed 90 female students.[63] Being put down by parents, favouritism, lack of care and overprotection all strongly correlated with being depressive. Furthermore, they correlated with the tendency to make negative social comparisons about the self and seeing oneself as of low status. Above all, being put-down and shamed by parents and a feeling of being a less-preferred sibling strongly correlated with submissive behaviour and a strong tendency to feel shame. Gilbert commented,[63] 'thus, in females, put-downs in mothers may incline the child, and later adult, to shame-proneness and to adopt rather submissive and low-rank self-evaluations'. He also stresses that the strong effect of feeling inadequate compared to a sibling in his study 'attests to the possible role of sibling relationships within the wider family for instilling a sense of inferiority'. He concludes: 'Our human sense of rank and status in the eyes of others is often influenced by how others value us and send signals that we are attractive to them . . . the central experience that might lead to a sense of confidence (having status in the eyes of others) and mitigate against the development of a subordinate, inferior sense of self and interpersonal problems, is the perception that one is valued.' Above all, Gilbert stresses elsewhere[15] that having too high standards set by parents which children take to heart and come to experience as their own leads to them constantly feeling they have failed to live up to an overambitious, unrealistic, now internal (although originally external, but now internalized) standard. Gilbert writes[15] 'If ideals are strongly aspired to but not reached we may feel we have failed, which is equivalent to the animal who experiences defeat. Indeed, patients talk exactly in these terms – e.g. "I feel defeated in life and cannot go on".'

But it is not only parents who set aspiration levels, societies do so as well, both directly and through parents. If a single change from the hundreds since 1950 that have contributed to the angst epidemic had to be isolated, it would be our increased and altered aspirations and their effect on our patterns of social comparison. Indeed, whole societies and classes can be organized in such a way as to stimulate depression through over-exacting standards. Two examples, where depression rates are exceptionally high, come from social anthropology. The Ojibwa Indians of Northern Canada believed that children were empty vessels who would be easy prey to malignant spirits unless disciplined and toughened by starvation and other deprivations.[65] The child was indoctrinated early into the pessimistic cultural beliefs of its tribe: he was made to feel responsible for misfortunes not his fault ('discounting' is prohibited) and taught that the deities could only be propitiated by self-induced suffering. The child remained close to a family unit that tended to be proud, jealous and competitive with other families. Finally, in adolescence, the young Ojibwa was required to have a vision proclaiming the future goal he had to fulfil. It is small wonder that depression was rife in the Ojibwa. A similar picture was painted of the Hutterite societies of the Dakotas and Montana.[66] After a reasonably loving early infancy, puritanism, self-control and duty were instilled from 30 months onwards through attendance at a strict nursery. Conformity to group values and identifying with the group were demanded. Education was highly moralistic and freedom, spontaneity and privacy denied in all aspects of their life. Encouragement and reassurance were always contingent on conformity and self-control. The child learned to fear his peers, his teachers and ultimately, God. As with the Ojibwa, depression rates were sky-high among the Hutterites.

These examples show how societies can directly pressurize children and indirectly overstimulate social comparison through parents. It is time to consider how changes in our patterns of aspiration and social comparison since 1950 have contributed to the angst epidemic – why more of us feel like 'losers'.

Chapter 3

Why We May Feel Like Losers Even If We Are Winners

How The Increasing Amounts Of Social Comparison,
And More Maladaptive Patterns Thereof Since 1950,
Contributed To The Low-Serotonin Society

A key issue for any analysis of the increase in the numbers of people with low serotonin is the fact that no sector of society has been spared. If status is such an important factor in our serotonin levels, common sense would suggest that those at the top of society would not suffer from the processes of subordination described by Paul Gilbert. It seems to be true that the lowest-status and income members of society do, on the whole, suffer more from low serotonin but it is also true that more people at the top are suffering than in 1950. This chapter offers an explanation of why, using by way of illustration the case of the British family who are by any reckoning the highest status.

The plight of our Royal family has been a striking feature of postwar British public life. In the persons of the Queen Mother (henceforth, the Queen Mum), the Queen, her children and children-in-law, we have examples from three generations all of whom have lived through the period since 1950. Many of the personal problems they have suffered are statistically typical of the kinds of problems suffered by their subjects. Three of the Queen's four children are divorced and like millions of mothers, with her husband Prince Philip, she has had to deal with the emotional fallout, probably despairing at the fecklessness and self-indulgence of 'the younger generation'. The future King, Charles, has made no secret of his personal unhappiness, his dissatisfaction with modern life and his aspirations for a better one. His wife Diana's depression, bulimia, unhappy childhood, dissatisfaction with her husband's 'cold, uncaring' personality and messy divorce – including a struggle for control of her sons' futures – strike such a chord with the many millions of modern women who have also suffered these problems that they are truly iconic. Her sister-in-law, Sarah Ferguson, is also emblematic, but of other features of recent culture including a lifelong struggle to control her weight, a tendency to spend beyond her financial means and the way she responded to a loss of sexual interest in her ex-husband. Finally, watching over these calamities with gin and tonic in hand, the matriarch of the family – the Queen Mum – provides a reference point for the grandparents who have witnessed their children and grandchildren flounder through a period of unprecedented peace and prosperity.

There are four changes I shall be singling out as the key causes of the increase in maladaptive social comparison. These are: increased aspirations and individualism; the advent of mass media; the increase in actual time spent in education and of classroom competitiveness; and the increase in competitiveness and assessment in the work-place. I shall end each section with an application of these changes to the three generations of the Royal family.

Rather than examining the effects of these changes since 1950 on all the members of the family, I shall focus on the three generations of women represented by the Queen Mum, the Queen, Princess Diana (henceforth Lady Di) and Sarah Ferguson (henceforth Fergie). This is mainly because the effects that I shall be presenting have particularly impacted on the lives of women, and to a lesser extent because there is most information available in the public domain about these individuals. In my treatment of these Royals, I am not intending that they be regarded as proper clinical case histories. I have met none of them in the flesh and many of the sources upon which I draw are probably unreliable. Rather, I am using them as symbolic of the problems and issues analysed in this chapter and as such, they could equally have been fictions. The advantage is that these stories (or the media's accounts thereof) are already well known to most readers.

THREE GENERATIONS OF ROYAL WOMEN

Before embarking on the main business of this chapter, I shall present some brief psychobiographies of the four Royals. The sources for my portraits are all in the public domain – newspapers, magazines, television interviews, biographies – and in selecting from them I have excluded those that have been exposed as downright fraudulent (I have not sourced what follows because they are of more or less dubious provenance, and unlikely to be of interest to readers). The portraits are a summary of my impressions, effectively fictions since what we know is based largely on commercially motivated mass-media accounts. They are intended purely as narratives of four public figures, whose lives are internationally known, which can be used for illustration of the scientific evidence that follows afterwards.

The Queen Mum

The extent of the fondness felt for the Queen Mum by her subjects predated her starring role in the Second World War when, during the Blitz of 1940, she visited the terrible scenes in the East End of London. From long before then she had been a Gay Young Thing and as such, featured in press accounts of Society Life during the jolly period (for the aristocracy – for the rest it was the time of The Great Depression) that succeeded the misery of the First World War. When the unexpected abdication of her brother-in-law, Edward VIII, occurred in 1938 she was like an understudy, ready made to take her greatest role of all – Queen. The preparation had begun in early childhood. She was already regal and charming by the age of four. She welcomed a visitor to her father, the Earl of Strathmore, with the words, 'How do you do Mr Ralston? I have not seen you look so well for years and years.' There are many other similar firsthand accounts of her desire to please and impress visitors. Asked to write her favourite childhood pastime she chose 'liking people'. A friend of the family said she was 'the most astonishing child for knowing the right things to say'. She adored dressing up and acting, and doubtless her precociously mannered greetings were part acting. One biographer wrote that 'had circumstances been different she might have elected to go on the stage'. Her favourite role was as the 'Princess Elizabeth'. This was her family nickname and she loved to wear her 'Princess Elizabeth' dress, acting the part in family plays. A visitor to the house remembered, 'I always addressed her as Princess Elizabeth, kissed her hand and made a low bow, which she acknowledged haughtily.'

Her desire to please and to charm, her love of acting roles and her desire to see herself as a princess may have partly stemmed from being the second youngest of ten children. The next eldest sibling was six years older and it must have been difficult to get attention. Like so many youngest children, charm was an effective weapon. She was also surrounded by adults for much of the time, and as the child of aristocrats, required to 'act' adult from an early age. But the need for approbation may have had deeper origins as well. Her nanny Alah, who was also to nurture our present Queen, was a strict disciplinarian. As described in the last chapter, such childcare can leave a child feeling love is contingent on good behaviour. It may have created a fear that she will not be loved for herself, only if she is pleasing to adults. There are some signs that the Queen Mum did feel deprived. Her mother Cecilia managed her ten children, an observer recalled, 'much the way she managed the staff'. She became depressed, following the deaths of two of her children. Depression in mothers leaves their children feeling insecure and bereft of attention. One biographer claims that the Queen Mum 'as a daughter, wife and mother craved attention. She needed the "fix" of public approbation.' Certainly, old age has done nothing to diminish her attention-grabbing dress sense. Her hats have never concealed her face, worn well back, and she still tends to have a heel on her shoes. When small she created a den where she hid chocolate and cigarettes and has had a life-long addiction to both. These drugs of solace may have been reliable sources of gratification compared with the adults who cared for her. As a biographer put it, 'from an early age she used food to fulfil her needs' and as a result, has always been slightly plump. This raises an interesting comparison – with the present Princess of Wales. She has also used food as a way of expressing deprivation and has also been the darling of the public. But the comparison is most revealing for showing the features that make the Queen Mum different.

Whereas Diana has chosen to make her difficulties very public and has sought therapy, the Queen Mum, coming as she does from a more circumspect, Stiff-Upper-Lip generation, has always maintained a silence. Had she been put through the media grilling that Diana has endured, would it have been a different story? One clue is the approach that the Queen Mum took to marriage. Originally, she had been offered up as a potential wife to the future King, Edward. It was only after he showed no interest that she was punted in the direction of his younger brother, Bertie (later George V), whose heart she quickly won. But he had to propose three times before she accepted and it seems that she was extremely reluctant until she was sure he truly loved her and had had no other entanglements. This scepticism may have resulted from a lifelong suspicion that no one really loved her for herself, from her childhood. But unlike Diana, whose childhood was considerably more disturbed, the Queen Mum did not take the hand of the first Royal to present himself. Her need to be loved was tempered by caution and a desire to be the only leading lady in the drama of her husband's life. It may be that if the Queen Mum had been placed in the situation of Diana, she might have handled it very differently. But as we shall see, there were also a great many social forces operating since 1950 on Lady Di which were absent during the Queen Mum's younger years.

THE QUEEN

As a small girl the Queen Mum's daughter, Elizabeth II, had symptoms of Obsessive Compulsive Disorder (called OCD). In a sensational book published in 1953, her governess from the age of five, Marion Crawford ('Crawfie'), unwittingly described the symptoms when she outlined the Princess's 'obsessions'. These included a night-time ritual involving 30 toy horses, one foot high, on wheels at the end of her bed. Crawfie wrote that 'Stable routine was strictly observed. Each horse had its saddle removed nightly and was duly fed and watered.' The preoccupation went far beyond a normal child's craze, lasting the whole of her childhood, and there were many other signs of OCD. At night, for example, she placed her shoes exactly under her chair at a particular angle with her clothes carefully folded on it. She would leap out of bed to check the alignment. She had an obsessive way of lining up the brown coffee sugar granules given to her as a treat after meals.

Elizabeth was a repressed, careful girl. Crawfie writes that she 'was a very neat, serious, perhaps unusually good child. Until I came, she had never been allowed to get dirty.' Her most personal relationships were with animals. She told Crawfie, 'If I am ever Queen I shall make a law that there must be no riding on Sundays. Horses should have a rest too.' She may have projected her suffering, her burden of being constantly bossed about and controlled by adults, onto the horses. She may also have sought animal company because she was lonely. Crawfie recalls, 'Other children always had an enormous fascination, like mystic beings from a different world, and the little girls [Elizabeth and Margaret] used to smile shyly at those they liked the look of. They would have loved to speak to them and make friends but this was never encouraged. I often have thought it a pity.' Elizabeth's personality was probably heavily influenced by the regime of her nanny, Alah Knight (who had also nurtured the Queen Mum). She only saw her parents for brief, daily snatches during her early years. Crawfie said of Alah's reign that 'the nursery was a State within a State. The Head of the State was Nanny.' Like the God, Alah was harsh. She saw her task as to suppress and channel the unruly instincts of the child. Crying babies were not to be indulged, hungry babies must learn to adapt to regular, externally defined feeding times. Potties must be introduced as soon as possible and regularly, always after breakfast. Given this obsessive regime, it is hardly surprising the Princess had obsessions, but in addition there were anxiety-provoking separations which can also have this effect. When she was nine months old, her parents disappeared on a State visit to the Antipodes. When they returned six months later she may not have recognized them at all. This may have caused 'anxious attachment', a fear of being rejected or abandoned by loved ones. It would have increased the attractiveness of animals since at least they could be relied on. Elizabeth's childcare also may also help to explain why she fixated on her husband at the tender age of 13, and why she persevered in marrying him against considerable opposition. Tommy Lascelles, a leading courtier, said the Court deemed Philip 'rough, ill-mannered, uneducated and probably not faithful'. Effectively orphaned at the age of ten, Philip had a severely emotionally deprived childhood, with separated parents. He was a cold, calculating suitor giving a chilling account of the motives for his marriage. 'After all, if you spend 10 minutes thinking about it, how many obviously eligible young men were available?' he said. He became a bullying father, according to Prince Charles, 'unable or unwilling to proffer affection and appreciation'. Elizabeth's childhood probably played a big part in attracting her to this pugnacious and unsatisfactory father to her children. Her obsessiveness very likely prevented her from considering other men. Once fixated at the age of 13 she could not let the idea go. Her anxious attachment meant she wanted to cling to someone. Her repressed personality may have been attracted to his delinquent, impulsive qualities such as his love of dangerous speeding in sports cars. According to Sarah Bradford, Philip has had countless affairs since the marriage, all with young aristocrats, including a princess, a duchess and two countesses. Bradford describes how 'on one occasion Elizabeth could see her husband dancing very close to her hostess' daughter. She sees but she does not want to know. Nor does she want to be told.'

Crawfie wrote that Elizabeth 'took after her father, reserved and quiet about her feelings'. Her uncle Lord Harewood said, 'It was a tradition not to discuss anything awkward' in her childhood home. Elizabeth's mother also believed in emotional repression. According to Sarah Bradford the Queen Mum 'always swept the awkward things of life under the carpet'. Elizabeth was therefore extremely ill-equipped to clear up the emotional carnage when her children's marriages fell apart. Above all, when Charles felt the need to put the record straight, he was virtually incommunicado with his mother. Perhaps because he could not communicate with her or his father, he spoke to a television camera and gave all his secret correspondence over to a biographer. Princess Diana's 'Queen of Hearts' transmission followed a year later and the monarchy has never been more exposed as a result. The repressive upbringing created a monarch who denies but, as Freud postulated, there is a 'Return of the Repressed': those who forget the past are condemned to repeat it. Few lives better illustrate this dictum than that of Diana, Princess of Wales.

LADY DI

The similarities between Frances Shand Kydd – Diana's mother – and her daughter are numerous. Both leggy blondes, they were born in the same room in Park House on the Sandringham estate which Frances' father was lent by his friend George V. Both had parents who were royal courtiers (Earl Spencer was an equerry to the Queen). Diana's husband was 12 years older than her, Frances' 14 years (there was a 26-year difference between her parents, Ruth and Maurice Fermoy). Both married young (Frances 18, Diana 20) and within a year had borne a child, under intense pressure to produce a male heir. Both found their first husbands' friends and pursuits dull. But there is one large difference.

Whereas Diana has been able to win a large amount of public support in divorcing her husband, Frances was publicly humiliated. When Frances began a trial separation from Johnnie Spencer in the summer of 1967 and subsequently was forced to sue him for custody of the children, she was depicted as a feckless 'bolter'. Enormous sympathy was won for Spencer because Frances was leaving him for another man, Peter Shand Kydd. But what no one knew at the time was that Spencer was almost certainly a wife beater. Erin Pizzey, founder of refuges for battered women, wrote a novel (*In the Shadow of the Castle*) about wife-beating in high society which is widely assumed to be based on accounts of the marriage. Diana has recalled witnessing vicious arguments between her parents and these escalated into violence. Her father was not on speaking terms with his own abrupt, irascible father for much of his life and may have been abused by him. Spencer appears to have been an emotional cripple. After his divorce he said of his marriage, 'How many of those 14 years were happy? I thought all of them until we parted.' He seems to have buried his emotions and was yet another person in the Royal Saga to prefer animals to people. When the children returned to Park House after visiting their mother in the holidays, Diana's nanny Mary Clarke wrote, 'After he made them welcome he would normally retire to his study and leave me to restore equilibrium in the house.' Frances was ripe for an affair when garrulous, witty businessman Peter Shand Kydd came on the scene. The divorce, even in swinging 1967, was a major scandal among the aristocracy as well as being Diana's first taste of what mass-media exposure can be like, and it provided an unsparing insight into the sort of person Frances' mother was.

Frances claims that she had 'a wonderful, happy childhood' but in the unlikely event that this is correct, it could only have been because she was raised by nannies and rarely saw her mother. Ruth was an austere, strict Scot who met Frances' father, Lord Fermoy, whilst she was training as a concert pianist in Paris. When her daughter's divorce occurred she totally betrayed her, giving evidence against her in the custody battle. According to Penny Junor, Ruth 'really could not believe that her daughter would leave a belted Earl for a man in trade'. Nanny Clarke claims that Spencer had 'a very close relationship with his mother-in-law' and that 'she gave guidance to Earl Spencer on the care of the children'. It was Ruth who decided to send Diana off to a boarding school at the tender age of nine against her father's better instincts. According to Clarke, Spencer was 'hesitant but he was persuaded that a new environment was just what Diana needed'. This kind of meddling in the upbringing of her children must have been extremely vexatious to Frances and after the divorce Ruth acted as a spy on Spencer's behalf. Before the children would go to see their mother Nanny Clarke reports that 'Lady Fermoy talked to the children about what they intended to do with their mother'. The divorce case hinged on a dispute about the cause of an injury to Diana. She had a fall from a horse shortly before going to join her mother for a skiing holiday. According to Clarke, 'although a little shaken, no damage was done' but according to Frances, the arm was damaged and an X-ray in a Swiss hospital proved this. Yet when Diana was returned to Clarke with her arm in a sling, Frances was blamed for the damage. With her own mother plotting against her and having been cited as the third party in Shand Kydd's divorce only two months before, Frances lost the custody battle. But Frances did not find happiness with Shand Kydd when, in 1972, they moved to a 1,000-acre estate in Oban, Scotland. Residents say he hardly ever visited and they separated in 1988 when he moved on to an affair with a younger woman. Frances became a Roman Catholic.

Given this disharmonious history, it is not surprising that Diana suffered from depression (for which she took the antidepressant Prozac and had psychotherapy), bulimia and suicidal thoughts. However, when she was interviewed on British television in 1995, she did not speak much of her childhood. Her performance was notable for its assertiveness. Again and again she used the emphatic 'I know'. Did she think her husband loved Camilla Parker Bowles (his lover of 25 years): 'I didn't think that – I **knew** it.' Did she believe she can help others in distress: '**I know** I can.' Yet she was impressively prepared to admit it when she did not know what she felt. One discerned the best effects of therapy in her refusal to attack and recriminate against her husband (although it is true that just by speaking out she was doing so) and in her explicit awareness of the problems her divorce could have caused her sons – she knew full well what it was like to have one's parents' divorce splashed across the newspapers. Only one thing was lacking from her account: the role of her childhood in breaking the marriage up and forming her present preoccupations.

Right at the start she mentioned that she had always been anxious to avoid inflicting what had happened to her on her sons. But she offered no clear reason why she has in fact done so – apart from the special pressures on a royal marriage and (implicitly) the emotional inadequacy of her in-laws. She was so busy exposing Charles' inadequacies that she ignored her relationship with her father. Everything she had to say about Charles was true of what we know of her feelings about her father and probably, of her mother's feelings about him too. Thus, she told us that Charles failed to be responsive when she suffered postnatal depression, para-suicide and bulimia. He never took her work at all seriously, never complimented her when she did well, only came down 'like a ton of bricks' when it went wrong. This was probably why she described herself as 'thick' at the time of her marriage. Perhaps all this was true of Charles (and then again, perhaps he was a little bit more encouraging than that) . . . but was it not also true of Johnny's attitude in childhood and later life? Her mother felt her father was emotionally unavailable and this is thought to have precipitated her leaving him. When Diana said of her own marriage, 'There were three of us' (referring to the presence of Charles' great love, Camilla Parker Bowles), was that not also true of her parents when her mother left and subsequently, when Raine Spencer moved in as the hated stepmother? Has Diana not always been surrounded by triangles and repeated this pattern in her adult life?

There was also nothing about feeling deprived of love by her nannies and parents in early childhood. Yet she believed that the 'biggest disease' today is 'people feeling unloved and I know that I can give love' (again the 'I know') by touching the members of the public she meets. This was heartfelt and will have gone straight to those of many viewers – at least half of them under age 50 have either divorced or had parents who have done so. Many feel the loneliness and despair she described. But when she went on to speak of wanting to be 'a Queen in people's hearts' rather than of the realm, you could not help pondering: Was the unloved baby and toddler Diana trying to use public adoration to replace what she missed? A common impulse behind wanting to give love unconditionally to nonintimates (e.g. in social workers and therapists) is the desire to receive it. Here was a woman crying out for it. This helps us understand her declared reason for giving the interview: 'I want to reassure all those people who have loved me and supported me throughout the last 15 years that I'd never let them down.' This and the desire no longer to be thought of as 'a basket case' and as 'unstable Diana' seem to have been the main reasons for speaking out. When she spoke of 'her' public, one was reminded of those A-list rock star interviews – an Eric Clapton or Madonna – with Barbara Walters or Oprah Winfrey on American television. They also made televisual cries for help directed at millions of people.

An obvious influence on her thinking was Susie Orbach, author of *Fat Is A Feminist Issue* and co-founder of the Women's Therapy Centre in London. When asked why the Palace had felt the need to mount a campaign of vilification (and one felt she was right that they had, not that she was being paranoid) against her, her reply was that of the modern feminist. 'Every strong woman in history has had to walk down a similar path, it's the strength that causes the confusion and fear,' she said. She may be right that men in general and The Establishment (as she kept referring to the royal hierarchy) in particular are scared of strong women. But one could not help feeling that she repeated that she is 'strong' and that she has 'chosen' her role (obviously not the case) a little more often than was necessary.

Asked if she had gone all the way in bed with the 'love rat' Major James Hewitt she replied 'Yes, I adored him. Yes, I was in love with him. But I was very let down' – as she has been by all the men in her life, but perhaps most crucially of all by Earl Spencer, of whom there was not one mention.

FERGIE

Fergie's financial problems (at one stage she owed her bank about £3 million) may lie in there never having been 'enough' in her childhood home: enough love, money or social status. By most standards Major Ronald Ferguson was wealthy. He inherited 800 acres of prime Hampshire farmland in 1966 and he must have had a sizeable income. Yet it never seemed enough. He is as fine an example of relative deprivation as you could hope to meet. To service his polo lifestyle he became increasingly like an upper-class Arthur Daley, involved with some very shady characters. He even sold himself – in the form of a tawdry autobiography. Added to this, Ron seems to have been something of a social climber, although by most people's standards, he started quite far enough up the social ladder. Along with his great-grandfather, grandfather and father he served in the Life Guards, the smartest of royal regiments. Yet he wanted more. He managed to be the first Ferguson to make the transition from parade-ground professional soldier to courtier. But to really feel at home in that role he needed a handle to his name and a multi-millionaire inheritance. He had neither. As *The Times* newspaper put it at the time of Sarah's engagement, his family was 'landed gentry rather than aristocracy, with old money but not much'. So, like the child of a Yuppie with negative equity, Fergie was raised by a father who was always stretched beyond his true social and material means.

The evidence that she was deprived comes from several sources. Many studies have shown that a mother's attitude to the care of her children reflects the kind of childhood she had. Fergie is said to have little maternal instinct, at least with babies. 'She is not into babies,' according to school contemporary Jules Dodd-Noble. Sarah has said that 'Parents don't really have any control over how their children turn out.' Not surprising, then, that she saw no problem about leaving her first-born at six weeks old to join her husband in Australia. 'Little babies are best left undisturbed so they can get into a routine,' she said. She left hers 'undisturbed' on a regular basis. This is, of course, exactly what her mother Susan and Major Ron had done. 'The advent of a baby did not curtail our lives,' wrote Ron in his autobiography. 'Susie did not seem to mind leaving them behind.' Their notions of childcare were uninfluenced by the then fashionable child-centred approach. 'I would never be over-indulgent. I tried desperately hard not to spoil her and I think I succeeded.' Yet again, as in almost all these sorry tales, animals apparently got the best deal. 'If you want to be well looked after round here, be a horse,' his staff used to joke. Horses rather than emotional involvement were also the key to Ron's choice of bride. 'Susie won my heart because she enjoyed going to polo matches and shared my love of horses and dogs,' he wrote. Somewhat unromantically, he cannot remember where or when the marriage was proposed or by which of them. When Susan met a man who loved her rather than her love of animals, the filly bolted – all the way to Argentina. Just like her sister-in-law, 13-year-old Fergie was left to be raised by her father.

A chubby child, she has always been prone to overeating. All too often the overweight use food as a substitute for love. Likewise, overconsumption of material comforts is usually a sign of feeling empty. Filling the void, whether with food or with expensive services or objects, becomes a compensation for feeling unloved. Like Lady Di, Fergie took Prozac for several years, only stopping when it reduced her sexual libido. According to schoolfriend Jilly Adams, she had low self-esteem at school. 'She had a massive insecurity problem.' At home alone with Major Ron – her sister Jane went to join their mother after the divorce – he does not seem to have been very aware of the problems. 'Sarah didn't react openly to her mother's departure. It affected her but I don't think it changed the way she was.' Her grandmother felt that suppressing the whole thing was for the best – 'We tried not to talk about it.' But, as noted above, those who forget the past are condemned to repeat it. Sure enough, Fergie found a husband similar in many ways to Major Ron. Even Ron noticed a connection: 'It did occur to me there were parallels between Sarah's marriage and my own first marriage.' Unlike Susan and Ron, Fergie and Andrew seems to have been a love match, but it was not long before it became a deprivation because he was away for the vast majority of the time, pursuing his career as a naval officer. His childish sense of humour and emotional frigidity also distanced her from him. So, just like her mother before her, when she met a racier, apparently more loving suitor, Fergie was off.

Having painted these pictures of three generations of royal women, we are ready to consider the effects of the four changes since 1950 on patterns and amounts of social comparison: increased aspirations and individualism; the advent of mass media; the increase in actual time spent in education and of classroom competitiveness; and the increase in competitiveness and assessment in the workplace.

WHY WE FEEL LIKE LOSERS
INTRODUCTORY: OBJECTIVE MATERIAL CHANGES SINCE 1950
It is often forgotten just how much more affluent the whole world – not just developed nations – is today and how rapidly this has come about. GDP (Gross Domestic Product) per head of population between 1900 and 1987 increased sixfold in the members of the OECD (Organization for Economic Cooperation and Development, the 16 wealthiest nations in the world), fivefold in Latin America, threefold in Asia and sevenfold in the USSR (a rarely mentioned, uncomfortable fact for critics of Communism).[1] For many nations, the period 1950-73 was the 'Golden Age' of growth. Whereas such nations as Britain and the USA were already relatively wealthy in 1900, and therefore had less distance to travel, the likes of France, Germany, Italy and Japan did their catching up during those decades.

Although population levels in most OECD nations had ceased growing by the mid-1960s (after the postwar baby boom was over), life expectancy rocketed, making ever-higher proportions of the population in older age groups. Whilst nearly one quarter of the OECD workforce was agricultural in 1950, this had fallen to 6% by 1980 and has stayed at that level. There was also a fall in industrial occupations as well (from about one third in 1950 to about one quarter), with service industries taking over as the majority employer. In many OECD nations government expenditure rose from being 20–30% of GDP to between 35% (in the case of the USA and Japan) and 58% (in the case of the Netherlands in 1983).

With these huge increases in wealth came corresponding expenditure on consumer durables. Average car ownership in European nations rose from about 50 per 1,000 citizens in 1956 to about 400 per 1,000 in 1989. In the same period in the USA the rise was from 300 to 600. The proportion of households with telephones rose similarly and has reached 90% in many developed nations. The proportion of European homes with bathrooms zoomed, 1950-81, from an average of 10% in 1950 to 90%, whilst the average number of persons per room fell. Sales of televisions, videorecorders, books and other leisure products rose hugely because (perhaps contrary to what one might have expected from reading the newspapers) the hours worked per working person per year fell between 1950 and 1986 by an average of about one fifth. However, this statistic conceals some sharp disparities. Within the EU as a whole 20% of men work an average of 46 hours a week whereas 40% of British men do so.[2] More precisely, in British dual-earner families one third of men work more than 48 hours a week compared with one in 16 of the women.[3] In short, although we may work fewer hours overall, some of us work a good deal more.

Not surprisingly, with a world so transformed by affluence, leisure and technology, the aspirations and values of the citizens also changed dramatically. This brings me to the first of the four changes that have altered our patterns of social comparison.

THE RISE IN ASPIRATIONS AND INDIVIDUALISM
CHANGING VALUES SINCE THE 1950s
For each decade since the Second World War there has been a book or several books which have captured the flavour of its values by advancing an iconoclastic thesis. For 1950s America it was Riesman's *The Lonely Crowd*, portraying slavish conformity. For Britain in the 1960s there was Booker's *The Neophiliacs*, scathingly denouncing that decade's fetish for novelty. For the 1970s it was Lasch's *The Culture of Narcissism*, lambasting our self-preoccupation. In the 1980s there was Dawkins' *The Selfish Gene*, a book which is often portrayed as providing an evolutionary justification of the 'Greed-is-Good' decade. But whilst these lively polemics sold well, we must turn to scientific studies of values for more measured analysis and reliable information.

In 1970, an American President stated that 'In the next ten years we will increase our wealth by 50%. The profound question is, does this mean that we will be 50% richer in any real sense, 50% better off, 50%

happier?'[4] Rather surprisingly, since he is better known as an atavistic advocate of raw capitalism, the speaker was Richard Nixon. Even he, it seems, had grasped the implications of relative deprivation theory. The previous year, a US government report had spelt out what is still today a fundamental tenet of almost all governments. 'Economic indicators have become so much a part of our thinking that we tend to equate a rising national income with national well-being.'[4] But international surveys were already underway which would reveal that this premise of modern life is false. By 1980, based on these surveys, one observer wrote of America,[4] 'It is our belief that this country is entering an era in which public aspirations can no longer be fully satisfied by simple increases in economic affluence . . . High income seemed to have less power to produce feelings of happiness at the end of the 1970s than it had had in 1957 . . . The population appears to raise its aspiration levels to keep pace when its achievements are rising.' In 1990, Ronald Inglehart, a much-cited authority, offered this conclusion:[5] 'In the short term getting what you want may produce euphoria; but in the long run it does not . . . After a while, people take what they have for granted and either want more or, when they reach saturation point, turn to the pursuit of other goals . . . One's subjective satisfaction with life reflects the gap between one's aspiration levels and one's perceived situation.'

These ideas were based on the large body of evidence (summarized in the last chapter) suggesting that once nations successfully meet the basic needs of most of their citizens, increased affluence does not increase well-being. As affluence has risen, aspirations have tended to keep a step ahead. In terms of social comparison theory, the increased aspirations constitute an increase in the amount of comparing *per se* and of upward comparing. There has also been an increasing tendency for people to want to feel they are distinctive, unique and individual rather than of the herd. But this also affects the tendency to compare – in order to feel different you must keep observing how you differ from others.

The evidence for spiralling aspirations and individualism comes from surveys of the general community conducted at regular intervals since the late 1950s, using comparable or identical questions at the different times. One of the most important, by Joseph Veroff and colleagues, compared answers to identical questions asked of 2,460 Americans in 1957 with 2,267 in 1976.[6] Overall, the 1976 sample were much more liable to evaluate themselves and their lives with reference to personal and relationship dimensions rather than social roles – to see themselves as an individual rather than in terms of their social position. They used the language of psychobabble far more in describing themselves. Whereas in

1957 the tendency was to see yourself as a role – a wife or mother or in terms of your class or educational background – in 1976 you were more likely to describe yourself using psychological words (e.g. introspective, outgoing and so on). This was especially so among the young. Compared with the class of 1957, the class of 1976 placed great emphasis on their uniqueness as a source of satisfaction. Alongside this new self-preoccupation, there was a greater interest in seeking expert help for problems, such as from therapists, a greater tendency to say they had had an unhappy childhood and a greater emphasis on intimacy and relation-ships as the cause of both satisfaction and unhappiness in their lives. They were far less likely to use moral concepts, such as good or bad, to define themselves or others. Not surprisingly, given all this, they were more likely to attribute both problems and successes to internal, psycho-logical aspects of themselves rather than to external aspects, such as social roles. They were much more likely to blame nervous breakdowns, for example, on traits within the individual or on relationships than on exter-nal, inescapable stress. So pronounced was the psychologizing tendency in the 1976 sample, Veroff was worried that 'to the extent that this more psychological approach puts an unrealistic and unmodifiable bind on people, then it may be a negative force on subjective mental health', a point to which I shall return.

Although the study showed that the 1976 sample was less worried overall about wealth and material needs than that of 1957, there was a substantial increase in emphasis on achievement and power-seeking as work goals. Long before the term 'wannabee' had been coined, young people had become considerably more aspirational. There was a much-increased reliance on work as a hoped-for source of satisfaction, espe-cially among young women. But in this they were often disappointed. Whereas 38% of young women had said they were 'very satisfied' by their work in 1957, 29% reported this in 1976 and the proportion at the opposite end of the scale, who were deeply dissatisfied by their job, had also increased in 1976. Both sexes reported wanting more satisfying work and lack of achievement as sources of dissatisfaction but especially young women (13% reported work as a major cause of dissatisfaction in 1957 compared with 25% in 1976). There was also increased conflict at work, more competitiveness and distrustfulness, which Veroff put down to[6] 'the constant pressure for more individuation, more achievement and more evaluation of performance in comparison with others'. Veroff also made explicit the possible effect of raised aspiration, especially amongst the most privileged groups:[6] 'In the process of becoming very ego involved in work, the more educated come to expect **too much** from that role. Do they develop such high expectations for individuation through a job that job gratification may be possible only in rare settings?'

Despite their dissatisfaction with their jobs, women had forsaken their traditional role, as shown by the fact that, given the choice, more of them than men would prefer to be 'excellent' at their work role than as a spouse or parent. Furthermore, more women than men would work even if they did not need the money. This high valuation of work by women was very different from the 1957 sample. As relative deprivation theory would predict, just when unprecedented job opportunities for women were opening up they became more dissatisfied on finding that really good ones (in terms of pay, promotion and job satisfaction) are scarce. Above all, the problem seemed to be that, in evaluating their satisfaction, women were not comparing themselves with their past conditions or with other women, but with men who were still at an advantage to them in many respects.[7] Other studies found that women were not so much dissatisfied with their individual circumstances as with the position of women as a whole compared with men.[8]

A very similar trend was reported for Blacks.[9] Equal rights legislation created new opportunities for them in the 1960s and 1970s but like women (this was the era in which John Lennon released a song entitled 'Woman is the Nigger of the World'), there were no signs that it was making them happier and there were signs of the opposite. Blacks in the North of the USA, for example, many of whom were doing better socially and materially, were more dissatisfied than those in the racist South. A number of studies showed that, just as dissatisfied women were comparing themselves with men, dissatisfied Blacks were comparing themselves with more privileged other Blacks or with Whites.[10] In explaining the seeming paradox of the racial unrest of the late 1960s and 1970s in America during a period of increasing rights for Black people, several authors cited Karl Marx's adage that 'A house may be large or small; as long as the surrounding houses are equally small, it satisfies all social demands for a dwelling. But let a palace arise beside the little house, and it shrinks from a little house to a hut.'

There have been numerous other surveys like Veroff's comparing values in the 1950s with the 1970s and extending the evidence into the 1980s, with similar results. Campbell[4] recorded the fact that in 1890, only 3% of American women were in paid employment. By 1951 it was one quarter and by 1978, half. Yet, writing in 1980, based on a series of surveys, Campbell concluded: 'Despite the considerable achievements of the women's movement during the 1970s ... there was very little change in the satisfaction with life expressed by women.' He presented further evidence for the seemingly paradoxical female dissatisfaction with both the role of homemaker and their job prospects. It seemed they were not satisfied by either. A more recent British survey[11] found that career aspirations were outstripping job opportunities in an alarming fashion. 55% of the 18- to 34-year-old single women wanted management responsibility and 67% sought 'greater possibilities for advancement'. Yet 42% reported no promotion opportunities in their present job. These statistics are a classic recipe for relative deprivation: high wants and sense of entitlement yet poor prospects of their fulfilment.

In 1990, Ronald Inglehart tried to make sense of the survey evidence since 1950, including one of his own, by arguing that there had been a 'Culture Shift' from 'Materialist' to 'Post-Materialist' values.[5] Materialists placed material well-being and physical security at the centre of their lives. Post-Materialists emphasized quality of life. Inglehart's argument was that basic physical requirements such as food, shelter and heat were by no means guaranteed for the whole population in developed nations before the Second World War. After it, they were. His surveys (of European nations) showed that post-materialism was most widespread in groups where material well-being was assured: affluent nations, rich classes and the young. By contrast, the more elderly generations – who still lived with their own and their parents' memories of pre-war material austerity and uncertainty – the poor and nations where affluence was not assured were still concerned with materialism. Just as the children and grandchildren of entrepreneurs who have built up large fortunes tend to be less preoccupied with acquiring wealth and more interested in quality of life (the arts, their inner lives), so with nations and classes.

Although commonsensical, Inglehart's thesis has been criticized heavily for overstating the causal role of post-materialism in producing the culture shift[12] and his methods have also been found wanting.[13] In 1991,[14] an international survey of 85 leading European analysts of social trends showed that they regarded increasing acquisitiveness, increasingly high and specific aspirations, and increasing individualism as the key trends in their countries at that time, not post-materialism. Trends such as the decline in birth rates and studies which showed that much higher proportions of people did not disapprove of keeping possession of a lost article found in the street were signs of the increasing extent of self-interest and the desire to look after Number One. In criticizing Inglehart's theory, David Halpern[15] pointed out that, compared with 1980, 1990 samples were substantially more concerned with pay and promotion and less bothered whether a job was useful to society. Whilst

Inglehart's theory might have applied to the Hippy generation of the 1960s and 1970s, the evidence is against it in the ('Breadhead, Brideshead') 1980s and 1990s. Halpern concluded: 'Higher expectations seem to be the reason why Europeans have become less satisfied with their work: levels of work satisfaction have fallen across Europe since 1981 . . . Overall, the picture of change for work values suggests not that people have become less materialistic, but that they have become more demanding. Consequently, pay is not enough: people today – and especially, young people – expect work to be interesting **and** well paid.'

Overall, the evidence shows that between 1950 and 1990 people's material and psychological expectations increased along with their affluence, yet their overall well-being did not increase and in some respects, for some groups, it decreased. As individualism grew, people were less and less prepared to settle for what they had and were liable to search for something better in the name of self-realization. Inevitably, such changes affected their patterns of social comparison.

THE EFFECT OF INCREASED ASPIRATIONS AND INDIVIDUALISM ON SOCIAL COMPARISON

The most fundamental change was an increase in upward comparison. As one author put it,[16] 'In Western culture, people not only wish to evaluate their abilities, they also feel pressure to continually improve them.' If, as happened after 1950, people are encouraged to believe that they can achieve more, to dream the American Dream, and if women are encouraged to believe that 'Having It All' (as Helen Gurley Brown's 1970s bestseller was entitled) is possible, they will inevitably look upwards for examples of what they might aspire to. Such groups as women and Blacks, who had once regarded their place in society as largely inevitable, were encouraged to aspire to the outcomes of far more privileged peers. Not only did they aspire, they had a sense of entitlement to the spoils of affluence. But upward comparison is a double-edged sword. As noted above, Blacks often compared their desired outcomes with Whites or well-to-do other Blacks, and many women compared themselves with men. The result was that many felt dissatisfied with what the system actually was able to deliver.

Of course, increased upward comparison alone need not in and of itself cause dissatisfaction. It can have positive, self-improving benefits. When people attempting to give up smoking or to overcome a phobia are given successful models to imitate, for example, it often helps,[17] just as, if I model myself on Jack Nicklaus in his *Teach Yourself Golf* video, it helps me. But upward comparison can also threaten self-esteem because one is in danger of feeling despondent at the gap between the model and one-self. If the gap between Nicklaus and me does not close despite hours of practice, I may end up blaming myself and feel like a failure. The key is whether and how I go about discounting the difference between us and perhaps the most significant change that has occurred since 1950 is that discounting has been increasingly disallowed as a way of coping with upward comparison.

Rampant aspirations and individualism encourage us to say 'I can do that', to collapse aspiration with entitlement, to feel it is our right to be anything we want to be by using magical thinking that leaves out the little matter of the instrumental steps between wish and fulfilment. They discourage making allowances for the difference between a desired model and our current state of performance. Some teenage Wannabees really believe they could be Madonna or Gary Lineker, not allowing for the fact that they might not have the necessary talent, discipline or real opportunity. Just as the British lottery uses the slogan 'It Could Be You' in its promotional material (obscuring the fact that there is only a 1 in 14 million chance that it will be), so with the raised aspirations of much of the population.

Citing the social historians Sennett and Cobb, relative deprivation theorist Jerry Suls has put the problem in an historical context.[18] 'The enlightenment encouraged a humanism which assumed that the capacity for civilized achievement lies within the grasp of any member of the human race, if only he could develop the rational powers nature instilled in him' (Sennett and Cobb, 1972). This humanism created societies in which unequal social strata still existed, but in which the groups were permeable. The 'rub' is that mobility was and still is considered to be based on the 'exercise of personal ability'. Sennett and Cobb (1972) explain: 'If I believe that the man I call "sir" and who calls me by my first name started with an equal fund of powers, do not our differences, do not all signs of courtesy and attention given to him, but denied to me, do not his very feelings being different in taste and understanding from me, show that somehow he has developed his insides, more than I mine? How else can I explain the inequalities?' The unfortunate consequence of a society that possesses the Enlightenment humanism but is also a system of unequal classes is that it renders self-evaluation (and upward comparison) problematic. As a result, large numbers of people feel deprived, but also somehow responsible for that deprivation. Other research bears out the damage done if there is an inability to change the outcome when comparing.[19] For example,[20] all the subjects in one experiment were told they had failed a test. Some were compared with models who had done better than them (upward comparison), others shown models who had done worse (downward). All were told there was to be a second test but some from each group were given to believe it would be impossible to improve, others that this was a possibility. The ones who were given upward comparisons as models and who had no chance of improvement became depressed and hostile, whereas all the other groups were unaffected emotionally. This accords with Seligman's Learned Helplessness theory. If more of us are making upward comparisons which we feel entitled to achieve but have virtually no likelihood of actually doing so, no wonder that more of us are feeling depressed because we are left feeling like helpless losers.

Suls also argues persuasively that the media have greatly exacerbated this process by blurring the differences between the wannabee and their role model.[18] For that vast majority unable to achieve their inflated aspirations and to obtain objective confirmation of their sense of their individual importance, upwardly comparing simply rams home their inadequacy and encourages depression. As Gilbert puts it,[21] 'If ideals are strongly aspired to but not reached we may feel we have failed, which is equivalent to the animals who have experienced defeat.' Just as vervet monkeys' serotonin levels drop after an encounter with a more dominant animal, so it may be with the wannabee who makes undiscounted upward comparison with an idol they are unable to emulate.

The ambitiousness of modern upward comparison is partly an unfortunate consequence of the removal of the blinkers which have restricted most of the population for most of the history of the world. As Inglehart puts it,[5] 'In a society undergoing rapid industrialization and expansion social mobility may be widespread. But in traditional agrarian societies, social status is hereditary.' Where there is little or no possibility of changing your social position through ability, such as in a feudal or caste system, you are unlikely to make undiscounted comparisons with your betters. Princes or kings are simply a different category of human to which you cannot aspire by the definition of your society. It would not occur to you. This may explain the ostensibly surprising fact that the most oppressed group of women in the developed world, the Japanese, are also by far the most satisfied compared with the men.[22] Unlike women in other nations, it probably does not occur to them to compare their lot with men and so they stick to comparing with other women. Jerry Suls has summarized the unforeseen damage that the postwar drive to include previously excluded groups has done.[18] 'Although there are vast disparities among classes, in terms of wealth, education and employment, the social credo dictates equal opportunity. Albeit good-intentioned, such reforms as desegregation and mainstreaming promote comparisons across different levels of attributes. Invidious comparisons can result and do! These reforms may be the only options our society has to correct past injustices, but they have costs, probably making some groups dissatisfied just when their circumstances are improving.' It will be interesting to see whether Japanese society will learn from our experience when, as is surely inevitable, their womenfolk begin to aspire to equal opportunities.

Alongside the humanist drive to open up opportunity to everything for all, the range of comparisons is also increasingly international. Exposed to media comparisons from early in life, young Europeans are far more global in their horizons. Many have 'been there', as well as having 'bought the T-shirt'. As high a proportion of 15- to 24-year-olds have travelled to another European nation as over-25-year-olds.[15] With the traditional shackles of class, gender, race and even geography removed, and the notion that 'anyone can be President' (or Prime Minister) oft repeated, although the real-world opportunities often do not match up, the aspirations are limitless.

Of course, as we already know from the evidence on 'positive illusions' and defensive mental manipulations, we have ways of sweetening the bitter pill of defeat when expectations are dashed. But these can also be destructive. There is today a growing appetite in the general public for media exposures of the personal shortcomings of politicians, pop stars, artists and all other categories of past and present high achievers. This may be a collective defence against the pain of increased and undiscounted upward social comparison. The publics of the developed world seem to want to demystify, unseat and subordinate their heroes after worshipping them, to downgrade them into pitiable or loathsome figures. But this leaves us bereft of role models (if 'Post-Modernism' is to be believed, everything today is merely a recycling of the past so no one can create anything new; there can be no more geniuses). Recent studies of the role of jealousy and envy in social comparison suggest that we may overcome the pain of upward comparison by enviously running down our heroes, thereby converting it into a reassuring downward comparison. Thus, if we admire Princess Diana but because, as wannabees, we are not discounting sufficiently and we begin to suffer from the comparison, we may become envious and therefore, all too pleased to read about her unhappiness in the newspapers or see her on television confessing to misery.

Jealousy is the feeling that something one possesses is threatened by another in some way. For example, a child may have a Christmas present but fear that it will be taken away by a visiting friend, or made to seem insignificant by a better or bigger version of it. In contrast, envy is the begrudging feeling that someone has something you want, often combined with the impulse to take it away or damage it. Whereas the jealous child is busy defending what they have got, the envious child may go over and grab the other's Christmas present or attempt to smash or belittle it. Peter Salovey[23] has extensively investigated the effects of social comparison on envy and jealousy. He asserts that they are likely to result when one's present self-evaluation is threatened by social comparison, especially if the comparison is liable to lead to loss of status. He writes: 'If we envy the genius in the next office we both wish we were as smart as he is but, perhaps secretly, wish he were not quite so smart. The envious person wants to have more and also would like others to have less. A goal of the envious person may be to be distinctive rather than similar to all others, as similarity can imply mediocrity.' Thus may the increase in wannabee individualists have led to more envious upward social comparison – they want to steal their heroes' special abilities for themselves and they want to feel that whilst the heroes may be more talented, their success has only made them pitiably miserable (drug addicts, philanderers or perverted paedophiles).

Salovey lists a number of methods we may use for coping with envy-inspiring comparisons, including running the successful competitor down. He cites one study which looked at how this works when we are confronted by a romantic rival.[24] In such situations, our self-esteem is put at great risk, should the object of our affection choose against us. Although we may have hostile feelings towards our potential lover for even considering another, these are poured into scorn for the rival, since to express them towards their real target would be counter-productive in the competition. The study found that in selecting aspects of the rival to criticize, the subjects were most likely to choose those aspects they believe the potential lover values highest. These are the areas where our self-esteem is most put at risk by the comparison and also the ones that would be crucial in influencing our potential lover. They are the aspects of the competitor about which the jealous subjects were most negative. If we lose the struggle, we are liable to explain away the defeat by 'sour grapes' – saying they 'were lucky' or 'played dirty'.

These processes of derogation of rivals may be operating in our feelings about public figures. We have a mental relationship with the people whose private lives we see exposed in the newspapers and baring their souls on television. It is not too far-fetched to speculate that we may be so pleased to see Michael Jackson exposed as a paedophile, or smug 'family man' OJ Simpson accused of murder, because unconsciously we see them as rivals.

Salovey points out that the amount of envy (rather than jealousy) may be less in 'traditional' compared with developed societies. In many traditional cultures there are elaborate structures and beliefs to minimize envy and the social harm it brings. In one study[25] of 67 cultures that believe in the 'evil eye', it served to discourage envy-promoting behaviour. Sharing wealth was believed to make the evil eye less likely whereas bragging about successes increased its likelihood. Myths told of the harm, disease and misfortune that came to those who aroused envy. 'In contrast', writes Salovey, 'Western culture, especially American society, has been criticized as being fuelled by envy as a way of maintaining a capitalist economy.' Several studies[26] suggest that the encouragement to define yourself through the opulence and extent of your wealth and possessions stimulates envious comparison. A study differentiating envious from unenvious cultures showed that the latter discouraged property rights, sexual possessiveness and marriage or progeny as high status. There were simply fewer possessions for people to get envious about.[23]

Another crucial change since 1950 is that we may be more prone to choosing criteria for comparison and aspiration on which we are more liable to fail. The evidence that we have become more self-obsessed and more liable to judge ourselves by our relationships and quality of life (alongside our increased lust for success at work) creates the danger that we are setting ourselves impossible standards. Veroff writes:[6] 'As many people have learned, it is often difficult to discover the authentic self.' He might have added that achieving a successful marriage or love life is 'often difficult' too, yet in a period when divorce increased nearly four-fold, we have been placing ever greater importance on this aspect of our life as a basis of social comparison. In his book *Solitude*, Anthony Storr provides a wealth of evidence that placing so much hope in relationships is misplaced. 'It is widely believed that interpersonal relationships of an intimate kind are the chief, if not the only, source of human happiness. Yet the lives of creative individuals often run counter to this assumption.' He goes on to list numerous great thinkers, from Descartes to Wittgenstein, who were unmarried and highlights many healthy consequences of solitude that are often forgotten.

Perhaps surprisingly, our greater tendency to be therapy-minded as part of our greater individualism and aspiration for higher quality of life actually increases the amount of reliance on social standards for evaluation of one's performance. Many studies have shown that greater self-awareness leads to greater uncertainty, at least in the short term, and to remove it, we may look outwards for definition.[22] Whilst therapy and talking about ourselves to friends may be reassuring and enable us not to repeat mistakes in the long term, they make us vulnerable to comparison. In addition, self-aware people are more likely to blame themselves rather than their environment when things go wrong.[27] Being self-focused, they assume it must be something to do with them.

These trends were exacerbated from the 1980s onwards by the vogue for individualistic explanations of social processes by politicians and some political scientists, eagerly retailed by the media, and by a sharp increase in inequalities in some developed nations. Robert Bellah[28] has put this point forcefully. 'Americans are united in this belief across lines of color, religion, region and occupation: the belief that economic success or misfortune is the individual's responsibility and his or hers alone . . . American individualism demands personal effort and stimulated great energy to achieve yet it provides little encouragement, taking a sink-or-swim approach to moral development as well as to economic success. It admires toughness and strength and fears softness and weakness. It adulates winners while showing contempt for losers, a contempt that can descend with crushing weight on those considered, either by others or by themselves, to be moral or social failures . . . members of the underclass have only themselves to blame: it's their resistance to all efforts to help them that has caused the problem. The underclass was actually created by the efforts to help them, above all by the Great Social welfare programs, which caused self-perpetuating, indeed permanent, welfare dependency . . . Even in the underclass, those who are not on welfare look down on those who are and those who are on the dole look down on those on it for a long time.' Bellah goes on to record that inequality in America had reached record levels by 1970 and that this continued to even greater levels by 1995. Thus, between 1973 and 1993 GDP rose by 29% yet 80% of Americans became poorer in real terms during that period. This was because the top 20% were the ones whose real incomes went up. The same trend has occurred in Britain[29].

Households Below Average Income (1994, HMSO) reveals that 25% of Britons were living with an income less than half the average in 1991–2, compared with 9% in 1979. The real income of the poorest 10% of Britons fell by 17% during this period compared with a 62% rise in real income for the wealthiest 10%. Only the top 30% of the population (ranked by income) achieved above-average growth in their incomes. Whereas 80,000 Britons earned more than £700 a week in 1979, 1.1 million did so in 1991–2, a huge change even allowing for inflation. The conclusion is that Britain is more unequal today than it was before the Second World War.

Regarding welfare provision for the lowest income sectors, benefits for the unemployed or the young have been reduced in real terms. The trend away from state provision of cheap housing by councils to private renting has also affected rates of homelessness. Perhaps most telling of all, the effect on health of the new inequality has been dramatic. The *British Medical Journal* (1994) devoted an issue to the subject, with several papers showing unambiguous correlations between inequality and poor health comparing European nations. Regarding Britain, an editorial summarized their view as follows: 'Growing socioeconomic divisions are likely to be an important part of the reason why average life expectancy in Britain slipped from 12th to 17th position among the 24 nations belonging to the Organization of Economic Cooperation and Development between 1979 and 1990 . . . Once it seemed possible health was best served by faster economic growth, which was incompatible with greater equity. Among the rich nations, however, little or no relation exists between growth and the rate of fall in mortality: the problem is relative not absolute deprivation. Indeed there is evidence to suggest that national infant mortality rises if the rich get richer while the real incomes of the poor remain constant.' The increased tendency to 'blame the victims' of increased inequality makes undiscounted, rampant upward social comparison even more injurious to self-esteem.

Thus, the rise in aspirations and in individualism have singly and in combination increased the amount of upward comparison and removed the get-out clause provided by discounting.

ROYAL ILLUSTRATIONS OF THESE CHANGES
Fergie and Lady Di both share their generation's emphasis on relationships as a source of satisfaction, the belief in self-analysis and in speaking about problems. Both married for love, have undergone therapy, have appeared on television speaking openly about their problems and both have contributed to books spelling out their view of their respective predicaments. Both would probably blame their emotional problems or the nervous breakdowns of others on psychological characteristics and relationships (Lady Di is explicit in blaming her bulimia and depression on her husband) rather than unavoidable factors such as their genes or 'stress'. By contrast, coming as they do from an older generation, it is almost inconceivable that either the Queen or her mother would ever do any of these things. They probably had no illusions about their marriages, fully expecting their husbands to be unfaithful, and regarded their roles – as mother, Queen and wife – not their emotional relationships as the foundation of their happiness.

A bizarre but intriguing possibility is that, despite their hugely privileged status, the younger royals actually upwardly compare with the individualistic ambitions of more ordinary women and feel subordinated thereby. Perhaps Lady Di looks at Susie Orbach or other successful female professionals and feels inadequate by comparison and perhaps Fergie does the same in the world of business, in which she has dabbled extensively. The very fact that they were born with silver spoons in their mouths, whilst still a source of envy for much of the population, has been rendered a source of pain by the new egalitarianism and ambition of women. By contrast, convinced of the primacy of social role and the traditional female role, the older royals probably look down their noses and see a woman professional as an object for downward comparison – 'poor souls, having to work so hard' or somesuch.

Even more remarkable is the way that Fergie went from being an object for upward to downward comparison, an unpleasant fate that may befall Di before too long. Since soon after her marriage Fergie (and since her television interview, Lady Di to a lesser extent) became the object of downward comparison for most of the populace, a figure to be despised and pitied – a fat, spendthrift, avaricious, publicity-seeking, sexually disloyal little rich girl. Her recent autobiography provides powerful evidence that she has internalized these projections. She repeatedly describes herself in it using the very same disparaging terms. At her wedding she had been widely perceived as 'sexy' and 'fun-loving' and this is how she says she saw herself at that time. But the new envy which turns admired public figures from undiscounted upward comparison objects into sad and reviled ones may have contributed to the change in Fergie's self-esteem. Since this trend only emerged after their youth, the Queen has been largely spared this reversal and her mother remains the one royal to be totally untouched by it.

By identifying herself with the sick and the disadvantaged, Lady Di may have used the classic methods of the depressed person of making self-enhancing downward comparisons with those less fortunate than her – recall the way that cancer patients made themselves feel better by identifying aspects of their situation which were comparatively good. But like Fergie, she almost certainly now wishes she could have what would technically be a lower social status – to be a doctor or a businesswoman. In both cases, therefore, the huge increase in female aspirations and individualism has profoundly affected them.

Most significant of all, the chances are that, had they been born 70 years ago, they would not have left their husbands when they became discontented because they would not have compared themselves with their 'Having It All' peers. They would have seen this as beneath rather than above them. But they have been as affected by the increase in comparing *per se*, as the rest of us, and with the collapse of social roles as the key to self-definition, unlike their elders, they see commoners as appropriate objects for upwards social comparison. They do not, as the Queen and Queen Mum probably do, use their royal status to discount the difference.

MASS MEDIA AND MALADJUSTED SOCIAL COMPARISON
THE INCREASE IN MASS MEDIA

As noted, we work about one fifth less than in 1950. The most common method by which we fill the extra leisure time is watching television. The timing of the introduction of television varied considerably between developed nations. In the US and Britain, a significant minority of households already had a set by 1953 whereas it took until 1960 for most European nations to reach the same level.[1] From then on there was a uniform and steady invasion of our homes and by 1965 half had a set in all the developed nations and ten years later, almost every household had one. Ever since 1975, on average, Europeans have spent between two and three hours watching TV – 13–19% of their waking lives. Average daily viewing in Europe is least in Switzerland (60 minutes) and highest in Spain (209 minutes), followed by Britain (189 minutes). Patterns vary according to age. Viewing increases steadily between ages two and eight, remaining constant until 13, then decreasing until early adulthood when it rises again, remaining constant until a further rise, on retirement. Across Europe, people with semi-skilled or unskilled occupations watch about twice as much as those with professional and managerial jobs (an average of 31 hours a week versus 18 hours).

Viewing is heavy in America. One survey[30] found that American 12-year-olds were watching 6 hours a day, and at the age of ten, spent more time watching TV than in the classroom. The version of reality they were viewing was considerably different from the real American world. About three-quarters of American TV characters are male, most are single, white, middle to upper class and in their 20s and 30s. The women characters tend to represent romantic or family interests. Whilst one third of male leads in TV dramas intend to or have married, this is true of two-thirds of their female counterparts. About 40% of characters in American dramas are employed in professional and managerial professions (compared with 20% in American reality). A remarkable 20% of characters are employed in law enforcement (compared with less than 1% in reality). Not surprisingly, given these distortions, heavy TV viewers are significantly more likely to estimate incorrectly when asked to guess these statistics (overestimating them) compared with light viewers.

There are an average of 7.5 acts of overt physical violence per hour on American TV, with major drama characters facing an average of five threats of physical violence or actual attacks per hour.

The increased amount of leisure time and affluence has led to increased consumption of many other media products, apart from TV. Whilst cinema attendance had almost halved by 1987 (although making something of a comeback in recent years), videotape machines and home computers (including computer games) are now widespread and sales of magazines are booming, although newspapers have seen a steady decline in the last 20 years. The number of books published in developed nations has risen from 220,000 a year in 1977 to over 600,000.

Of all these developments, the emergence of television is the most significant and in what follows, I shall concentrate mainly on this medium.

THE EFFECT OF THE INCREASE IN MASS MEDIA ON PATTERNS OF SOCIAL COMPARISON

In 1978 I spent three months studying Borbon, a village in Northwest Ecuador with few inhabitants that could read or write, no televisions, radios, newspapers, magazines or books. No one there had heard of England. The Borbonaise only knew the people they had actually met or knew of relatives and friends they had been told about in nearby villages. By contrast, I 'know of' or am 'acquainted with' many more people. If I was to write a list of all the people I know a good deal about it might run to a thousand. There are all those I have spoken to on the telephone many times but never met. There are the (terrifyingly numerous) people I have read about in newspapers and magazines, the people I watch on TV and listen to on the radio, the stars I have watched in films. Indeed, you might say that my mind is a pit of useless information. I have built up this trivial database over many years, whole galaxies of stars and celebrities whose personal histories of achievement or emotional development I am more or less aware of depending on how much detail has come into the public domain and how much they have attracted my interest. They include politicians, TV performers (including entertainers and current affairs presenters), actors, sports stars (soccer, cricket, rugger, snooker, golf), rock stars, novelists, academics (as well as reading their thoughts, in preparing this book I have formed telephone relationships with dozens of academics, mostly in America) and so on. There are all the ordinary people I know about who became 'famous for 15 minutes' for various reasons, including murderers, victims thereof, civil rights *causes célèbres* and curiosities (such as the 32-year-old man who passed himself off as a 16-year-old and retook his 'A' levels at school, or the woman who revenged

herself on her unfaithful husband by cutting off the arms of his suits).
What is more, these galaxies are international – I know of many people
who live thousands of miles away in different cultures from mine.

A key aspect of this change is the way it blurs the actual and the imaginary, the people who I have met in the flesh and the people whom I feel
I know but have only experienced as celluloid images or as a pattern of
dots that look like a person on a TV screen or as a picture in a newspaper
or whose voices I have heard on the telephone or radio or whose words I
have read. Television is especially powerful at creating the illusion. I have
interviewed many stars from soap operas in the flesh, all of whom have
met members of the general public who seemed to have suspended their
disbelief so completely that they talked of the world of the soap as real
(interestingly, nearly all these stars seemed uncommonly like the characters they portray and I am told by soap producers that this is no coincidence – the actors are carefully chosen because they are like the
characters they will play and the scripts are subsequently adjusted to the
actual mannerisms and speech patterns of the actor to further improve
the fit). Of course, all the people I know – whether I have met them or not
– are imaginary in the sense that they are constructed by me in my mind
based on sensations of sight, sound and so on. Whether the sources of
these sensations are facsimiles of people (celluloid, electronic, etc.) or
their real bodies, you might say, is irrelevant – in the end, they are all real
in that they exist as patterns of electrochemistry in my brain, whatever
the external source. But the blurring has important implications in terms
of social comparison because it creates a sense of familiarity which fudges
the fact that I do not 'really' know them. This familiarity reduces difference and crucially, encourages me to see them as similar, as people who
inhabit my social world. As we saw in the last chapter, if upward social
comparisons are not to result in a depressing sense of inadequacy it is
important that we recognize difference – that I discount when comparing my golf to Jack Nicklaus' by reminding myself that he is a pro, prac-
tises all the time and so on. But if I experience Nicklaus as someone like
myself, a person who I know and have a relationship with (albeit a one-
way relationship), I am more in danger of not discounting.

Some of the huge difference in the size of my acquaintanceship compared with the Borbonaise in 1978 existed for British adults in 1950. The
radio, Pathé News at the cinema, the movies that followed them, newspapers, magazines and books meant the average person in 1950 'knew' a
great many more people than the average Borbonaise. As far as I know the
study has never been done, but I suspect that if the average number of
'acquaintances' between the three groups (today vs. Borbon in 1978 vs.

97

Britain in 1950) had been measured, it would be substantially different for all three. Suppose the average Borbonaise could name 150 people in all (I doubt it would be much more). The average 1950 Briton might have managed four or five hundred. I suspect that the average 1996 Briton would manage twice that, including several times as many foreigners than in 1950. In short, mass media since 1950 have supplied vastly more people with whom we can compare ourselves and have hugely expanded the number of societies from which they are drawn.

It is likely that the blurring effect of this change – especially television – has profoundly affected our patterns of social comparison. Regrettably, there has been surprisingly little research directed specifically at this issue. Many researchers mention it, but only in passing. They emphasize that media models are forced onto us, thereby increasing the dangers of unwanted upward comparison and involuntary subordination. Paul Gilbert points out that[21] 'Individuals select the sources of their comparison . . . On the other hand, the environment can impose sources of comparison (e.g. television continually shows us people in better houses and with considerably better resources).' Another influential researcher writes,[27] 'The media (e.g. television, magazines, movies, etc.) provide many salient opportunities to engage in social comparisons. To avoid social comparison would require an almost total withdrawal from society.' Whilst most social comparison and relative deprivation researchers seem to believe that the media stimulates social comparison and, reading between the lines, seem to suspect that its effect is to increase maladaptive patterns, very few have done empirical studies to establish whether this is really so.

One reason may be that most research has concerned the effect of celluloid violence on real-life violent behaviour because research funding for this kind of study is readily available. A survey of 2,500 studies of the social effects of television in 1978[31] found that 80% of them had been devoted to this subject. A similar problem arises with the effect of advertising in general and TV advertising in particular. Whilst there is a large body of information regarding how people react to particular categories of advert and to specific campaigns, even in the vexed matter of the effect on children there is deplorably little known about the wider consequences, including for patterns of social comparison. Whilst it is understandable that commercial organizations are not in the business of promoting lines of research which might point to damaging consequences of their selling methods, it is shameful that governments have done so little to find out about such a crucial and potentially destructive aspect of their citizens' lives.

Having said this, however, there are some important and telling studies to which we can turn. Although rarely referred to, perhaps the most dramatic demonstration of the effect of media is the series of studies conducted by Douglas Kenrick over the last 16 years. They were concerned with the ways that media portrayals might cause us to be dissatisfied with the attractiveness of our partners and might stimulate depressive feelings about our own looks.

Kenrick prefaced the first study, published in 1980, by pointing out that the models used to sell goods and as actors and TV presenters in the media are rarely less than stunningly attractive.[32] Given the evidence that our judgements are influenced by the extremes and by comparative contexts, he hypothesized that being exposed to extremely beautiful women on television would influence the short-term standards of women's attractiveness of young male viewers. To test the theory, audaciously, he and his confederates burst in on groups of male undergraduates whilst they were viewing *Charlie's Angels*, a 1970s TV series which had three classically beautiful young women as its lead characters (starring Farrah Fawcett Major, the Pamela Anderson of that era). The undergraduates were asked to break off briefly and to rate the attractiveness (on a scale of one to seven) of a photograph of a young woman previously selected by 11 other undergraduates as being of average attractiveness. Their scores were compared with the attractiveness ratings of the photograph provided by other male undergraduates who were burst in on whilst watching other TV shows that did not include beautiful women. A total of 81 undergraduates participated.

Sure enough, the *Charlie's Angels* viewers were significantly more likely to give the photograph of the average woman lower attractiveness ratings than the viewers who were watching the other (babe-free) programmes. In two further studies in 1980, Kenrick showed a similar effect from observing slides. Students shown a series of photographs of average women rated their attractiveness and dateability lower if a magazine picture of a model was included in the series – the model seemed to raise the attractiveness standards of the students and caused them to give the average women lower scores.

The conclusions that Kenrick drew from these studies are worth quoting in full. They 'support the suggestion that our initial impressions of potential romantic partners will be adversely affected if we happen to have been recently exposed to posters, television, magazines or movies showing highly attractive individuals . . . Let us imagine a scenario involving a college-age male who is engrossed in an episode of a television show containing unusually beautiful females in the central roles (the examples are not hard to come by, especially given the recent conscious and concerted effort of TV network producers to place highly attractive women in starring roles). He is briefly introduced to a neighbour who happens to be a female of average physical attractiveness. Our data suggest that his immediate assessment of her attractiveness and dating desirability will be lower than might otherwise be expected . . . Given the male college student's vast history of exposure to (media) visual female stimuli and a tendency to selectively attend to highly beautiful females, our results suggest that "chronic" standards for physical attractiveness may be somewhat inflated, particularly among individuals who are exposed to relatively more mass media.' Kenrick speculated that young men exposed to large amounts of such material might find themselves preferring to recall images thereof (I assume he means for masturbation) to the reality (i.e., in colloquial terms, to become 'wankers'. And this prediction made 15 years before the invention of the archetypal wankers of American TV, Beavis and Butthead, two cartoon students who sit in front of the TV ogling 'babes' but who are paralysed with fear when confronted by the real thing).

Having established that young men's judgements are influenced in the short term by media beauties and proposed that heavy media exposure could cause them to inflate their standards beyond the average found in the real world, Kenrick's next series of studies examined the effects on women and included the whole body, not just the face.[33] Male students exposed to slides of *Playboy* and *Penthouse* centrefolds subsequently rated averagely endowed women lower than men who were shown slides of either abstract art or average-looking women. In contrast, women students' judgements were unaffected by the pornographic slides. The study was repeated with a different set of students but this time they were asked to rate their real-life partners after seeing the slides. Sure enough, in a landmark finding, Kenrick showed that the men who were exposed to the centrefolds rated their partners lower, both in terms of attractiveness and how much they loved them, than the men exposed to abstract art or average women: the effect transferred to real relationships.

The next study[34] examined how exposure to media beauties affected mood. 80 male and 80 female students were shown slides of faces of male and female magazine models or of averagely attractive people. For both sexes, viewing opposite-sexed models raised mood and viewing same-sexed models lowered it. Kenrick concluded the negative reaction was due to 'unfavourable comparisons with the self'. This added to a growing body of evidence (cited by Kenrick)[34] that women exposed to images of very attractive other women suffered a lowering of self-esteem (although not, it seems, a downgrading of their view of their own attractiveness). So powerful was the effect of being unusually attractive that exceptionally attractive real people were found to be more likely to suffer social rejection from same-sex peers, presumably because they made them feel bad just by existing.

In a final experiment,[35] Kenrick gave a dramatic demonstration of the different effects media exposure may have on the sexes. 407 male and female students were shown profiles including a photograph and information about the personality of the person portrayed. These personalities were either dominant (powerful, authoritative, masterful but not aggressive) or submissive (obedient, yielding). The students were then asked to rate how much they would like to date the profiled person. Some were given photographs of models, others given only averagely attractive people. When this was over, they were asked to rate their current real-life partner.

As before, the men who were shown models rated their current relationship lower than the men shown average women. However, the men were only influenced by a model's looks if the models also had a submissive personality profile. Men shown dominant but highly attractive women did not rate them as highly and did not regard their current relationship in a worse light. The findings regarding the women were equally stereotypical. They did not seem to care what the men looked like – their judgements about dateability did not vary according to whether the men were models or looked average. However, if the men were profiled as being dominant then – regardless of what the men looked like – the women were more likely to give their current relationship a lower rating afterwards. In short, men thought worse of their current partner if exposed to beautiful, submissive women and women did the same when exposed to high-dominance men, regardless of looks.

Leaving aside the political incorrectitude of the results of these studies (see Chapter 6), their implications for the effect of media on social comparison are considerable. In the first place, they show that TV programmes and magazines presenting beautiful women raise the standards of what young men find attractive. Although they do not prove that this effect is long term, it seems highly probable that the repeated exposure to media beauties makes men more demanding of women in terms of looks. Secondly, the studies show the adverse effect of exposure to same-sexed images of good-lookers for both sexes. Both men and women find it depressing to see a series of stunners of their own sex because the enforced upward comparison highlights their shortcomings. Thirdly, whatever the reason (and it is a matter of heated debate), these studies form a small part of a large body of evidence that compared with women, men are hugely influenced by women's looks and that women are more concerned with other aspects than looks in evaluating men[36] (see Chapter 6). Given that women want men to be attracted to them and given that the media are dripping with attractive females, it places far more pressure on women than men to aspire to be attractive. Constant comparison with these images is likely to affect the self-esteem of even above a averagely attractive women, let alone those who are below average. Although it is almost a cliché, the findings of these studies must help to explain why women are far more preoccupied with their appearance than men, are more likely to suffer from eating disorders and twice as likely to report feeling depressed. Finally, the findings on the differing roles of dominance may put an equivalent, if different, pressure on men. In choosing dates, women appear to be as influenced by a man's dominance as men are by women's looks. Whilst women may suffer at the hands of their absurdly good-looking sisters on the TV, let us not forget the statistics with which we began: three-quarters of characters in American drama are prosperous Whites in their 20s and 30s; 40% of male leads have professional or managerial jobs. Spare a thought for the many millions of American males who are none of these and for whom the enforced comparison when they watch the TV may be a wound to self-esteem.

The net implication of Kenrick's work for social comparison, then, is that the media raises the aspirations of women to be attractive, raises men's standards as to what they regard as attractive, raises aspirations for men to be dominant and raises women's standards in terms of the amount of dominance they desire in a male. The mood of both sexes may be lowered by the comparisons and both sexes may find themselves less satisfied by their existing partner as a result of involuntary adverse comparisons provoked by constant media exposure. Small wonder, it might be said, that the nearly fourfold rise in divorce has coincided with the introduction of television (although, as we shall see in later chapters, there are many other factors involved as well). It is also worth mentioning as a final corollary of all this that many studies have shown that physically unattractive people have a higher incidence of psychiatric problems than attractive people[37] – one cannot help wondering what role media images play in this.

Desirability is only one of many domains of social comparison that are affected by the media. As noted, most of the research into the effects of television has been on the propensity to act violently. I do not propose to climb this mountain of evidence since this has been done many times

102

before by others better qualified than I.[38] Instead, I shall offer a brief summary of my view of it.

Few social scientists today would maintain that the increase in celluloid violence has played no role whatsoever in the parallel rise in real-world violence throughout the developed world (with the exceptions of Switzerland and Japan). The question is, how much of the increase can be attributed to this cause? It is abundantly clear from the research that if normal boys and young men are exposed to violent footage, in the immediate aftermath their levels of aggression are liable to be increased compared with subjects shown nonviolent footage, but there is little convincing evidence that this effect lasts long. It is also clear that compared with peaceable males, violent ones are more inclined to watch violent films and TV programmes. The trouble is that almost all of us are exposed to a substantial diet of celluloid violence (e.g. the rate of 7.5 acts per hour in America) but only a small minority of us become violent in the real world. If merely being exposed to celluloid violence caused real violence invariantly, the members of the British Board of Film Censors would be homicidal maniacs. In fact, real violence is largely confined to very specific groups: the young (three-quarters of recorded violence against the person is done by 14- to 29-year-olds); males (an average ratio of eight males to every one female throughout the world); and people with low incomes and little education attainment (at least five times as many low-income males are convicted of violence against the person compared with high-income males). The difference between the poor, young males who commit most of the violence and the ones who do not is also well established. The violent are more likely to come from homes in which they were severely physically abused, witnessed a great deal of parental disharmony and had parents who were extremely irritable and hostile. These patterns of childcare are much more common in families where the parents are living with the stress of a low income.[29]

My conclusions are twofold. Firstly, the increase in celluloid violence has almost certainly increased our general tolerance to it in the real world, compared with 1950 (of course, our intolerance then was a very new phenomenon in the history of the world; the further you go back in history, the more violent the society; in the past, violence was so commonplace that it was a widely accepted feature of everyday life). Secondly, based on the research evidence, I am doubtful that viewings of specific violent images have provoked many specific imitations thereof, directly causing a man to rise up after watching a particular film and recreate the fiction in reality. However, it is highly probable that those poor, young men who come from a family with violence-inducing patterns of childcare are generally disinhibited by celluloid violence. In particular, the images may seem to legitimize violent acts as a way of expressing frustration and anger, and as such, enable the man to override any conditioning he has had to regard violence as unacceptable. If you idolize Clint Eastwood and his main method of dealing with people who oppose or disagree with him is to blow them away with a large gun, it would be surprising if this had no effect on your behaviour if you had a childhood which predisposes you to this method in the first place. But what should never be forgotten in this debate is that most violent men (all but two of the 150-plus whom I have interviewed) have starred in a horrendous, unending violent movie of their own: their childhood. In conclusion, it is likely that there would be less violence today if the torrent of celluloid violence had never happened, although we cannot estimate how much less. But it is also likely that there would be considerably less violence than this if there were no low-income parents: low income plays a far larger part in causing violence than TV and films.

Interestingly, at least in the early days after the introduction of television, its effect on crime may have been greater on larceny (i.e. 'larceny theft', including pickpocketing, shoplifting and stealing property from cars) than on more severe crimes, such as violence. There is one definitive study which suggests this. Karen Hennigan[39] took advantage of the fact that television in America was not introduced at the same time across the nation but over a period of five years to examine how its gradual introduction correlated with crime. She prefaced her report of the study in 1982 with the following rationale: 'There are several reasons to predict that television viewing has powerfully affected instrumental criminal behaviour over the last three decades. First, television advertising purposefully (and television programmes inadvertently) may stimulate desires for material goods. Television advertising has been used successfully to stimulate desires for more and better products of all sorts. In addition, television programmes have been populated by relatively wealthy characters whose occupations, activities, homes, cars, clothes, and other possessions are indicative of upper- and middle-class lifestyles. On the other hand, viewing surveys reveal that persons from lower socioeconomic levels have been the heaviest viewers, even in the 1950s. As a result, most viewers have fewer and lower quality or less luxurious possessions than the television characters they regularly view. Viewers may become frustrated by an inability to satisfy desires heightened by TV commercials or to purchase the possessions characteristic of the wealthier life-styles seen on TV.

'Second, television programmes have encouraged lower- and middle-class viewers to compare themselves with the wealthier TV characters. Viewers have been invited to feel similar to TV characters in some basic ways and to find characters likeable and attractive. Such factors are thought to encourage social comparison. Heightened desires and social comparison with better-off others are crucial ingredients in relative deprivation. Viewing television regularly may have increased relative deprivation, which is thought to result in feelings of unfairness and resentment, acts of protest and instrumental behaviour aimed at acquiring the goods of which one has been deprived. For some viewers, legitimate (legal) means to acquire the goods they lack may be extremely limited, so they may resort to illegitimate means such as theft and burglary.

'Third, television is an important source of normative information. It is perhaps the most accessible and the most powerful source of common culture in the United States. The normative information that TV provides aids in socialization through social learning of the activities featured on TV. Individuals can learn from these shows that turning to crime to solve personal problems is common and often (at least somewhat) effective.'

To test these ideas, Hennigan correlated FBI statistics for crime rates with the introduction of television in 68 cities where the sale of sets was extremely rapid once transmission began (reaching 50% of households within the first year). Comparison was made between rates of crime in 34 cities that had TV introduced in 1951 with 34 cities which were then TV-free. Hennigan found that rates of violence, burglary and car theft were unaffected a year later but rates of larceny rose significantly in the cities where TV was introduced. A further comparison was made in 1955. Again, the 34 cities who had previously had no TV but now had it saw an increase in the rate of larceny by the end of the first year after introduction, compared with the cities that already had had TV for four years, whose rate of increase did not markedly change. Hennigan estimated the degree of impact as follows: 'The impact of television on larceny seems to have been to increase it by at least 5% in the year television saturation reached 50% (of households)'. She offered this interpretation of her findings: 'The lower classes and modest life-styles were rarely portrayed on TV, yet the heaviest viewers have been and are poorer, less educated people. It is possible that in the 1950s television caused younger and poorer persons (the major perpetrators of theft) to compare their life-styles and possessions with (a) those of wealthy television characters and (b) those portrayed in advertisements. Many of these viewers may have felt resentment and frustration over lacking the goods they could not afford, and some may have turned to crime as a way of obtaining the coveted goods and reducing any "relative deprivation".'

The finding that violence and burglary were unaffected by the introduction of TV may have been due to the fact that TV in those days was more tame (older British viewers will recall the moral homilies with which the cop show *Dixon of Dock Green* began and ended). It was some time before shows adopted the full-blooded 'social realism' which is often used today (e.g. *Hill Street Blues, NYPD Blue, St Elsewhere* and so forth). Thus, Hennigan argued that the increase in larceny was unlikely to have been due to direct imitation (known as 'social learning') of TV characters since TV portraits of larcenists were rare. Rather it was the result of adverse upward social comparison, stimulating aspirations and entitlements to consumer goods and wealth that many viewers could not legally obtain. Social learning of crime may, however, have resulted in the last 20 years from the large amount of TV and movie dramas and news, providing realistic role models of criminals of almost every conceivable variety.

A crucial – if nebulous and difficult to research – aspect of all this is the way television encourages viewers to make unrealistic, undiscounted upward social comparisons by blurring differences and underplaying contexts of achievement. Very often, television drama offers magical connections between desired wishes and outcomes without the intervening means. Impressive, attractive and sympathetic characters with formidable self-discipline or intelligence are shown achieving improbable goals without us seeing how this person worked to develop their attainments and downplaying the improbability of what they achieve actually happening in real life. We are skilfully drawn into their world, we identify with them, and this process by definition removes discounting. The suspension of disbelief causes undiscounted upward comparison and gives us access to a world where anyone can do and have anything.

Reiterating and building on Hennigan's conclusions, Jerry Suls writes that[18] 'Different eras and different cultures may encourage or discourage different comparisons with dissimilar or similar others . . . To the extent that the possessions and lifestyles of persons who are advantaged are visible to less advantaged individuals, the opportunity for comparison is increased . . . I would propose that media, like television, by representing the riches and luxury of the upper class and by attempting to sell them to the less advantaged, have the effect of blurring the significance of related attributes. As a result, it becomes unclear whether years of education, family background and the like are actually legitimate bases upon which to make social comparisons. That is, individuals in the lower strata begin to assume that differences in background factors are not relevant to acquiring a job that requires substantial expertise, and so forth. In short, they compare with people who are dissimilar. That is bound in many instances to produce a sense of resentment, anger or alternatively, depression . . . Actually, one may be surprised that there is so little protest and resentment in our society at present, given pressures to compare upward prompted by the mass media.'

These comments are especially applicable to TV advertising. TV often seems to be telling the viewer that just by wishing something is the case, it will be. Magic dressed up as realism is rife and unwarranted implicit associations are made between all manner of products and desirable outcomes: 'buy this pension and you will look like a mini-skirted model in her early twenties if your husband dies', 'possess this car and you will become a wise, admirable and independent man', 'buy this washing-up liquid and you will have a harmonious relationship with your child'. Whilst we may know this is nonsense, consciously, if the associations did not work at some level the adverts would have no effect and it is unlikely that shrewd business executives would waste their money on them.

Exposure to this Hocus Pocus starts early in life – by age 12 the average American will have seen 200,000 TV adverts. Studies of children[40] show that between the ages of four and seven they become aware that advertisements are not the same as other TV material and that as they approach the teenage they are increasingly likely to be aware that the true purpose is to sell a product. Nonetheless, it seems likely that adverts gnaw away at our grip on the differences between reality and fantasy and in doing so, increase the likelihood of undiscounted upward comparison. In fantasy, as we know from our dreams, almost anything is possible and the normal relationships of cause and effect need not apply. It is possible for us to fly, to inhabit another's body or to have sex with anyone. Advertisements exploit that part of us which is happy to suspend our capacity for causal analysis.

For example, an internationally successful advert for a deodorant portrayed a model walking past a man who immediately dropped what he was doing, rushed into a florist and charged after the woman to give her the flowers.[40] A study of this advert showed that until aged seven, children who saw it said the man followed the woman 'because he liked her'. But from age nine onwards, the children gave the reason 'because he liked her smell', correctly divining the manufacturer's intended message. The fact that men almost never behave like this because of the smell of a deodorant (and especially the one that was being advertised!) no longer concerned them. But in many ways, the unsophisticated seven-year-olds were closer to the mark, in that, on the rare occasions that the scenario portrayed actually does happen, it is because the man 'likes' the woman, not her smell – is attracted to the woman's face, legs and outward appearance. Although most nine-year-olds are probably aware that smell is not the main consideration when it comes to sexual attraction between adults, 200,000 repetitions of this kind of crackpot worldview must have some effect on their sense of reality.

Anecdotally speaking, it is worth mentioning in passing the curious statistics from surveys of the American population that appear in British newspapers from time to time, such as that '40% of Americans believe that Elvis Presley is not dead' or that '50% of Americans believe they have met an alien from outer space'. Amusing as these are, they may also be signs that, despite decades of universal secondary education, pre-scientific thinking may still be commonplace. If so, we may be sure that exposure to 200,000 adverts by age 12 has played a part. America is, after all, the country whose leader (President Reagan) actually did consult an astrologer before making certain important decisions.

As we shall see in Chapter 9, urbanization and technological development tend to correlate with increased education and therefore, the supplanting of religious and mystical worldviews with scientific ones. However, running in parallel with this development is a massive increase in lack of understanding of even the most basic elements of subsistence. How many of us understand why and how the electric light which may be illuminating your book at this moment works? What about the central heating which is making it warm enough to sit comfortably, or the car you used to go shopping? In this sense, magic has increased rather than decreased. In rural, traditional pre-capitalist societies all adults could do almost all the things necessary for subsistence and had a working knowledge of how they worked, if not why. Whereas we flick dozens of switches every day without having a clue why the televisions, computers, washing machines and so on work, until relatively recently in the history of man, we understood the basic cause-and-effect relationships in our daily existence – milling flour, where eggs come from and how to encourage hens to lay more, getting water from a well. Perhaps it is no wonder that the leader of the most powerful nation on earth could have effectively believed that pigs could fly (and begun the 'Star Wars' programme, a military fantasy conceptualized in the language of a science-fiction feature film) if he lived in such a magical world of technological wonders.

Be this as it may, in terms of social comparison there is little doubt that adverts encourage the viewer not to employ analytical or discounting skills. An advert that presents the sequence 'the problem is pain, the solution is a pill and pleasure is the result' discourages any consideration of changing your lifestyle to avoid repeated headaches or stomach aches. Much has been written of how the very genre itself is mind-rotting and morally depraving.[40] Whilst many of these authors offer little scientific evidence for their claims (perhaps, partly, because so little research exists on these issues) and are clearly influenced by political ideologies in their arguments, they are often plausible. Defenders of the genre sometimes counterattack by citing the evidence that children quickly learn to disbelieve adverts. For example, in one study[41] two-thirds of 126 12- to 14-year-olds believed that adverts 'often or always lie and cheat'. You might conclude from this that they are streetwise and healthily sceptical. But you might also wonder what deeper message they are receiving about lying and cheating: if the society accepts and institutionalizes mendacity on TV to attempt to trick you into buying goods, then presumably it is not all that wrong to lie, whatever your parents and teachers say. In this sense, a higher-order social comparison is being made by the child when it evaluates the morality of the genre as a whole, legitimating antisocial behaviour.

Of course, not all the effects of TV on our comparative schema have been negative. In Britain, the BBC continues to offer educational services and part of its commitment to Public Service Broadcasting can be characterized as providing models for upward comparison that are positive and self-enhancing. Programmes that teach viewers how to cook, for example, often show ordinary people stuggling with the real problems thereof (e.g. BBC2's *Can't Cook, Won't Cook*), providing similar-comparison others who do not leave the viewer feeling inadequate. Other BBC cookery programmes (e.g. BBC1's *Masterchef*) are implicitly sympathetic to the likely gap between the viewer's competence and that of the participants, thereby discouraging undiscounted, demoralizing upward comparison. However, commercial TV often exploits comparisons to humiliate participants and stimulate viewers' envy and destructiveness (e.g. almost anything by Chris Evans). This is especially apparent in the perverse programmes based upon attractiveness. ITV recently achieved a low point in this kind of programming with *Man O Man*, a series in which men are pushed into a swimming pool by sexy models after an audience of baying women has voted which one to reject. Such programmes may reflect a genuine and growing antagonism between the sexes but they also play their part in stimulating it (thankfully, even ITV was able to recognize that this programming was unacceptable and cancelled the second series).

In conclusion, there are good reasons for believing that the maladaptive effect of media in general and television in particular on social comparison has been considerable. It has encouraged undiscounted upward comparison, lowering the esteem of men and women as regards their attractiveness, and encouraged unrealistic standards thereof. It has helped to disinhibit potentially violent boys and men. It has fuelled consumer aspirations and increased larceny. It has encouraged a blurring of the real differences between classes and types of people and obscured their true causes, conjuring up an irrational, magical worldview in their place. Through these effects on social-comparison processes, it is probably a major cause of the increase in the proportion of people with low serotonin levels compared with 1950.

ROYAL ILLUSTRATION OF THESE CHANGES

It is interesting to speculate about what today's media might have said about the Queen Mum's pear-shaped, bulbous figure when she married the future George VI, given the attention that Fergie's bottom has attracted. Although the vogue for thinness started in the 1920s, the Queen Mum probably found it easy to sidestep the fact that she did not resemble a Flapper or a showgirl comparative other. For one thing, although magazines and newspapers of that time were full of slender girls, without television the sheer volume of images was far less, nor was there the uniformity and internationalism of tastes that exists today – there was still widespread enthusiasm for the fuller-figured woman as well. On top of this, with her daughter, she will have been able to rely on her social role and status to ignore unflattering comparisons, and most of all, it is only in recent years that the media have become so unsparing and explicit in its observations about the royal body.

Perhaps the most important effect on the younger royals has been the capacity of TV to blur differences both in their minds and in their subjects'. This democratizing effect may have played a part in Lady Di and Fergie's use of professional women as upward-comparison targets. Although TV offered few such comparative models before the 1980s, there are now many more. By identifying with these characters, they would have been discouraged from discounting them down against their royal status.

I would speculate, for example, that if the money-hungry, glitz-attracted Fergie watched Joan Collins in the 1980s classic TV series *Dynasty*, she may have felt that this woman's power and wealth were to be admired. Not for nothing was the newly built home that the Queen gave Andrew and Fergie as a wedding present dubbed 'Southfork' by the tabloid press, because of its similarity to the opulent ranch house from that other quintessential 1980s TV series, *Dallas*. The house is widely believed to reflect Fergie's tastes and some support for this comes from the fact that several of her marital infidelities were committed with Americans (and even Americans from the Deep South, where *Dallas* was set) and that she has several times stated her love for that country and its culture. Although it may seem extraordinary to many Britons, despite her exalted status, an affluent American lifestyle almost certainly ranks higher than living in Buckingham Palace on her comparison hierarchy. Indeed, she has spoken publicly of how unpleasant an environment the Palace was, criticizing the fact that the miles of passages were only lit with 40-watt bulbs. This may have developed partly as a response to the hammering she took in the British press in the years after her marriage. In her mind, she may have derogated British taste so that she could feel its proponents were to be pitied – created a downward comparison.

The main press assault, of course, concerned her figure. The comparison with Lady Di's svelte shape was a permanently subordinating one but like all other plump women, every time she switched on the TV or opened a magazine it was rammed home. Thus, Kenrick's evidence concerning the effect of images of beautiful women on the esteem of other women directly applies to Fergie in the strongest possible way.

But interestingly, the avalanche of beauty affected Lady Di as well. For one thing, she was as worried about her weight as Fergie, developing bulimia. For another, as interviews with many a beautiful woman show, very few of them are fully satisfied with their appearance. Despite repeatedly reading of herself as 'the most beautiful woman in the world' it is very likely she does not feel beautiful. The pictures of her as a child and adolescent show a gawky girl, uncomfortable with herself. She suffered from depressed moods and low self-esteem even then. Unless she was very unusual, this will have extended to her feelings about her body. In all probability, the universally admired blushing innocence and conspicuous nubility of the 19-year-old bride had developed as her only method for attracting praise and attention and may have been a cover for deep insecurities. Thus, hard though it may be to believe, it is possible that she was as distressed as Fergie by media beauties – they were the competitors in what she may have regarded as being the only field in which she excelled.

On top of this, egalitarian TV images presenting professional men as ideal may have helped to undermine their respect for their husbands. When they compared the 'silver spoon', inherited careers of Charles or Andrew with the glamorous self-made businessmen or intelligent, masterful-yet-caring doctors and detectives that filled the screens, they may have compared upwards and downgraded their husbands. Again, the blurring power of TV combined with their adoption of 'New Woman' aspirations may have meant they did not discount these differences by reminding themselves that they had married princes, especially when figures from other highly valued fields who appear regularly on TV are added to the equation. Beside Sting or Jack Nicholson, what was a mere prince?

Such thoughts would, of course, rarely if ever pass through the older Royals' minds. If they did, an instant discount would be provided: 'these men are common', 'Americans!', 'entertainers'. By contrast, Fergie and Lady Di's partners would come off badly from such comparisons and in the process, they would subordinate themselves still further: if their husbands are not as admirable as these men, then they must also be of lower status.

A final point concerns the representation of the older compared with the younger Royals in the media. All would compare themselves with each other and within their pecking order, suffer, but more fundamentally, we can only wonder at the effect on the younger Royals of seeing images of themselves and words describing them. What does it do to yourself to be used extensively as a major object of social comparison? Whilst this applies to all leading public figures (John Major, Tony Blair) an oddity for the younger royals might be that neither is in the public eye for exhibiting a talent. They are there because of who they married. When Fergie reads about herself in *Hello!* or Lady Di watches her interview broadcast on TV, is it possible that they compare themselves with their aspirations and end up feeling even worse? Filled as they are with the aspirational and individualistic zeal of young women, they must sometimes perceive the lack of 'real' achievement compared with other prominent women, be it Madonna, Mrs Thatcher or Benazir Bhutto.

TOO MUCH TOO YOUNG: INCREASED, MORE COMPETITIVE SCHOOLING AND SOCIAL COMPARISON

INCREASED, MORE COMPETITIVE SCHOOLING SINCE 1950

Compared with 1950, we spend much more of our childhood in classrooms and for most children, the competition is substantially fiercer. With the realization by governments that education was crucial to economic growth, the average number of years' schooling in the developed nations doubled between 1913 and 1983.[1] In most developed nations, the substantial increase in secondary and higher education occurred after 1950. Between 1950 and 1980 it almost doubled in France and Japan. In some nations the main acceleration was in the 1980s. In Holland, for example, the proportion of 21-year-olds in higher education rose from 14% to 32% between 1975 and 1986. On average half of 19-year-olds in developed nations are in some form of higher education today and 25% of 21-year-olds compared with a tiny fraction of this prewar. In Britain in 1979, one in eight school-leavers went on to higher education; today it is one in three.

Although there can be little doubt that standards have risen, at least among higher-achieving children, there is doubt as to how much. In the last 20 years in Britain, for example, there is evidence that literacy and basic mathematical abilities have actually fallen, at least in children educated at those state schools with high numbers of children from low-income families.[42] There is also good evidence that grade inflation has reduced the standards of secondary and graduate qualifications.[42] However, at the top end of the scale competition has never been tougher. In many cases it starts at birth. Parents reading modern baby manuals are encouraged to evaluate the 'progress' of their infants towards 'developmental milestones'. The competition to get the baby walking, talking, potty trained and so on is extreme in some social circles.[8] Penelope Leach, a child psychologist and bestselling author of baby manuals, has provided a telling critique of such hothousing.[43] 'Child development is a process, not a race. In the first years each infant recapitulates the evolutionary stages that produced humanity, so major landmarks like walking and talking are important and exciting. But that does not mean it is necessarily better to reach them faster and pass them sooner. The modern infant is human and therefore **will** become a biped and communicate in speech. She is not a better example of her species because she does these things at an earlier age than average, nor does infant precocity predict adult excellence. We behave as if the child who walks earliest will walk fastest, as if exceptionally early single words predict meaningful later sentences, and as if children's prospects as intelligent, independent and socialized people can be improved by speeding them through the age-appropriate illiteracy, dependence or incontinence. It is not so and there is abundant evidence to prove it.' Leach provides an example of a father of a two-year-old whom she met at dinner. He said of his son's development that ' "coming along nicely" just won't do and "average" is an insult. I don't want him to be average, I want him to be the best . . . He's quick at everything and always has been . . . you can't tell me he's not bright.' Leach comments: 'Nobody had told him his son was not bright. His paediatrician had told him he was normal and since he wanted to be told his son was a genius, he found that insulting.'

Reflecting this hunger for good marks among the wealthier classes, in the private educational sector children must have their names put forward virtually at birth on the lists of sought-after nursery and primary schools. Where there was no entry exam for these schools in the 1970s, there is now often a stiff test to be passed. Examination is now much more frequent and rigorous throughout school life.

The increased overall competitiveness in the higher echelons of the education system is only to be expected since for five decades enormous efforts have been made to encourage the participation of groups previously largely excluded from advanced education – women, and children from low-income families. In Britain in the 1970s, one quarter of graduates were female, today it is one half. It should also be recalled that it is only very recently that access to universities was significantly dependent on academic prowess. The principal requirements were a public school education, being male and parents wealthy enough to support you. Prewar, the majority of such people achieved the low standard required to attend The University (as Oxford or Cambridge were referred to among the upper classes – other institutions were not often considered by them). But most public school leavers did not bother, opting to go straight into the Army, the City, industry or to do nothing at all. If they did attend at The Varsity (Oxbridge), as anyone who is familiar with fictional accounts of life there between the wars (e.g. Evelyn Waugh's *Brideshead Revisited*) will know, the main object seems to have been to have a jolly time, not to acquire knowledge.

But with the postwar increase in competitiveness, grades at GCSE and A level rose steadily, particularly sharply in the 1980s. Whilst it seems highly probable that this was partly due to a dropping of standards, it must also have been the result of more focused and disciplined schooling. This is well illustrated by the way grades have changed at Eton College (the 'top people's' school, as it is often dubbed in the newspapers).[44] In the 1970s about half the boys were sons of alumni whereas today it is more meritocratic – about 30%. Boys who would once have been accepted – despite the fact that they would never be academically very able and dragged down the overall ranking of the school – are now weeded out by the rigorous entrance exam. The consequences of these new entry criteria, combined with tougher teaching, show in the results. In 1977, 31% of Etonians obtained a grade D or worse in one of their A levels, whereas today only 7% do so. In 1977, 46% of boys achieved one B grade or better at A level whereas today the proportion is 84%.

One stimulus for these changes was that competition for the top universities to which Old Etonians have traditionally gone had also increased and once there, the competitiveness was substantially greater. Whereas many students in the 1970s spent little time doing academic work, industriousness increased steadily from the 1980s onwards. By the mid-1990s, students were twice as likely to graduate with a 2:1 or First compared with the early 1970s. Whilst this was due to grade inflation to some extent, it is unlikely that the whole of the difference can be so explained. Such a rise is exactly what would be expected, given the huge increases in the number of competing able girls and children from low-income families.

Overall, then, two major changes have occurred in the educational life of young people, at least among the higher social classes, since 1950: they spend a great deal more time at school and their schooling is considerably more competitive, from ever-younger ages. Because these changes are so widely assumed to be 'a good thing' by all political parties and by the media, their potentially dire effect on the self-esteem and well-being of many children – both high and low achievers – is rarely discussed.

THE EFFECT OF INCREASED, MORE COMPETITIVE EDUCATION ON PATTERNS OF SOCIAL COMPARISON

There is a large body of evidence showing that social comparison and competition at school cause a lowering of self-confidence, optimism and self-esteem in most children starting from age seven onwards. Prior to that age, children are largely unconcerned about the performance of school peers; afterwards, they are at risk of becoming hyper self-critical and if not as extreme as this, there is a dousing of their enthusiasm for school activities and of their mood.

Popular culture is replete with attempts by artists to convey the distress that school life can bring and it is nothing new. Whilst there are many examples from before this century (e.g. the works of Charles Dickens or *Tom Brown's Schooldays*), Herman Hesse's novel *The Prodigy*, published in 1905, is perhaps the single most chilling account of how high expectations can affect a child. Hans, a precocious young boy, learns that the only way to win his parent's love is through doing well at school. He passes into a top academy and embarks on an unending diet of hard work and competition. His teachers and parents are relentless and insatiable. Eventually, plagued by thoughts of rebellion but equally by guilt and shame at not performing in the ways demanded of him, he drowns himself (perhaps this book should be compulsory reading for parents as well as children in Japan, where rates of suicide among hard-pressed schoolchildren are legendary). Almost as heartrending is George Orwell's essay 'Such, Such Were the Joys', describing his days at a snobbish preparatory school in the 1920s (also attended by the likes of Cyril

Connolly, Cecil Beaton and my father – who confirmed Orwell's account). In this case, academic standards are less the cause of the sense of comparative inadequacy than adverse comparison with aristocratic pupils who are given special treatment. More recently, Alice Miller has provided a best-selling, psychoanalytically based account (*The Drama of Being a Child*) of the damage wrought on clever young children who become the medium for the aspirations of adults who force high comparative standards on the child from birth onwards. She describes the false self which the child must develop in order to deal with these demands and the swings between grandiosity and depression which, she claims, result in later life. One could also list many rock music songs over the last 30 years which have tackled the ill-effects of competition at school (John Lennon's 'Working Class Hero' would be one, beginning as it does with the words 'Soon as you're born they make you feel small, by giving you no time instead of it all'. Another would be the Pink Floyd 1982 hit 'Another Brick in the Wall'. Sung by schoolchildren, the chorus was:

> 'We don't need no education,
> We don't need no thought control.
> No dark sarcasms in the classroom,
> Teacher: leave us kids alone!')

But it is not only artists who have noticed the damage that can be done by social comparison at school. Although rarely given wide publicity, many academic studies have demonstrated it too. Somewhat less poetic, Veroff nonetheless bears out the thesis of 'Another Brick in the Wall' or 'Working Class Hero' when he writes that[6] 'We would note that our schools systems and vocational ladders are ones where comparisons are constantly demanded. This focus on comparison cannot help but translate into some doubts people in our society have about the adequacy of their lives. We are unwilling to talk of ourselves in extremely praiseworthy terms – especially in doing things well compared with others.' Paul Gilbert describes how high parental aspirations can create involuntary subordination and depression.[21] 'Suppose your family have groomed you for high office (e.g. to be a famous brain surgeon) but in your heart you would like to be a painter. Here you would like to back down and give up your status but are constrained from doing so (e.g. don't wish to disobey your parents or feel you must continue to work in medicine). In this sense, you cannot voluntarily yield. But eventually our surgeon may get depressed and have to yield.'

According to Diane Ruble,[45] the most active researcher of this specific subject, social comparison starts young in life. 'Anyone who observes 3, 4- and 5-year-olds will see them make comparisons all the time. Sibling rivalry starts very young.' She goes on to present evidence that 'preschool children seem to want to make sure they are getting their fair share of rewards, readily engage in competition and make overt comparison statements'. However, until about age seven, children are very indiscriminate in who they choose to compare themselves with, as happy to pick an adult as a peer.[46] They seem to have a minimal grasp of the comparative dimensions for many characteristics and therefore, do not grasp that they have done worse than others.[47] Ruble concludes that 'Children's assessments of their relative performance in classroom are quite unrealistic until after their early school years.' There is usually a large discrepancy between their own view of their status, in such skills as alphabet acquisition and reading, and their teacher's view.[46] They ignore information about the performance of contemporaries and therefore, feel no sense of inadequacy. They are much more likely to assess themselves by reference to their previous performances on a task – to say they have read a story better than last time rather than a peer. They also compare more to absolute rather than relative standards – of sums they will say, 'I got them all right.' At this stage, they are not backward in coming forward about their achievements. Comparing the utterances of three- to six-year-olds with seven- to nine-year-olds, Ruble found the youngsters more likely to give voice to their successes.[46]

But aged seven comes a big change. Studies of utterances at this age show much less positive statements about one's own performance.[48] Indeed, successful children who rub their peers' noses in their success lose friends.[46] Children stop talking about their successes because they begin to realize that doing so disturbs their peers. As Ruble puts it, 'there is a shift from rather boorish braggadaccio to questions requiring little self disclosure'. But at the same time, there is a steady increase in social comparing with peers as the means of self-evaluation, rather than using past personal performance or indiscriminate others, like adults.[49] If now more circumspect about their own, they are more likely to request information about peers' performances.[50] As a result, they become more realistic and the gap between their appraisal of themselves and their teachers closes. They become increasingly preoccupied with competition and beating peers,[51] and teaching methods become increasingly designed to exploit this, using techniques that encourage public victories and defeats.[52]

But these changes are not without their cost to the child's well-being. Perhaps because they do not compare with peers and are largely ignorant of their performance relative to them, according to Ruble[45] 'preschool and primary grade children show impressive resilience in the face of failure. They maintain persistence, self-confidence and expectations of future success.[53] By mid-elementary school, however, such optimism and positive responses to failure largely disappear . . . with increasing disinterest in school-related activities appearing as children progress through elementary school.[54] When self-consciousness is induced (about their standard relative to other children), seven- to nine-year-old children are not satisfied unless their performance surpasses other children.'[55] Ruble argues that[45] 'because there are only a limited number of "winners" in any competitive system, children may experience a dissatisfaction with themselves . . . Comparison can promote a sense of relative deprivation and inadequacy, affecting interpersonal relationships and self-esteem.' From ages seven to nine, self-esteem, self-confidence and optimism decrease at school.[56]

Ruble emphasizes the crucial fact that schoolchildren who feel they are failing (even though they may be doing well) have no escape from the comparative system.[57] She suggests some mechanisms that attempt this, such as 'disengagement' – becoming less engaged with school activities.[54] Another method is the development of anti-academic school cliques, to provide a counter-culture with alternative means of gaining self-esteem than the prevailing academic standards.[45] But despite these evasions, the most common effect of all, as Gilbert's rank theory of 'involuntary subordination' would predict, is lowered self-esteem and the reason seems to be increased social comparison.

Writes Ruble,[45] 'The drop in self-confidence and achievement expectancies found during the early school years may be due to the incorporation of comparative standards into the self-concept.' Children who do badly do more social comparing than those who are succeeding, because they are searching for clues as to where they are going wrong[58] and because they feel uncertain.[59] Ruble states:[45] 'children may develop a poor opinion of themselves because they compare frequently, or they may socially compare more because they have a poor opinion of themselves . . . They may begin to look for additional information but along the way the perception of the self as poor comes, in part, from negative conclusions they draw from social comparison information. Taken all together, the data suggest that the period from seven to nine years is a very important one for self-definition and self-evaluation.' Children who do badly, as well as compounding the problem by increased social comparison, are more likely to show signs of learned helplessness – to act as if their actions cannot make any difference.[60] Experimental studies bear this out. When children were given low scores – regardless of performance – on tests, they began to display signs of helplessness.[61]

Crucial in all this is the unavoidability and objectivity of the comparisons in the classroom. By contrast, adults are often able 'to move the goalposts' if they are failing. Ruble illustrates this neatly with a study of 153 male and 84 long-distance adult runners.[45] They were classified into three groups: improving, declining and stable. Ruble discovered that the ones who were improving were eager to measure themselves by reference to the time they were taking over the course. By contrast, the runners whose performances were not changing or were declining avoided thinking about how fast they were going relative to past performances and the whole field and instead, concentrated on how well they were doing compared with other runners of about the same standard. In this way they could avoid the uncomfortable fact that they were not improving and continue to feel good about themselves. But such redefinitions are not available to a schoolchild who is regularly assessed and told where they stand in their class or what grade they have achieved in exams, almost whatever steps they may take to avoid the process.

On top of all this come the expectations of parents. Studies show clearly that children tend to develop the same expectations as their parents and that these can significantly affect real-world performance. For example,[62] parents generally tend to expect their daughters to find mathematics harder than their sons, regardless of how well the children are actually performing. Children's expectations tend to duplicate this, even if a daughter is doing better than a son in reality. In another study,[63] a sample of disabled children were tested for depression and hostility. It was found that some parents were using healthy, able-bodied children as the basis for comparing their disabled offspring's performance. Such offspring were significantly more depressed than those of parents who used other disabled children as the standard. The importance of which comparison groups are used – whether by the child, their parents or teachers – is further shown by the many studies[64] comparing self-esteem of Black children in racially mixed and all-Black schools. Esteem is lower in the racially mixed schools because the pupils compare themselves with White pupils whereas in the all-Black schools, this is not stimulated.

An important aspect of the damage done by the effects of higher standards and longer exposure to schooling on social comparison is that it affects high achievers as well as those who fail. For example, one study[65] related the average ability level in several differing schools with self-esteem. Esteem was lower in schools with higher-ability pupils, suggesting that if you are surrounded by very able people, it tends to lower your self-valuation. Another study found that high achievers in top American universities had lower views of their value and career aspirations than high achievers from less exalted universities.[66] The author of this study dubbed the phenomenon 'the campus as frog pond; for the frog in a shallow pond aims his sights higher than an equally talented frog in a deep pond'. Stevens and Price[67] have elaborated this point. 'Critics of [the] Rank theory [of depression] are fond of pointing out that not all people who are in subordinate positions, or who are low in social resources, suffer from depression, while people in a high social position (such as a Head of State) may do so. What is critical is what people perceive their social status and power to be and what they themselves believe to be the critical level below which it must not be allowed to fall.'

This is exemplified by a common experience for educational high flyers. In Britain, their academic career is a sequence of becoming the biggest fish in a pond followed by diminution to a tiddler in a shoal of equally big fishes. First of all, they must do well at their primary school. They may get a scholarship to a top public school but on arrival there, unless they are extraordinary, they will find there are plenty of other pupils as able as them (for even a prodigy there is no escape: the major public schools have mostly had even more prodigious prodigies than you in the past; being this outstanding you will rapidly be passed to university-level teachers, upping the ante; in mathematics, for example, you will quickly find yourself compared with the great minds of the past and sooner or later, in almost every case, be found wanting). If they succeed in being the *crème de la crème* at their public school (always remembering that there can only be one – by being first a dozen or so other pupils are in danger of feeling subordinated), they will move on to a university where there will be peers who are just as good and the whole process starts again.

A recently completed in-depth British study following and comparing 19 middle-class girls with 19 working-class ones from age 4 to 21 powerfully bears this out.[37] All the middle-class girls, without exception, were considerably more anxious and stressed than the working-class girls. Despite mostly having done very well academically, they felt they had not achieved enough. Valerie Walkerdine, the researcher who did the study, told me that 'Expectation more than actual achievement coloured the middle-class girls' view of their performance. The majority of them went to schools where high performance was the norm and therefore high performance came to be regarded as average. A young woman who did well would not see herself as particularly outstanding because achievement was what was expected of her. By contrast, a working-class girl who did well would be held up as a good example by friends and family, whereas the talents of middle-class achievers were largely unsung.' Walkerdine's finding was familiar to Elspeth Inch, the head teacher of a leading girls' school (King Edward VI in Birmingham). 'Even our really clever girls do not realize how clever they are. All their friends are bright and intelligent and they do not realize everyone is not like that.'[2]

I can offer anecdotal illustration of these points. 'St Luke's is one of the most competitive all-girl British schools, the one that Juliet (described in the Introduction) attended. I have met many alumni from there and it seems to me that they often have a far lower view of their abilities and personal charms than is warranted. The problem is that not only must these girls be academically outstanding to feel convinced of their intelligence, but there is also a culture which demands two extra ingredients: that they be highly individualistic and that they be appealing to men. This is an extremely tall order that almost none can rise to. Thus, a Luker who by virtue of her outstanding academic prowess (even by the lights of her peers) feels reasonably confident of her intelligence might have chubby legs (despite her pretty face) or a large nose (despite her long and slender legs) which mean she feels unattractive to men by comparison to the best-looking of her peers – with whom she is liable to compare herself. I have also met many dazzling-looking Lukers who did not particularly shine academically (although they may nonetheless have gone to Oxbridge) and consequently, doubt their intellectual abilities. Even if you stand out on both looks and brains, you will probably fail on the originality count, since it takes a certain conformity to be good at your lessons. In short there is nearly always a girl better than you at St Luke's. It seems to me a system for creating high achievers who feel like losers.

Then there is the strange phenomenon of Oxbridge. Nearly all the students who gain entry to Oxford or Cambridge were big academic fishes in their particular school ponds yet suddenly they are surrounded by ambitious, hard-working, more impressive peers who outshine them. People deal with this in different ways. The most common is to belittle the institution: to claim disappointment at the low standards of teaching, to whinge at the 'medieval' practices of the individual colleges, to decry the quality of fellow students, or to be scathing about the 'upper-class pretensions' of the place. Others go in for extreme modes of dress, eccentric patterns of speech or wild behaviour to make themselves feel special. Others still associate themselves with the adult world and affect disdain for the antics of mere students – pay frequent visits to 'enviable' parties in London, perhaps take a merchant banker for a boyfriend. Many students drink heavily in the first few terms to deal with their social insecurity. A significant number simply retire from social life altogether to avoid the comparison pressures. Of course, all these patterns are probably to be found to some degree at other universities, but they are exaggerated at Oxbridge. The net result, I would hazard, is that despite being members of an academic élite who might be lauded at another university, very few students there feel very good about themselves, at least for the first year.

Of course, the account I have given so far of the effects of educational social comparison is one-sided. It also has benefits, most notably, in creating a sense of fairness and social justice and in giving some pupils cause for satisfaction and a motive to persist in their studies. Also, even in the most lackadaisical of societies, all children must pass from the 'egotistical' state (that most of the Great Psychologists, such as Freud and Piaget, have described in their different ways) which prevails until about age five to an acceptance of the existence of an outside world that is frustratingly and implacably independent of their magical wishes. This transition is made gradually, over many years (and arguably, our unconscious never submits to it – witness our dreams), but if the person is not to be thought of as what is commonly known as mad, it is a journey that must be made. Thus, every child must come to accept that for its whimsical desires to be fulfilled in reality, it cannot merely wish them, and education plays a key role in this.

It is not my intention at this stage to discuss the rights and wrongs of the effect of the increased, more competitive schooling since 1950. Suffice to say that there is abundant evidence that exposure to harsh and unavoidable social comparison in the classroom lowers the self-confidence and optimism of children around the age of seven throughout the developed world. This is not necessarily an inevitable consequence of being forced to relinquish childish egotism. It seems highly probable that different educational systems soften the blow to the child's natural grandiosity and omnipotence more than others. Above all, given the evidence presented above, the increase in the raw amount of time that children spend in classroom environments *per se* has increased social comparison and when coupled with the increased competitiveness that now characterizes the education system, there can be little doubt that these changes have helped to create the low-serotonin society: a great many of us were permanently subordinated to some degree by our education.

ROYAL ILLUSTRATION
These points are poignant and have many resonances for our Royal women.

Apart from a brief period of a few months, neither the Queen Mum nor her daughter attended a formal school, being taught instead by governesses. The problems of social comparison facing a girl at St Luke's were completely unknown to both. Neither is likely to have suffered the drop in confidence and ambition seen in normal seven- to nine-year-old children. Education was not regarded as of much importance at all in either case, since both were being prepared for careers as wives, not as professionals. The rise of the highly educated woman, in all probability, poses no threat to their self-esteem because they simply do not regard a detailed knowledge of scientific subjects and suchlike as being a domain in which they have ever competed or are ever going to.

By contrast, both Lady Di and Fergie attended schools. Whilst Fergie did better than Lady Di, neither did well academically at schools with conspicuously low standards. Lady Di was shipped off to a girls' boarding school after attending local primary schools when she was nine. At secondary school, she was popular but did not scrape a single O level, leaving for a brief sojourn at a Swiss finishing school. There is firsthand evidence that these experiences lowered her self-esteem: it was soon after her engagement to Charles that she described herself as 'thick'.

Fergie went to boarding school aged 13 and fared somewhat better. She was well liked and in her last year became joint Head Girl and obtained six O levels. However, her self-esteem was not good even then. According to a peer of that time, Jilly Adams, 'She was a real stunner even then, but she was convinced she was hideous. Fergie was always wailing, "Oh just look at the state of me. I'm so fat and my bottom's so huge. And I'm so spotty. What boy would look at me? I'm so ugly."' Given that the capture of a good husband was the principal basis on which alumni of this school were judged, to feel so unattractive was to rate oneself low in the most important regard.

During their courtships and the early years of their marriages both of them may have felt that the fact that they had managed to marry the two most high-status men in Britain was a proof of their ultimate value. However, they cannot have been unaware that they were academic low achievers whilst at school and many of the comparison processes described by Diane Ruble may have applied. Whilst their immediate peers at their schools were also low achievers, they must have met other girls of their age who were more successful. Eventually, in both cases, they must have felt out of kilter with the academically ambitious generation of women of which they were members, adding to their sense that they were 'thick'.

INCREASED COMPETITIVENESS AND ASSESSMENT IN THE WORKPLACE AND SOCIAL COMPARISON

The increased competition continues beyond the classroom. There is today considerably more competition for jobs in the developed world and as a result, increased attention paid by employers to assessing the suitability of job applicants. Where once the process of being accepted for a post was relatively uncomplicated, today's applicants must go to great lengths to establish their credentials. Inevitably, this increases the amount of social comparison and stimulates relative deprivation.

Unlike the other processes considered so far, the increase in competitiveness and assessment dates back to the 1970s, rather than 1950. Since 1973 there has been increasing unemployment throughout the developed world1, especially among the young. Job insecurity has also increased, at least for the bottom 60% of the workforce.[68] At the same time, jobs have become increasingly highly skilled. For all these reasons (the causes and rights and wrongs of which are, of course, hotly debated)[68] it is now a 'buyer's market' for employers, and for most posts there are an abundance of suitable applicants. Needing methods for predicting which will be the best bet, ever more refined tools for selection have been devised. Employees have responded accordingly, especially the young, who are taught at school and university how to represent themselves in the best possible light in their curriculum vitae and through their interview technique. Job-seekers now devote considerable time to establishing how they can define themselves in the eyes of the employer as more attractive than the other applicants. This can only be achieved by extensive comparison of self with others, both real and imagined.

Techniques for measuring human capacities first emerged during the World Wars when there was a sudden need to find a reliable way to assign millions of servicemen to different branches of the armed forces. By 1950 there were several tests of intelligence available and since then, the 'science' of psychometrics has produced thousands of tests of personality, work capacity and motivation. The British Civil Service developed an elaborate system of assessment in the 1960s and today nearly all large employers have an assessment procedure for graduate and nongraduate applicants. Tests concerned with mental ability are not the only ones, personality is often evaluated as well. The British Institute of Directors estimated that 47% of companies used personality tests in 1989, and this rose to 57% by 1991. They are often used as one of the criteria for firing as well as hiring.[69]

Many of the changes already described in this chapter overlap with these ones. Increased aspiration and individualism have made employees more job-focused, more eager for responsibility and for better pay and promotion prospects. Television fuels the hunger and competition for better-paid work in order to buy the lifestyles portrayed in dramas and advertisements and by hugely overrepresenting managerial and professional occupations, encouraging aspiration towards them. The large increase in the proportions of people with further educational qualifications has greatly increased competition for the inevitably limited number of professional and managerial posts. The effect of having a more aspirational, better-qualified workforce chasing fewer jobs, and of elaborate assessment procedures, must be to increase social comparison as employees strive ever harder to establish precisely what attributes are desired for particular posts or careers. This, in turn, 'ups the ante', as standards of self-presentation in interviews and skills in taking tests are practiced and honed by failure. The workforce becomes deeply preoccupied with the performance of peers.

Studies of the effect of qualification on expectation and sense of entitlement illustrate this. In one,[70] children were led to believe they had performed a task either well or badly. When they were subsequently all told they had done badly – regardless of actual performance – the children who believed their performance had been better than this displayed manifest aggression: if the child felt 'qualified' by their performance they were more likely to be resentful. Another series of (five) experiments[71] showed that high qualifications in adults increased both entitlement and expectations of success, and under certain conditions, failure to be rewarded for qualifications increased resentment. For example, students were asked to read a description of an individual who was either unemployed or underpaid and to picture how that individual would feel if competing with another for a post or a pay rise. If the students were told that the individual was as well or better qualified than the competitor, they were more likely to say the individual would feel resentment if the competitor was awarded the post or the pay rise. The implications of this for the modern job market are obvious: since more highly qualified people are chasing fewer jobs, there must be more people about feeling relatively deprived.

Overall, the increased assessment of employees is the culmination of a trend which, for many young people, begins in childhood. It demands of us that we compare more and as we have seen, over-stimulated comparing contributes to low self-esteem.

ROYAL ILLUSTRATION
Again, these changes will not have affected the senior Royals one jot.

'What need have I of qualifications and credentials when I am who I am?' they almost certainly would reason. Not so the younger Royals.

The question of the right of any of them to rule us has become a matter of increasing public debate. Whilst the debate may be water off a duck's back in the cases of the Queen and Queen Mum, Lady Di and Fergie are all too aware of it. Lacking any formal training and without even an O level to her name, Lady Di must be aware that she would have trouble in gaining even the lowliest of employment. Likewise Fergie, who despite having worked as a publishing assistant, has little qualification compared with the vast majority of other girls from similarly privileged backgrounds. Comparison with their thrusting and more sucessful peers must leave them feeling subordinate. The thought of completing a curriculum vitae and of taking the various tests required by large organizations might cause them to break out in a muck sweat. The reality is that if either of them were to apply for even a menial post in one of the large food retailers – such as Sainsbury's or Marks and Spencer – other, far better qualified applicants would win. Whilst neither of them probably ever thinks consciously about this, both were competitive children and have shown themselves to be ambitious in their own way. Their exposure to the usual competitive processes of schooling must have done much to lower their basic self-confidence in their aptitudes – like so much of the general population.

CONCLUSION

It should not be forgotten that both Fergie and Lady Di have taken the serotonin-raising antidepressant Prozac. The four changes focused on in this chapter may all have played a part creating the necessity thereof. Unlike the older Royals, they may have been typical of their generation of women in having aspirations which tended to outstrip their opportunities or real capacities and in a newfound lust for individuality (encouraging them to reject their traditional roles and husbands). They may have been influenced by the mass media to make undiscounted, upward comparisons, promoting negative feelings about their bodies, their careers and their husbands. They may have been humiliated by comparisons in the schoolroom, creating lifelong feelings of intellectual inadequacy. They may have found themselves lacking credentials and qualifications in an increasingly meritocratic and competitive labour market.

However, changes in social comparison are only part of the reason why these privileged young women found themselves reaching for the Prozac. They also illustrate the other great change since 1950, which is the subject of the next chapter, the increase in anxious attachment. For there is an aspect of their biographies which, thus far, I have ignored: both were neglected as small children; both suffered rancorously divorcing parents, with their mothers having affairs; and both, in turn, have themselves gone on to have deeply unhappy marriages, affairs and divorces. Their stories are also archetypal of the second respect in which modern life fails to meet our primeval needs: the need for stable attachments.

Chapter 4

Losers In Love

The Increase In Broken Emotional Bonds Since 1950

Jean Paul Sartre's play *Huis Clos* (1944) begins with a man alone in a bare room. More people arrive gradually, until there are four. They comprise a specifically ill-assorted group, each an embodiment of what the others most hate. The clues mount up until you realize that they have died and are in Hell: they have been put together to torment each other for eternity. The point of the play is encapsulated in the memorable phrase 'Hell is – other people', and so it is, if they subordinate and undermine you, and if they are part of a social system that stimulates patterns of comparison in which everyone feels like a loser. But this is only one aspect of the modern hell that other people represent. The other concerns the absence, as well as the presence, of others. Losing loved ones can make us feel like losers too and although there have been no major wars since 1950, we have been losing each other so frequently that, in terms of the emotional effects, it is as if we have been living through a psychological Third World War.

The increased emotional and physical separation of child from parent, of lover from lover and of elderly parent from relative is a wail of anguish which crescendoes to the furthest reaches of our society. Everyone knows heartbroken, bitter and depressed divorcees, distressed children who are not receiving adequate care, elderly people who are isolated and hopeless. It may be objected that compared with the life-threatening wars, diseases and slavery that destroyed the relationships of our ancestors until very recently, these new problems are as nothing. But this takes no account of the high expectations and intensity we bring to our relationships today. I will present evidence below that the epidemic of broken bonds is so damaging because we form more, more intense, intimate relationships than hitherto, only to break them.

128

We can console ourselves that as a result of breaking these bonds, compared with 1950, fewer people are trapped in loveless marriages, women have more equal opportunities and the care of elderly parents is less likely to impede the lives of their offspring. It is also true that many parents (especially fathers) are more open in the expression of love to offspring. These are welcome improvements but we have not yet learnt how to balance the equations they represent and at present, they are achieved at a heavy cost, are a major cause of the low-serotonin society. It is a vicious irony that, just when our physical needs were unprecedentedly well catered for and our physical security never greater, in order to achieve this, disruption of our need for stable and lasting bonds has been the price.

This chapter examines the broad picture of modern attachments and the succeeding two explore the problems that have arisen between the sexes since 1950, leading to rancorous relationships which damage both adults and children. I begin with an example of the damage that unresponsive parenting and divorce can cause in a child.

SALLY'S STORY
Sally was born to wealthy and privileged parents but she had very unresponsive care in her early years. She suffered terrible deprivation at the hands of her mother, who was an alcoholic, and she had a distant relationship with her father when she was small. He was driven to divorce her mother by her heavy drinking and chronic depressive mental illness. From the age of nine Sally lived with this sick woman and was sadly neglected. She was regularly beaten up by her older brother. To her father's huge despair there was little he could do to protect her.

In adulthood, although she graduated from a top university and managed to present herself as reasonably stable for much of the time, she was emotionally deranged by these deeply disturbing and disrupted attachments. When she was 26 she wrote a brief account of her life, which I reproduce here.

'I took my first drink at the age of eight. I thought it was going to be a glass of ginger ale but instead I had a surprising yet extremely pleasant, far-away feeling. I liked it immediately and for the wrong reasons – that it detached me from my surroundings – and it's one reason I'm convinced that I was born with a genetic disposition towards addiction.

'But it is also true that my surroundings were of a kind to encourage detachment. My alcoholic mother had by this time separated from my father. Aged nine I had my second drink just before getting on the school bus, but it was not until age 13 that I made a habit of taking my mother's Mogadon to use at boarding school.

'During holidays, until about my 16th year, I would smoke marijuana, as did many of my friends. But I did very well at my public school and finished up with high-grade A levels and every chance of getting into a good university.

'I also finished up very unhappy indeed.

'I first took heroin the night before my A levels. I was visiting a friend who I knew was a frequent user. As I saw them smoking it I said, "Can I have some? I feel really nervous and it might help." Looking back, I actually believe he thought he was acting in my interests when he replied, "If I don't give it to you someone else will, and you'll get ripped off and into all sorts of trouble."

'I inhaled the smoke from the silver foil. I felt totally sick. Then, after about two minutes, I felt as if I'd taken five steps back from reality. I experienced that warm feeling which addicts always talk about and – cliché of clichés – I felt as if the gap, that had been inside of me and hurting me for 18 years and that had been created by my parents being apart, had closed.

'At this time in Britain use of this drug was extremely common and I'd often seen it used around me. At that stage I thought that drugs were Cool and that heroin was the Coolest Of Them All. Today I feel physically sick when I remember how my mind worked at that time.

'Of course I got into a good university. How could someone so wholly absorbed in the task of pleasing others do otherwise than "satisfy the examiners"? Putting on faces to meet the faces that I met was a piece of cake. Expressing even a small part of the real me to the world was my problem. My real feelings were not expressed through my behaviour. Not surprisingly therefore, I felt completely dissatisfied – I wasn't doing anything to please my self. Except that is, to take drugs.

'Everyone said that university would be a wonderful time for me. But there were no happy parties and I found the other undergraduates intimidating. I became literally unable to walk into the dining hall at mealtimes. I withdrew. I spent most of my time on my own or on the train to London.

'At this point my mother got cancer and I used this to deceive myself that this was the reason for my going to London.

'It was also how I justified the fact that I was spending increasing amounts of my time alone in my room smoking heroin. My mother recovered but I continued to use. By the end of my three years as a student I was practically immobilized by fear and panic, unable to face lectures or lecturers. Amazingly I just managed to get a degree.

'I set off to Asia for a year. The plan was to write articles and to live a healthy outdoor life. I soon ended up using heroin again.

'Back in England, I began to realize the seriousness of my problems. That I didn't feel or behave like other people. Since the age of 14 I'd been to a succession of analysts, psychiatrists and behaviourists and had been prescribed huge quantities of tranquillizers, antidepressants and so on. I went back to these doctors and asked them, "What can you do to make the pain go away? I want to be like other people."

'With the help of their pills I got back to the appearance of stability with a job in Public Relations and a thoroughly kind and respectable boyfriend. At this stage I was using prescribed pills combined with alcohol to change the way I felt. Although from time to time friends would gently hint that "perhaps you did drink a little bit too much last night" no one seemed to realize that alcohol was just as big a problem as heroin.

'Things continued like this for the next three years. On the face of it I was alright, not very far beneath the surface I wasn't. I was chronically depressed and filled with a corrosive self-doubt. I had everything a girl could want yet for no logical reason I often felt suicidal.

'Then a sequence of tragedies gave me some real reasons to feel that way. My response was to go back to heroin. A few months later my mother died, in her mid-40s.

'I knew I needed help, I didn't know what kind. I suggested a health spa to our family doctor, he said, "A drug dependency clinic." In my desperation I admitted to my father for the first time that I'd been living a double life.

'For the first time, too, I realized I had an illness. I was not a bad girl trying to be good . . . I was a sick girl trying to get well.

'That certainly helped me but I was still prone to acute bouts of depression which left me in bed for days on end. I kept off heroin and stuck to alcohol as my medication, especially when the going got tough in my love life.

'At a wedding I met Tim, a man I had seen from afar as a teenager, when he'd been my first crush. I was in a fragile state, having just split up with my boyfriend of two years.

'Although I was attracted to Tim, it was hardly the moment to rush into another affair. But as I found myself spending more and more time in his company, his exceptional warmth and kindness was compelling. And yet how did I feel?

'Increasingly depressed. Worthless. And this time, seriously suicidal. So it's back to different shrinks, different pills, a new diagnosis (of manic-depression) but it's still the same old story with the same ending – heroin.

'Except for one thing. This time there was someone who was prepared to go to the ends of the earth to help me.

'To start with, he was smart. Heroin addicts are notoriously good at lying their way out of trouble and for a time I managed to con him. But bit by bit he let me know that he was on to me as he uncovered more clues of what was going on. At first when he confronted me I shouted and screamed my way out of trouble but in the end he forced me to admit – to myself as much as to him – that I was using again.

'For most men that would be it. Who wants to go out with a junkie, especially in an AIDS epidemic? But Tim never faltered . . .'

Here the essay ended, but for a few notes: 'NOT ENOUGH TO DEAL WITH THE ADDICTION HAVE TO DEAL WITH THE EARLY CHILDHOOD FACTORS – MUM ABUSE/DEPRIVATION, DISTANT DAD, *DIVORCE*.'

Alas, heroin won out over Tim and no therapists were able to sustain a relationship with Sally for long enough for her to 'deal with the early childhood factors'. Some two years after writing this account of her life, she began to go a bit mad, becoming slightly delusional, something she had always feared, and she took a fatal overdose.

It seems probable that Sally's genetic inheritance contributed to her unhappiness but far more significant were those 'childhood factors' and chief among these was her parents' disharmony. Like Princess Diana, Fergie and millions of other of their generation, Sally's parents did not get on and she paid a price. Divorce, gender rancour and the isolation of children from depressed or absent parents have all increased since 1950 and between them, play a large role in increasing the numbers of low-serotonin people.

WHY BROKEN BONDS MAKE US LOSERS

Recall the words of the evolutionary psychiatrists Anthony Stevens and John Price, quoted in Chapter 2: 'It seems likely that the various neuroses, psychopathies, drug dependencies, the occurrence of child and spouse abuse, to say nothing of the ever-rising crime statistics, are not unconnected with Western society's inability to satisfy the archetypal needs of our kind . . . the number of people in whom these basic needs are not met is large and growing, as indeed is the psychiatric problems which they represent.' The 'archetypal needs' were for status (discussed in the last two chapters); and for emotional attachments. The failure to satisfy these needs was related to two basic pathways to depression. The status path was[1] 'marked by excessive personal demands for accomplishment and control accompanied by relentless self-criticism, guilt and sensed inferiority when one fails to satisfy personal standards'. On the attachment path were to be found[1] 'persons whose intense need to be loved, highly esteemed and prized by others leave them precariously sensitive to real or perceived slights, abandonments or withheld esteem by significant people in their lives'. Changes in our society since 1950 have directed more of us down both paths.

There is a vast body of evidence proving a fact of which few can be unaware: that we have a powerful drive to form intimate relationships and that if these relationships turn sour or end, it puts us at risk of a variety of problems, most notably depression but also violence and compulsions such as eating disorders.[2] Since people with these problems are more likely than people without them to have low serotonin, attachment is clearly implicated therein.

Attachment behaviour in animals is related to serotonin levels. High-status, high-serotonin male vervet monkeys were more sociable – akin to securely attached humans in many ways – than the low-status, low serotonin ones, who more resembled 'anxiously attached' humans. The anxiously attached have an irrational fear of rejection or abandonment in relationships (see footnote 65 for more detail). The high-serotonin male vervets approached the females for social contact more, stayed in close proximity for longer and engaged in mutual grooming more. When put in isolation, with no opportunities for social contact, their serotonin levels fell. Given drugs that raised serotonin levels, males who had previously been relatively subordinate and antisocial became much more sociable. When these same males were given other drugs which lowered serotonin levels, they became markedly more unsociable.

The effect of drugs which raise serotonin on human attachment behaviour may be similar. Although these drugs are mostly prescribed to treat depression, increased sociability is often one of the results. Depression undoubtedly causes disrupted attachments and when a drug lightens the black mood, the person becomes more able to relate to others. However, it is also clear that it can work the other way around – that disrupted attachments can cause depression. Three studies of married couples have shown that members of disharmonious ones who were undepressed at the start of the relationship are more likely to become depressed a few years later[3] (see next chaptere). Since people with anxious attachments are more likely to be part of a disharmonious marriage, it suggests that anxious attachment can cause depression through disharmonious marriages, and therefore, low serotonin levels. As far as I know there are no studies directly testing the idea in humans but when they are done there is little doubt that they will demonstrate that disrupted attachments are a significant cause of low serotonin. Adults who are violent,[4] who suffer from eating disorders,[5] low self-esteem[6] and depression[7] have all been shown to be more likely also to be anxiously attached than people without these problems. A number of studies of various species of monkey have demonstrated conclusively that if they are separated from their mothers whilst young, their serotonin levels are lower than the unseparated.[8] It is highly probable that the same would be true of humans aged six months to three years if they are separated from their primary caregivers with inadequate substitute care. In human adults, if levels of serotonin were measured in the divorced, the recently jilted or the bereaved and compared with levels of people who had not recently suffered these misfortunes, they would be extremely likely to be lower, given the evidence that these experiences are liable to be depressing. Just as McGuire's defeated vervets have lower levels after being subordinated, these people have been defeated by love and life: both rank and attachment pathways to depression entail a form of defeat. It further follows that any social changes which increase the amount of anxious attachment would also increase the number of people with low serotonin. Such social changes are precisely what have happened since 1950 throughout the developed world.

THE EPIDEMIC OF ANXIOUS ATTACHMENT SINCE 1950
INTRODUCTION: DENIAL OF DEPENDENCE AND OVERVALUATION OF RELATIONSHIPS

Since 1950, across the life cycle, dependence within personal relationships has been increasingly frowned upon and denied in practice. At the same time and in total contradiction of this trend, there has been a wholly new valuation placed on personal relationships as a fount of happiness. Many long-term adverse consequences are related to these paradoxical changes. One is to increase our sense of discontent. Another is the dramatic rise in addictive behaviours of all kinds, including the compulsive use of 'solaces', such as illegal drugs, alcohol and gambling. At least in part, addictions are one of the substitutes for unmet emotional and social needs.

The denial of dependence begins with a refusal on the part of a significant section of the present generation of parents to acknowledge the needs of small children. Infants are left crying at night and forced to fit their feeding regime to the convenience of parents who tell themselves that infants 'have got to learn they can't get away with it'. The demand for a premature self-sufficiency is part of a swing away from child-centred care to patterns which suit busy, working parents. Instead of being able to rely on the carer to feed or comfort it, the infant has to learn what the carer wants. It grows into an adult who looks outwards to others for definition of what it wants and of who to be. Its sense of self is undeveloped because biologically based needs such as 'I feel hunger in my stomach' were hijacked in infancy. Instead, it was 'my carer defines whether there is hunger in my stomach, not my bodily sensations'. The development of 'I' is impaired.

The denial of dependency continues into toddlerdom. Aged six months to three years, there has been a trend towards leaving children in the care of overworked or unresponsive substitutes, especially in America. The evidence shows that if the substitute is responsive and does not change during these years, then no emotional damage ensues. Indeed, women who do not wish to care for children full-time are liable to become depressed if they stay at home, with dire consequences for their charges, so it is better that they find adequate substitute care. But unfortunately, this is all too rarely possible.

On the one hand, some parents recklessly chop and change childminders without regard for their children's mental health. They may be envious of minders whom their children become attached to and sack them like an incompetent secretary. Others are unable to afford adequate substitutes or are insufficiently careful in searching for them. There is now a substantial body of evidence that when the substitute care is not adequate it causes 'separation anxiety' and that a few years later, the child is liable to suffer from 'anxious attachment'.

On the other hand, millions of mothers since 1950 have become depressed by the new conditions under which motherhood takes place: unappreciated – even scorned – by the wider society and often isolated from any social support and intimate relationships. Between 1960 and 1989, 90% of Americans relocated to a new town and almost half of all individual Americans had moved house between 1986 and 1990. In Britain, a recent survey showed that two-thirds of children had moved house at least four times before they reached their 16th birthday.[9] No wonder, then, that so many mothers find themselves distanced from their close kin and community.

The denial of dependence extends into middle childhood and early teenage, with parents increasingly likely to turn their offspring into 'Latchkey Kids'. The newfound freedom of teenagers, won by their parents in the 1960s, offers opportunities for fulfilling experimentation to those who have had stable, loving childcare and have enough psychological boundaries to know when to stop. But for those who lack inner controls and strong identity, increased choice carries great dangers. As the age of puberty drops, sexual intercourse is increasingly frequent at ever-younger ages (especially among girls), accompanied by drug taking and heavy alcohol use. Many teenagers have adult patterns of sexual life and recreation before they are ready to do so. It is 'too much too young' because in many cases, as well as aspirant adults, they are still dependent children who need parental nurture and guidance.

Running in the opposite direction to this collective abnegation of personal obligations is the huge expectation now placed on relationships as an almost religious salvation. The ideal of exclusive, intense, long-lasting relationships which many parents strive for with their children and with each other today may be a relatively new development in the history of humanity. Most of us take for granted the material conditions which make our unprecendented focus on relationships as a source of fulfilment possible. Reliable, effective medical care, hygiene, plentiful food, home comforts and so on leave us free to concentrate on each other, but until very recently, life was not only a great deal more nasty and brutish for all but a tiny élite, it was also a great deal shorter for everyone. A person born in England and Wales in 1841, for example, could expect on average to live to the age of 41. This had only risen to 45 by the turn of the century, climbing sharply to the 60s by 1950 and to its present average in the mid-70s.[10]

I believe that a crucial implication of these differences may have been that in the distant past, humans formed fewer, less **intense** attachments. That life was so relatively short may have acted as a discouragement to many people to become too attached to others. Not only was physical illness much more prevalent, life was also a great deal more dangerous. Parish records show that the risk of being murdered in London in the thirteenth century was 10–20 times greater than the present day.[11] Likewise, the generalization holds that the less developed the nation today, the greater the likelihood of being assaulted or murdered,[12] with the overall risk being twice as great in the developed compared with the developing world. This suggests that in the days when most of the world was as poor as the developing world is today, it was more violent. If you live in a world where a plague, a war, a murderer or just a simple bacterial infection is liable to carry off your intimates at any moment, repeated as an experience over dozens of generations it could act as a disincentive to get too involved. Those who avoided too great attachments would be favoured because they would be less encumbered by repeated mourning. Added to this, there was simply less time and opportunity to sit around intensifying attachments – the struggle for survival was much fiercer and the warmth, food and so forth which provide the opportunity were less available.

This does not contradict the evolutionary advantages of social bonding, it is merely to suggest that **intense** bonding may have been rarer. Survival and reproductive benefits of bonding and the evidence that all humans everywhere form attachments in small groups are not in doubt. Nor am I suggesting that intense bonds were never formed. We know from historical sources that intense love has existed since written records began but I argue that this was more common among the tiny élites who had the time and nourishment for such things. For most of the population, survival was a tremendously practical struggle, in the absence of the technologies we take for granted today.

As further support for my argument I adduce the extremely high morbidity among small children before modern medicine had developed. Until recently, at least one quarter of children died before age five.[10] In evolutionary terms, it is hard to believe this did not have an effect on the preparedness of parents to become intensely attached to small children. Since women in most societies began reproducing soon after they came into puberty giving birth to an average of eight children, the high infant mortality rate would have afflicted them at least twice during their childbearing years. This could have militated against parents becoming too intensely attached to children during our evolution.

Historians have hotly debated whether the records prove that the history of childhood is a nightmare from which we are just awakening or much the same as ever. The truth probably does not lie somewhere between the two. Lloyd de Mause, the most influential proponent of the nightmare scenario, summarized his view thus:[13] 'The history of childhood is a nightmare from which we have only recently begun to awake. The further back in history one goes, the lower the level of childcare, and the more likely children are to be killed, abandoned, beaten, terrorized and sexually abused.' Over the last 20 years De Mause has provided a steady flow of evidence to support this contention, although not without his critics.[65]

Some support for De Mause's view comes from my 1978 study of the village of Borbon in Western Ecuador,[14] which was typical in most respects of what life was like for the majority of the world's population before 1900. Infant mortality in Borbon is at a rate of one in four and basic subsistence is a constant struggle. Fathers are not expected to play any role in childcare except to contribute to the family income where possible.[15] They are migrant workers, moving up and down the river on which the village sits, with several partners in different villages – women bear children from several different men. The burden of childcare falls wholly on the mother but because she has to work hard to scrape a basic living, the care during early childhood is erratic: grandparents, siblings as young as age three, in fact anyone does it who happens to be able and willing. This constantly changing rota dilutes one-to-one relationships and there is little or no time for play or personalized interaction. Compared with the North American mother-infant dyads who I used as a comparison group, there was little interaction. Few of the carers become especially close to the infant, who is attached to no particular person. But given the high infant-mortality rate and given that most mothers have at least six children, this makes sense. If they fell in love with their babies, becoming intensely attached, as mothers in technologically developed societies are supposed to do, they would be putting themselves at grave risk of suffering repeated bereavement. The mothers anyway come from the same pattern of multiple care, and are probably less prone to intense attachments with other adults or offspring as a result.

Jay Belsky, the American developmental psychologist, offers an analysis of the evolutionary purpose of child maltreatment which also supports my observations regarding Borbon. He states that 'if one looks across the animal kingdom, it becomes apparent that the mistreatment of progeny is so widespread that it would seem to be as much a part of the "natural" condition as is sensitive, solicitious parental behaviour. One reason that maltreatment strikes so many of us as an aberration is the implicit assumption that it is natural for parents to love children and that harming them, intentionally or inadvertently, would not be in the parent's best interest, so they would not do it.

'Such a romanticized view of parent-child relations fails to acknowledge that, from the perspective of contemporary evolutionary biology, the interests of parent and offspring are not always one and the same ... for example, whereas it may be in the toddler's best interest to maintain breast feeding to ensure his or her physical well-being, for a mother needing to return to the fields to secure food for her entire family or seeking to conceive another child, her reproductive interest may be served best by weaning her child. In such circumstances conflicts of interest can generate actual conflict, leading to abuse ... under conditions in which the provision of sensitive and responsive care adds nothing to the reproductive fitness of parents – and more likely still, actually undermines it – abuse, neglect or both should occur; or at least would have done so in the environment of evolutionary adaptedness in which such behaviour is presumed to have evolved.'

Belsky goes on to present extensive evidence that where instability, unpredictability or unavailability of resources exist for parents, they would be more likely to maltreat children. Thus, poverty and low income correlate strongly with abuse and neglect: 'By physically abusing the child, the parent may be seeking to prevent the child from coercing them to allocate resources in a way that are more in the child's best interest than in the parent's.' Unemployment and low educational achievement are also correlated with high abuse and neglect rates because they reduce the parent's ability to obtain resources. Likewise, young mothers who have unplanned pregnancies with more closely spaced births are more likely to have large families and this is strongly correlated with abuse and neglect, because they divide limited material and emotional resources into smaller and smaller parcels. In many pre-capitalist societies, the greater the number of offspring, the greater the chances of having surviving offspring to help with subsistence and to care for you in old age. That this would increase the likelihood of abuse and neglect is consistent with De Mause's version of the history of childhood.

Belsky further points out that abusive, neglectful childhood experiences may actually be adaptive if the environment for which the child is being prepared is a hostile, tough one. 'It may well be the case, in fact, that the interpersonally opportunistic orientations that have been found repeatedly to characterize the behaviour of maltreated children (i.e. aggression, lack of empathy) may enhance their ability to reproduce when they confront, as they grow up, the very same adverse environmental conditions that led to their mistreatment in the first place.'

This is well exemplified by the case of Borbon. By the standards of developed nations, the children there are severely emotionally deprived but because of the society they are born into, this does not mean they suffer mental illnesses or angst as a result. Indeed, it can be argued that the Borbon pattern of childcare is a successful adaptation to conditions of life there. The social system reflects the material realities. The people of Borbon, like many of the inhabitants of the strip of coastline running down the Western side of South America, are of West African origin, enslaved by the Spanish and shipped over in the sixteenth century.[15] After 50 or so years of very deliberate deculturation, the slaves escaped to the coast and have been there ever since. Perhaps because their culture was so thoroughly suppressed by the Spaniards, the Borbonaise have a fairly low level of organization, neither having inherited their African traditions nor having set up many new ones. Political, religious and economic systems are basic and as a despised minority (10%) in the wider Ecuadorean state, they have little chance of improving their circumstances.[15] There is little 'division of labour' so that skills are basic and almost all the villagers can do what the others do to a similar standard. This lack of differentiation is reflected in beliefs about the world.

Overall, in societies where they work hard, the mothers' concept of the child is of an entity not requiring great emotional and interpersonal investment for it to develop healthily, a hardy creature who does not need mollycoddling. By contrast, mothers who have few demands on their time other than childcare conceive of infants as requiring a large emotional involvement. This is commonsensical – we would expect that people would develop models of the world consistent with their objective circumstances. Thus, anecdotally speaking, full-time working mothers today will often tell you that a baby has few emotional and social needs until it is old enough to talk, at which point it requires plenty of mental stimulation, such as that to be found at a nursery. Full-time mothers, by contrast, have often read books by experts suggesting that how they relate and meet the needs of their infant is critical to the mental health of their offspring.

Childcare beliefs and practices knit into the wider society. In developed societies no two people sitting on a bus would be likely to subscribe to the same beliefs. Astrology, atheism, Christianity, New Age holism, therapy and many other basic worldviews would be likely to be represented in any 40 people on a London bus. By contrast, all the inhabitants of Borbon have roughly the same ideas about how the world works and a similar morality. What Emil Durkheim called a 'conscience collective', a shared worldview, prevails.[16] This inevitably reduces individualism and questioning of the status quo. Feeding into this consensus is the uniformity of the patterns of childcare. Because their needs were not met reliably and personally in childhood, they do not have high expectations of life, which, it could be argued, is just as well since the opportunities for material advancement or for challenging the status quo and fostering individuality are poor.

The situation in developed nations since 1950 is very different. In Durkheimian terms, the glue that bonds them together is not the 'conscience collective' and 'mechanical solidarity' of Borbon but what he called 'organic solidarity'.[16] Rather than shared beliefs, developed societies are bound together by networks of economic obligation often enshrined in law. This reflects an advanced division of labour with different occupational groups specializing in exclusive skills that often take years to develop. The diversity of work experience promotes very different cultures, structures and classes which are themselves multiply subdivided. The childcare patterns reflect this diversity further, with many different variants, but they do have one fundamental in common: a commitment to intense one-to-one personal relationships in early childhood. These are extremely useful to the system which evolved them because they promote individuality and ambition.

As described in the last chapter, the drive towards individuality has steadily broadened out from the wealthiest élites during this century, at least in principle, to embrace all citizens of developed nations. Advanced capitalism demands continual economic growth and this is only possible if needs are constantly diversifying to create new markets. As many authors have pointed out, there is a demand for ever more diverse needs so that ever more specific new products can be devised to meet them.[17] In fact, individualism is a recent development in the history of the world. The anthropologist Sir Edmund Leach,[18] for example, refers to 'the ethos of individualism which is so central to Western society but which is notably absent from most of the societies which anthropologists study'. It was not until 1674 that the word 'self' took on its modern *Oxford English Dictionary* definition of 'a permanent subject of successive and varying states of consciousness'. It was only around this time that words linked to self, such as 'selfish', 'self-conscious' and 'self-determination', entered the language.[19] The word 'individualism' originally denoted 'indivisible', not its present meaning. It could be used for the Holy Trinity or of a married couple, meaning 'not to be parted'. The author of a thesis on the subject points out that[19] 'The gradual inversion of the meaning for the word "individual", moving from the indivisible and collective to the divisible and distinctive, carries within itself the historical development of self-consciousness . . . from a sense of unconscious fusion with the world towards a state of conscious individuation.'

In developed nations, close attachments are essential between parents and children and between partners to foster individualism. The child must have its needs met to a reasonable degree in order to have the stable set of specific and personal preferences which make for a good consumer (and good worker). The home fosters uniqueness. As noted in the last chapter, the pressure on a child as it passes through the school system is enormous, requiring individual ambition to compete with other pupils. When the child emerges into the workplace the strains are just as great to be individual and it must develop its own unique style to attract a mate. In the central emphasis on marrying and having children, it is often argued, capitalism offers the worker a small area of autonomy compared with their relative powerlessness in the workplace and the love and affection are seen as rewards for the more impersonal work life.[20]

Above all, the spread of the affluence which results from all this individualism and ambition widened dramatically after 1950. As Inglehart's work (discussed in the last chapter) suggests, there has been a 'culture shift' from 'Materialist' to 'Post-Materialist' values, with personal relationships taking centre stage, in affluent compared with poorer nations, and among the wealthy and the young compared with the poor and the elderly in affluent nations. The tragedy, as we are about to see, is that just when this new focus on personal relationships began, so did a dramatic increase in the likelihood of them being broken or disrupted. In fact, the drive for individualism is one of the main forces that has promoted an almost phobic fear of dependency, whether it be of self on others or others on self, which runs parallel to, and largely in total contradiction of, our new concern with relationships. The tragedy is that we place much greater importance on our relationships with lovers and children and yet, having become more intensely involved in unprecedented numbers, we make ourselves miserable by breaking these relationships up.

BROKEN BONDS IN CHILDHOOD

John Bowlby's theory of attachment proposes that between six months and three years of age children pass through a 'sensitive' phase in the development of patterns of attachment, with important implications for their adult mental health[21]. Anxious patterns, in which the child becomes enduringly fearful that people they are close to will suddenly abandon or reject them, are created by two possible childcare circumstances. Firstly, anxious attachment is promoted if the main people upon whom the infant depends keep changing or are not there for extended periods of time on a regular basis, are not 'accessible'. Secondly, it occurs if the main caregivers are not responsive when they are present – do not respond sufficiently or appropriately. This second possible cause is often forgotten in discussions of Bowlby's theory and as we shall see, separation from caregivers may actually be a less common cause of anxious attachment than unresponsiveness.

There is nothing new about separating very small children from their biological parents. The historical record suggests that for much of history in much of the world it has been standard practice for mothers to farm their infants out to all manner of substitutes (most commonly of all, to wet nurses).[13] What is new is that we encourage our infants and toddlers to become intensely attached to us on an unprecedented scale, only to break the bond and all too often, supply inadequate substitute care. Equally significantly, however, those mothers who do stay with their infants are no longer valued for doing so, become socially isolated and may be separated from their offspring by the mental barrier of depressed thoughts and feelings – be unresponsive. Finally, fathers are increasingly likely to disappear out of the child's life as a result of divorce and separation.

A recent analysis of 39 studies of the effects of being cared for by someone other than a parent (known as nonmaternal care) on over 14,000 under-three-year-olds concluded that about half of them suffered from anxious attachment compared with a general average of less than a third (an increased risk of 66%).[22] The authors stated that 'This is a remarkable effect that should be of concern. If this were a disease or illness due to environmental effects this effect size and increased risk would be considered extremely serious among medical people.' Nonmaternal care was also shown in this study to significantly increase the risk of emotional and behavioural problems. Whilst there are other less recent reviews of the evidence which find less cause for concern,[23] most students of the subject agree that at the least, nonmaternal care of a six-month- to three-year-old promotes anxious attachment where the ratio of children to carers is over two to one, where the substitute is a poor caregiver and where insufficient time is provided in order for the child to get to know the substitute.[24]

There is good reason to believe that this is often the case in the USA. In just the ten years after 1975, the proportion of infants with a mother who worked outside the home rose from 31% to 52%.[25] Most significant of all, three quarters of these mothers worked full-time with substitute arrangements that are a cause for concern.

In 1985, 37% of American under-one-year-olds with a working mother were cared for in their homes, nearly all by relatives, arrangements that are often as satisfactory as maternal care; 18% were also cared for by relatives, although not at home.[26] The good news, therefore, is that over half of the one half of under-one-year-olds whose mothers worked were cared for by a relative. But this leaves 37% who were cared for by nonrelatives, outside their home (23% in paid minders' homes, 14% in daycare centres) and 8% who were looked after by their mother on the job (unlikely to be a very satisfactory arrangement).[26] If we assume that the latter groups are at risk of anxious attachment, it would suggest that 17% of all American under-one-year-olds are put at increased risk by inadequate substitute care (see footnote 27 for the basis of this calculation).

Penelope Leach, the British child psychologist and bestselling author of Babycare books, has written eloquently of what this might mean for the babies concerned. She states:[28] 'Every baby needs at least one special person to attach herself to. It is through that first love relationship that she will learn about herself, other people and the world; experience emotions and learn to cope with them; move through egocentric baby love into trust, and eventually towards empathy and then the altruism that will one day enable her to give to another person what she needs for herself now. At least one person. More is better, safer. Babies do not have a fixed quota of devotion: if there are several adults around and available to an infant, she will usually select one for her primary, passionate attachment (and, even today, that will probably be her mother), but each and all of them will be special to her and any one can serve as a life-raft when the mother's absence would otherwise leave her drowning in a sea of deserted despair. Every baby will sometimes need a human life-raft. The grieving of a baby who loses her one and only special person – her lone mother who dies, for example, or the lifelong foster mother from whom she is removed – is agonizing to see because we know we are looking at genuine tragedy. But the pain of the separations we arrange and connive at every time we change caregivers or leave a baby in the daycare centre that has new staff – again – or with an agency babysitter she has never seen, may not be as different as we assume. In her first six, nine or even twelve months, that baby has no way of knowing that the parent who leaves her will come back; no way of measuring the passage of time; no way of holding the parent's image in her mind so as to anticipate her or his return. Only another known and beloved adult can keep her happily afloat.'

Leach continues in a section entitled 'Why Nurseries and Daycare Seldom Meet Those Infant Needs', as follows. 'That vital continuous one-to-one attention can rarely be achieved by group care, however excellent the facility may be . . . In North America the annual turnover of childcare staff (in daycare centres and nurseries) is 42%, and aides come and go even more frequently. It is not uncommon for a group of children to have three "mother figures" in a year.' Arguing that under age one, anything less than a one-to-one ratio is problematic, she points out that in America the recommended ratio of carers to infants ranges from one to three in three states to one to eight in four others. Leach cites estimates (in 1988) that the cost per child in American daycare should be $150 per week but the average paid by parents was $55. She further argues that nannies are not necessarily better than group care because they are also liable to change and because they often have not been mothers themselves, relying on a training of whose value Leach is sceptical. The 'least worst' solution (apart from relatives), according to Leach, is a minder who has had children of her own.

In general, fewer mothers of small children in Europe work than in America. In Britain, 10% of married women worked in 1931 and 30% did so by 1951.[29] This had doubled by 1987 and the proportion of all mothers (with a child under 16, as opposed to married women *per se*) who worked was 59% in 1993.[30] However, these statistics are misleading because, as Catherine Hakim of the London School of Economics has recently pointed out, all the increase in female labour in Britain has been in the part-time sector.[31] Astonishingly, according to her, there has been no increase whatsoever in the proportion of British women working full-time for 150 years (for a full discussion of these claims, see the next chapter). This creates two crucial differences to the American picture: fewer British mothers with small children work at all; and the majority do so part-time (compared with the three-quarters of American mothers of under-one-year-olds who work full-time). Thus (see Table I below), the proportion of British under-one-year-olds with working mothers in 1996 was 28% (compared with the American 50%) and of this 28%, only one quarter were full-time (compared with the American three-quarters). Nonetheless, in the last decade there has been a substantial increase in the proportion of British women with small children who work. As recently as 1986, only 18% of under-ones had a working mother (compared with the 1996 28%). Further broken down, 8% were full-time in 1986 compared with 11% in 1996. 10% were part-time in 1986 compared with 17% in 1996 (the Labour Force Survey provided me with these figures directly; similar proportions are reported from the other main source on this subject, the General Household Survey – see *The Impact of Subsidizing Childcare*, 1995, Duncan, A. et al, London: Equal Opportunities Commission):

Table I: Percentage of all mothers with a youngest child aged under one with a full- or part-time job, 1986 and 1996 compared

	1986	1996
Full-Time	8%	11%
Part-Time	10%	17%
Total Working	18%	28%

(Figures supplied directly to the author by the Labour Force Survey, Department of Employment, London)

From the standpoint of attachment theory, the most critical figure is for all under-threes (see Table II). In 1986 a total of 25% had a working mother compared with fully 40% in 1996. The 1986 breakdown was 8% full-, 17% part-time; in 1996 this had become 13% full-, 27% part-time.

Table II: Percentage of all Mothers with a youngest child aged 0–2 with a full- or part-time job, 1986 and 1996 compared

	1986	1996
Full-Time	8%	13%
Part-Time	17%	27%
Total Working	25%	40%

(Figures supplied directly to the author by the Labour Force Survey, Department of Employment, London)

That there has been such a substantial rise in the proportion of small children in nonmaternal care must have given rise to some increase in the amount of anxious attachment, although it is extremely hard to estimate precisely how much. Leach reports a survey of 18 British daycare centres in which the ratio of carer to child was an average of 1 to 4.6, which by her reasoning would cause considerable damage. However, daycare centres provide only a small minority of the substitute care in Britain, where more of the substitutes are relatives – and therefore likely to be consistent and responsive – than in America: only one quarter of the children of working British mothers of under-fives were cared for by paid substitutes such as childminders, nannies and daycare centres in 1993 (up from one fifth in 1980). The remainder were mostly cared for by grandmothers and friends.[28] Furthermore, most of the mothers work part-time in Britain and many authorities argue that below 20 hours a week work, the risk of anxious attachment is significantly less.[24] Since about half of the maternal part-time work is less than 20 hours, it means fewer children are likely to be at risk in Britain than America (with its higher rates of full-time work).

Yet another important point is that there is a very marked difference in the kind of employment between mothers in professional-managerial jobs and the unskilled. In 1992, 32% of mothers of under-fives with skilled jobs worked full-time, whereas only 1% of mothers with unskilled manual jobs did so.[28] Given that skilled mothers would have more cash than unskilled to employ good-quality substitute care, it seems likely that this reduces the potential damage of full-time working.

There is, then, considerable room for debate as to what all these statistics portend for patterns of attachment in modern Britain. Only the most ideologically motivated of theorists could maintain (in the face of the mass of evidence to the contrary) that **any** working by mothers of under-threes is worse than no work.

Although the evidence is far from clearcut, there is no doubt at all that some mothers are actually depressed by full-time childcare and become less so when they obtain part-time work[31] (see the next chapter for a detailed analysis). There is some evidence that the groups most at risk of depression are mothers who are full-time at home or at work; the part-time may be least at risk[32] (helped by the social contact and status a job accords but not overstretched by full-time work). An unresponsive, depressed mother is just as likely to foster anxious attachment as one who works full-time with inadequate substitute care. In those cases where, if the mother did not work, she would become depressed, it is better for the child if she does so and finds adequate substitute care. Thus, in terms of the best interests of the child, there is a balance to be found between mothers staying at home and becoming depressed and mothers leaving their children in inadequate substitute care.

For, just as separation has increased, so has the number of small children raised by depressed mothers. As noted in Chapter 1 and Appendix I, women born after 1955 were some five times more likely to suffer depression than those born before 1925[33] and those with small children were much more at risk than comparable childless women.[34] 30-40% of the poorest mothers of small children are depressed at any one time[37] and the effect on the children is indisputable – in one survey of two-year-old children with depressed mothers, 61% showed marked signs of emotional disorder.[35]

The causes of maternal depression are increasingly well understood (see Chapter 5). Women who lost a parent before the age of 14, who have three or more children under age five, who are poor and who lack social support are most at risk. Because there have been no increases since 1950 in the first two factors they could not account for the rise in depression, but since 1979 in Britain there has been a sharp rise in the number of low-income parents. Then, 19% of children were being raised in such a home but from 1981 onwards, to the present day, the proportion has been about 30% of children.[36] I believe we are already seeing the effects of this change in the form of increased rates of violence against the person by young men.[37]

Regarding lack of social support, the number of mothers in this position has risen steadily since 1950. Of the many causes some of the most commonly advanced are the increasing disdain shown for the mothering role among young women, the alienating architecture of modern public housing (e.g. high-rise blocks), increased geographical mobility that takes women away from their family support systems and above all, 'the break-up of the family'.[38] In the next chapter I shall present persuasive evidence that sex role strain is also a major cause of depression in both men and women.

Many are the ills of modern society that have been laid at the door of The Single Parent and The Absent Father. In Britain the most vocal advocate has been Norman Dennis. However, his contention that much of the substantial rise in crime since 1950 is directly due to father absence is not supported by the evidence (indeed, close inspection of the lack of substance to Dennis' claims makes it hard to comprehend why, even today, he is given so much space in certain newspapers).[39] Dennis fails altogether to take proper account of the effects of parental divorce and separation. It is these, not single parenthood or absent fatherhood *per se*, that give rise to the consistent finding that children of single parents are more at risk of criminality, depression and educational underperformance. Parental break-up is damaging to children for three main reasons: the witnessing of parental disharmony up to and after the separation; the mother's loss of income afterwards (on average, women have half as much income a year later); and the loss of the father. This latter is often deeply distressing for the child and since about half of fathers lose touch with the family, it is extremely common. Doubtless Dennis is right that the absence of a male authority figure and role model is damaging to some children in some cases. But in the poorest homes, where the father may offer criminality and violence as a model, it may sometimes be a distinct bonus (two famous examples of this Liam and Noel Gallagher, of the highly successful rock group Oasis. Their father was a violent alcoholic and according to his sons, they were delighted when their mother left him).

Another development since 1950 has been the increasing lack of parental supervision of teenagers – the emergence of the Latchkey Kid. In America, 12- to 13-year-olds who care for themselves after school for 11 or more hours are twice as likely to use cigarettes, alcohol and marijuana than those who do not care for themselves after school at all.[40] Whilst this effect is due in part to low income and lack of education of parents and to a greater incidence of emotional problems in the kind of family that hands out latchkeys,[41] just not having parents around much in adolescence is also important. One effect seems to be to make the teenager more susceptible to peer pressure at this age.[42]

A UNICEF publication entitled *Child Neglect in Rich Nations* (1993, Hewlett, SA) presents a damning indictment of child care in several wealthy nations. Apart from highlighting the large increases in the proportion of parents with low incomes in the 1980s in America, Canada, Australia and Britain, it examines the decreasing time and energy parents have to devote to children. These nations devote far greater proportions of their budgets to the elderly than to children. This is contrasted with continental Europe and Japan, nations which 'share a wider and deeper vision of collective responsibility for children'.

The author states: 'It is important to stress that growing economic pressure on families with children, particularly young families and single parents, is at the heart of the parental time shortage. Many families are squeezed on two fronts, dealing with falling wages, while at the same time they are also facing sharply higher living costs. In the United States, mortgage payments now eat up 29% of median family income, up from 17% in 1970, while college tuition consumes 40% of family income, up from 29% in 1970.

'Trends are similar in the United Kingdom. House prices there tripled between 1970 and 1990; indeed, for first-time house buyers, mortgage payments now consume 40% of net household income, up from 18% in 1970. It is no wonder that most British families need both parents in the labour force.'

To meet these economic pressures, working hours have increased. In America, the average working week went from 41 to 47 hours between 1973 and 1989. Entrepreneurs in small businesses worked an average 57 hours a week and professionals, 52 hours. In Britain the average male works five hours more a week than his continental counterpart and executives worked an average 55 hours a week. Less than half took their full holiday entitlement and one quarter worked every weekend. The UNICEF report spells out the potential effect of all this work on parenting skills.

'In contemporary Anglo-American societies, children not only have two parents at work, they also have mothers as well as fathers who routinely work 55-hour weeks and who come home preoccupied and exhausted, unable to give much of anything to their children . . . Research by Pittman and Brooks has shown that the hard-edged personality cultivated by many successful professionals – control, decisiveness, aggressiveness, efficiency – can be directly at odds with the passive, patient, selfless elements in good nurturing. The last thing a three-year-old or a 13-year-old needs at eight o'clock in the evening is a mother – or father, for that matter – who marches into the house in his or her power suit, barking orders, and looking and sounding like a drill sergeant.

'Compare the ingredients in a recipe for career success with those for a recipe for meeting the needs of a child, beginning with the all-important ingredient of time. To succeed in one's career may require long hours and consume one's best energy, leaving little time to spend together as a family and precious little enthusiasm for the hard tasks of parenting. Mobility and a prime commitment to oneself are virtues in the job world; stability, selflessness and a commitment to others are virtues in family life. Qualities needed for career success also include efficiency, a controlling attitude, an orientation towards the future and an inclination towards perfectionism, while their virtual opposites – tolerance for mess and disorder, an ability to let go, an appreciation of the moment and an acceptance of difference and failure – are what is needed for successful parenting.'

Taken as a whole, whether it be early separation, parental depression, loss of father, teenage neglect or overstretched parents, the bonds of child and parent are broken more today than in 1950. Singly and in combination, these experiences provide the seeds for a low serotonin citizen. But of all the misfortunes that befall modern children, the new tendency of their parents to separate and divorce is probably the most influential.

INCREASED DIVORCE AND SEPARATION SINCE 1950

The chances of a British couple who married in 1950 subsequently divorcing were 12 in 100. The proportion who marry today who will divorce is 40%.[43] Whilst Britain has one of the highest divorce rates in Europe, the figures for other nations are similar, averaging around one in three marriages today compared with one in eight in 1950. In America, half of marriages end in divorce.[44]

It is difficult to convey the quantum of misery that these statistics represent. Both divorce and bereavement provoke depression, aggression and psychiatric problems in vulnerable people, all associated with low serotonin. It is not mere hyperbole to compare their effect to that of a World War because a divorce has many similar psychological consequences to a bereavement (indeed, Colin Murray Parkes,[45] a leading authority on bereavement, has shown that bereavement resembles a great many other losses than death, including the loss of a limb and of a home). A total of 470,000 British military personnel and civilians were killed in the Second World War,[46] causing deep distress to relatives and friends. Since 1950 there have been approximately two and a half million divorces[47]. Using these crude criteria, the emotional impact of the World War may not have been much greater than that of the explosion in divorce.

Studies comparing bereaved and nonbereaved groups show that death within six months is approximately six times more probable among the bereaved, with the rate at least twice as high among widowers compared with widows.[44] Studies of divorcees also reveal a substantially increased morbidity compared with those in intact marriages. The bereaved and divorced are both at increased risk of psychosomatic illness, suicide, alcohol abuse and of psychiatric disorders. Divorcees are between three and 22 times more likely than persons in intact marriages to be admitted to a mental hospital. Bereaved versus nonbereaved are between four and eight times more likely to suffer this.[45]

An important difference between the divorced and the bereaved is that most deaths occur in old age, whereas the majority (55%) of divorces involve children under 16 years old.[48] About 15% of British children today come from a divorced family and in America it is estimated that half of all children today will experience the divorce of their parents by age 18.[49] The effects of divorce on children are causing increasing alarm as the results of studies which have followed families from before divorce to the present day have become available. For boys, increased risks include aggressive, delinquent behaviour and depression, as well as becoming a divorcee themselves. For girls the effects seem to be even worse: increased risk of underperformance at school, depression, teenage pregnancy, youthful marriage (which greatly increases the risk of divorce) and divorce in adulthood.[50]

Perhaps partly because of disillusion with the marital state, the last 20 years has seen a huge increase in the proportion of parents who do not marry at all. In Britain, the proportion of children born out of wedlock rose from 10% to 30% between 1980 and 1991.[49] Two parents registered these children in three-quarters of cases, mostly living at the same address, so the truly lone parent was a rarity (only 7% of all births). In about 30% of out-of-wedlock cases, the mother was married within two years, although not necessarily to the biological father. An estimated 30–40% of children are conceived outside marriage across Europe but only a minority of these women are unmarried at the time of the birth – pregnancy is still a spur for marriage in many cases.[51] Nonetheless, a substantial proportion of British children are now raised by unmarried, cohabiting couples and the worrying fact is that their relationships seem to be more unstable than those of the married (40% of whom divorce, it should be remembered). In Sweden, where only half of parents marry at all, the rate of separation among unmarried couples is three times higher than among the married.[52] Similar rates have been found among British unmarried parents[53] although there appears to be a subgroup of well-off couples who stay together more than the low-income couples who make up more than half of all unmarried couples.[44] Couples who cohabit before they marry and who marry in a registry office rather than a church are more likely to divorce.[54] It seems probable that those who never marry, or who do so in less conventional circumstances than the non-cohabiting, church-wed, are less committed to the concept of marriage as an inviolable state and therefore, when the going gets tough, are more likely to break up. It is also plausible that the more unconventional are a self-selected group of less stable individuals, although this is a highly debatable matter.

Another possible indication of scepticism about forming attachments is the remarkable fact that 20% of women born immediately after the war in Britain, America and Australia are predicted to remain childless.[55] In most cases this is voluntary and commonly by women of advanced education and higher social classes. In the past there have been cohorts in which 20% of women were childless, such as the women born in 1920, but this was not through choice but because of low marriage rates and a shortage of men due to wars. The current increase in voluntary female childlessness helps to cause a fertility crisis throughout Europe.

Added to this, we form a great many more intense sexual attachments to the opposite sex than previous generations. Although these create great joy, they also bring with them a great load of sadness. The carefully conducted British Sexual Survey asked detailed questions of over 20,000 representative Britons aged 16–60 in 1990–91.[56] Almost twice as many women aged 25–34 had had sexual intercourse with three to four partners than 45-59 women (23% versus 13%). Two and a half times as many of the younger group had had sex with five to nine partners (17% versus 7%) and nearly three times as many with ten-plus partners (10% versus 4%). Whilst the differences for men were less dramatic they were still considerable. These statistics represent a very welcome reduction in sexual inhibition and dysfunction but behind them can also be found a great many broken hearts. It is no coincidence that tragic, sad or angry responses to the end of a sexual relationship are an abiding theme of the popular music that pours out of the juke boxes and stereos which form the backdrop to most encounters between courting couples.

THE CAUSES OF INCREASED DIVORCE THIS CENTURY

The recent unprecedented rise in divorce is part of a century-long trend in most developed nations. As a leading historian of the subject has put it:[57] 'In all Western countries where divorce is permitted, divorce rates have risen steadily over the century, have fluctuated following each of the World Wars, and have accelerated from some time in the 1960s or early 1970s until the early 1980s.' This is well illustrated by the example of England. The scale of change is staggering. The number of divorces in 1857, the last year in which divorce was achieved only by Decree of Parliament, was just five. With courts able to decree divorces, this had risen to an average of 215 per year, 1870–4, to 590 per year by 1900–4 and 710 for 1910–13. In short, until the First World War, divorce was virtually unheard of.

The average for the four years immediately after the First World War was four times greater than immediately before it. The rate then settled down to a slower rise, reaching 4,000 by 1930, but rocketed again after the Second World War, stabilizing at around 25,000 to 30,000 per annum, 1952–60. In other words, there were about 40 times more divorces in 1952 than at the start of the century, most of the increase occurring 1945–52. In the 1960s the numbers doubled and they doubled again in the 1970s. In 1995, in England and Wales there were 165,000 divorces, 280 times more than in 1900. With different timing, similar trends occurred in Germany, the USA and much of Europe.

The reasons for the increases immediately after the wars are no mystery. The danger of imminent death speeded up courtship; the long separations weakened relationships, even previously stable ones; the opportunity and temptation for adulterous unions were numerous, especially for women; and during the war years couples who were anyway liable to divorce put it off until afterwards. Nor is there much dispute about why there was little growth in divorce during the 1950s. Most authorities agree that it was because those who had been raised in the 1920s and 1930s had their aspirations fulfilled by the relative affluence and stability of the postwar years. Compared with the poverty and economic instability of the prewar years and the terrors of the war itself, the 1950s were a haven of peace and prosperity.[58] The debate is over the hundred-year trend and the rapid increase that began in the 1960s.

The explanation is best presented at several different levels. On the first, there are the reasons that divorcing couples themselves give. Like characters from situation comedies, the genders offer predictably different ones. Wives tend to cite physical violence, verbal abuse, financial problems, mental cruelty, drinking, neglect of the home and children and a lack of love. Husbands are more likely to cite parents-in-law and sexual incompatibility. However, most students of the subject treat these explanations as superficial symptoms of root causes.

The next level consists of a series of conditions or antecedents that have been identified as correlating with divorced compared with intact couples. The most commonly listed include being young when married (a woman who marries before the age of 20 is two to four times more likely to divorce than one who marries after age 25); having a low income or being uneducated (in England, people from unskilled professions are four times more likely to divorce); large differences in social class, age or education between the partners;[59] marriages where the wife has a job or the man is unemployed; marriages where there is premarital pregnancy or cohabitation; marriages solemnized in registry offices rather than a church; and marriages where one or both parties come from a family with a history of divorce.[60] Whilst all these factors seem to be important, they are not necessarily explanatory in themselves. That registry office weddings are less enduring, for example, is not caused by the kind of ceremony in itself but is widely assumed to indicate less commitment to the concept of marriage and therefore, less preparedness to stick it out if the relationship sours. Another complication is that many of these 'causes' are explained by each other. For example, the finding that youthful weddings are more at risk is complicated by the fact that such couples are more likely than older ones to have premarital pregnancies and to be of low income. Likewise, American Black couples are often reported to be at greater risk than white ones but when the effects of low income, family size, home ownership and other similar factors associated with divorce are taken into account, they are actually *less* likely to divorce than equivalent Whites.

The final level of explanation includes a variety of kinds of factor, most significantly (in no particular order): urbanization; erosion of traditional family relationships; rising expectations of what marriage can supply; liberalized divorce laws; increased numbers of working women; the women's movement; the decline of religion; shifts in moral and social values; demographic changes such as the decline in the mortality rate; improved education and social welfare; and reduced stigma as more people know divorcees and media reflect the trend. Of course, many of these changes also overlap and several are secondary effects of increased industrialization. It is from this list that most explanations for the rise in the second half of the century are drawn.

THE CAUSES OF THE INCREASE SINCE 1960

The 1969 English parliamentary legislation which introduced 'no-fault' divorce is often blamed for the rise but the numbers had already doubled in the eight years beforehand – if anything, the new act was an effect rather than a cause. Indeed, there seems little doubt that the legislation which gradually made it easier to get divorced during the course of the century reflected changing social mores rather than caused them, although once the changes were in place they are thought to have accelerated the rate of increase. An extremely influential aspect of the legislative changes was the increased access to legal aid because it eased divorce for low-income classes and women. Changes to the rules of eligibility in 1914, 1920, 1949 and 1960 meant that by 1966, one third of all divorcees were from unskilled manual professions. Where once divorce had been only affordable by the rich, it was available to anyone – including women with no independent means.

The increased participation of women in the workplace was equally critical in making divorce a realistic financial plan. Where once a woman with a poor husband might have found herself with no income at all after a divorce, the new acceptability of women in the workplace made them more confident about starting a new life. Although there is no clear causal relationship, divorce and female employment are correlated. In 1980 in the USA, for example, 50% of married women worked, whereas 75% of the divorced did so. Important too was the potential for employment. In the 1960s and for much of the 1970s, the easy availability of work meant that even if a woman were not actually employed, she felt confident she would find a job. Jobs may also have provided a psychological buttress – a protection against loneliness and isolation – and continuity during the separation and divorce process. On top of this, the newly established welfare state provided a safety net for the divorced woman that would not have been there to catch her mother in the 1920s and 1930s. This almost certainly gave confidence to previously excluded groups – low-income people and the average woman – when considering divorce. But at least as significant was the change in values and morality.

As one authority put it: 'The various limitations [on divorce], which had been slowly eroded during the previous three-quarters of a century, seemed to collapse within a few years during the late 1960s and early 1970s.'[61] There was a sharp decline in church-going and belief in formal religions (although belief in such concepts as a god and an afterlife, often customized to suit individual tastes, remain surprisingly robust, even today).[61] This reduced the stigma of divorce, a change that itself increased divorce. With the increasing tendency for people to live alone and apart from family networks, social controls and pressures to conform to moral edicts of the older generations were lessened. These changes, coupled with the others listed above, meant that more people knew someone who was divorced and it became more acceptable to have this status . . . so more people felt able to follow suit. As television tightened its grip on the public imagination and replaced radio as the main broadcast entertainment, it reflected these changes, also further reinforcing them.

At least as important as these changes, there was a revolution in perceptions of the importance of relationships to happiness, as expectations rose (see Chapter 3). One authority summarized the significance of this change for divorce: 'Recent decades have seen an unprecedented emphasis on the emotional content of marriage and deriving emotional fulfilment from it . . . that aspect of marriage which is arguably the most fragile. The stress on romantic love, emotional intensity and sexual satisfaction that has long been associated with premarital and extramarital relationships has spilled over into marriage . . . the higher these expectations rise, the less they are likely to be fulfilled.'[57] This change is linked by most analysts to the change in women's attitudes and expectations. A typical analysis is provided by the distinguished British historian, Lawrence Stone.[62] 'The egalitarian ideology of feminism has had a major impact, in that it has drawn attention to the gross injustice to women of unequal opportunities for jobs. The result of this pressure has been an opening of doors to married women, who have poured into the labour market on a large scale. These ideas have radically transformed the personal relationships of males and females in marriage and the relative allocation of responsibilities and powers within the family unit. Beneficial though this has been in many ways, it has put modern marriage under greater stress than ever before.' Stone goes on to point out that the advent of washing machines, prepared supermarket meals and other such technological changes enabled the average woman to cope with the practicalities of everyday domestic life and to have paid employment at the same time. In the end, although he is tactful about it, he leaves us in no doubt that he regards 'the egalitarian ideology of feminism' as having played a significant role in causing the increased divorce rate. Other, somewhat less diplomatic and less scientifically based versions of this view are to be found in the newspaper columns of 90% of the British press. Hardly a day goes by without one or other columnist (some of them divorcees or notorious extramarital philanderers themselves, mostly men) lamenting the effect of feminism on modern marriage. The effect of these changes in gender roles is the subject of the next two chapters, along with the possibility that the greater freedoms resulting from the 1960s may have made people with pre-existing personality problems more likely to divorce. There is some evidence that divorcees were more neurotic 16-year-olds than non-divorcees[63] and in the next chapter I present the substantial but unfashionable and largely overlooked evidence that people with neurotic and impulsive personality traits are more at risk of divorce.

In summary, then, these are the conventional explanations for the increase since 1960: greater financial and legal ease of divorce for previously excluded plaintiffs; changing social values and morals; and the new role of women at work and home. To these, in the next two chapters, I will add another stage on the road to divorce, gender rancour, and explore how its increase may be both cause and effect of the increased rate.

Taken overall – married and unmarried parents – the picture is not a pretty one. If parents do marry they divorce at an ever-increasing rate, and if they do not, the relationship is even more liable to end. The effect on the participants is undoubtedly profoundly depressing in many cases, a major cause of low serotonin. Whilst there are happily separated couples today who would have had to suffer the agony of a loveless and acrimonious life together in 1950, there may be a great many more whose lives have been wrecked by the pursuit of 'greener grass' which in the event turned to straw. On top of this, there is a sizeable proportion of children who have been damaged by their parents' behaviour. In all, at least half of under 40-year-olds today have been directly touched by divorce, either as parents or children.

BREAKING BONDS WITH THE ELDERLY
If parents with small children are increasingly unable to meet the attachment needs of their offspring and each other, they are also finding it harder to cope with those of their own elderly parents.

Medical advances and better primary health care mean there are more old people and they are living to older ages. In 1901, 5% of Britons were over 65, today it is 16% and there are ten times more over-85-year-olds (from 0.15% in 1901 to 1.6% today).[48] But as their numbers rise their circumstances become increasingly isolated.

The fundamental shift is away from living with relatives, towards living alone or in residential homes, especially amongst the eldest. The proportion of over-85-year-olds living with relatives fell from 31% to 19% between 1971 and 1991.[64] The numbers of 85-plus in long-term residential care rose by 25% after 1981 and living alone increased from 30% to 49%, 1971–91. That this reflected fundamental changes in how our society is ordered is shown by the fact that in 1962, 75% of over-65s had one child living less than 15 minutes away whereas only 40% were in this position in 1986. The isolation is still increasing rapidly: one third of over-65s saw a friend or relative daily in 1985, whereas only six years later, this had fallen to one quarter. The changes most affect women because they live longer than their husbands.

These trends are part of the atomization of social life described by Durkheim, accelerating since 1950. The tendency for people to live alone extends to younger age groups as well. Whereas 17% of households contained only one person in 1971, for example, the proportion was 27% in 1991.

CONCLUSION: LOSERS IN LOVE
Until very recently in the wider sweep of history, the premature death by murder or disease of intimates was a routine part of life. It has often been suggested that modern life is so angst-ridden because most of us have never had to confront these harsh realities and instead, we invent new perils as a substitute. We are supposed to have become a society of Woody Allens, obsessing about trivia and unanswerable philosophical dilemmas to fill the void left by war and plague. The truth is that between them, modern patterns of childcare, divorce, separation and care of the

elderly have created at least as much if not more mourning, especially when combined with the greater numbers and intensity of our attachments. By the end of the Second World War the relatives and friends of 470,000 Britons were wrestling with the sadness and anger that death brings. But the statistics for broken bonds listed above suggest a tide of melancholy every bit as high. Alongside the distress caused by excessive and maladjusted social comparison and relative deprivation, the tidal wave of broken bonds explains a significant part of the rise in depression, violence and compulsion and the new pervasiveness of low serotonin.

Chapter 5

Gender Rancour,
Part I

*Are Working Mothers 'Unnatural' Or Are Men Just
Bad Losers?*

When I put the above question to my 80-year-old mother she answered
with a single word: 'Both.'

In the 1960s and 1970s it was widely felt that, psychologically speaking,
men and women should be assumed to have the same basic potentials
despite the fact that on a great many psychological tests women and men
tended to score differently. It was believed that, given truly equal opportunities and if we were not treated differently in childhood just because of our
sex, there would be no patterns of sex difference in intelligence, aptitudes,
patterns of emotion, personality and extent and kind of sexual desire. In
such a society, what was between your legs would not affect how stupid or
clever you were, whether you were better at maths or art, whether you were
prone to depression or aggression, what kind of sex you wanted and how
often. Equal opportunities and socialization would mean that in future,
when social scientists were investigating a subject there would no longer be
a need to 'control' for sex in the selection of samples, there would just be
different categories of individuals, regardless of gender.

At that time, for example, if you wished to examine whether children
of violent parents were more at risk of depression than children from
nonviolent homes, it was necessary to have equal numbers of boys and
girls in the sample because other studies had shown that there were differing outcomes of parental violence for each. Unless you controlled for
these by selecting representative samples of both sexes, you would not be
able to tell if your results reflected gender rather than parental violence.
But it was felt that if, for a few generations, boys and girls and men and
women were not treated differently because of their sex, 'sex differences'
would be eradicated.

Similar arguments were applied to social class and to race and today it is still widely believed that, given the same chances, classes and races would not differ. But recently there has been a shift in many people's feelings about gender. This is for many reasons, including a long period of political conservatism in most developed nations and the increasing popularity of biological theories of society (known as 'sociobiology'), the former perhaps playing a part in causing the latter. But it is also because for most behaviours, it is as necessary to control for sex when carrying out research today as it ever was: men and women continue to be very different despite three decades of concerted efforts to equalize their conditions. In particular, as will be discussed in some detail below, women continue to be much more likely than men to suffer from depression, despite all the improvements in their opportunities.

My mother qualified as a psychiatric social worker in the 1940s and as a psychoanalyst in the 1950s. In the 1960s she probably subscribed to the egalitarian view of gender for a time (although she hotly denies that she ever really did!). Whatever her beliefs then, like many others she now believes that in terms of psychological potential, men and women are 'equal but different' and that genetics are the reason why. I am not sure that I agree with her – the jury is still very much out on this point, in terms of scientific evidence, as we shall see – but the relevance of the issue to the main subject of this book is that many authors have claimed that the rise in depression since 1950 has been significantly influenced by the attempt to equalize the sexes. It is argued that these attempts were bound to create a great deal of distress because they were pressurizing the genders to feel and behave in ways that did not come naturally to them. In particular, the increase in working women and in working mothers with small children is on trial as having soured the relations between the sexes and increased rates of depression.

ANECDOTAL EVIDENCE OF THE NEW GENDER RANCOUR

I do believe that relations between the sexes have never been more acrimonious and rancorous and that this is partly due to changes in patterns of work for both sexes. However, it is much less clear to me whether this bloody phase in the battle of sexes is a necessary stage on the road to a better way of living or whether it is the consequence of organizing our affairs in a manner that is Against Nature.

Whilst we know that sex antagonism has been considerable throughout history, there has been an unprecedented intensification of hostilities since 1950. The most obvious sign of this is the increased divorce rate. The greater preparedness to go to war and to fight to the death (sometimes literally) on the part of both sexes – rancour – is both a cause as well as an effect of increased divorce because the bad feeling often does not end with the Decree Nisi, it poisons subsequent relationships . . . causing still more broken bonds and rancour . . . and more divorce. Since rising divorce is an important cause of increasing depression, rancour may be linking the two. But as we shall be seeing, depression also can cause divorce, as well as being an effect of it. Depressed people are extremely rancorous towards their intimates so the factors (such as relative deprivation) other than divorce already discussed in this book which have increased depression can be said to have increased divorce through increasing depression. In what follows, I will demonstrate that depression, gender rancour and divorce are all highly combustible elements that ignite each other and have inflamed an ever more brightly burning bonfire of misery and rage since 1950.

The contribution of new patterns of employment to this conflagration – especially the new trend for working among mothers of small children – is controversial and debatable. To suggest, as some authors have, that it has been the match that first ignited the fire is grossly inaccurate, but as we shall see, it may have fanned the flames. Put crudely, many husbands are depressed and confused by their wives' work. For their part, many mothers (especially of small children) have been depressed by the strain that working puts on their sense of identity and on their practical resources. This has created ill-feeling and increased the divorce statistics,helping to create the low-serotonin society. But the resentment of men at the new status quo combined with the problems for women of defining what they want from it – given that as girls they were socialized into a female sex role – are at least as likely to be the main cause of the resulting rancour as any supposed genetically implanted differences.

INTIMATIONS OF NEW GENDER RANCOUR IN POPULAR CULTURE
In Britain, the new rancour has been institutionalized in the television programme *Blind Date*, which started out in the mid-1980s as a compelling investigation of what attracts men and women but in the 1990s has become a vehicle for unvarnished sex hatred. The events of the date are always filmed and edited in such a way as to emphasize conflict. The woman is shown laughing at the man as he tries to impress her with his water-skiing or horse-riding skills, whilst he is usually shown ogling her scanty bikini or soaked T-shirt, mocking her attempts at 'blowing' (snigger, snigger) glass and throwing clay on a wheel (one which looks like a penis, haw, haw). The separate interviews at the end of the date where they say what they think of each other are edited for maximum personal

opprobrium. Back in the studio, Cilla Black acts as agent provocateur for the final humiliation. A shy man is teased in front of 10 million viewers, an uneducated woman is portrayed as thick. Beautiful or handsome participants are encouraged to explain why their date was not up to their standard. The impulses to humiliate, to hate and to display contempt for the opposite sex are given free rein.

Sex hatred has always played a big part in popular television but it has previously been mostly confined to the situation comedy. George and his belittling Mildred, the guerrilla warfare of the bourgeois couples on holiday in *Duty Free*, the misogyny of Alf Garnett, the *Likely Lads* and now *Men Behaving Badly* . . . the list is long. But *Blind Date* is not fiction, or not supposed to be, and nor is it the only 'factual' programme now promoting sex hate. Such programmes as *Beadle's About* depend largely on the desire of lovers to make their partner's worst nightmares come true in front of one fifth of the adult population. It is not an obvious way of expressing affection, but the women who conspire with Jeremy Beadle to bulldoze their partners' prized car into a harbour or the men who help to wreck their lovers' pride-and-joy kitchen seem to regard the whole thing as a super prank. That sex hatred has come out of fiction into reality as entertainment indicates its power.

It can be argued that all this illustrates is that we have become more open about our hatred – that men and women would always have loved to see this kind of thing. Literature is littered with evidence that men and women have always hated each other, with a gradual crescendo in the volume of misandry (man-hating). Chaucer's fourteenth-century men and women are often in lifelong struggles to exploit and defraud each other ('The Wife of Bath'); Shakespeare's sixteenth-century sexes are usually at war, as are the characters in Jacobean tragedy; in the nineteenth century, innumerable authors could be cited, including Balzac, Flaubert (Madame Bovary would have enjoyed *Blind Date*), Trollope and Henry Arthur Jones (with his play *The Case of Rebellious Susan* – 'Men are Brutes,' she says), demonstrating a steady growth in fictional women openly expressing their distaste for men and the status quo, and of distressed and vengeful men.

Male enmity has always been more visible than female and continues apace today. It is to be found in countless 'sexist' films, TV dramas, novels (including several whole genres) and most conspicuously and explicitly of all, newspaper columns. What is new is the extent to which the women are fighting back.

The middle- and up-market women authors of today paint a bitter, discontented picture of heterosexual relationships, with men emerging as for the most part despicable: Fay Weldon, Joanna Trollope, Mary Wesley, Anita Brookner, and the Americans Anne Tyler and Alison Lurie, to name only a few of the more literary kind. Men in blockbuster novels do not fare much better – be the author Jackie Collins, Julie Burchill or Jilly Cooper. It is hard to recall one fictional couple drawn by a modern woman author that is contented, honest and loving. Not so long ago I met Fay Weldon. I asked her why she seems to portray sex wars in every book: men and women who betray their best friends by sleeping with their spouses, deceitful and selfish people who are for the most part amoral, not a happy couple in sight. 'Because that is what all the people I know are like,' she replied. When I told her that I know many people (such as my three sisters) who have stable and lasting relationships unblemished by sexual treason and providing sane home lives for their offspring, she said that might well be true and that her experience could be exceptionally bleak. 'But where I live,' she went on, 'divorce and infidelity are the rule.'

There is also a new perception of males as disposable. This was all too obvious in a BBC2 discussion of the subject in 1995 between some prominent female luminaries, including Germaine Greer, Janet Street Porter and the *Guardian*'s (now the *Independent*'s) Ms Angry, columnist Suzanne Moore. 'What is the point of this [male] sex except for impregnation?' asked Greer. Moore answered that she used to see DIY as one, but that since she has become wealthy enough to employ tradesmen (through the earnings from her weekly newspaper onslaught on masculinity), sex was now the only point (she had tried and rejected lesbianism). The attitude displayed to men was patronizing and contemptuous: they were children who did not want to grow up, women were evolving at a much faster rate; men were being left behind and at best to be pitied.

Perhaps the clearest indication of all this is the acceptability of nakedly sexist jokes against men, where the equivalent joke about women would cause a tumult of outrage. Thus, Channel 4's *The Girlie Show* feels entitled to nominate a man as 'Wanker of the Week' – imagine the outcry if Channel 4 had a programme called *The Laddies Show* which nominated a 'Fat Slag of the Week' (or suchlike). Another example is the best-selling women's magazine, *That's Life*, with its regular item 'Rude Jokes of the Week', always attacking men. A recent example was 'Q: Why is sex with Englishmen like a fight with Mike Tyson? A: It's all over in two minutes.'

Of course, all of these observations are unscientific anecdote and it might be possible to construct an equally persuasive case for the exact opposite – that we live in an age of unprecedented harmony – but a few examples may give a more specific picture of the sort of thing I am driving at, before returning to a scientifically based approach.

ONE MAN'S REACTION TO HIS WIFE GETTING A JOB

One of the most significant changes since 1950 has been the increase in working women, especially mothers. As we shall see, there is abundant evidence that men are not altogether happy about this and that it depresses and angers some of them. As we shall also see (in the next chapter), men are much more likely than women to be traumatized at the thought of their partner having sex with someone else. It is also the case that more men now have low-grade jobs, that full-time male posts have decreased and that changes in employment patterns mean there are many fewer of the 'jobs for life' which used to be the mainstay of the male breadwinner. The following story may be illustrative of these developments, although there is nothing new at all about a man beating his wife.

Now aged 32, Tim was born into a family of 12 children, and learned at an early age to show independence and self-sufficiency. He prided himself on being his own man – someone who needed no one. He was confused, then, when he found himself to be intensely dependent on his future wife. Soon after they married, she became pregnant. When the child was about a year old, she decided to return to her part-time job at a supermarket. Tim was extremely displeased about this and he beat her up for the first time. He says now that he was terrified that she would have an affair, although the main reason he gave to her at the time was that he had never expected her to work and did not accept this was the right way to bring up their child (who was cared for more than adequately by his wife's mother when she was at work). That they needed the money because Tim was unemployed and that he could have cared for their child in her absence did not persuade him that her job was reasonable and necessary, in the least.

Before long the beatings could be triggered by almost anything, but most of all they happened if she had refused him money for drink – he had a serious drinking problem. On one occasion, 'She said no, so I took the money anyway. As I was going out the door she grabbed me to try and stop me going out, because I'd stolen her money, so naturally I attacked her.' At other times, he would complain about the way she had done her household chores or because he thought she was looking at another man. He says now that he was scared of losing her and in some 'twisted part' of his mind, he believed that beating her could force her to stay with him and, just as importantly, make her subservient. As long as she was subservient he was able to ignore the dreadful knowledge that he needed her more than she needed him.

When Tim had first met his wife, the attraction had been instant. 'In public we're both extroverts and I'd make her laugh, she'd make me laugh. She fitted in with my idea of keeping everything at the level of being a laugh. She still does, because if I didn't laugh I'd cry and go back to drinking. Behind closed doors though, Liz was an introvert. I suppose I used that to dominate her. After she went back to work she started to become more assertive and the more she became like that, I would try to dominate more. She would attack me with words and when she beat me on the verbals, I could always beat her with violence. For instance I would say I needed money and she would sit there and try and persuade me to stay home and cut down on the drinking. I didn't want to admit that she was right, that I did have a drink problem, so I would dive across the room and start hitting her until I felt that she'd had enough punishment. I didn't hit her because I wanted to hurt her. I just wanted her to fit into my view of what a wife should be. I think she should be totally subservient, doing the cooking and cleaning and everything like that. So sometimes I'd punish her because I thought she'd failed in her duties; especially if she spent too much on shopping so there wasn't anything left for me to have a drink with.

'A lot of it was also jealousy. You'd be walking down the road and someone would put their arm up and wave to her and I'd give her the third degree. I didn't actually believe that she was sleeping with other men but it was a good way of digging at her without actually hitting her. But then after a while she stopped rising to the bait – we'd got to the level where there was no insult I could throw that could hurt any more, so then the violence would start. Because if you lose the row verbally, you lose your manhood, so violence creeps in. Yet if she'd ever left me I'd have been pole-axed. Some of the beatings were to stop her from going. They came out of frustration because she was leaving and I knew I couldn't make her stay.

'In the end it was because I was afraid of being dependent. As a child I thought of myself as an island. My best mate died at that time and I felt as if he'd betrayed me by bloody dying. So I never got close to anybody again because if you depend on someone they let you down. And here I was dependent on someone again . . .'

There is nothing new about Tim's psychology or the fact that he beat his wife. What is different compared with 1950 is that she had a job and that she became more assertive. As we shall see, there are many couples in which this change has led to rancour.

NOT ONLY UNEMPLOYED MEN FIND FEMALE CAREERS THREATENING

There is abundant evidence that men with ambitious, high-powered careers are especially likely to want their wives to conform to a traditional role as a support system. Such wives are increasingly infrequent and the next story illustrates the problems that resulted between a chief executive and his spouse.

He recalls that the relationship began at university. 'I was very intense, wouldn't take no for an answer, played a lot of games to get her, which made her feel I cared. I wasn't everyone's cup of tea physically but it didn't matter to her. Of course we were ridiculously young – children – to be getting married. But you did get married in those days.'

They moved to Scotland for his first job, as a trainee in a large manufacturing company. Twenty years later he was the chief executive. A lot had changed in between.

'At first we had most weekends together. I think I honestly believed I was going to be a family man. But by the time our fourth was born we had moved house five times already. By then my work came before everything else. From about, say, the age of 27 I was just never ever there. I don't just mean weekends. Evenings. Mornings. We hardly ever saw each other. And even when I was there I wasn't, if you see what I mean.

'My personality changed. I went from being a rather enthusiastic, slightly insecure, lovable sort of type to a much more secretive one. But the real revolution happened when I became a national figure. When I hit the headlines I started to really value myself – my ex-wife would say that I came to believe I was The Almighty.' She does.

Soon after he had reached the top of the company, his wife knew he had started an affair with his assistant. She chose to put up with it for the sake of the children. However, national events thrust him onto television and front pages and he became a highly recognizable public figure.

'I became increasingly confident about myself – my ex-wife would say that I was going berserk. I called up one of her best friends after a dinner party and suggested she and I go out for an evening alone. My ex-wife confronted me about this. She asked me what was the matter, why I was being so outrageous. I said I did not expect to live to a very old age and was determined to enjoy what time I had left.'

There were many more such rows. 'I often propositioned the wives of dinner guests the next day, over the phone. Some were astonished and very embarrassed to receive the call, some succumbed. I made up for a lot of lost time.'

He made advances to their sons' teenage girlfriends and had an affair with the young daughter of family friends. The wife of another very famous public figure was also a lover. On top of all this, through his membership of a health club he made many other conquests.

Much of the blame for all this is laid by this man at his ex-wife's door: she had developed a career of her own. 'I did not marry a career woman and I felt she was reneging on our marriage vows by spending so much time on her qualifications and subsequently, at work. I have nothing against women working, but I just do not happen to want one as my wife. Justifiably, I felt neglected and extremely angry. She made no attempt to fulfil her part of the bargain. I really do feel resentful at the way she behaved, at the way she blames it all on me and at her attempts to paint me as a Lothario to our children. It's outrageous. Our sons suffered and so did I.'

His ex-wife takes a different view, although she also believes her career upset him. 'I think that what happened was that the fame and the power completely went to his head and he became a total megalomaniac. To put it mildly, he was not the man I married. Because he was well known he thought he could sleep with anyone he wanted, and he was the first to say he was making up for lost time. The man I married wasn't much of a ladies' man and kept his nose to the grindstone. The Almighty was a very different matter.

'But I think a large part of the change was to do with my career too. He hated it in every way. He had become used to being obeyed and winning in his career and he could not take the fact that I was doing something against his will that made me more knowledgeable than him in a particular domain. On top of that, he wanted me to be at home at his beck and call.'

According to her, their story is not unusual.

'The lifecycle of the top executive follows a predictable course, like that of the moth. They rarely have that normal adolescent stage in which they are "rebels without a cause". They are too busy from their teens until well into their thirties, frantically getting ahead. What they are running away from varies but there is no time for fun.'

Once they have made it to the top, she believes they divide into two types. 'About half just carry on paying lip service to their families and pursuing their careers. A few of these are genuinely committed to their families. But of the remaining half, most suddenly start trying to catch up emotionally. They enter a middle-aged adolescence . . . which often means sexual experimentation.

'Being so emotionally immature, they are particularly attracted to girls who are emotionally the same age as them – late teens or early twenties.

Fiona Wright's sort of age [19] at the time Ralph Halpern had his affair with her. But they also want to keep their wife. They want her at home as a mother figure (which is what she often was originally; I was). They want the support system as well and if the wife starts working they become very upset.'

ARE SOME WOMEN TURNING NASTY TOO?

Compared with their mothers, women born after 1945 are more assertive, individualistic and have higher expectations. They are more likely to be breadwinners and to be supported by the wider society if they object to male maltreatment. Men like Tim feel that their desire for dominance is being challenged. Some authors have argued that there is a very real risk that traditionally reared, old-fashioned males will become even more likely than hitherto to resort to physical and sexual violence, the more that women come to occupy positions of personal and professional power. The husbands of the same couples 50 years ago might have been exactly the same, but the wives would probably have been more long-suffering and subordinate. The fact that these women were not prepared to put up with such behaviour is an important change.

However, there may be another, darker side to the increased assertiveness of women. Exactly in the same way that it is impossible to arrive at truly accurate estimates of the amount of sexual and physical domestic violence by men against women, so the reverse is true. Surveys of the general community are notoriously poor at counting real rates of violence,[1] which may help to explain how a BBC poll could have found that there is more female-to-male violence than vice versa.

Nonetheless, my reading of the official statistics does show that there has been a significant increase in the amount of court cautions and convictions of females for violence against the person, so that women now account for 15% of all such crimes compared with 10% in 1987.[1] The rise is especially steep among young women. Whilst the significance of this increase has been blown out of all proportion by media hungry for a new trend (in Britain in 1995–7 there was a spate of particularly silly and ill-informed scaremongering newspaper articles and television programmes warning of the dangers of 'girl gangs'), it is true that if the rate of increase in cautions and convictions did increase at the present rate, women would be as violent as men within 20 years. I do not believe this will happen, and concentration on female violence should not be allowed to distract from the fact that it is almost certainly still largely a male problem and likely to remain that way. But it should be admitted that, logically, as women become more assertive it would make sense if a larger minority express anger and frustration in violence than hitherto with an increased rancour by men towards women resulting. The story of husband beating which follows may not be as uncommon as one might think, although we have no way of knowing if such cases have increased since 1950 – they could have been going on behind closed doors at just the same rate as ever, with the only change being in the preparedness of men to speak out.

A rockfall is the perfect metaphor for mining engineer Jim's marriage: 'The unloading of stress makes the rock turn into plasticine, the ground wobbles and turns to jelly. Suddenly the roof warps and wows and the timbers begin to shift. Rock underground is not a static medium, there are dynamic pressures which make it utterly unpredictable.' Much like his ex-wife Sally: 'It was so instantaneous it could be terrifying. She would melt down in a few seconds and become incoherent, blubbering, babbling, striking out, lashing at anybody who was around, children, friends, family. She would use cutlery, bits of furniture, squash rackets, any weapon. She had the strength of three men, a tremendous release of energy. Once she hammered her fist down on a writing desk and split a three-quarter-inch oak top with four blows.'

For almost 20 years, Jim (now aged 40) endured the kind of mental and physical battering we are well used to hearing men having inflicted on women, but which always seems incongruous when the boot is on the other foot. He carefully protected her and never reported her violence. His reward today is to be accused of committing all the obscenities that his wife committed – abuse of their children, marital violence, sexual sadism.

The violence would last whole weekends. It would be three to four hours of aggression until she tired herself out and slept for 20 minutes, then another three to four hours, then sleep, and so on. They would go without sleep for 48 hours and it was like this every weekend for the last few years of the marriage. Much of her behaviour seems to have been designed to create fear. She would prowl around him and threaten and shout and circle and scream and bang objects to the floor or wall. He used to hide away a particular kitchen knife because she would hold it to his throat or body, visibly exulting in the fear that this caused. All responses other than total passivity inflated the violence. At other times it was a case of bare-handed physical assault, usually strangulation. She would grab Jim around the throat until he was turning blue. Their children (John aged 10, Mary 13) witnessed this often. On one occasion they came upon her doing it and he made a gargled noise – 'not in front of the children, please'. She banged his head against the wall so hard that it is indented to this day.

On other occasions it was the fingernails raked across the back and face, eyes punched black and nose bloodied. He might be asleep in bed and she would punch him in the face or knee him in the groin. She would mock his manhood for having undergone a vasectomy. Once, she hooked her fingers into his cheek and threw herself backwards onto the floor. This detached the cheek from the jawbone on the inside, leaving it hanging open. It took several weeks to heal. If it were a woman claiming a man had done this to her we would be quick to believe her claims. When a woman is the perpetrator we immediately feel sceptical. Our instinct is to dismiss it as a freakish thing, that the man must be a weirdo if he allows himself to be beaten up.

This incredulity is regardless of class or race. Julian Nettlefold, author of a self-help book on the plight of men married to mentally ill and violent women (*Saving The Situation*, London: Family Practice Press), is one of a number of Old Etonians who have felt hard-done-by as a result of court custody cases in the last few years. Yet, however posh and able to buy the best legal advice, according to Nettlefold it is almost impossible for the man to get custody of the children in these cases. Courts and welfare officers need a lot more convincing evidence that a woman has been violent than a man. The fact that the man often has the physical capacity to stop the violence seems to distract from the essentially psychological nature of what is happening. The courts are thinking, Why did he put up with it – he must get a kick.

Jim's wife was a large woman (size 18 and 5' 8") but he acknowledges he could easily have bettered her in a straight fight. He is six-foot tall, boxed at school and survived many fights, including riots, whilst mining in remote regions of Africa. Yet he only tried to calm and restrain her and he put up with it for years. 'I had been browbeaten into believing that my actions were causing this. I genuinely loved her and when I signed up for life on the marriage register I was determined that that was what it would be. I was prepared to do anything to help her – and to protect the children.'

The violence to them began early. It started against their daughter Mary 'when our son John was only a toddler and below swiping height'. But Mary got tall and strong and could increasingly defend herself and John became the main target. His wife would use John's body like a flail, throwing it across the room, against the walls, across the furniture. Jim would come back to find John sitting on the stairs bruised and crying – 'Why did Mummy hit me?' John was the most sensitive to the clues, could tell when she was going to explode. He could hear in two words if it was about to happen and would escape to somewhere safe in the house to sob his eyes out. Jim was doing his best to protect them and as a result of his coaching, they were protecting her: 'We don't want to get Mummy into trouble,' he would encourage them to feel. There were no limits to how far he would go to try and help her, all the way into sexual sadism. He says, 'I kept asking, "Is there not some other way of directing this need to hurt?"' She leapt at the idea of sadistic sex. 'It was as if it had been lying dormant in her for all these years and that she needed someone to take her to it. I didn't really like someone hurting me in order to get their jollies. But here at last was something that really did strike home and it did work for a while. Bondage, humiliation, unagreed violence, all sorts of domination, everything you can imagine. Using her speed and strength she used to grab me by the balls and just pull. This woman was definitely trying to do me harm.'

Jim hoped that by letting off steam humiliating and attacking him in the bedroom, she would become nonviolent outside. 'But it wasn't possible to keep this in one arena, she had to do it in all arenas. She was a true control freak. That was when I knew the relationship was doomed.' She would always blame others for her actions, anything to avoid the idea that she could be at fault. This was to be the nub of her case against him after she insisted that they separate. Jim foolishly agreed to move out of the matrimonial home. He admits now that his behaviour throughout was very unwise. 'I didn't report the violence to the children soon enough and I should have. I should never have left them alone with her in the matrimonial home.'

In the divorce petition she inverted everything. Jim had to defend against claims that he was the sadist, a pervert, a homosexual and molester of the children. He believes this is her final act of cruelty. Today he is powerless to extract his children from the hands of a woman who is clearly suffering from a chronic mental illness. Over the years he tried to get her to a psychiatrist but she always refused. Their GP gave her sleeping tablets but otherwise there was no recognition by the authorities that she has a problem. This is because she has a tremendous ability to calm down as soon as any authority figures arrive. She puts up an affable, sane-seeming front and her GP has no idea of what she is really like. Jim's claims about her violence are viewed with scepticism and because he never reported the injuries to the children, there is no evidence.

'Unless one of the children is bleeding to death and there's enough admirers over the body nothing can be done. The authorities are frightened to diagnose her because it would show she is not fit as a mother. It is the cruellest thing imaginable to have to stand back and watch my children being ruined, like seeing them dragged off to a concentration camp.'

Or being trapped in a rockfall down a mine.

Of course, this story can be dismissed as the kind of extreme case that hardly ever happens. Surely the woman was mentally ill? Surely the man was masochistically lacking in basic self-protective tendencies? These may be fair questions, but as we shall see, depressed women – of whom there are a great many more today than in 1950 – are often vicious and hostile to their intimates, although not necessarily physically so.

Bearing these anecdotes in mind, let us now return to a more scientific approach to the issues.

DEPRESSION AND GENDER RANCOUR

There are sound scientific, as well as anecdotal, grounds for supposing that the increases in depression and aggression since 1950 have resulted in a rancorous disharmony between the sexes. That there is so much more recorded violent crime is a self-evident indication that aggression has increased. The role of increased depression is a less commonsensical indicator of increased rancour.

DEPRESSED PEOPLE MAKE DEPRESSING, HOSTILE PARTNERS

Until the publication of Myrna Weissman's (co-authored with Eugene Paykel) classic 1974 account of *The Depressed Woman*, it was widely assumed that depressed people were passive and withdrawn[2] (it should be stressed that most of Weissman's findings probably apply to depressed men as well). Their aggression was turned against themselves, as was evident in the savage negativity they displayed towards themselves mentally, and at its most extreme, in the physical attacks they made against their bodies, not just in suicide attempts, but in such self-destructive illnesses as the eating disorders bulimia and anorexia nervosa, both of which are more common among the depressed. The assumption was that outwardly directed hostility must be reduced since it is all turned against the self. However, this view had to be modified after Weissman's careful comparison of 40 depressed women with 40 nondepressed ones.[2] It showed that depressed women are anything but unaggressive in intimate relationships. They displayed 'significantly more overt interpersonal hostility in most relationships, and the intensity of these feelings ranged from resentment, general irritability, through arguments of increasing intensity, to physical encounters'.[2] The brunt of this hostility was borne by their children, with whom they had twice as much friction as their spouses. However, they were also significantly more hostile to their spouses than to their extended family members, friends and professional colleagues: 'Marital relationships become an arena for the depression and

172

are characterized by friction, poor communication, dependency and diminished sexual satisfaction. The depressed woman feels a lack of affection towards her husband together with guilt and resentment. Communication is poor and hostility overt.'[2] That this marked viciousness was confined to intimates explained why researchers had not noticed the pattern before. Not being intimates the researchers doing the studies did not evoke it: 'The depressed patient's behaviour at interview is a poor sample of her actual behaviour outside. In the initial psychiatric interview she is cooperative, compliant and not hostile.'[2]

Given that depressives are like this, the finding that depressives create unhappiness in their intimates is no surprise.[3] Partners of depressives are themselves more likely to be depressed, to get ill, to abuse alcohol and to commit both suicide and homicide. The relationship suffers. Compared with couples where neither party is depressed, in couples with one depressive, the depressed one is more likely to be domineering and overbearingly insistent in solving disputes.[4] The couple are likely to use destructive methods for doing so, to feel miserable about their relationship, be secretive and incommunicative and provide little support to each other.

This miserable list could double up as a fair definition of the word 'rancour'. Given that there has been a large increase in the number of such depressed adults, it is almost certain that there has been a concomitant increase in the number of disharmonious couples and therefore, in the amount of gender rancour.

DOES DEPRESSION CAUSE DIVORCE, OR VICE VERSA?

An important effect of such increased rancour may be on the divorce rate – itself an important cause of the increase in depression since 1950, as we saw in the last chapter. One study of 56 married depressives followed over a two-year period found they were nine times more likely to have divorced than the general population.[5] Not only do couples with a depressive member show more disharmony, they are more at risk of divorce.[6] This is not surprising if depression is such a powerful cause of gender rancour. At the same time, as noted above, other studies show that marital disharmony and divorce are a cause as well as an effect of depression.[3] Disentangling them is not done easily and there are two very different theories.

The first, which became extremely fashionable during the 1960s and 1970s and remains dominant today, is the 'marital compatibility' view. Troubled marriages are seen as the product of ineffectual communication patterns resulting from personal incompatibility. John Gottman,[7] for example, asked over 100 newly-wed couples to pick a perennial bone of contention between them and videotaped the ensuing discussion. How they dealt with the problem predicted whether they were still together four years later. In this view, successful marriage is a case of finding the right person for you and making sure that destructive patterns of problem-solving do not develop – unsuccessful marriages cause depression.

That this perspective became so popular during a period (after 1960) when millions of dissatisfied husbands and wives were asking themselves if they were with the right partner may be no coincidence. The perspective is also supported by considerable evidence[8] and there is little doubt that unhappy marriages can cause previously stable and well-adjusted individuals to develop depression and other problems. However, this view has become so dominant that the alternative has been almost totally forgotten: that emotional problems, often dating back to childhood, in one or both of the partners could cause the marital problems. In this view, there are people whose personalities would have put them at high risk of divorce whoever they had married.

As one author bluntly put it back in 1935,[9] 'One would hardly expect a man and a woman, both highly neurotic, to achieve a very high order of marital happiness.' In order to test this theory properly a study would ideally have followed a large sample from childhood to late adulthood. Only then would it be clear how much any emotional problems during marriage preceded the union. No studies have gone as far back as that, but there are no fewer than seven which tested the personalities of couples before they married and followed up what happened to them subsequently.[10] In all of these, 'neuroticism' (in these studies, 'neuroticism' includes mild or more severe depression as part of its definition) and lack of 'impulse control' (in the male partner) predicted subsequent disharmony and divorce compared with people without these traits before marriage. There are also several other studies suggesting that males with poor impulse control are more likely to have marital problems[11] (it may be recalled that low impulse control correlates strongly with low levels of serotonin). To this can be added a British study which found that high neuroticism among girls at age 16 predicted subsequent increased risk of divorce.[12] Furthermore, since children of divorce are at greater risk of a large variety of psychological problems, these may be one of the reasons why they are also at least twice as likely as children from intact marriages to divorce themselves. Taken together, this body of evidence suggests that predisposing personality and emotional problems could cause divorce.

There is also an eighth (and the most recent, in 1987) study of this issue which repays close inspection.[11] It followed 300 married couples from before they had married in 1940, to 1980. Those that divorced were significantly more likely to have had psychological problems before they married (back in 1940) than those who stayed married. Divorcees of both sexes started out higher in neuroticism and the men were higher in lack of impulse control. The women were more likely to have said at the outset that they came from unstable families which lacked emotional closeness, a predictor of subsequent emotional problems. Altogether, these factors predicted which couples would be divorced 40 years later. Furthermore, among the couples who stayed married, the personality factors also predicted which marriages were likely to be the happy ones. The authors concluded: 'The husband's impulsiveness and the neuroticism of both spouses are potent predictors of negative marital outcomes ... in marital relationships, neuroticism acts to bring about distress, and the other traits of the husband help to determine whether the distress is brought to a head (in divorce) or suffered passively (in a stable but unsatisfactory marriage).'[11]

To some, the idea that depressed, neurotic and impulsive people are more at risk of divorce might seem to be plain old-fashioned commonsense. But so deep rooted is our reluctance to 'stigmatize' individuals that we dare not suggest that one individual has got a problem. Rather, we blame it on The Relationship. Others might also feel that it may be true but best left unsaid since it seems very negative. Yet many marriages might be greatly helped by this understanding. Where one individual is clearly suffering from depression, rather than encouraging both to agonize over their compatibility, it can be extremely helpful for the disturbed person to seek treatment for their individual angst. It is particularly so with depressives, who (as Weissman's and subsequent studies prove) are especially liable to be paranoid and to blame everything on their intimates and then to launch a barrage of hostility and aggression towards them. The 'personal incompatibility' model is very convenient to such people but they may find the same problems recurring with subsequent partners – divorcees are more likely to divorce if they remarry than first-time unions.

This is not to say that incompatibility never happens or that there are not men and women who treat each other intolerably badly and from whom divorce is the only sane response. Both statements are true and incompatibility and poor communication skills remain well-established causes of divorce. It is simply that the emphasis on relationship rather than individual pathology has been so all-consuming in recent years that it is important to redress the balance in explaining divorce.

RELATING THE INDIVIDUAL TRAIT PERSPECTIVE TO THE RISE IN DEPRESSION, RANCOUR AND DIVORCE SINCE 1950

The Individual Trait approach helps a great deal in explaining this rise. Firstly, given that there has been a large increase in depression since 1950 and given that we know depressives are hostile and aggressive partners and that they have higher rates of divorce, it could be that the increase in depressed people has partly directly caused the increase in divorce. Secondly, we saw in the last chapter that the divorce increase is also due to a significant extent to changes in values, especially to changing sex roles, increased individualism and increased expectations of relationships as a source of gratification. It seems highly probable that the new freedoms and accompanying values will not have affected everyone in the same way. Neurotic and impulsive people may always have had a greater risk of unhappy marriages but in the past have been protected by social pressures from expressing them in ultimately self-destructive attacks on their marriages. Furthermore, such people may have been made even more neurotic and impulsive by the excitement and overheated expectations of the prevailing *Zeitgeist*. This might have caused their marriages to become even unhappier and increased the likelihood of divorce in an era when it was fashionable to believe the relationship was to blame and there was a better partner somewhere out there just waiting to meet you.

Thus, the rise in depression, the increase in gender rancour and the ascending divorce rate may have all impacted on each other to create a firestorm of rage and despair. But the impact of these changes did not fall equally on both sexes.

SEX DIFFERENCES IN THE INCREASE IN DEPRESSION AND THEIR EFFECT ON GENDER RANCOUR

THE SEX RATIO OF DEPRESSION SINCE 1950

It will be recalled that women are twice as likely as men to describe themselves as depressed. It follows that if there has been a large increase in depression since 1950, it would have entailed twice as many women as men – unless there has been a change in this ratio. In fact, there is some evidence that the ratio may have changed slightly. Whereas rates of depression are still rising rapidly among young men, some observers (although not all)[13] claim they have stabilized among younger women, born after 1945.[14] This may have resulted in a slight decrease in the sex ratio, at least in America, from 2:1 to 1.7:1 (see footnote 15 for further analysis). Whatever the precise details, there is no doubt that women are still considerably more prone to depression than men and that much more of the increase since 1950 is accounted for by women than men. On top of this, women have been consistently more likely to attempt suicide than men, and since most attempters are depressed this is a further indication of a real effect. A recent analysis of four large community surveys (in 1993 by Myrna Weissman), for example, reported the following sex differences for percentages of men and women likely to suffer a major depression or suicide attempt during their lifetime:[14]

	% Lifetime Prevalence Depression		% Lifetime Prevalence Attempted Suicide	
	Males	Females	Males	Females
USA (n = 18,000)	3.5	8	1.7	5
CANADA (n = 3,258)	7.5	13.2	2	5.3
GERMANY (n = 481)	4.9	17	0.7	3.3
NEW ZEALAND (n = 1,500)	8.6	17	2.6	6.2

If we can identify what causes these difference between the sexes it may help us to pinpoint what has changed since 1950, for whatever caused this increase has presumably been affecting women more than men. There are five main explanations commonly offered for the sex differences in depression.[16]

Firstly, it has been claimed that there is, in a sense, nothing to explain, that the gender difference is an illusion because men are more unwilling than women to admit to, or seek help for, depressive symptoms. It is true that men are more likely than women to express depression outwards through 'acting out' behaviours, such as violence and alcoholism. This almost certainly conceals the true rates of depressed mood among men, since three-quarters become depressed when these options are not available to them: that is the proportion of imprisoned violent men who are depressed compared with nonviolent offenders.[17] If you had met these men prior to their imprisonment, many fewer would probably have admitted to depression. However, studies investigating precisely this point do not find it has a major effect on the overall reporting of depression[17] and most authorities doubt that much of the sex difference in depression is explained purely by male reluctance to admit to it. The most plausible interpretation is that men do suffer from psychiatric problems every bit as much as women, but they express them differently.[17][18] For every depressed woman there is probably an antisocial or alcoholic man.[19]

Since there have been no known major changes in our basic biology since 1950, it is unlikely that changes in it could explain the increase since then (any more than they could explain the rise in violence). Biological arguments anyway remain very much 'case unproven'[16] although it is hard to believe that biology and genes play no part whatsoever since major depressive illnesses are almost certainly caused by genes to some degree. Nonetheless, molecular genetic studies have not as yet proven any significant gender difference.[20] There are a few studies seeming to suggest that female animals of various species have **higher** levels of serotonin than males[21] but these need to be replicated. Even if this effect is shown to be a real one, it may not translate across to humans since it is not at all what human studies would predict – depression correlates with low, not high, serotonin. Studies of hormones give a conflicting picture, although the fact that women are at high risk of depression at precisely those times when they are undergoing profound hormonal changes (puberty, after childbirth) has been suggested as a likely contributory factor.[22] Thus, whilst biology probably plays some part in the sex differences, it is unclear if this is minimal or substantial, and it is unlikely to have played much, if any, part in the increase since 1950.

Psychoanalytic explanation of the difference focuses on the social pressure in early childhood for girls to be like their mothers, the constraints placed on the expression of female aggression and the conflict between a supposed innate desire to bear children and the drive for independence.[16] These theories have gone largely untested but overlap with the remaining two.[16] The Learned Helplessness theory (outlined in Chapter 2) suggests that as girls and adults, females are discouraged more than males from believing that their actions will achieve desired results, thereby creating a negative expectation of helplessness. But this does not seem, on the face of it, to help us much with the increase in depression since 1950 because increased equality and working opportunities mean that fewer, not more women are in positions of helplessness.

The last theory, that of sex roles, is the only one of the five where there have been relevant changes since 1950. It also relates directly to changes in patterns of employment and childcare.

THE SEX ROLE THEORY OF DEPRESSION

The theory comes in several shapes and sizes. Walter Gove is the chief advocate of the most popular variant which dates back to the 1970s and was heavily influenced by the women's movement. In 1979 Gove listed six reasons why the social role of modern women should make them more depressed than men.[23]

First, full-time housewives have only one potential arena for gratification – the home – compared with men who have their job as well. If a man is unhappy in one arena, he can turn to the other as an alternative source of gratification. This is not an option for a housewife.

Second, for most full-time housewives their primary focus is childcare and homemaking but these activities do not require a great deal of skill and are of low status. Women with high educational qualifications and intellectual abilities would find such unprestigious and undemanding work frustrating.

Third, the lack of structure and invisibility of the housewife role makes it easy to let things slide into a brooding, ruminative state which then feeds on itself. There is no workplace to distract her from her problems and the work is held to be inherently depressing.

Fourth, for those women who do work, it is usually ill paid and of low status, seen as secondary to that of the man. Coupled with their arduous childcare and housework, they end up working longer hours than their man, yet are accorded less reward than him.

Fifth, the female role is unclear and contingent compared to that of males. It leaves women feeling uncertain and lacking in control.

Sixth, in the past families were larger and women were responsible for childcare for most of their adult lives. Housework required considerably more skill and the houswife was seen as being an integral part of a family enterprise. With the advent of small families, modern equipment and industrial employment, the homemaking role lost respect.

Gove concluded with the following prediction: 'If this analysis is correct much of the presumed stress on women is a relatively recent phenomenon . . . given the present changes that are occurring in the role of women, their roles will become more commensurate with the roles of men and the two sexes will (again) experience similar amounts of stress, with the consequence that their rates of mental illness will become relatively similar.'

Another important advocate of this view was Ronald Kessler. In 1983 he made a similar prediction:[24] 'Since sex roles are related to mental health it is likely that rates of distress for men and women will change as sex roles change. In fact, looking at the dramatic changes that have occurred since World War II there is good reason to predict that the mental health of women, relative to that of men, has improved. Women increasingly are deferring childbearing, having smaller families and planning to have children at times that fit their career plans. They are marrying at later ages and combining employment outside the home with being a wife and mother. These are all changes that should . . . improve the mental health of women relative to men.'

However, Gove and Kessler's predictions do not appear to have been fulfilled. Ratios of male to female depression have either not changed at all or have changed only slightly. Despite decades of increased opportunity, education and changing sex roles, women are still much more prone to depression and attempted suicide than men. True, rates of depression among young women may have stabilized whilst men are becoming more depressive. Women are also showing more male patterns of drug use, sexual behaviour and criminality. But the basic ratios for depression have remained the same or similar and in a recent publication (1992), Kessler explicitly changed his views, questioning the validity of his sex role theory (see footnote 25). It is particularly noteworthy that he should now reject the theory since, alongside Gove, he has been a chief advocate for over 20 years.

However, other variants of sex role theory which emphasize the strain that has been placed on both sexes by a period of rapid change can accommodate the continued sex ratio. In 1977 Myrna Weissman offered an influential analysis of the effects of historical change and rising expectations.[26] What records there were suggested that women have always been more likely to be depressed than men and she also presented evidence that periods of social change may be particularly likely to exacerbate this. Depression was reported to have reached epidemic propotions in late Elizabethan and early seventeenth-century England during a time of rapid social change. Likewise, a supposed rise in mental illness in late eighteenth-century England was reported at the time to have been due to the 'wear and tear of civilization'. Weissman goes on to apply relative deprivation theory to the particular case of women since 1950 and I shall quote her comments in full.[26]

'Rising expectations, access to new opportunities and efforts to redress the social inequalities of women have been suggested as further explanation for the recent increase in depression among women. Depressions may occur not when things are at their worst, but when there is a possibility of improvement, and a discrepancy between one's rising aspirations and the likelihood of fulfilling these wishes. The women's movement, government legislation and efforts to improve educational and employment opportunities for women have created higher expectations. Social and economic achievement often have not kept pace with the promises, especially in a decreasing job market where long-standing discriminatory practices perpetuate unequal opportunities.

'These new role expectations may also create intrapsychic personal conflicts, particularly for those women involved in traditional family tasks but who also desire employment outside the family. While the women's movement has mainly involved middle- and upper-class and educated women, it has had an impact on women from other social classes where opportunities for work outside the home, management of money, dominance in the marriage, etc., may be crucial. Even for the educated and economically comfortable women, ambivalence and conflict continue about careers not conventionally seen as feminine. The documented increase in suicides and suicide attempts among women suggests that social changes may be exacting social costs for many young women. In this regard, Gove and Tudor (1973) note that communities that are extremely close-knit, stable, traditionally family-orientated and culturally isolated have lower rates of mental illness in general, with the women having even lower rates than the men. Although support can be adduced for the hypothesis that participation in the women's movement is associated with psychological distress, it is unlikely that this is the major factor for the excess of depression among women. The differing rates substantially predate the women's movement. The short-term changes may be disruptive, but in the long term a new equilibrium may be reached and the high female rates may decrease. Such a reduction would be indirect confirmation of the hypothesis that the female excess of depression is due to psychological disadvantages of the female role. As behaviours become more similar between the sexes, females may begin to employ modes of coping with stress that are similar to those of men. There are some indications that this may be occurring in that the female rates of alcoholism, suicide and crime (predominantly male behaviours) have begun to rise. Alternatively, the sex ratios for depression could become equal because of an increase in depression among men due to the stress produced by the change in the roles of women and by the uncertainty of the male role.'

Twenty years on there are few signs of Weissman's 'new equilibrium', with the rates of depression and attempted suicide among women still high and much higher than those for men. Some feminist authors have seen this absence of equilibrium as a direct challenge to their beliefs. Susan Faludi, for example, in her polemical 1991 text *Backlash* (London: Vintage), tried to deal with the problem by arguing that the increase in depression itself is a myth. Citing various antifeminist media commentators who claim the increased rates since 1950 are real and are caused by feminism in general and the rise in working mothers in particular, Faludi rebuts them, thus: 'The actual evidence – dozens of comparative studies on working and nonworking women – all points the other way. Whether they are professional or blue-collar workers, working women experience less depression than housewives; and the more challenging the career, the better their mental and physical health.' Faludi goes further. She asserts that the changes have actually improved mental health and that women are less rather than more depressed compared with the 1950s. 'By helping to widen women's access to more and better employment, the women's rights campaign led to vast improvements in women's mental health over the last three decades, as several landmark US surveys have shown. The famous 1980 Midtown Manhattan Longitudinal Study found that adult women's rate of mental health impairment had fallen 50 to 60 per cent since the early 1950s. Midtown Manhattan project director Leo Srole concluded that the changes "are not mere chance coincidences of the play of history, but reflect a cause-and-effect connection between the partial emancipation of women from their 19th-century status of sexist servitude and their 20th-century advances in subjective well-being." '[27]

Unfortunately, the true position is considerably more complex than this and if Faludi had referred to all the relevant studies of these subjects, it is hard to understand how she could have reached such a simplistic and erroneous conclusion. She cites only those few studies that support her case and even then, is sometimes incorrect in doing so. Her heavy reliance on the 'famous' Manhattan Midtown study is an example. It is one of only two studies that did not find an increase in rates of depression since 1950, a blip in comparison to the much larger body of evidence that there has been a substantial rise (cited in Appendix I). Worse still, as an analysis of changing trends in sex ratios of depression the Manhattan study suffered from a serious shortcoming which has led the leading researchers in this area to disregard it as a reliable source of evidence on this issue (see footnote 28 for details).

Faludi gives no sign that she is aware of this problem or of the extensive literature that contradicts her, maintaining that the claim that women are more depressed is part of a 'backlash' against the gains made by women since the 1960s. 'Behind the news, cheerfully and endlessly repeated, that the struggle for women's rights is won, another message flashes. You may be free and equal now, it says to women, but you have never been more miserable . . . the prevailing wisdom of the past decade has supported one, and only one, answer to this riddle: it must be all that equality that's causing all that pain. Women are unhappy precisely *because* they are free. Women are enslaved by their own liberation. They have grabbed at the gold ring of independence, only to miss the one ring that really matters. They have gained control of their fertility only to destroy it. They have pursued their own professional dreams – and lost out on the greatest female adventure. The women's movement, as we are told time and again, has proved women's worst enemy.' Although this backlash is not a conscious conspiracy, according to Faludi that makes it all the more invidious. 'Although the backlash is not an organized movement, that doesn't make it any less destructive. In fact, the lack of orchestration, the absence of a single string-puller, only makes it harder to see – and perhaps more effective.'

Conspiracy or not, Faludi is incorrect in her conviction that the rising depression rates are necessarily a threat to the gains of feminism. Of course, it is disappointing that the gains have not yet included the improvements in female mental health that Gove and Kessler hoped for but that does not mean they will not do so. As Weissman pointed out,[26] it could be that we are simply passing through an uncomfortable and painful period of change that will ultimately prove very fruitful. Nor does Faludi advance the debate by oversimplifying and misrepresenting the evidence. The true complexity of the effect of changes in sex roles on increasing depression emerges more clearly when we examine the differing social conditions under which women are most likely to become depressed.

SEX ROLES THAT DEPRESS WOMEN, OTHERS THAT DO NOT

It so happens that there are a number of social groups in which there are no differences in the amount of depression between the sexes. This suggests that differing social conditions and sex roles can affect the ratio. One study[29] showed no sex difference in rates of depression between student teachers followed over a five-year period. The group turned out to be very similar in their 'social profile' during the period of the study – i.e. they lived similar sorts of lives – so that their sex roles remained constant. The authors concluded that it was this lack of change in role that accounted for the lack of sex difference in depression. There are several more studies of students (aged 18 to 25) which also find no sex differences in depression[16] whereas nonstudents in this age range do display the standard 2:1 ratio. Another source of evidence is from communities where sex roles are unambiguous and fixed, as opposed to flexible – where there is little room for confusion. There are no sex differences in depression in the Old Order Amish community in America, who live a highly structured life with old-fashioned sex roles.[30] A recent study of 182 Orthodox Jewish women in England also found no difference in rates compared with 157 Jewish men, repeating the result of a previous one by the same researchers.[31] Again, the presence of highly prescribed and valued traditional sex roles were thought to be significant (however, an American study comparing Orthodox and Modern Orthodox Jewish women found that the more liberated, modern group had even more equal sex ratios;[32] this suggests that cultural differences can be important even within ethnic subgroups and that it is not traditional roles *per se* that diminish differences). Equal depression sex ratios have also been found in several rural communities in 'nonmodern' societies, including a Nigerian tribe and a group in rural Iran,[16] with traditional and predictable sex roles. Taken together, these studies suggest that where roles and lifestyle are the same (students) or where they are clear-cut (and strictly enforced), there is no sex difference in depression rates.

The uniting factor may be lack of 'role strain' – the lack of conflicting demands. Several theorists[33] suggest that women who attempt to succeed in jobs may face disturbing conflicts between their traditional role as an emotional support for their family and the demand to be independent and competitive in their job. A woman may be expected to be both passive, unselfish and supportive in line with her traditionally feminine role and yet also to be assertive, self-sufficient and demanding – traditionally masculine – if her career is to progress.[34] The woman may feel forced to ignore one or other set of expectations or try to be both people at the same time. As one influential author put it,[16] 'It is not so much the number of demands put on women because of their sex role that makes them more vulnerable to low self-esteem and despair, but the conflicts or radical changes in the expectations for women and the society's devaluation of the stereotypical female role.'

The social conditions and roles where sex ratio differences in depression do emerge are all consistent with this role-strain theory.

Marriage, employment and motherhood are all critical, in various combinations. In general, dozens of studies show that married people are less likely to be depressed than never-married, divorced or separated and widowed people.[35] However, there are a great many ifs and buts behind the statistics. A crucial element is whether or not a wife is employed, whether she has small children and what both partners' attitudes are to the division of labour. One study identified four different kinds of marriage in a sample of 680[35] couples.

In the first type, the wife does not have a job, she and her husband believe her place is in the home and she does all the housework and childcare. The wife was more likely to be depressed than the husband in this kind of marriage but less likely to be depressed than in the second type . . .

This is the same as the first except that the wife has a job – even though both of them disapprove of her doing so. This is bad for both parties. The wife is more depressed than in any other condition and *the husband is actually considerably more likely than the wife to be depressed*: the opposite of the usual ratio.

In the third type, the wife also has a job but both partners approve of it and the wife does all the homemaking. Here, the man is contented but the wife is about as depressed as in the first type: whilst her husband approves of her job, she ends up having to run the home and feels this is neither sensible nor fair.

Finally, in the fourth type both spouses approve of the wife's employment and share the running of the home. The wife is still considerably more prone to depression than the husband, but this is the least depressing for both sexes and the ratio between them is (only by a small margin) the smallest.

This study suggests that role strain is extremely important for whether a woman (and a man – see the next section) feels depressed and the size of the sex difference ratio. There are many studies showing that on the whole, employed wives are less depressed than unemployed ones[36] but the significance of this difference is not simply a matter of 'women like working and find homemaking depressing'. The more that there is tension about the woman's employment – from the woman as well as the man – the worse it is, and there are many other studies showing the centrality of this role strain: the importance of both partners' attitude to the principle of a mother working and of how much the husband helps out with childcare and housework if she does work.[37]

Only comparing 'employed' with 'unemployed' wife in isolation is to ignore another critical factor: whether or not there are small children. Generally, women with small children are dramatically more at risk than women whose children have grown up or with no children. The more children and the younger they are, the greater the risk.[38] The most at risk from children are lone or divorced mothers, largely because of their low incomes.[35] Among the married, satisfaction with marriage decreases with the birth of the first child and as the number of children grows, so marital satisfaction declines. But the crucial relationship is between mother's employment and children.

Until George Brown's study in 1990 the evidence on this point was ambiguous.[39] Brown selected a sample of 354 low-income mothers with at least one child under 18 still living at home. None was depressed at the time of first being interviewed and they were assessed again a year later. Brown found that the groups most at risk of having developed depression in the interim were the nonworking housewives and the mothers who worked full-time (defined as more than 31 hours work a week). The group least at risk were the part-time workers. When Brown took a closer look at the full-time workers to understand why they should be more at risk than the part-timers, role strain seemed to be critical. The depression of almost all the full-timers was provoked by a major event involving either their children (e.g. a son caught stealing or the discovery that a young daughter was on the pill) or their partner (e.g. a husband's infidelity or bankruptcy) and in most cases, the women explicitly stated that they felt torn and guilty at continuing to work full-time through a crisis when they were needed at home. In analysing the reasons for the higher rate of depression among the nonworking mothers, Brown discovered that they were particularly likely to lack social support from their partner and to perceive that relationship to be insecure, possibly because they did not have the buttress of a job to reduce their fear of abandonment.

One problem with Brown's sample was that nearly four times as many (74%) of the nonworking mothers had a child under age five compared with the part-timers (19%). Since small children themselves are a major predictor of depression in mothers, this may have heavily influenced the findings. Brown does not provide figures for how many of the full-timers had young children and this may have influenced the results as well. The non-working mothers were also nearly three times as likely to have been married less than ten years than the part-timers and twice as likely to be under age 36. Both of these predict a greater likelihood of marital instability and consequent lack of emotional support, which in turn predicts greater risk of depression. Brown is careful to acknowledge these points in his discussion of the findings (see footnote 40 for quotation). In short, for the results of this study to be even more convincing, Brown would have ensured there were three sufficiently large samples of mothers all with under-five-year-olds.

Interestingly, where studies have compared full-time, part-time and nonworking mothers with small children, the full-timers are often more prone to depression or dissatisfaction than the part-timers.[41] Studies merely comparing 'employed' versus 'nonworking' mothers which do not state the ages of the children are consequently of little value, since this is a major factor. Equally, it is important to know whether the mothers are primarily committed to childcare or to their work (although, of course, these are not mutually exclusive). Where does their basic identity lie? Women whose first love is childcare and who work full-time are liable to feel very torn. Women for whom work comes first and who do so will have less role strain. If they were nonworking housewives wishing they were at work they could be frustrated and liable to strain. For these women, the new opportunities and greater support for working mothers is a godsend and in many cases, the same may be true for their offspring. Such women would be at high risk of depression if they stayed at home and there is a large body of evidence that children of depressed mothers are at grave risk of subsequent problems. So long as these women are able to find adequate substitute care (not easy in such a child-hostile environment as modern Britain), it is in the best interests of all concerned that they work. As George Brown put it,[39] 'the obvious policy implications . . . of our results would involve making it easier for women to pursue their **desired** status, whether as workers or nonworkers'. On top of this, men could be playing a far more constructive role than is currently the case (see below), perhaps even adopting the role of homemaker themselves in some cases.

An important illustration of Brown's view is provided by a longitudinal study of 292 mothers which examined how these basic preferences for work or childcare affected the mothers' attitudes to being separated from their children when they were still very small, both in terms of their fears for the child and the distress it caused the mother.[42] The mothers were interviewed on four occasions before their children had reached age three and a half and they were asked in depth about their basic preferences as between childcare and a career. The authors stated that[42] 'women who prefer employment are psychologically different than those who prefer to be home, regardless of their actual employment status' (i.e. whether or not they have a job). Their study identified two groups. 'The women with a home preference were highly invested in their role as mothers and only moderately interested in jobs and careers. If they were employed, they were working primarily because of financial reasons and were relatively unmotivated by personal benefits (e.g. prestige) of their jobs. This group, then, defined motherhood as their primary *raison d'être* and relegated employment to a rather insignificant place in their lives.

'The women who preferred to be employed reported a very different relationship between motherhood and employment. These women were strongly committed to their careers and usually worked for personal as well as financial reasons . . . they were not as strongly invested in the role of mother as women who preferred to stay at home . . . they seemed to define motherhood as only one of their many interests.'

Not surprisingly, given these differences, the two groups had very different attitudes to leaving their children. The mothers who preferred staying at home were much more anxious about it than the career women. Full-time career women were more likely in actual practice to leave their child in a daycare centre, something the home bodies were most reluctant to do. The authors analysed why the career women were so much less concerned about leaving their children, as follows.[42] 'First, they may have achieved a psychological balance between their own needs and their infants' needs that allowed them to act without guilt and anxiety about their desire to be employed. Alternatively, the ego defense mechanism of denial may be in operation; these mothers may be denying their concerns about nonmaternal care and separation in order to be able to deal with issues of employment. In either case, their lower anxiety about separation is consistent with their less intense investment in the role of mother and their greater involvement in employment.' This finding harmonizes with the numerous cross-cultural surveys, showing that where there is a heavy work burden on women, they are more likely to believe that small children are resilient and do not require intensive, one-to-one nurture.[88]

As we also saw in the last chapter, at present the number of European women who opt to work full-time while their children are very small, or at all, is relatively few (in Britain, 89% with an under-one-year-old do not work full-time, 87% with an under-three). The evidence suggests that in most cases this is out of choice rather than necessity, although this is debatable (see below). Less so is that work occupies a different role in the lives of men and women, as shown by the many studies which indicate that most women's overall satisfaction is little affected by how much they earn or how successful they are. They emphasize the social pleasures of the workplace far more than achievement. By contrast, men place a high premium on power, status and income. This has remained the case for a long time. Writing in 1982, Ronald Kessler (an enthusiastic supporter of the women's movement in his research, it should be recalled, and highly commended by Susan Faludi) stated that[43] 'The meaning of employment differs for men and women. Women are satisfied with less-well-paid jobs and draw their sense of job satisfaction from characteristics of work less directly tied to objective job achievements than do men. They have a lower expectation of work.' Whilst young women conform less to this portrait than their mothers did at the equivalent age, it remains an accurate one.[44] The question of why – after three decades of feminism – it should still be a true one is, of course, highly contentious and debatable (see below).

It may be seen that sex differences in depression are a considerably more complex matter than Faludi would have had us believe. It is beyond dispute that in general, women are more prone to depression than men and contrary to her claims, there is little doubt that the amount of female depression has risen substantially despite – but not necessarily because of – three decades of feminism. To assert that women's mental health as a whole has not yet gained from greater opportunities is not, as Faludi suggests, to be part of an unwitting conspiracy to chain mothers to the nearest kitchen sink, it is to accept Weissman's wisdom[26] that the new roles may, for the time being, have created some unattainable expectations in many cases and considerable guilt, uncertainty and confusion in many others. Nor is it only women who have suffered.

SEX ROLES THAT DEPRESS MEN, OTHERS THAT DO NOT

Men have been reluctant to accept their wives' careers and male mental health has suffered accordingly. In Ronald Kessler's 1982 paper analysing the effect of having a working wife on the happiness of 1,086 couples, the husbands were more likely to report depression and low self-esteem if their wife worked.[43] That this may have been related to an inability on the part of the men to accept their wives' working status was shown by the fact that men who helped their wives out with the childcare were less at risk of these problems than those who did not – these may have been traditionalists who resisted a working wife and found her work depressing. But why should they find it depressing? You might imagine they would have welcomed the extra income and have been pleased if it made their wives happier (which it did – on the whole working wives were less likely to be depressed than unemployed wives, so long as the husband helped with the childcare).

Perhaps men were upset by wives' success at work, as a 1984 study suggested.[45] In America and Britain, divorce is generally more common the lower a couple's income and level of education. However, a big exception to this rule in America was the rate of divorce among women who had had five or more years of higher education. Their divorce rate was almost as great as that for women who did not even graduate from high school (there is also some evidence that some groups of professional women suffered from remarkably high rates of depression, at least in the 1970s and in America).[46] The study examined the marriages of 663 women with five or more years of higher education. The authors concluded that these women's careers placed a large strain on their marriages. The women themselves were torn between home and work and, as in many other studies, found themselves heavily overstretched in the struggle to meet all the conflicting practical and emotional demands. But one of the most important factors was the way their husbands reacted to their careers. Where a husband was unwilling to relocate for the wife's career progression and where he was not understanding about the demands that her career placed on her, the marriage was in greater danger. Since highly educated women were divorcing in large numbers, this might suggest that many husbands were not reacting well to having an ambitious wife.

Another 1984 study addressed this problem more precisely by examining 31 marriages in which all the wives actually had a higher occupational status than their husband (the author also cites six previous studies which suggested this reversal of the usual inequity causes marital strain).[47] According to the respondents, they were seen as deviant by friends, coworkers and relatives. 'Husbands were perceived as losers, e.g. lazy, irresponsible and unmasculine . . . wives were deemed unladylike, domineering and manipulative.'[47] Nearly half the men complained about their wives' frequent absences, their lack of housework and involvement in childcare. Again, the men seemed to find their wives' success a role strain.

This issue of husbands feeling put down by the wife's work came into still sharper focus in a 1986 study which interviewed 1,025 couples, comparing homes where the man was the single earner with dual-earning ones.[48] Men in the dual-earner setups were less satisfied with their leisure time, personal lives and jobs. Interestingly, the dual-earner men who had high status jobs were particularly dissatisfied (as other studies suggest).[48] It emerged that this was because they were more liable to marry highly educated women who were committed to their careers and less prepared to accommodate the husbands' careers. This was acutely galling to the high-status men because, ironically, even more than low-status men, they wanted a wife who fulfilled the traditional role by providing a home base for their career (perhaps partly because an executive is expected to have a Little Woman at home and 'failure' to do so might diminish his status at work – his wife was not sufficiently a 'trophy'; this finding is reminiscent of the anecdotal account of the chief executive's marriage with which this chapter began). The authors concluded that[48] 'as long as men are diminished in the status hierarchy by wives' employment . . . role change will be distressing even for, perhaps especially for, the most able and educated men. Avoidance of housework, inadequate parenting, domestic violence and high divorce rates may be among the consequences of men's sense of relative deprivation.'

In 1987, another study attempted to pinpoint this feeling of a diminished breadwinner status.[49] Previous studies had shown that husbands with nonworking wives tended to feel more successful (regardless of actual status) than ones with working wives and husbands with working wives were more likely to say they were dissatisfied with their jobs.[49] This study proposed that men experienced their wives' work as reducing their sense of adequacy as breadwinners. 408 husbands with nonworking wives were compared with 333 whose wives worked. Sure enough, the latter group of husbands complained more about a lack of challenge, financial rewards, promotion and personal resources at work compared with husbands whose wives did not work. Further examination of the results revealed that the husbands were not upset by the increased domestic burdens placed on them, or because they opposed working wives on principle or because their wives' jobs prevented them relocating to better jobs. The reason seemed to be that it reduced their sense of their adequacy as the breadwinner.

These and other studies[50] suggest that men are suffering role strain too. They also strongly imply that men are making matters considerably harder for their working wives, increasing their guilt and in the case of wives who outperform them, actually divorcing.

The analysis so far suggests that both men and women are suffering sex role strain and that husbands are making it harder for wives, which taken altogether is creating a poisonous cocktail of depression, gender rancour and divorce. However, up to this point I have not presented the evidence of what has actually changed in the realm of work. The facts are most surprising, at least to this author.

PATTERNS OF EMPLOYMENT AND ATTITUDES TO WORK SINCE 1950

In a 1996 paper, shortly followed by a book, Catherine Hakim of the London School of Economics claimed to expose 'Five feminist myths about women's employment', every one of which is relevant to the increase in gender rancour and depression.[51] The alleged myths which she claimed to explode were:

1. That women's full-time employment has been rising
2. That women's work orientation and commitment is equal to men's
3. That childcare is the main barrier to women's employment
4. That part-timers are exploited in poor-quality jobs
5. That women's stability of employment is equal to men

Hakim argues that all these statements are false and for the most part, her critics have been unable to prove her wrong. Her explanations of why are more debatable and have been heavily criticized.[52] Nonetheless, the debate generated by her controversial claims addresses all the key issues that need to be considered here, especially the core one of whether women's current tendency not to work full-time reflects nature or nurture. I shall therefore present her arguments and the critiques of them, in full.

Hakim claims modern women fall into three employment profiles.[53] About one quarter have **Continuous Employment** in the primary sector. From a young age they have a strong sense of a career, complete with a workplan for their future progress. From leaving education onwards they stay in employment continuously, many of them full-time. They do not permit marriage or childbearing to interfere with their career. A strong predictor of this pattern is whether a woman has a plan when young. Among 14- to 24-year-old women asked what kind of work they would like to be doing when aged 35, those who answer positively (compared with those who had no idea) are significantly more likely still to be working full-time at 35.[54]

By contrast, **The Homemaker Career** entails one period of continuous employment, if any at all, between the end of education and the beginning of marriage or childbirth. For these women, Hakim observes that 'Higher educational qualifications may be acquired to ensure a girl marries a partner of at least equal status rather than with a view to acquiring marketable skills for long-term employment. The [practical] returns of education in this group consist of the husband's earning potential rather than personal earnings potential. Women in Europe can still achieve greater social mobility through marriage than through their own employment. The popularity of apparently nonvocational degrees in the humanities among young women in Western societies is attributable to these subjects being appropriate for the homemaker career . . . the homemaker career has long been the ideal for the majority of girls, especially working-class girls, in Britain and for a substantial proportion of one-third to two-thirds of women generally in industrial society . . . this [full-time homemaking] profile has been rapidly declining in recent decades.'[55]

Finally, **Intermittent Employment** entails either two continuous periods before and after marriage and childcare, or numerous brief periods until retirement. This pattern is now by far the most common across the whole of Europe and Hakim argues that in many ways, it is really the Homemaker pattern updated to fit with modern values and practicalities. This is debatable, since Intermittence as a trend could equally be a step towards the Continuous pattern, as it looks like being in the USA, where all the growth in women's employment has been in full- rather than part-time jobs. Whether this pattern is a harbinger of the new or adaptation of the old is a crucial question, because it is the most common in Britain today and it goes to the heart of the debate about whether women are 'naturally' prone to see homemaking as their primary focus or whether this is largely an artefact of social conditioning. If it is natural, then we should assume that most women will continue to see work as a secondary activity in their lives; if it is conditioned, then we should expect that women will take advantage of increasing opportunities to join men full-time in the workforce.

Hakim's thesis is that, contrary to the general perception, most women are choosing – rather than being coerced into – essentially traditional roles for themselves and she shows implicit sympathy for the idea that women have a natural tendency towards homemaking. Central to this is her contention that, although the proportion of ever-married British women who work rose from a quarter to three-quarters between 1951 and 1994, this figure conceals the fact that most women work part- rather than full-time and have done so for a long time. According to Hakim, on average throughout Europe, only one third of women have worked full-time since 1851 and there has been no significant change. She writes that 'All the increase in employment in Britain in the post-war period from 22 million jobs in 1951 to 25 million in 1988 consisted of growth in female part-time jobs . . . In reality the female full-time work rate remained constant for over a century and is still only half the male rate: 36% compared to 70% in 1994 for people of working age. The only innovation is that another 29% of women aged 16–59 years are working part-time . . . there is no evidence that women have been taking full-time jobs from men or that changes in female work rates could account for the loss of men's jobs.'[56]

Hakim believes that most women **actually prefer** part-time work. Of part-time women's jobs only 10% are professional or managerial (versus 27% of full-time working women). 77% are low-skill and low-paid, like clerical posts (secretarial, 21%) and serving in shops (retail sales, 18%). Hakim offers a number of reasons for why many women prefer it this way. One is that work serves a different function for part-time working women than men. 'Wives working part-time in Britain can regard work almost as a kind of social club, a place to meet people, to get out of the house while earning additional income.'[57] She cites several studies that support this claim, including one of 120,000 employees of the computer company IBM in 66 countries[58] which showed that the women and the part-timers (who tended to be one and the same) were much less likely to regard their job as a career, as a test of ability or skill or be concerned with promotion, and more likely to see it as a secondary source of income to that of their partner or husband and as a social activity. Full-time workers and men (also statistically coincident) were opposite on all these dimensions. Hakim cites several studies following women over time from the ages of 14 to 24 which showed that only one quarter are 'career planners'.[54] A further quarter decide early to be full-time homemakers and half are 'drifters' who have no specific career inclinations. Whilst more recent studies suggest that today's young women are more likely to be planning a career, as the figures cited above show, only 10% of part-timers actually end up in professional or managerial posts (compared with 27% of full-time working women). Of course, feminists could and do argue that this is strong evidence that women are still being discriminated against.[52] But this is becoming less and less true. For example, in the developed nations, for several years now, about half of trainee doctors, accountants and lawyers have been female.[59] Whilst there is still evidence of 'glass ceilings' in these professions, so that if these women persevere in their profession it is harder for them to reach the very top, the fact that there has been no increase in full-time employment could be taken as evidence that many of them are not motivated to do so because, as we shall see, when they fall pregnant, they either work part-time or not at all for several years. However, it can be countered that the women drop out of the workforce because of the 'glass ceiling', feeling that the odds are stacked too heavily against them, creating a vicious circle: not enough women break through the glass ceiling because there are not enough to be seen when a woman gazes up through it.

Hakim goes on to argue that the effect of marriage and childbirth on women's employment is still huge. As noted in the last chapter, only 11% of all women work full-time continuously before and after the birth of a baby and only 13% are doing so when their child is under three. Put the other way around, 89% of mothers of under-ones and 87% of mothers of under-threes either do not work at all or only work part-time. Whilst the proportions of pregnant women notifying their employers that they intend to return to work after the birth almost doubled from 26% in 1979 to 47% in 1988, many had no intention of actually doing so: one third in 1979 and one fifth in 1988 admitted this to researchers. In practice, two-thirds (in 1979) and one half (in 1988) of all working women actually did not return to work and many of these dropped out soon after returning. Another sign of the disruption of women's work is the much greater likelihood of mothers, compared with men, moving in and out of the workforce during the childcare years. In the USA, for example, Hakim calculates that 25- to 50-year-old women are two to five times more likely than men to enter or leave the workforce and 35- to 39-year-old women five times more likely than men to leave the workforce and four times less likely to re-enter it.

It can be objected that more mothers would return to and stay at work, and do so full-time, if better and cheaper childcare facilities were available. However, this seems unlikely to be the whole story if Hakim's claims about what women say about their motivations are correct.

She cites numerous large surveys suggesting that part-time women workers are very different from full-time ones in their view of traditional sex roles. One large-scale study showed that 80% of British part-timers agreed with the proposition that 'the female partner should ultimately be responsible for housework', compared with 44% of full-timers.[60] This was true in practice as well as theory: part-time women workers did as much housework as full-time housewives, which was twice as much per week as full-time working women. Furthermore, the proportions were 60% part-timers and 29% full-timers, respectively, agreeing that 'the male partner should ultimately be responsible for breadwinning'. Hakim's (not undisputatious) question regarding these statistics is 'So where does the idea come from that women are challenging the traditional sexual division of labour? From the minority of women working full-time, it would appear, the group most likely to include the media reporters, social scientists and other opinion leaders who claim to know the trends . . . [but] women full-time workers are seriously unrepresentative of the views of the majority of adult women.'[61]

Hakim also maintains that evidence purporting to demonstrate that women are keen to work full-time and to forgo traditional roles is based on an overrepresentation of the views of younger rather than older women, as well as of full- versus part-timers. Europe-wide, only 15% of 15- to 24-year-old women approve stereotypically different gender roles for housework and breadwinning whereas it is 40% among the over-55s. Given that women in all surveys everywhere become increasingly conservative and stereotypic in their view as they age, she argues that when the young women have had a chance to prove themselves in the workplace (and perhaps be disappointed by what it has to offer – through relative deprivation) it is likely they will follow that trend. Hakim uses this argument to explain the inconvenient (to her thesis) fact that the proportions of women who say they would work even if they had no need of the money increased from 58% in 1981 to 67% in 1992:[62] she argues that these surveys do not include women who have already dropped out to become housewives or taken early retirement and overrepresent young working women who are more liable to be attached to working than the average.

Hakim's overall view seems to be that the desire for women to be intermittent in their employment profile is deep-seated. To further test it, she examines countries where concerted efforts have been made to change attitudes and provide practical opportunities for women to be exactly the same as men. The proportion of Swedish women believing in separate, traditional sex roles decreased from 16% to 13% between 1982 and 1993.[63] Whilst accepting that this seems to prove the power of egalitarian policies to change attitudes and behaviour, Hakim claims this as support for her views by stressing that despite 30 years of applied egalitarianism, a stubborn minority of women (13%) still do not subscribe to it. More convincingly, she shows that when a totalitarian insistence on a low-wage, full-time-employment-for-all policy regardless of gender, was relaxed in China after several decades, one third of wives still regarded the traditional division of labour as ideal and 80% of both men and women felt that the woman should stay at home full-time whilst children were small.[64]

Hakim's broad view is summarized in the following passage.[65] 'The great majority of women working part-time see themselves as house-wives, whose primary responsibility is keeping home, with employment fitted around family life. Despite their short hours, women part-timers are far more likely than full-timers to take unpaid time off work for domestic reasons . . . The disproportionate job satisfaction of many part-timers has been observed in so many surveys in so many countries that the pattern is no longer disputed. Although some of the "excess" satis-faction is attributable to the fact that part-time jobs offer more conve-nient hours, produce less stress and exhaustion at the end of the day, and generally offer pleasant social relations at work, there seems to be an additional factor over and above these, which must be due to the differ-ent perspective of the secondary earner.

'It is sometimes argued that women are forced into part-time work by the need to combine employment with their childcare activities. While plausible, the evidence does not support the idea. The vast majority of married women take a part-time job in preference to a full-time job; among unmarried men and women many of the part-timers are still stu-dents. Virtually all part-time work is voluntary in the sense of being pre-ferred over a full-time job, in Britain, Germany, Italy, Denmark and the Netherlands, all countries with high levels of part-time work, apart from Ireland. Although childbirth may be the initial stimulus to taking up part-time work, most part-timers feel their combination of employment and domestic work gives them "the best of both worlds" and continue with part-time work long after children have left home or their husband has retired. The choice is simply not available to primary earners who are obliged to work full-time throughout the lifecycle . . . For this reason

men only do part-time work during the transition from full-time education into the labour market, or during the transition out of employment
into full-time retirement.' Perhaps the most significant claim here is that
part-timers volunteer to work that much rather than to work full-time.

Hakim rejects the notion that women have taken jobs away from
men.[66] Full-time jobs fell from 21 million to 19 million between 1951 and
1995. Virtually all the occupants of these lost posts were male but Hakim
argues that the change was away from masculine-friendly occupations
towards gender-neutral, higher-skilled ones, rather than towards traditionally female ones. Thus, the proportions employed in manual work
fell from 81% to 47% between 1900 and 1995, demasculinizing the job
market, and the proportion of (gender-neutral) professional, managerial
and clerical posts rose from 19% to 37% (from 1911 to 1971), with 54%
predicted for 2001. But women's jobs shifted from being one third
domestic service and one third dressmaking and sewing, to 77% clerical,
retail and so forth – also gender-neutral. Hakim comments that 'the fem-
inization of the workforce gave women great expectations which have not
materialized. Reviews of post-War trends repeatedly note the paradox of,
on the one hand, an enormous growth of female labour force participation and, on the other hand, an intensified segregation of women into
lower grade, lower paid jobs.'[67]

Perhaps curiously, given this wealth of evidence that, apparently, most
mothers prefer things the way they are, either dividing their time
between an unambitious part-time job and childcare or being full-time
mothers, Hakim seems cautious about offering theories as to why. A clue
is provided in this passage:[68] 'Some feminists argue that the ideology of
motherhood is part of patriarchal ideology, serving to keep women subordinate to and dependent on men. Women who reject motherhood are
rejected as unwomanly. However all the evidence is that in modern
industrial society the social pressures towards parenthood are equal for
men and women, and that it is typically women who are the prime movers
in seeking or rejecting childbearing within couples. Many women welcome motherhood as a confirmation of their sexual and social identities.
Some gain an irreversible sense of achievement from childbearing,
reducing the motivation to seek achievements in the labour market. But
homemaking activities are also treated as an expression of femininity, so
that the homemaking role can be actively retained, even in the absence of
children, in competition with a paid job.'

What are we to make of Hakim's thesis?

A critique of it by 11 feminists suggests that many of her facts are not
in dispute.[52] Only on the role of childcare as an impediment to women's

work is there a substantial disagreement as to the actual facts (see footnote 69 for more detail). The debate concerns interpretation and explanation. Above all, 'The 11' criticize Hakim for not spelling out her explanation of the facts. They state that 'Our main disagreement with Hakim is over the reasons for the persistence of gender inequality in full-time employment. Hakim tends to place unwarranted emphasis on women's attitudes and orientation to work, blaming the victim as indicated by the epithet "Grateful Slaves" [a reference to a paper with this title by Hakim].' Hakim rebuts the criticism of her lack of an explanation for the reasons for persisting inequality by stating that 'there is evidence to support all three main theories explaining women's subordinate social and economic position, so that they must be seen as complementary rather than competing'. In summary she presents 'the three main theories' as follows:

- Goldberg's theory of the inevitability of male patriarchy, which claims that hormonal differences cause men to seek to dominate in all settings. In contrast, women's hormones cause them to seek relatively subordinate roles, at home and in the workplace.
- Hartmann's (feminist) theory, which presents men as an interest group who use class and occupation to dominate and exclude women against their will and nature.
- Becker's Rational Choice theory, which concludes that the man-breadwinner, woman-childcarer pattern is a rational use of energy which predominates because it works.

Hakim offers far more evidence supporting the theories that maintain the status quo (Goldberg's biology and Becker's rationality) than the theory which challenges it (Hartmann's patriarchy). Again and again she emphasizes the pervasiveness of the female adoption of the homemaker, mothering role throughout history and modern society, although she is nearly always careful to avoid actually stating that she believes this is because of a genetic difference between the sexes. On only one occasion does she come close to explicitly stating this (consistent as it is with her acceptance of Goldberg's biological theory). The final words of the conclusion to her chapter on the incapacity of laws to socially engineer women into the workforce and out of childcare are:[70] 'The law can change the treatment of women in the workforce; it cannot change **women themselves** [my emphasis].'

Although she is extremely careful to avoid over-simplified conclusions, I believe she is tentatively hinting that women have a biologically based greater tendency than men to want to care for children and to be the homemaker. Whilst she fully accepts that a minority of women are not like this and embrace a male pattern of employment, her central thesis is that most women do not and there are enough clues that she does not believe this difference is only caused by differences in upbringing.

Space does not permit a detailed discussion of the claim that it is in the genetic nature of women to be homemakers but I believe there are strong grounds both for accepting and for rejecting it and that we shall have to wait several generations before we find out the truth: we are in the middle of a massive experiment to see how much advantage women will take of the egalitarian opportunities now opening up for them. In the meantime, if we treat Hakim's work as ultimately supporting the biological view at least in part, against it (as a recent United Nations report showed)[59] is the indisputable evidence that women are still significantly discriminated against at work in all sorts of ways (evidence which, to be fair to Hakim, she acknowledges), both in the developing and developed worlds. Prejudice and stereotyping continue to be widespread.[71] Women are left holding the baby as well as sometimes wanting to do so, and despite Hakim's selective use of the examples of Sweden and China, we do not really yet know how many women would prefer to work full-time if they had truly equal opportunity, which most do not[72]. Nor can we be sure that women's 'satisfaction' with low-paid and low-status work is real[73] and how much their unstable work pattern is really to do with gender rather than characteristic of the sort of jobs they tend to do[74] (see footnote 75 for a brief summary of the evidence that women are still socialized very differently to men).

IMPLICATIONS OF CHANGING EMPLOYMENT AND SEX ROLES
What does this analysis tell us about sex role strain and the new gender rancour?

THE IMPLICATIONS FOR MALE ROLE STRAIN SINCE 1950
If Hakim's facts are broadly correct, it would appear that women have not been 'stealing' men's jobs. Any feeling that this has been occurring is a matter of perceptions rather than reality. Nonetheless, this perception would not be surprising since more men are out of work or can only find low-level, 'unmasculine' posts than in 1950, and more women are working (albeit part-time and in gender-neutral jobs). Thus, the decrease in traditional 'job-for-life' posts and of unskilled 'masculine' jobs may have created more men who feel emasculated by, and rancorously envious

towards, their partners' (mostly part-time) jobs, even though the increase in female working has nothing to do with the man's lack of work. The evidence (cited above) regarding male touchiness about being the breadwinner makes this change a plausible cause of male rancour.

Although there is a perception (often fostered in the media) that women are becoming the new bosses, this also seems to be incorrect to a large extent. More than three-quarters of female jobs are low in pay, status and power, two-thirds of them part-time. Whilst the proportion who have higher-quality jobs who work full-time has increased compared with 1950, they are still a small minority of all bosses; only one tenth of part-timers and one quarter of full-timers are professional or managerial. Again it is a matter of perceptions rather than a consequence of a larger number of men actually having to obey a woman's orders every day, if female success in the workplace is upsetting men. But as the studies of husbands with more successful wives suggest (above), men do not seem to find the idea at all congenial. Perhaps it takes only a few women in positions of power for the men in that organization to feel threatened and for this to generalize out into a vague, paranoid sense that 'the women are taking over'.

Third, it would seem that many women are not interested in competing with men at work in conventional terms. If Hakim is correct, many of them are satisfied by their existing jobs and do not remotely correspond to media stereotypes of the female workplace predator. Rather, their primary focus is childcare and homemaking. Yet again, if men are feeling threatened, it is about perceptions. Perhaps this shows just how intolerant husbands still are of the idea of working wives. Even part-time, poorly paid women with unambitious goals may pose a threat.

Taken together with all the other evidence in this chapter, it is possible that all these changes have increased male role strain and contributed to rising male depression and rancour. If so, this would be an important catalyst in the toxic mixture of depression, rancour and divorce, both through direct aggression and indirectly, by increasing any doubts women may have.

THE IMPLICATIONS FOR WOMEN

Role strain may affect Hakim's full-time homemakers as well as the continuous career women. Although it is clear from George Brown's work that a significant part of the homemakers' problems come from low income and lack of social support (especially if they are divorced or lone parents), their status has suffered a serious demotion since 1950. This is illustrated by the many surveys of young women demonstrating their increasing disdain for 'mere' childrearing as an occupation.[77] Anecdotally, this can be observed down the pub or at the dinner table when mothers are asked what they do and reply 'bring up my children': all too often this reply results in a perceptible lack of subsequent interest from the questioner. Magazine and newspaper articles implicitly rejecting the homemaking role abound. In addition, as we have seen, in some societies sealed off from the norms of modern life where the mothering role is accorded high status, such as the Amish and Orthodox Jews, women do not suffer more than men from depression, perhaps because they have less role strain and are more highly valued. On top of this, the full-time homemaker is liable to threaten her full-time working peer, and vice versa. Not only do the two groups have to grapple with role strain, they may also have to deal with some antagonism from their own sex as well. Thus, some homemakers today may actually feel guilt and depression at not having the ambitious careers that they imagine their sisters pursue – although if Hakim is right, only a minority (about one quarter) of women actually do pursue a 'masculine' career path, in practice.

As regards these women, the role strain can be severe and they are even more at risk of suffering the relative deprivation of unfulfilled high career expectations described in Chapter 3 – not, it should be noted, so much of a problem for men, whose aspirations have not risen as much. The centrality of changing female identity since 1950 in driving up rates of depression and eating disorders among ambitious young women was explored in an intriguing series of studies by Brett Silverstein.

Pointing to the substantial increase in eating disorders among young women since 1950, he established that the modern 'thin standard' for female bodily attractiveness has fluctuated during this century.[78] Popular magazine photographs of women demonstrated that in the mid-1920s and from the mid-1960s to the present day, standards became very thin (as measured by a low ratio bust and hip measurements to waist measurements). Bustier women were in vogue from 1900 to 1920 and from 1930 to 1960. Silverstein went on to demonstrate that the thin standard periods were the ones in which eating disorders seemed to have increased.[79]

In exploring the reasons in subsequent studies, he pointed to the strong connection between masculinity and academic or career achievement in most societies. In accord with this, there is a well-established relationship between physique preferences and achievement in women:[80] curvaceous women are perceived to be less competent and less intelligent than noncurvaceous ones. It followed that women who wanted to be successful would want to minimize their visible femininity. Responding to silhouettes of female figures, women who preferred smaller breasts and smaller buttocks were also more likely to choose 'masculine' careers and desire high academic achievement. Women who were dissatisfied with their figures tended to be more concerned about reactions of others to their efforts at achievement. Historical evidence also supported this association. An investigation of archives of medical literature and case reports describing symptoms related to eating disorders in women found references in every single one to strivings for intellectual or academic achievement by the women concerned. In those past times it had been extremely difficult for any women to achieve recognition in these fields and the desire to be masculine may have been intensified.

A modern clinician who had treated many cases wrote that[81] 'though few express it openly, they had felt throughout their lives that being a female was an unjust disadvantage and they dreamed of doing well in areas more respectful and worthwhile because they were masculine'. Disordered eating is indeed particularly common among adolescent women who strived for high achievement academically and professionally.[82] In Britain, girls from fee-paying schools (such as St Luke's, where Juliet went) are more at risk than those at state schools[83] and upper-class girls are more likely to desire to be slimmer (whatever their actual weight) than lower-class ones.[84] Pressure for academic success is greater on girls in these groups.

This is related to parental expectations, which are themselves influenced by the wider society. In a study of 326 women undergraduates, Silverstein demonstrated that they were more likely to engage in binge eating if they felt that their mothers were dissatisfied with their career performance.[80] Interestingly, if the fathers were dissatisfied, it made no difference but if fathers said they thought the respondents' **mothers** were 'not at all' or 'only slightly' intelligent, the respondents were more likely to be a binger. For those women who had brothers, bingeing was more likely if the father but not the mother felt he was more intelligent. Following up on these complex results, Silverstein examined gender identity in a sample of 188 women students.[85] Women who aspired to nontraditional, masculine sex role aspirations were more at risk of eating disorders. Likewise, women who said they wished they had been born a boy were more at risk.

Silverstein also suggested that if his theory was correct, girls who feared they were incompetent or stupid would be particularly at risk of eating disorders. He found that those who claimed that their father (but not their mother) had not thought them intelligent were more concerned about their weight than girls whose fathers thought them bright. Mothers were found to have a different effect. As noted, eating-disordered women often attribute their feelings about food to their femaleness and tests of their gender identity reveal more conflict than normal. This conflict was found to be most common of all in women whose own mother did not achieve academically.[80] A possible implication is that the daughters were under such pressure to achieve on their mother's behalf that some developed eating disorders in the attempt to avoid seeming female and therefore, being labelled incompetent or stupid. Another implication is that paternal criticism of daughters' intelligence or of their wives increases fears thereof, promoting masculinizing dieting.

Silverstein further tested this theory by correlating the bust-to-waist ratios of models in magazine photographs since the beginning of the century with the proportion of women working as professionals at the beginning of each decade up to 1980.[79] When women professionals were numerous, magazine photographs showed thin models. A similar significant relationship was found between thinness in the photographs and the number of women graduating from universities. During periods when women were pushing to be taken seriously in terms of careers and brain power, they dieted.

This set of studies make a lot of sense in the context of modern female aspirations and the pressures on them to succeed. Although Catherine Hakim may be right in claiming that the majority of women opt for part-time and relatively low-status occupations in practice, there is still considerable pressure on the New Woman to seem competent and intelligent. One way of doing this is to be thin. The studies also neatly augment the evidence presented in Chapter 3 of the pressure placed on women by television images.

Silverstein extended this correlational approach to the increase in depression among women since 1950.[86] He prefaced this study with the fact that many girls with eating disorders also suffer from depressive symptoms, that both problems are more common among girls and that the sex difference in rates of both emerge from puberty onwards. His hypothesis was that gender differences in depression are larger in generations that reached adolescence when women had greater opportunities for educational and career achievements than their mothers – consistent with the predictions of relative deprivation theory that raised expectations will increase the risk of disappointment and with his earlier studies of eating disorders.

Women in pre-1910 and 1930–39 cohorts reached adolescence in years when females were less likely to graduate from college than their mothers had been. It was found that the sex ratios of depression were smaller for women who were adolescent during these periods when the women reached age 30. Depression ratios were larger during the other decades. Thus, small differences between the sexes at the beginning of the century were followed by two decades of larger differences, then another decade of smaller differences and a final period of large differences.

Silverstein's work is only correlational but it is suggestive. The root problem it raises is that there are still powerful stereotypes and prejudices about women which may cause severe distress when attempts are made to challenge them. Busty women are assumed to be incompetent and stupid and it should be no suprise if this groundless idea makes women who want to be taken seriously diet. Likewise, as was described in Chapter 2, women who feel under severe pressure to succeed from parents or from the wider society are at risk of depression (the 'dominant goal' variety, identified by Arieti and Bemporad).

Role strain is clearly an important cause of female depression. We have seen in this chapter that a good deal of the depression that women suffer may be due to being in the wrong role at the wrong time. Once mothers have given birth, working full-time places considerable strain on those who would prefer to be at home. Equally, mothers who are at home who would prefer to be at work are at risk. On top of this, both groups have had their expectations and sense of entitlement raised substantially, and as Weissman suggested in 1977 (and as we saw in Chapter 3), they have suffered considerable relative deprivation. Silverstein's study correlating depression with high aspirations is consistent with this theory.

SEX ROLE STRAIN AND GENDER RANCOUR: LINKS BETWEEN DEPRESSION AND DIVORCE

It will be recalled that women and men generally give different kinds of reasons for divorcing. Studies of these reasons can give us an insight into the differences between the sexes as to what has provoked disharmony and gender rancour. A review[87] of several studies found that 'lack of communication/understanding' was ranked first by both genders as the reason, but here the agreement ended. Tied for third place on the women's list were 'extramarital sex', 'immaturity' and 'drinking' as complaints about the man, whereas these ranked 12th, 14th and 19th respectively for the men as complaints about the women. 'Being out with the boys' was 6th as a complaint by women whereas 'Being out with the girls' was 16th by men. 'Conflicts about independence, having a life of one's own and desires for freedom' came 2nd for women, whereas these were 6th for men. By contrast, 'issues of gender role' (such as disagreements over who does what in the home and complaints about being nagged and bullied) were placed 2nd by men. Men blamed women's overcommitment to their work (8th) far more than the reverse (25th on the women's list). Problems with relatives came 6th for men and 18th for women. For men, 'not sure what happened (with an attempted explanation provided)' came 3rd in their list of reasons, whereas this was 29th in the women's list (as the many studies suggesting that men find it harder than women to express and articulate their feelings would predict). Equal 3rd on the male list was 'different backgrounds/sexually incompatible', whereas this was 8th for women.

The authors found two basic trends beyond the gender differences, one of which may be important for understanding the growth in gender rancour. In studies conducted in the 1940s, the reasons tended to be more instrumental and practical, such things as physical and verbal abuse, finances and refusal to get involved in childcare. In the later studies, mostly in the mid-1970s, the reasons were more expressive, such things as emotional satisfaction from the marriage, value clashes and personality differences. These differences are what we would expect from surveys of changing values (see Chapter 3).

Overall, these findings are consistent with the notion that modern women who divorce feel constrained by the marital state and get fed up with traditionally male characteristics of their husbands, such as infidelity, drinking and going out with the boys, which in previous generations, they might have tolerated more (or even, in some cases, have admired). Men, on the other hand, have probably not changed so much, being as inarticulate as ever about their emotions and proffering time-honoured complaints about such problems as sexual incompatibility. The main innovation in their complaints concerns gender roles, where they feel women are not playing the game. We can only speculate as to how many of the men who complained about their wives' reluctance to perform traditionally female functions in the home turned to them (like the chief executive described at the start of the chapter) and said, 'You're not the woman I married.'

Thus, real and perceived changes in sex roles are putting a huge strain on modern marriage, and much of this is focused upon the desire of mothers to work. The resultant increases in depression, rancour and divorce are feeding the flames of our unhappiness.

The failure of modern society to meet status and attachment needs has affected both men and women, but not in the same way or to the same extent – except that both sexes seem to be feeling more rancorous towards each other. From the lofty hill-tops of sociobiology, gender rancour is best understood as an inevitable consequence of ignoring alleged genetic differences between the sexes, such as the tendency of men to seek dominance through the workplace and of women to 'instinctively' gravitate towards childcare. Alternatively, viewed from the rolling plains of sex role theory, the new gender rancour has little or nothing to do with genes and is merely an unfortunate and temporary side-effect of necessary and welcome changes, as women take their rightful economic, political and social place alongside men. There is evidence to support both explanations and we shall have to wait at least 50 years to see which is correct. Only then (assuming that present trends continue) will we know what happens when several generations of men and women have tried to make a society work based on an assumption of sex equality.

The debate is continued in the next chapter, as applied to sexuality and attraction.

Chapter 6

Gender Rancour, Part II

Sex And Attraction As Further Causes Of Gender Rancour

Worldwide, there appear to be substantial and consistent differences between the sexes as to what attracts them, what they fantasize about sexually and what they want in bed. Let it be said at the outset that men will probably tend to be more enthusiastic about these findings than women, that most of the research on which they are based was done by men and that some women may even find them insulting and offensive. Despite these disclaimers, there is not much doubt that what you are about to read is true of the average man and woman all over the world today.

COMPARED WITH WOMEN, MEN . . .
- Value physical attractiveness higher than women whether it be for marriage, a date or casual sex
- Prefer partners who are younger than them and marry younger partners
- Care less about the social status and wealth of partners if they are physically attractive or actually prefer lower status and wealth in partners
- Place a higher premium on sexual intercourse
- Are keener on the idea of casual sex, more indiscriminate when considering it, think more often about sex, are more unfaithful and have more partners in practice
- Fantasize about a greater variety of partners, masturbate more, are more explicit about sexual acts during fantasies, picturing precise features of partners' anatomies, such as genitalia, and are more likely to base their fantasies on real people and situations
- Fantasize more about 'doing things to', rather than 'having things done to'

– Are more jealous of sexual infidelity

COMPARED WITH MEN, WOMEN . . .
– Prefer and marry partners who are older than them
– Place a higher value on the wealth and status of potential mates – even if they are themselves of high status and wealth
– Are more influenced by negative information about a potential mate
– Place less emphasis on sexual intercourse as a goal, are more faithful and have fewer partners overall
– Fantasize less about sex, are less sexually explicit in the fantasies, focus more on the build-up than the climax, focus more on the emotions and settings of the fantasies, are more likely to ascribe the partners a profession and personality and are more likely to base the fantasy on their imagination than on real people or situations
– Are more jealous of emotional rather than sexual infidelity

When I began to research this chapter, I was amazed at how abundant and robust is the evidence for these assertions, cross-nationally and historically (it will be presented in the second half of this chapter). Despite several decades of intense debate and pressure for equality, apart from in a few respects, what women and men want sexually does not appear to have changed very much. The cliché that 'men use love to get sex and women use sex to get love' still has more than a little truth to it (as we shall see, it seems that you could equally substitute 'status, power and wealth' for the word 'love'). Why are men and women still so different? Will the differences remain, say, 50 years from now? Above all, has the durability of these differences affected gender rancour and therefore, rates of depression and serotonin levels since 1950?

That these differences have endured has led some sociobiologists to go so far as to claim victory in the gender debate: 'despite decades of feminism, genes will out'. As we shall see, this is premature. There is still a long way to go before we know for sure what, if any, psychological differences in this area have been inherited. There are still good grounds for supposing that they could be largely a matter of conditioning, and evidence regarding the first two questions is inconclusive. But in the meantime, I do believe that the durability of these differences, coupled with recent social trends, is causing a good deal of gender rancour and adding significantly to our unhappiness.

The heart of the matter is that they cause considerable role strain for both genders in the sexual realm as well as the others described in the last chapter. The media still exploit these differences in films, magazines, advertisements, popular songs and books. Put crudely, the women are portrayed as wanting rich, powerful men, the men as wanting 'babes', and the products sell because these narratives play to audiences' real preferences to a surprising degree. Yet alongside this commercial exploitation of our desires (whether natural or nurtured), there is also another pressure from the media which is telling us that it should not be so and offering a new way. Men are under considerable pressure to value women as people and as equals, and women to become independent and thrusting. Both sexes are being pulled in two directions and this increases aggression and depression. For, if it is true that most men still basically want to have sex with young, pretty women, think about sex more, want it as often as possible and still tend to be focused on intercourse as the goal, then these desires will clash with the contrasting desires of women listed above and with the prevailing ideology that men 'should' value women as human beings. Most men want the old traditional femininity in women and are upset by the New Woman. Some men react angrily when their predilections are criticized or rejected by women and in the media; others conceal their 'true' predilections behind a carapace of New Man attitudes and feel dissatisfied; others still feel guilty or even 'unnatural' when they find themselves fantasizing about what they really want.

Meanwhile, if most women still basically want a 'good catch' – a relatively well-to-do, high-status, older man – who will make a solid breadwinner and father and if they are less focused on sex in general and intercourse in particular, these desires will also conflict with the desires of men listed above and the prevailing ideology that the New Woman should be an independent equal with the sexual appetites of the New Woman in *Cosmopolitan* magazine articles. In some cases this leads to a self-contradictory position in which a woman may be cursing 'the lack of real men who are not just wimps' in one breath and complaining of the overbearing arrogance or intransigence of men in the next. Some women are furious when men exhibit classically male desires; others pretend to be New Women in front of their girl friends but act Old Woman with men; and others still act New Woman all the time and guiltily nurse Old Woman fantasies.

Yet again, both sexes end up losers.

As in the last chapter, I shall attempt two routes through this minefield: the anecdotal; and the scientific.

ANECDOTAL EVIDENCE OF THE PROBLEM
In his report of his 1987 study of sexual attitudes and behaviour in 20 male and 20 female American medical students, aged 22 to 27, John

Townsend included some interesting extracts from his interviews.[1] Since all the students were advancing towards a well-rewarded, prestigious profession, Townsend reasoned that gender differences should be least in this sample: there was no practical, evolutionary reason for the women to seek older, wealthy mates and no necessary reason for the men to seek younger, lower-status ones.

THE FEMALE MEDICAL STUDENTS

Admitting that his sample was not a representative one of all women in that age group, Townsend's purpose in quoting them was to illustrate what he believed, nonetheless, to be typical conflicts. The women had for the most part been averagely promiscuous until their early twenties but as they got older, were beginning to seek more commitment from partners. Of course, it would be a simple matter to find innumerable examples of women who would have very different feelings from the ones selected by Townsend – indeed, Shere Hite[2] has made a good living out of doing so – but these voices give a good impression of the issues.

CASE 1:

This woman was chosen by Townsend as a prime example of someone who was hearing loud ticks from her 'biological clock'.

'There's a phase of your life where people are watching what you do in a professional environment, and you're at the "marrying age". You're 24 and you should be more serious. You can't rationalize one-night stands to yourself any more. I would do it two years ago and I wouldn't do it now. There was nothing at stake then. Now every man is a potential mate. When you get to this age and see other friends your age getting married, you wonder, "What's wrong? Why aren't I getting married?" I went to seven weddings this summer. By the time we finish residency [qualify as doctors], our fertility is about to take a nose dive. So you think about these things. I think the idea is that guys will go for the young, pretty girls. We'll be 30 and 35; they'll want women 20 to 25. As an undergrad, I didn't see it in the same light as I do now. Everyone around me seems to be getting married now. I've started to think about it.'

CASE 2:

A woman who had been dropped by a boyfriend decided to sleep with him again. She thought that if he could handle sex on a casual basis, so could she, and they spent a night together.

'He didn't call the next day and I finally called him that night. He was studying and after we talked a bit he said, "Well I've got to get back to studying!" I felt brushed off and . . . I shouldn't use that word. Why should I feel that way if he doesn't?'

Interviewer: 'What word?'

Subject: 'Used. I feel used even though I don't think I should. It's irrational. If we had just gone out to dinner and talked, I would have felt he was interested in me. Or if he had called the next day, I wouldn't have felt bad. But I called him and went over and slept with him and he got what he wanted and I didn't. He says he wants a friendship but I think he just wants to keep things friendly so it won't be uncomfortable in classes – and to sleep with me occasionally. That really bothers me. That's not even enough for a friendship. I thought I could handle it the way he does, but I couldn't, and I feel pretty bad now about going over there.'

CASE 3:

After a series of affairs and an unreciprocated love, this woman adopted a new 'no sex on the first date' approach with a lawyer. They went out five times before they slept together, and even then she refused to have intercourse, feeling it was still too soon.

'In fact, I don't know what made me say no. It's very unusual for me. I guess I didn't consciously plan it this way. I'm trying to protect myself by taking things slowly. I've learned that if you're interested in a man, it doesn't pay to sleep with him the first night. He probably won't call you again if you do. Sex is something they want and you give. The more difficult it is to achieve something, the more the person wants it. If a woman gives it away at the first shot, she's given up the game point. It's hard to go back and say no after that. You've given up your leverage and you probably won't get what you want, which is commitment. If I just wanted an orgasm, I could do that more easily myself, so obviously I want more than just sex. I know I'm taking a big chance by not having sex with him because I might not hear from him again but I have a feeling I'm trying to gain respect and keep the upper hand – call the shots this time.'

The lawyer did not call but the woman was glad to have established a precedent.

THE MALE MEDICAL STUDENTS

In contrast to these tales of an increased desire for commitment, according to Townsend, the males were increasingly keen to avoid it. Whereas 90% of the women in his sample answered 'yes' to the statement 'I would prefer to have a serious relationship but I have not met the right person', only 10% of the men did so.

CASE 1:
He had a girlfriend with whom he had negotiated an open relationship
but she started to push for greater commitment. He was even more reluctant because, as he had moved further through the medical training, he
began to sense he would have many more opportunities for sex as his
status increased.

'I could see my status was rising rapidly. I'm only a student now but
I've already gotten my name on some articles and people know who I am.
Every year my status seems to go up, and it's like, "Whoa, I'm really
somebody now." People are starting to realize that, and I'm starting to be
able to take advantage of it. It's really becoming a very powerful tool.'

He feels that his present relationship must end because it does not
meet his need to feel free, although he would like a relationship that helps
him get through a tough period in his career.

'But at the same time I can't have the same sort of hassles I'm having
with my girlfriend now. I wouldn't be able to deal with it. So I am not
ready for any commitment right now and frankly, I want to look around.'

CASE 2:
A student from a conservative background had associated sex with
marriage but this changed after losing his virginity to a nurse. As their
relationship progressed, differences in their background and annoyance
at her feelings about a previous boyfriend made him doubt its worth. He
still sleeps with her occasionally but feels sad because she pressures him
to become engaged.

'I realize that I learnt a lot about life from this relationship, how to
relate to a woman sexually, and I am a lot more comfortable now along
those lines. Before, any girl I went out with for a long period of time I was
sizing up for marriage. Now I want to go out and have a great time and
not think about a woman's marriage potential. I think I better play it cool
for a while as far as getting really involved with anyone because I just got
out of a lot of trouble. My next couple of years will involve a lot of long
hours working and awful lot of moving and I don't want to get married.'

CASE 3:
Unlike the previous two cases, the next man was actively involved in radical politics and described himself as a feminist. Nevertheless, his relationship with an undergraduate he met a political rally has a traditionally
male sound to it.

'We see each other a few times a week. She comes over about 10.30 and
we hang out for an hour and then go to bed. She complains that I'm not

giving her enough except in bed. She wants more time, more from me. I tell her I'm busy with my work and political activities and I am. Ideally, I would like to have a deeper relationship with someone, create something that's working, that's stable, because this relationship is not going anywhere. If she weren't hassling me, I could coast and just enjoy it. It's better than nothing, especially sexually, having someone there, to hold. Having sex regularly is definitely important – letting out all that frustration. Having sex builds you up and you need that outlet. Friendships are important too but there's something special about a sexual relationship: women will nurture you. This relationship fills a need even when I know I won't marry her. I'm not even thinking about marriage now and I don't want to marry before I finish my residency.'

He is 'frightened' that his girlfriend will cut off the relationship because she is so dissatisfied. Asked why he could not reassure her that he loved her and try to make more of a commitment he said, 'Oh no way! I'm not into that!' He said: 'When you're in a relationship like this and it's cut off it's devastating . . . even when you're not in love and not especially committed, it's a big loss.' This echoes the research finding that males more than females resist ending relationships even when they are less involved than their partners, and are more upset by breakups.[3] Contrary to what you might imagine, men are also generally more starry-eyed and less pragmatic about relationships.[4] They are less likely to plan their relationship 'career' and to freewheel, whereas women keep a close eye on where the relationship is leading and often know long before the end that it will not last. This man illustrates these tendencies.

'So I don't want to cut it off. I would like to coast for a while. She's fairly physically attractive. That's definitely a major part of it. I would like to meet some other women, and I do occasionally sleep with a woman I know from before, but the ones I'm really attracted to are all attached.'

CASE 4:
Although males in this sample tended to see their opportunities for both casual and serious sexual relationships expanding with their increasing status, fear of opprobrium limited their attempts to initiate casual sex with female classmates.

This student said Medical School had been 'a bit of a bonanza' as regards sex, having gained a bit of a reputation as a carouser and lecher. After a casual encounter with a classmate, he approached the woman the next day to ensure she was 'cool' about their sexual activity. To his surprise, she was eager to see him on a regular basis. He told her he did not want to get 'involved'. He said he was so frank because she was a classmate; if she had not been he might have 'let it ride and let the woman figure it out for herself'. He divided women into those he wanted for sex only, and those who inspired commitment, and she was in between. He saw her for a month and slept with her several times. Although she was not pushy about it, she made it obvious she wanted more commitment so he had to 'blow her off'. He reports that it 'was a bad scene' and he is now 'paranoid about getting involved with women in my class'. However, he ended up necking another of his classmates who encouraged him to stay the night but he decided not to do so when she said she had had a crush on him for some time.

Overall, he claimed that two factors militated against male students going for classmates: the female students generally had a low level of attractiveness; and the opprobrium resulting from one-night stands.

'When I get a few drinks inside me I'm a walking erection, but I try to control myself. To seriously date someone in my class I'd have to find her really attractive and interesting and I don't know if there's anyone in the class I'd be willing to date. As far as looks go, we're hitting the bottom in my class but I'm interested in some of these women as friends. There are so many guys who say, "No way would I go with anybody in class." If the women were more attractive you'd be more inclined but you'd still be less inclined than if there were in the general population. There are plenty of guys who would be more than willing to seriously date the two or three best-looking girls in the class, but they don't want 140 pairs of eyes watching them and if things don't work out there's all this shit you have to deal with: gossip, friends who know you both and their different loyalties. So it's an added burden. If you go to bed with someone in your class and then blow her off, the woman feels fucked over. People gossip, word gets around and pretty soon not only are the other women not attracted to you, they hate your guts!'

Townsend makes no claims for these anecdotes as scientific evidence *per se*, but he believes they are illustrative of wider patterns. He writes that[1] 'In their behaviour and attitudes the men quoted above did not exemplify a stereotypical macho desire for sexual conquests, but their increasing status and experiences convinced them that they could seek and enjoy more transitory relationships in the future and such a course would be less damaging to their mental balance and career aspirations than would more involved relationships. Their experiences, the lessons they drew from these experiences and the resulting strategies stand in marked contrast to those of their female peers, whose increasing age, status and experiences led them to precisely the opposite conclusion: transitory relationships were deleterious to their mental balance, their marital goals and their careers. On the basis of these exploratory interviews, at least, it does not appear that equalizing and increasing male and female socio-economic status substantially reduces sex differences in the tendency to associate coitus with emotional involvement and marital aspirations.

'Female subjects tended to be concerned that their pool of acceptable partners was declining with their own increasing age and rising status. These concerns are not groundless. Demographically, women's chances of marrying begin to deteriorate rapidly after age 25. The problem of finding an acceptable partner is especially acute for women over 25 who are highly educated and have ambitious careers because most women still prefer to marry men of equal or superior status and the pool of higher-status, single men is small. Higher-status males, however, are not averse to marrying "down" in terms of age and socioeconomic status – particularly when the woman is exceptionally pretty. These interviews with medical students suggest that upwardly mobile men can use their increasing attractiveness to women to engage in more casual sexual relations until they find acceptable partners and are ready for marriage. Some women subjects showed a keen awareness of these dynamics and **expressed considerable resentment in this regard** [my emphasis].'

Townsend's view of the cause of these differences between the students, in which the women are seeking commitment and the men to be freer agents, is that this reflects evolution. This is highly debatable: it could equally be that social conditioning causes men to seek younger mates and women to feel pressured to get married. But in terms of increased gender rancour the important point is his last one. In 1950, women may have been considerably less resentful of the fact that men seem to prefer young women to older women (for whatever reason). Today, the fact that the cards are stacked against older women is no longer seen as inevitable or 'natural'. It is perceived as an inequity imposed by a social system which promotes youthful girls as models and which handicaps older women seeking mates. Whatever the truth about this, it undoubtedly builds resentment and contributes to gender rancour.

SEXUAL ATTITUDES AMONG YOUNGER WOMEN

One objection (of many) to Townsend's view is that most of the women in his survey were already in their mid-twenties and therefore – without any need to posit unconsciously evolved needs for commitment – they might have been thinking consciously and practically about their futures. Since there is no biological time clock for men's reproduction, the same pressure does not apply to them. Consistent with this criticism, there is considerable evidence that as women have become more equal with men, their sexual behaviour has become increasingly similar when they are young. Young (14- to 24-year-old) women are far more likely than older women to reject a traditional role, although this nonconformity decreases with age. This trend to more similar sexual patterns for both sexes had already become marked when Townsend did his interviews in the mid-1980s (and was acknowledged by him). Throughout the developed world the number of partners of young women has been steadily increasing and the age at which they first have sex has decreased.[5] In Britain and the USA, boys still tend to have begun intercourse younger than girls and to have more partners, although the gap is closing fast and is unlikely to exist in ten years' time.[5 6] In Sweden, where a concerted effort to create sexual equality has continued for four decades, as many girls as boys (95%) had had sexual intercourse before marriage by the 1960s and *by 1982*, a representative sample of 93 Swedish schoolgirls (average age, 15.6 years) had not only had their first intercourse earlier than the 88 boys (average age 16.0), but the girls had also had more partners. 44 of the girls had had intercourse (= 47%) compared with 27 (= 31%) of the boys.[7] What is more, the girls were much more likely to say they were satisfied with the amount of intercourse they were having than the boys, who seemed to be masturbating a lot instead. A very similar picture emerged in a 1981 survey of 1,952, 20- to 30-year-old German undergraduates, which had the added virtue of being a follow-up of an earlier study of 3,666 students in 1966 (both surveys were claimed to be representative of the then populations).[8] The change was dramatic. In 1966, 39% of the 20- to 21-year-old women in the sample had had intercourse in the previous 12 months, compared with 42% of the men. However, in 1981 in the same age group the figures were 78% for women and 60% for men. The women had also accumulated more partners than the men and were generally more sexually permissive. Only in masturbation did the men outdo the women. This evidence could be said to broadly contradict an evolutionary view, or at the least, shows that female sexuality is more plastic and influenced by social systems than a gung-ho genetic determinism would suggest. It is certainly not clear whether men still favour coitus more than women and are relatively unemotional about casual sex. The picture has almost certainly been complicated by the AIDS epidemic,[5] where women feel (and are) more at risk from penetration than men.[6]

Consistent with the evolutionary view are the considerable number of studies showing that women and men give different reasons for having sex. In one, twice as many women say they were in love with their first sexual partner.[9] 95% of a sample of American undergraduate women compared to 40% of the men stated that emotional involvement was 'always' or 'most of the time' a prerequisite for intercourse.[10] In another, answering the question 'What was your most important reason for having sex on the most recent occasion?', 51% of women and 24% of men gave love/emotion reasons; by contrast, 9% of women and 51% of men gave lust/pleasure reasons.[11] Finally, in a 1989 sample of 580 men and women (average age 35) men attached more importance to pleasure, pleasing one's partner, conquest and relief of tension as reasons for having sex whereas women emphasized expressing emotional closeness.[12]

It may be that age is a crucial factor in women's attitudes to penetration. With the advent of efficient contraception and the sexual liberation of the 1960s, young women no longer have any great reason to regard it differently from young men. As they age and as reproduction begins to concern them more, they become more concerned with commitment and less interested in experimentation. In 1994 I conducted a series of 20 unstructured interviews with 19- to 21-year-old British female undergraduates. They did seem to regard sexual intercourse differently from males. However, unlike Townsend's (older) medical students, these women seemed keen to avoid commitment. In accord with surveys, when still this young, women tend to have high career ambitions and to be eager to avoid marriage or pregnancy. Yet if Townsend's evolutionary theory were correct in a simple sense, these women ought to be hankering for pregnancy since their fertility is at its peak aged 17–22 and their nubility is also time-limited.

CASE 1:
From a remote rural area of Britain, this 20-year-old London University student kept a childhood sweetheart at home. This did not prevent her having innumerable sexual adventures whilst away from him at university. She was paying her way at college working as a successful part-time fashion model and she was not short of sexual offers.

'It's only for a limited period that I'm good looking. Right now I'm like a child with the run of the sweetshop, but it won't last for ever. Of course if I ate all the sweets I'd get fat. To me full sex is the icing on the cake. But I would never forgive myself if I ignored the opportunity altogether.

'Guys get pretty obsessed with me. They keep on and on. It seems to mean so much more to them than it does to me. We have no girls ringing our flat up, it's all boys. I'm really quite rude in giving them the brush-off and they never seem to get the message, they get so hurt. I'm often called extremely selfish by boys I have snogged. But I take it as a compliment, I'm quite chuffed, it's not negative. You have to be ruthless while you've got it.

'If I do go out I'm the one that lays down the rules. I say, "I'm not going to sleep with you but if you enjoy my company that's fine." It's clear to them: I'm not just getting off with one guy, I'm getting off with loads of guys and if you don't like it, sod off.

'It doesn't in any way deter from my relationship with my boyfriend. You do it, there's no guilt about that. You're young, you do what you like but you're not stupid. My boyfriend doesn't stop me from doing anything. I make no compromise, so if it's a holiday I'll do it, if I want to be at university in London then I'll go there, if I see somebody else I want to snog, I'll do it. Because I'd feel so bad if I was missing out. I'm not going to be tied down by anyone.'

Given this feeling of freedom, it is interesting that she did not regard intercourse in the same way as many men would: despite being in a position of apparently unconstrained choice, she did not do it often.

'Sex [intercourse] would leave me feeling I had no worth, bad about myself. I'd feel it was wrong, I'd hate myself, to prove something by going the whole way. Maybe sometimes I do want to go the whole hog, I do want to sometimes. Sometimes I'm very tempted but as soon as I speak to my boyfriend I'm glad. The regret would be a bloody nightmare. I couldn't betray my boyfriend. AIDS is just rampant and you can't just do what you want all the time. My boyfriend thinks I'm really selfish. It must be very hard for him, but he has to accept it. I'm quite good at controlling myself in all areas of my life, not just sex. I do believe I will sleep with men more in ten years' time. At the moment I'm just taking advantage of the fact that a huge number of men are available to me.

'I never feel dissatisfied at the end of a night's snogging because I get my thrills and the men never meant anything to me anyway. I think, "If I was some old 30-year-old boiler you wouldn't be talking to me at all," and that makes you realize how shallow it all is anyway. While I was away on holiday I was getting off with people but not sleeping with them. It was a bit of fun. I'm confident enough not to have to go the whole way.

'I don't touch the man, I just let him touch me in a limited way, maybe heavy petting. I say to them, "You go now or you know the score – not any further than this." They always push to get as much as they can from you.'

CASE 2:
This woman, also a part-time model at London University and from a small town, had adopted a similar strategy when it came to intercourse.

'In the 18 months before I started my present relationship, I got off with 20 to 30 men but I only had full sex with one of them, an ex-boyfriend. The classic scenario is when you go out with somebody you quite like and you sit looking at him across the dinner table and you think, I do really *quite* like you, and it's that problem of the "quite" that keeps coming into your mind. You're not desperately keen, not thinking, If I don't have sex with you I'm going to die, yet at the same time, you're thinking, If you don't make a pass at me I'll be disappointed. It's that limbo between desperation and "it would be quite nice". So you take the middle way path and you snog 'em.

'Snogging's a case of "suck it and see". With sex you rarely get it right the first time round, so you have a snog and if you quite like it you might have another go. If you don't like it then at least you've tried and you can dismiss it. When you snog someone you put a question mark over their head – "maybe". You put them on a shelf as potentials for sex one day.

'Snogging is a small break from reality and that's why it's so exciting. It's no problem to get an orgasm from it. Mental attitude takes you 95% of the way almost regardless of who the person is on the other end and what he does. Sometimes it's much better to leave things in the realm of fantasy rather than pushing things into reality where they're not going to work. Fantasy is great. You can have a Fantas-tic time without doing hardly anything. Life's so boring and a snog does make it more exciting. Boredom is a big factor, I sometimes just do it because I'm bored.

'A big thing is that you know you are going to have no repercussions. Nobody's going to hold you to ransom over a snog. You can't do anybody down for having a snog. You were on for it and so were they. You can snog your friends and there's no comeback.

'Now if you had sex it's a completely different kettle of fish, because suddenly either you owe them something or they owe you something or you have to be nice to them in the morning or you have to ask how their grandmother is and you're really not that interested in how their grand-mother is, and all you really want is a fabulous snog. It's as far as you ever wanted to go with them, it was not something you ever wanted to take any further.

'What's new is that girls have the confidence to say, "I think you are really nice, your mum's fabulous and I like your four sisters, but I don't want to sleep with you." There's all these men who want a piece of the action so you give them a small piece of it where once they might have got the lot.

'It's the pudding theory: you don't worry about having starters and you may go on to a main course but you think very hard about having pudding because you might get fat and live to regret it. It's whether or not to go the whole way.

'Say I go to a party and I see a couple of possibles. The reason I won't sleep with them is Danger: emotional and physical. Emotional is that you wake up in the morning and can't stand them, physical is that you wake up pregnant or with the clap.

'There's a question mark in the back of your mind: "What am I doing?" if I start to go all the way. You can have all your kit off, it doesn't make any difference. You feel quite territorial about yourself. You have to really like somebody to let down the barrier.

'There are some people a thousand million horses wouldn't drag you away from. With others it's like going to Brighton for the weekend rather than Barbados. It boils down to how much you fancy them.

'Are we smarter now than in 1970? The fact is that we're more scared. We've learnt that all the people in the Sixties actually took more drugs than was good for them, and did not end up very happy. So now you don't sleep with people lightly, I don't. I really have to like someone to sleep with them.

'In our society we've decided that mouths are fine and hands are fine but if you have sex you are giving something away. It's rather like the Indians who won't look in mirrors because they think it's going to take away their soul. We're working on the same principle.'

CASE 3:
This Cambridge undergraduate was doing a traditionally male course and very ambitious in her career aspirations. She had had less sexual experience than the previous two cases and also seemed to regard men somewhat dismissively.

'I have a boyfriend now but I want this really international career. I wish I had met him five years later than I did. Our relationship is going to influence my decision about whether to go abroad for the next step in my career but I don't think that when it comes to the final crunch that will influence it really. I am curious about men, what they would be like, it's inevitable at my age and in the end that will affect my sex life. There's a lot I still have to experience.

'Men are just competitors in —— [her course]. You can't both get better grades and snog the other classmates. It would be degrading to me. I'm not having them think of me as less than a man.

'All the men in Cambridge are such cowards. I don't know one who has a girlfriend who wasn't chased by her. We are led to believe that it's the man who does the courting and the woman who is chased. That's rubbish. It's not a case of the innocent girlies waiting to be swept off their feet. Cambridge men are so inhibited and socially inept.

'At school I didn't need men. Soon after I left I snogged my best friend and I went downhill from there. I snogged every man I met for a time after that. I realize how insecure they were now, although at the time I thought their nervy reactions were my fault. Now I only get involved with men who I know reasonably well.'

CASE 4:

This woman was very reluctant to get seriously involved with any men and used snogging as a tool for keeping them at bay.

'I had a guy for two months but I suspected he was seeing other people as well so I did not feel obliged to be faithful. We didn't sleep together because I didn't trust him. So I have a lot of short on and offs, snogging which may or may not lead to heavy petting, but I will not go all the way. Some get persistent but to me it's just a fling, a bit of fun. In Val D'Isère on the University skiing trip I got off with seven different men but I didn't sleep with any of them. On holiday it's completely different. You won't be seeing them next week, whereas I'd be seeing my close friends at university at lectures or parties all the time, I couldn't just leave it as a casual bit of fun. When I got back I thought I had behaved terribly but they were all fine about it. It's the fact that everyone's in the same boat, drunk, ignoring the usual constraints.'

These interviews provide some grounds for questioning the evolutionary theory of sex differences. Whereas the older, female medical students were seeking commitment, the younger women were generally concerned to avoid it, yet if the evolutionary theory were correct, their 'selfish genes' should have been eager to capitalize on their youthful charms by converting them into rich, high-status husbands and offspring. At the very least, this suggests that social changes can override any genetically evolved tendency to seek commitments. Nor is there any necessity to propose such tendencies to explain the older women's attitudes. The ageing process alone would put pressure on them to seek out more stable, committed relationships if they were considering reproduction and in a society where men tend to earn more than women and girls are raised to make a 'Good Catch' for a husband, together these influences could account for their marriage aspirations.

However, it would not be fair to judge the evolutionary argument on such slim evidence and anecdotally based reasoning, for there is a great deal more to it than that.

221

THE SCIENTIFIC EVIDENCE FOR, AND EXPLANATION OF, SEX DIFFERENCES IN ATTRACTION AND DESIRE

In 1989 David Buss, an American psychologist, published the results of an analysis of differences in preferences between the sexes in mate selection.[13] The study examined results from 37 samples drawn from 33 countries on six continents, including 10 from developing nations, with a total of 10,047 people having been studied.

Based on evolutionary theory, Buss hypothesized that women would be more concerned than men with the ability of a mate to provide food, shelter, territory and protection. In demonstrating his capacity to supply these, the male would indicate that he would be able to support her during the vulnerable period of childcare and also that he was of good genetic stock to pass on to her offspring. Therefore, women would place a higher priority on 'good financial prospects' and 'ambition-industriousness' in a mate than a man.

For their part, men would be more concerned with the reproductive value of women as indicated by a preference for youth and physical attractiveness. As Buss put it,[13] 'Features of physical appearance associated with youth – such as smooth skin, good muscle tone, lustrous hair and full lips – and behavioural indicators – such as high energy level and sprightly gait – have been hypothesized to provide the strongest cues to female reproductive capacity.' Since younger women would be more fertile and have a longer reproductive period ahead of them than older women, across the span of the evolutionary millennia men not pursuing youthful characteristics in women would have ultimately produced fewer offspring. Buss summarized his predictions as follows:[13] 'Females, more than males, should value attributes in potential mates such as ambition, industriousness and earning capacity that signal possession or likely acquisition of resources . . . Males, more than females, will value relative youth and physical attractiveness in potential mates because of their links with fertility and reproductive value.'

The results of the study emphatically supported these predictions. In 36 of the 37 samples females valued 'good financial prospects' significantly more than males and the same was true of women's valuation of 'ambition-industriousness' in 29 of the samples. In contrast and as predicted, in 34 of the 37 samples men valued 'good looks' significantly more highly than women and in all the samples, men preferred a younger woman (on average, 2.66 years younger). In addition, although Buss had not included this prediction, women preferred older men in all the samples (with an even greater gap preferred, of 3.42 years). As a check that these preferences were expressed in actual behaviour, Buss examined the marriage statistics of the 27 countries from the sample in which they were available. The men were on average 2.99 years older than the women, confirming that preference was put into practice. In summarizing the findings, Buss claimed that they were 'among the most robust psychological sex differences of any kind ever documented across cultures'.

Clearly, the results were consistent with an evolutionary, genetic explanation of these differences between the sexes although Buss was careful to emphasize that culture was still an important influence and that they are not ' "genetically determined" in the sense of being inevitable or intractable'. Thus, in his Nigerian and Zambian samples, where polygamy was practised, he noted that the preferred age gaps for both sexes were considerably larger than the average for developed nations because as men aged they were socially sanctioned to continue choosing new wives increasingly younger than them. He also noted that the preferred age gaps tended to be less in European nations. Likewise, a prediction that men would generally prefer chaste virgins was not supported, and unlike the other mate selection factors, varying social norms produced a great variety of results for this. Nonetheless, Buss was able to claim these results as strongly suggestive of an evolutionary basis for the sex differences he had presented.

But it is one thing to demonstrate that men and women consistently differ in some respects, it is quite another to prove that these are due to genetic evolution rather than other causes. Just because a pattern is found almost everywhere does not prove it is genetically inherited. That other interpretations are possible was evident from the 'open peer commentary' published immediately following Buss' article in which scientists from a wide variety of disciplines were given the opportunity to respond. Several of them suggested that there was no need for a recourse to evolutionary theory or genetics to explain the findings because social and economic explanations could do the same job with a great deal more rigour and less speculation. One stated:[14] 'Consider an alternative account of the relationship preferences males and females show for financial prospects in a mate. Both sexes want the same financial resources, but because women are denied independent access to them, we may conclude that (a) women select the most practical remaining option – marriage to men who have the resources – and (b) men do not use irrelevant criteria for their preferences.' This author drew attention to the convenience of the evolutionary theory for men and for the status quo: 'Why should the resources of a society be used to provide women with good financial prospects of their own when their "natural" preference is for men with such prospects?'

Another author[15] reasoned along similar lines in considering why women may go for men with ambition and industriousness. 'Male economic control makes male economic status critically important [to a woman] in selecting a mate, because it ensures her economic future and that of her offspring. In turn, females, lacking economic influence, may use their sexual attractiveness as an avenue to social and economic power. Similarly, males may use their higher economic status to gain sexual access to females. Thus, males may value "good looks" more highly than economic potential in mate selection because females in most present cultures offer more of the former and less of the latter. This relationship might be different in dowry-orientated cultures where females have gained a substantial measure of economic parity.' This author went on to point out that Buss' theory was most applicable in the Asian countries in his sample and in Iran, where female control of resources is least. In a reanalysis of Buss' data, it was further established that it was the region, not the gender which showed the strongest association with female preference for 'ambition' and the predicted preferences for age differences and male desire for chastity. Gender only predicted the male desire for 'good looks' and female desire for 'good financial prospects'. In another reanalysis[16] of Buss' data, it was shown that the preferred age differences, the importance of good looks to men and the female desire for ambitious men were less pronounced in the industrially developed nations compared with the primarily agrarian ones.

All these arguments suggested that social and economic explanations could account for the results completely, or as well as evolutionary ones. Added to these, it was pointed out[17] that for Buss' study to have been a real test of how much sex differences prevailed across different cultures (and therefore might be supposed to be genetic), he would have needed a more diverse sample: 27 of the 33 cultures were either European or European-influenced. Another critic,[18] an anthropologist, claimed that 'there are times and places in which older-female marriages [by males] are socially and statistically significant', taking Buss to task for ignoring them (although providing only one concrete example).

There were also fundamental criticisms of Buss' methods and of the scientific status of evolutionary theories as applied to human behaviour. One contributor[19] began by pointing out that 'attempts to explain human behaviour using evolutionary models routinely applied to other species have a chequered history. What applies to animals may not apply to humans.' Another pointed out that Buss effectively presupposed his conclusions and sought evidence to support them rather than testing a scientific hypothesis that could be confirmed or disconfirmed either way.

She stated.[14] 'Psychologists will find Buss's article problematic, largely because the traditional "rules of the [methodological] game", from hypothesis to conclusion, are contravened to no apparent purpose. The evolutionary hypotheses do not describe some heretofor unnoticed but significant behaviour, nor are they contrasted with nonevolutionary hypotheses. The same predictions [about mate preferences] could have been made from a random sample of newspaper advertisements, magazines or soap operas.' She concludes that the basic theory is 'open to serious doubts as to the ultimate disconfirmability of the sociobiological framework'.

Although not mentioned by Buss or in the peer commentary of his paper, there is another serious criticism of sociobiology. Wealthy and successful people tend to reproduce less than the poor and unsuccessful. Given that the key premise of sociobiology is that we are ultimately motivated to reproduce our 'selfish genes' and that the battle for status and wealth is assumed to be waged to this end, it is a fact that takes some explaining. Daniel Vining, the man most responsible for pointing up this problem, described it thus:[19] 'Sociobiology predicts that individuals will behave so as to increase their genetic representation in the next generation. Individuals, then, should exploit positions of power to increase their number of descendants relative to those below them. Rarely, however, do we observe such behaviour in modern human populations . . . the striving for, if not the actual possession of, status and power seems, on average, to deter rather than stimulate reproductive effort among modern humans.' In other words, chief executives, top politicians and so on are so busy becoming powerful and wealthy (in order to attract good mates and ensure maximal reproduction, according to Buss) that they do not get around to actually spreading their seed as much as poor and low-status people. He goes on to describe this fact as 'a direct violation of sociobiology's fundamental premise'. It might be added (as noted in Chapter 4) that the most educated and successful women are increasingly childless. It was estimated that 20% of all women in the cohort born after 1950 will not give birth. Since childless women are more likely than average to be of high social class and attainment, this hardly squares with a 'selfish gene' perspective.

A commentary on Vining's paper by his peers (immediately following it) did not dispute his fundamental facts and it is widely accepted that the well-to-do in modern society have considerably fewer children than those at the bottom. However, various arguments were offered as to why this fact did not contradict sociobiological theory, of which Fox's is the most widely cited. He maintains that it predicts that we are motivated unconsciously to maximize our resources and copulate as much as possible, not to actually have children as such. Since the highest-status people in modern society still seek as much wealth, power and access to sex as possible, the fact that they no longer seek to have large families (or even any children at all) does not disprove that theory.

Richard Dawkins' contribution to the peer commentary is to fall back on a 'general disclaimer'. He states that 'Natural selection can only favour behavioural rules of thumb which, without the behaver being aware why, tend to have the effect in the environment where most of the selection took place, of maximizing reproductive success. Change the environment and, of course, you'll be lucky if the rule of thumb works.'

What is interesting about both Fox and Dawkins' arguments is that they demonstrate the endless flexibility of evolutionary theory, reminiscent of psychoanalysis. In Fox's case, confronted by an awkward set of facts, he simply redefines the unconscious proclivities that humans are supposed to have inherited from maximizing the number of offspring to doing the things most likely to achieve this. Perhaps he is right that this is what we have inherited but for his to be a scientific theory, it must be disconfirmable and what is to stop me or anyone else cooking up an equally credible alternative theory: how do we choose between them? Dawkins' position is even more obviously unscientific and akin to that of a Freudian defending psychoanalytic therapy: he can only offer 'rules of thumb' and if some detailed facts happen not to fit his theories he can fall back on untestable claims about what the evolutionary environment was like and how humans adapted to it. By this reasoning, no facts about humans today can disprove his theories yet he is happy enough to advance them if they support him.

At least these authors recognize there is a problem. Others simply deflect its seemingly awkward implications for the status of sociobiology by turning the problem into an opportunity by incorporating it into their model. The iconoclastic Richard Herrnstein and Charles Murray, enthusiastically confirmed that the pattern exists but argued that the relative lack of reproduction by the ruling classes poses a serious threat to the intellectual capital of modern societies.[20] Claiming that intelligence is largely genetically inherited and that by virtue of their greater ability, the brightest in a society cluster at the top, the fact that they reproduce less is presented as a watering-down of our collective mental powers (a remarkable intellectual sleight of hand: Herrnstein and Murray convert a fundamental challenge to their sociobiological edifice into a brand new conservatory!).

A final reason to reject rampant biologizing of social and psychological patterns is that, at least on one reading, evolutionary theory itself would predict that humans would be highly adaptable. It makes sense that we are born with certain basic, species-wide proclivities such as to seek out mates, food and safety. But it also makes sense that we are born with a great potential for individual differences in how we express these instincts. Evolution occurs because we adapt, after all. If individual humans were as tied into specific ways of cognizing the world and behaving as, for example, cats, we should not be where we are today – able to survive in all of the world's very various ecosystems. It is precisely the fact that we are so adaptable and so influenceable by the whims of our parents and societies in childhood that we knock spots off cats, ants and all other species when it comes to the survival of the fittest. The tendency for sociobiologists to posit ever more specific genetically inherited thoughts and feelings actually runs counter to Darwin's theory of evolution.

Thus, there are several different persuasive reasons for questioning Buss' interpretation of his findings. But having acknowledged this, it must be added that the peer commentary of his paper was unable to find fault with many of the most fundamental findings. He was able to claim that 'No one proposed alternative explanations for the sex differences found across cultures in terms of (1) why males prefer younger females and (2) why males value physical attractiveness more than females do.' Undoubtedly, the sheer pervasiveness of these tendencies does pose a considerable (though not, as we shall see, insurmountable) problem for social or economic explanations and suggests a genetic propensity. Perhaps this is why prominent feminist authors often duck the issue[21] of why men prefer young and attractive women (every bit as much as sociobiologists ignore the fact that very successful people are less reproductive).

Buss counters the economic explanation of women's preference for wealthy and older men by citing a study he conducted of 100 American men and 100 women.[13] He found that the more money women earned, the more they valued high earnings and professional status in men, even though these women had less practical need of such men. Furthermore, in this study, for the men, the wealth and status of a woman made no difference to his preferences – even poor men cared more about the looks and age of women than about their wealth. This is certainly a crucial issue.

If women's preferences for wealthy men are determined by their upbringing and the relative lack of opportunity for them to obtain wealth other than through marriage, then as greater equality prevails, their preferences should follow suit. John Townsend augmented his study of medical students (described above) by exploring the mate selection preferences of 212 female and 170 male first-year psychology undergraduates, aged from 18 to 21.[22] Introducing the study he stated: 'Numerous authors have attributed women's greater caution and selectivity, and a greater emphasis on emotional involvement and marital aspirations in sexual relationships, to differential access to power and resources. This explanation can best be summarized as follows: (1) women tend to acquire socioeconomic status through their choice of marriage partners; (2) until recently women's opportunities for economic independence were restricted; (3) consequently, in the past, economic necessity forced women to be more selective than men in choosing partners, to put more emphasis on the partner's status in selection, and to maintain greater marital aspirations in relationships; (4) as sex differences in status weaken in the future, sex differences in sexuality and mate selection should begin to dissipate . . . Presumably women entering medicine should not feel forced by economic necessity and inferior occupational status to exhibit these sex differences.' The purpose of his study was, therefore, to test the proposition that 'increasing and equalizing male and female socioeconomic status tends to reduce or eliminate sex differences in the tendency to associate coitus with emotional involvement and marital aspirations'.

In both samples (medical students and undergraduates), the results showed that women did not want a spouse of lower social and economic status than themselves (whether measured by their background or current career status). By contrast, the men actually preferred the idea of a wife who earned less than them and who was of lower status (a result that reached statistical significance). Among the women medical students, 30% came from a home with a total income of less than $34,000 and 40% from one of less than $54,000. Since all of them expected to earn $60,000 or more on qualification, these women were clearly on their way up. Yet unlike the men, all of these women wanted a spouse of equal or greater status and wealth than themselves. No woman in the study preferred a husband of lower status and income than she had and no man preferred a wife with higher status and income. As the women's individual achievement raised their own status and wealth, their aspirations for a mate followed suit but this was not the case with the men. Interestingly, the same differences were found as robustly among the undergraduates. Even aged 18 to 21, the women preferred a man with a successful career to one with a good body, whereas the men were much more likely to say that a spouse should be very physically attractive. These findings are, of course, consistent with evolutionary theory: even when women have no need of men's wealth and status they continue to want it.

However, this explanation is no more necessary than a simple social one: as girls these women were socialized to believe they must make a 'good' marriage; perhaps this idea is so pickled into them that they continue to believe it even when they are as likely to have a high income as men. Millennia of unequal opportunities cannot be overturned in a couple of generations.

Whatever the explanation, the differences between the sexes do not stop with patterns of attraction – they are found in sexual desires as well. Elaborating on his 1989 paper,[23] Buss has stated that 'Dozens of studies confirmed the existence of large sex differences in the desire for sexual variety. When asked how many sex partners one would ideally like to have over the next couple of years, men reported eight on average, whereas women reported one or two. Men reported having more frequent sexual fantasies than women report. Men's sexual fantasies more often involve the switching of partners during the course of a single fantasy episode.

'In one study on a college campus[24] students were approached by an attractive stranger of the opposite sex ("Hi, I've noticed you around town lately, and I find you very attractive") and asked one of three questions: "Would you go out on a date with me tonight?", "Would you go back to my apartment with me tonight?" or "Would you have sex with me tonight?" Of the women approached by an attractive man, 50% agreed to the date, 6% to go back to his apartment and 0% to have sex with him. Of the men approached, on the other hand, 50% agreed to date the attractive woman, 69% to go back to her apartment and 75% to have sex with her.'

Buss claims that this is but one of 'hundreds' of studies showing that men have a greater desire for more frequent and varied sex and that such studies conform with the prediction of evolutionary theory that men would be more so inclined because the more women they can impregnate, the more they can spread their selfish genes. By contrast, because impregnation takes up nine months of their potential reproductive life and because they are usually the ones who are left holding the baby, women are more choosy about who they sleep with. This was Kinsey's basic finding in the 1940s: women were less concerned with genital sex, and emphasized foreplay and emotional contact.[25] A study of over 5,000 couples in the 1980s found the same,[26] including an accentuation of these patterns when lesbian and male homosexual patterns were compared: gay men had far more partners and a great deal more casual sex, focused more on the genitals and with considerably less emphasis on emotions; in all these respects the lesbians were the opposite. Homosexual unions of both kinds are taken by Buss to express that sex's basic sexuality more freely because there is no need to compromise in order to fit the opposite sex's different sexual agenda. Whereas in heterosexual sex there is a process of negotiation over fore- and afterplay, with the man keener than the woman to get on to coitus and afterwards to 'roll over', it seems that homosexuals have less need for such compromises[26] (however, some people might find it puzzling to offer up homosexuality as being arche-typical of a gender's desires . . .).

A 1990 study by Bruce Ellis reviewing the literature concerning gender differences in sexual fantasy[27] supports Buss' claims that there are considerable differences, all of them consistent with evolutionary theory. American teenage boys are twice as likely as teenage girls to say they have fantasized about sex one or more times a day. Studies in Japan, America and Britain found men have twice as many sex fantasies as women (although two other studies found no such difference). Men have more sex-packed dreams than women. Female fantasies are more likely to include descriptions of the contexts, settings and feelings associated with the sexual encounter, which is less explicit. They are much more likely to be only emotionally rather than sexually aroused by their fantasies and they contain more affection and commitment, emphasizing themes of tenderness. Females are more likely to imagine themselves as recipients of sexual activity, as the objects of sexual desire.

By contrast, males fantasize others as the recipients of sex acts, imag-ine many more sexual acts, more organs and a greater variety of visual content, especially of minute physical details of partners' anatomy. They picture strangers and multiple or anonymous partners more and they are more likely to base their fantasies on actual people they have seen than women, who are more likely to invent imaginary figures and situations.

Having presented substantial numbers of studies to support each of these points, Ellis reported the results of a study of his own.[27] He admin-istered a written questionnaire asking about sexual fantasies to 182 female and 125 male first-year students at a California university in order to test two hypotheses. The first was that partner variety would be a more central aspect of male rather than female fantasies. Evolutionary theory claims that women evolved to be more cautious and choosy in their sexual partners in order to find men who would support their childrearing activ-ities. Thus, Ellis hypothesized,[27] 'selection favoured females who were discriminating and slow to arouse sexually, since reflex-like sexual arousal on the basis of visual stimuli would have tended to undermine female choice . . . Female sexual attraction and desire should incorporate a wide range of information about male quality and the quality of the specific male–female relationship in question.' By contrast, within this hypothesis, 'since males can inseminate females at almost no cost to themselves, males should also have been selected to become easily aroused by the sight or thought of females (especially novel females). It follows therefore that males have been designed by selection to experience sexual arousal largely on the basis of visually detected cosmetic qualities and to focus outward on their sexual partners as objects of desire.' Thus, the second hypothesis was that visual images would be the primary focus of men's sexual fantasies, whereas women's fantasies would emphasize touching, feelings and partner response.

The results supported both hypotheses. Men had significantly greater numbers of fantasies, got sexually aroused more often and imagined more different partners in a single day. Men pictured the genitals of fantasy partners much more than women did and switched partners during the fantasies more. For women the look, textures, sounds and smells of the fantasies were significantly more important than for the men. There was much more caressing and nongenital touching and the emotional mood of the fantasies was more important for the women. Women were more likely to accord their partners a profession or personality and to have a long build-up, with much enticement and interplay before any sex occurred.

In analysing these results, Ellis pointed to the consistent differences between male and female literatures of erotic fantasies. In male pornography sex is sheer lust and physical gratification, devoid of encumbering relationships or emotional elaboration. By contrast, although modern female literature has increasingly accorded the heroine an interesting career and explicit sex scenes, the basic formula has not changed over the centuries. As an historian of the genre states,[28] 'In all romances, the love story is the central action and the most significant motivating force . . . romances assert and reinforce a woman's desire to identify and marry the one right man who will remain hers for the rest of her life.'

Ellis acknowledges that these consistent differences in fantasies are influenced by social as well as genetic factors. Nonetheless, he emphasizes that their precise nature does fit neatly with what an evolutionary perspective would predict. A 1990 study by Douglas Kenrick provides further evidence of the relative caution and pickiness of women.[29] It examined differences in how demanding the sexes are when asked to contemplate scenarios containing various degrees of commitment. The questions went from criteria for a date, to having sex, to steady dating, to marriage. Men were far less fussy than women when it came to sex, but for dating, steady dating and marriage there were relatively few differences. Kenrick infers that sex means something different to men and women and that it was the different implications of impregnation which caused that difference. However, when a relationship beckons and the outcome could involve investment in a child, both sexes take a more careful look at the partner's personality and other, nonphysical attributes.

In accord with this evidence of women's greater caution are the studies suggesting that women are more influenced than men by their peers in mate selection. A series of four,[30] for example, showed that women were more likely than men to give low scores for dateability of photographs of men if they were told negative things about him. Whereas men were only influenced by how attractive the women in the photographs were, women were more concerned to obtain additional information. The authors concluded that since men are so influenced by looks (supposedly for evolutionary reasons), as far as they are concerned, all they need is to see the potential mate. Women, by contrast, are supposedly seeking a potential support system and they need more information than just a pretty face. Because they are concerned to maximize their offspring's chances, they are especially attuned to negative information which may, in the long run, be more crucial than the positive (a man may be rich but if he is also feckless and wild, it may be more important to know about this than his bank balance).

Another difference is in sexual jealousy between the sexes, found in studies in America, Japan, Germany, Holland and Korea.[31] Samples were asked which of two scenarios would upset or anger them more: (a) imagining your romantic partner having sexual intercourse with another person, or (b) imagining your romantic partner becoming emotionally involved with another person. 85% of women were more worried by emotional involvement, whereas this was true of only 40% of men. Again, the inference made is that men are more worried about another man stealing their chance to reproduce selfish genes whereas women are more concerned if their support system – which is assumed to rely on the man being emotionally involved with them – is threatened.

Evolutionary theorists maintain that all these findings are remarkably consistent with their explanation of the differences between the genders. They also argue that the sheer extent of the evidence and the pervasiveness of these patterns throughout history should be taken into account in assessing whether theirs is the most plausible explanation. However, the argument is far from being over.

As noted, there are major methodological objections to this theory, most notably, that it is not falsifiable and whenever it encounters apparently insurmountable contrary evidence (such as that high-status people reproduce less than low-status people), the theory simply changes to accommodate the new facts (or in the case of Herrnstein and Murray, brazenly incorporates it as support for a subsidiary argument). Just as Freud and Marx's theories were criticized by Karl Popper[32] because they did not allow the possibility of disproof, there is a suspicion that the same is true of sociobiology.

But equally important, social, economic and even biological explanations may also account for all the evidence presented so far, without any need to posit evolved inherited tendencies at all. This becomes especially clear in the discussion of why it is that men prefer younger partners and women, older.

Douglas Kenrick carried out a series of related studies to address this question, followed by a peer commentary.[33] Three of the studies analysed preferred age differences stated in dating advertisements in singles magazines in America, Germany and Holland. Three others examined actual age differences upon marrying in different time periods and towns in America, and in a Philippine island. In all the studies, women preferred older men and did so at all ages. For the men, however, Kenrick identified a new finding: the preference for younger women did not become pronounced until the men began to age. Whether marrying or seeking a date, the older the man, the greater the discrepancy in age, but when young they were as likely to prefer an older woman as a younger one. As they got older, they sought relatively older partners so that the age gaps increased and the age of preferred mates rose. Kenrick explained this new finding by the fact that when a man is in his teens or early twenties, it does not matter if a woman is slightly older than him in evolutionary terms because she still has many years of potential reproduction ahead of her. It is only when a man reaches his late twenties or older that his female contemporaries cease to be as fertile and have a shorter reproductive career ahead of them.

In the peer commentary on Kenrick's paper, a basic objection was that his theory of why men preferred younger women is untestable[34] because Kenrick states that the motivations of men in seeking younger mates are unconscious. 'We do not envision a male saying to himself: "I am interested in young women so that I can have more offspring." ' Their behaviour 'reflects adaptations that may operate below the level of consciousness'. The ironies of such a position are considerable for psychoanalysts who have had to deal with the criticism that there is no way to test their theories of unconscious motivation, or Marxists criticized for arguing that the proletariat's participation in the capitalist system can only occur so long as they suffer from 'false consciousness'. Exactly the same objections can be raised about the status of Kenrick's theories as were directed at them by Popper: how can such claims be tested?

Another damaging argument,[35] as with the critique of Buss' paper, raised by one of Kenrick's critics is that there is no need to posit these hypothetical unconscious motivations because the pattern may reflect simple economics. 'If women tend to value economic security and so seek a man who will be a good provider, and if younger, more attractive women are more likely to achieve this goal, a young wife is a sign to the world that a man is a good provider, and that he has wealth and possessions. The young wife is a symbol of material success just like a prestige car, and is valued for the same reason.' This is a perfectly feasible explanation: over history, societies nominated youth in women as a prized commodity and men competed for it; women, unable to achieve wealth or status in any other way and recognizing that youthful beauty is what men most want, offered it to the best of their ability or settled for low wealth and status. Although greater equality of the sexes is gradually coming about, perhaps the continued pattern shows that old social habits have not yet died out.

Of course, this theory does not explain why, of all the possible other attributes (such as height or weight), it is youth and beauty that have been given such primacy by males. Nor does it explain why almost every society everywhere has always apparently placed this premium on these attributes. But it remains a perfectly plausible theory and all sorts of evidence that is normally wheeled out to support the evolutionary position can be used to support this one. Numerous studies of social mobility, for example, reveal that women are more likely to rise up the social system through marriage than men and there is abundant evidence that this occurs because of a bartering of female beauty for male status.[36] In a study of girls in the USA in 1920,[37] they were rated for attractiveness in their teens. By 1958 most of them had married and it was found that the more attractive the girl had been in 1920, the greater her likelihood of having married upwards, particularly for originally working-class girls (although it applied to middle-class ones too). Just how large a weight is attached to beauty in this society may have been demonstrated by a more recent study of mobility in the early 1980s.[38] It showed that a woman was more likely to rise up the class system through marriage than a man was through his occupation. Another study showed that the more attractive a woman was in high school, the greater her likelihood of marriage, the younger the age of marriage and the higher her household income 15 years later.[39] A straightforward correlation between the occupational status of men and the physical attractiveness of their wives has been shown.[40] Also in accord with the 'beauty as status symbol' theory is the fact that males tend to be given higher status evaluations by both male and female peers if they have an attractive partner.[41] In another study,[42] unattractive men compared with attractive ones were actually seen as having the highest income, occupational success and status if they had a beautiful partner – they gained directly from the association. This was not at all the case for unattractive women paired with attractive men. The women achieved no increase in perceived value of any kind.

There is no need for recourse to evolutionary theorizing to explain all this, it can be argued, if the well-established 'equity theory' of attraction can do so.[43] All men and women exist in a marketplace of desirability, so this theory goes, and there are numerous currencies for evaluating one's value. Everyone positions themselves on a hierarchy of attractiveness and seeks out a mate of similar value. To aim too high would be to risk losing the partner to a higher-status competitor and to aim too low would be to undersell your value. Men trade their power, status, wealth and personality, females trade their facial and bodily beauty. Thus may a wealthy, fat and unattractive middle-aged male be coupled with a thin, young and attractive female. That the currencies used by the sexes are so consistently different may have to do with the way anatomical differences became expressed in social systems, rather than a psychological gene insisting on this preference. In past times, the superior physical strength of males made that a virtue in the hostile and dangerous environments and as societies became more sophisticated, this was translated into symbols of power and wealth in men. For women, the need to start reproducing young was paramount in a world where one in four infants died and where life was liable to be short. Thus, women's youth and male status came to have a premium but there is no need to assume this was ingrained in our genes – it was inherited through social systems.

Another theory that dispenses with the need for unconsciously evolved psychological traits points to the simple fact that women of reproductive age are always in much shorter supply than men. The menopause removes the option of conception for women in their forties or early fifties whereas men can continue to fertilize an egg, at least in theory, throughout their life. Inevitably, this creates a practical pressure on both men and women to reproduce whilst the woman is young, and over many millennia, this pressure would be incorporated into social systems and cultures. There is no need for an unconscious mechanism to be inherited genetically if all societies have to adjust to these facts to survive.

Against these critiques of Kenrick's paper, there were several peer comments in support of his thesis. A number disputed his evidence that young men do not prefer younger partners and argued an even more extreme evolutionary case: that all men everywhere actually desire pubescent girls, if only they dared admit it. One[44] pointed out that when men are young, younger females are often 'stolen' by older men, reducing the numbers available. When males are in their early teens, anatomy and social taboos prevent them chasing pre-pubescents, leaving no option but to go for same-aged or older women. These practical limits, it was suggested, might conceal a basic preference for nubile, pubescent girls since in evolutionary terms, these ought to be at the highest premium because they are most fertile and with the longest reproductive future. The fact that older men raise the age of their declared preference might reflect fears at losing a mate to a younger man. One author[45] presented a list of reasons why older men would be reluctant to admit even to themselves that they preferred 13-year-old girls: the laws relating to underage sex, the likelihood of rejection by such girls, the stigma of lechery and social taboos against large age gaps such that a wife might be younger than a daughter. As he put it, an advertisement stating 'Rich male octogenarian seeks 13-year-old virgin' would be more likely to attract the attentions of the police than suitors fitting this description. The real test was provided by societies where these constraints and stigma do not exist and he listed 11 references to polygamous, patrilineal societies, mostly in tropical regions, where this was the case. 'In those societies, men, irrespective of age, clearly prefer pubescent girls, and the value of women (expressed in bridewealth) declines with age.'[45] In this 'system of unconstrained male preference', men often took girls as wives who were younger than their granddaughters. Supporting this view[44] was another author who analysed 26 similarly structured subsistence societies. Arguing that men will always seek partners as near to puberty as the system will permit, she cited non-Western societies in which the average male age at marriage is in the early twenties with wives an average four years younger. In five such societies where the average male marrying age is in the thirties, the average wife was 12 years younger. As regards the fact that preferences are older in more developed nations, it was pointed out that the average 25-year-old woman is able to make herself seem much younger than her developing-world peer of the same chronological age. In poor societies, the ravages of childbearing start at a younger age, protection from the elements is less, nutrition and health is worse and there are no cosmetics (or cosmetic surgery) for enhancing youthfulness. Thus, in stating a preference for 25-year-olds the man in the developed nation may actually be preferring the equivalent of a 16-year-old from a developing nation.

Many studies show that men of all ages favoured child-like, very youthful features in women.[46] Michael Cunningham, for example, asked 75 male undergraduates to rate the attractiveness of black-and-white pictures of the faces of 23 averagely attractive women and 27 Miss Universes.[46] He carefully measured how much the faces corresponded to the typical features of small children. The males were most attracted by faces with combinations of large eyes, small nose areas and widely spaced eyes – all infantile characteristics. A second study reproduced this result and also showed that men made more positive assumptions about attractive women with such characteristics, believing they would be better at raising children, would be more self-sacrificing and so on.

A final contribution to the peer commentary of Kenrick's paper pointed out[47] that males are more rigid and specific than females in their sexual propensities and that the evidence of what these are for all age groups is to be seen in *Playboy*, *Penthouse* and other soft-porn magazines: youth is prized. If older men truly preferred older women, rather than simply adjusting their standards according to what is realistic, there would be separate magazines for the older man with pictures of older women, since there are magazines for almost every imaginable sexual preference. This argument could also be applied to women's consistent lack of interest in pornography directed at them. Despite innumerable attempts over the years, no publisher has succeeded in devising a way of packaging naked men's bodies or explicit sex scenarios which sell to women, nor is there any market for pictures of pubescent boys directed towards women.

This question of what men would do if unconstrained can also be asked of women. As noted above, Buss' study of 100 men and women found that the richer women became, the more they valued high earnings and status in potential mates. Kenrick presented a study of dating advertisements in the upmarket magazine *The Washingtonian*.[33] It showed that the wealthy women still preferred similarly aged or older men despite having no economic necessity to do so (cf. Townsends's female medical students' and undergraduates' preference for high-status men). The wealthy men, by contrast, preferred much younger women. One respondent[48] to Kenrick's paper reported a study of 1,800 couples from the Herero-speaking peoples of North-West Botswana as a further example of unconstrained womanhood. In this society, the women inherit as much as the men from their parents and only half of them ever marry. Marriage is seen as particularly irksome by rich women and they have freedom to do as they please in sexual matters. Nonetheless, in this situation – where the rich women have no practical social or economic pressure to choose an older man – they still prefer same-aged or older men.

CONCLUSIONS CONCERNING SEX DIFFERENCES IN ATTRACTION AND DESIRE

It is far from clear to what extent the consistent differences in attraction and desire are explicable by nature or nurture or a combination of the two. Some of the facts fit more readily into an evolutionary explanation, others fit better with the social and economic theories.

The attraction of women for older, wealthy men, for example, fits at least as snugly into the economic model as the genetic one. Given that men control wealth and status, and older men control more thereof, it stands to reason that this would be attractive. The fact that women who were raised to make 'a good catch' for a husband continue to try to do so even when there is no need could easily be a matter of conditioning. Why posit an unscientific unconscious genetic tendency to be so attracted when such a commonsensical alternative exists?

Other facts are less easily explained away. Why is the desire of men specifically for youth and beauty so pervasive? Why are there no societies in which other physical traits, such as extreme tallness, or psychological ones, such as quick-wittedness, are not more valued by men? Likewise, the differing attitudes of women to sexual intercourse would seem to have, at the very least, a biological basis (fear of pregnancy or sexual disease). How else can we explain the endurance of these differences after 30 years of widespread access to the contraceptive pill?

If present trends towards greater sexual equality continue, the answers to many of these questions will become clearer in 50 years' time when the great-great-granddaughters of feminism are grown up. In the meantime, there are a number of unhappy implications arising from what has been presented above.

EFFECTS OF SEX DIFFERENCES IN ATTRACTION AND DESIRE ON GENDER RANCOUR

Men are at odds with themselves, with each other and with women over their sexuality. So are women.

The enduring sex differences combined with the enlightened attempts to change them have created a duality in modern culture. On the one hand, most couples still have a conventional age gap and the old battles of the sexes in and out of bed continue apace – the annoyance of women that men are not more romantic, the wish of men to be allowed to get on with watching sport on TV and to roll over after sex. This is faithfully and constantly reflected, as well as reinforced, by mass popular culture – BBC1, ITV, the tabloid newspapers. On the other hand, there is a strong tendency for women to protest that they want a new order and for men to pay at least lip service to this ideal. This new agenda is strongly reflected in the 'quality' media – BBC2, Channel 4, the broadsheet newspapers – and it trickles through to the mass media from time to time (e.g. it is part of the hidden agenda of the once Alternative Comedians who are now part of the mainstream, such as Ben Elton, Dawn French and Jennifer Saunders, Lenny Henry and Harry Enfield). The new agenda is also enshrined in equal-rights legislation and finds its way into mass consciousness through teachers, welfare and health workers, local government and other state-funded agencies.

But it creates a great deal of criticism and aggression which can become self-criticism and depression. If men admit to themselves that they are most attracted to young and pretty women, they risk feeling guilt and frustration. If they admit these predilections to other men, they risk criticism or alternatively, becoming part of 'Men Behaving Badly', defensively 'sexist' cliques. If they admit their feelings to women they risk alienating or upsetting them.

If women admit to themselves that they are attracted to older, wealthier men, they are in danger of feeling they have 'sold out' or that they are 'not being true to myself'. If they admit such leanings to other women they risk sneers or hostility. If they admit such feelings to men they risk feeling dominated and powerless.

The issue of dominance is a pivotal one. Whether caused by nurture or nature, there are innumerable studies showing that women are attracted by it as a personality characteristic in men and equally, that men seek to display it. For example, in a series of three studies in which large samples of young women were shown scenes in which men behaved dominantly or subordinately, the women were far more likely to deem the dominant attractive.[49] Studies examining adjectives associated with being 'male' stress dominant ones like 'assertive', 'self-confident' and 'leadership'.[50] One study identified four characteristics as strongly male: achieve success; do not be dependent; be aggressive; and avoid classically female behaviour.[51] The equivalent lists for women either omit dominance or specify 'low dominance'. Where people behave in ways that run counter to these stereotypes the studies find they pay a social price. Passive, dependent men and aggressive, assertive women are liable to be unpopular.[52]

However, there is a crucial difference between male dominance as opposed to aggression or bullying behaviour.[49] Women are distinctly unimpressed by these latter but unfortunately, these are precisely the behaviours that men are most likely to display when their attempts at dominance are thwarted. Thus, as women become more assertive in and out of bed during the courtship process and as they are increasingly perceived as a threat in the workplace (however illusory this may be, as we saw in the last chapter), so men may feel threatened and be more likely to become aggressive, at its worst, becoming violent or sexually abusive.

As an illustration of this I will end with a disturbing story.

An attractive, assertive 22-year-old woman recently picked up a barman from a late-night drinking den in Notting Hill, attracted by his 'fantastic bum', 'tough, no-nonsense attitude' and 'all-round hunkiness'.

They went back to his place and, divested of her outer clothing, she announced that penetration was not on the agenda, as she sometimes does. The man began shouting but soon they settled down and resumed snogging. The cycle was repeated twice more with a gradual increase in the intimacy after each outburst. Finally, down to her knickers, she decided to call it a night. The man was absolutely incensed and she had to make a run for it, finding herself standing almost naked on the pavement in Ladbroke Grove with clothes and abuse raining down from his window in equal measure.

She feels some contempt for men, as well as enjoying their desire for her. She despises them for being motivated by lust and wanting to 'use' her; yet this is often true of her attitude to them. She was perfectly well aware that her behaviour with the man was likely to provoke him and was open about enjoying frustrating him.

To a certain extent, this was just a case of a New Woman setting limits. Sometimes she does not feel like intercourse and it is surely a healthy development that a woman like her does not feel she has to go 'all the way' just to please the man. However, she did say that the whole scenario was given added spice and made more explosive by the fact that the man was black and from a working-class background, whereas she is upper-middle-class and white. Whilst this precise kind of incident may still be relatively rare, there can be little doubt that more and more sexual relationships entail a women of higher status, power and wealth. The complicated interplay of the woman's attraction to a man's dominant characteristics and her desire to be in control is undoubtedly making it harder and harder for men and women to get along.

Whatever the truth about our fundamental proclivities, let us hope that the period we are living through is a transition to something more harmonious, so that men and women can feel more on each other's sides and less at each other's throats.

Chapter 7

Pills

Solutions For The Low-Serotonin Individual,
Part I

Preceding chapters identified a wide variety of ways in which advanced capitalism fails to meet our needs for status and attachment, thereby lowering serotonin levels, but, as Americans are rightly wont to say, 'If it ain't part of the solution, it's part of the problem.' The time has come to offer the practical implications of my analysis.

Some readers may feel that any serious suggestion that antidepressant pills be considered as a 'solution' is preposterous, reasoning along the following lines: 'Pills are merely elastoplast for the soul; advanced capitalism wins at both ends, not only profiting from making us miserable but making money from treating the sickness it has nurtured, as well. By stoking individualism and expectations, advanced capitalism stimulates widespread discontent, deprivation and insatiability, creating ever more diverse consumers in search of ever more fetishistically precise consumer predilections. But these material solutions to emotional, spiritual and social lacks leave us perpetually dissatisfied. It is outrageous to suggest that the "solution" to this emotional holocaust is to swell the coffers of the drug companies.'

I shall make my view of these and other general issues clear in Chapter 9. In the meantime, I believe there is a pragmatic case to be made that antidepressants are a 'least worst' short-term expedient for a suffering individual, even if they are not The Answer for society-wide relief. However unsatisfactory either antidepressants or therapy may seem to the reader, these are the two most effective and least damaging recognized methods for raising individual levels (I shall not attempt to evaluate the innumerable 'alternative' and 'New Age' methods, all of them largely scientifically untested, some – such as the role of diet – with a

241

more plausible theoretical foundation than others – e.g. astrology – useful though I believe some of them can be).

In fact, the evidence concerned with pills and therapy leaves a great deal to be desired. Whilst there is sound proof that both can reduce symptoms of depression, there is little known about why they do so and the studies are lamentably crude for the most part. Because the vast majority of the studies of pills are funded by commercially motivated businesses, they are very carefully directed towards obtaining the information necessary to convince the relevant government bodies that the product is sufficiently safe and effective to warrant a licence to be sold. Vast areas of scientific knowledge are ignored altogether in favour of these goals and government research bodies have done nothing to fill the gaps. For example, for wholly political reasons, very little research has been done to see if antidepressants that raise the serotonin levels of violent men make them less so – despite the fact that almost all experts in this area are convinced that they would do so. Or, to take a broader issue, virtually nothing at all is known about the subjective experiences and implications of different brands because the drug companies seem totally uninterested in this matter, either because they want to fund only the bare minimum necessary or more probably, because they fear the questions that such studies might provoke. Given that tens of millions of citizens in the developed world are already taking antidepressants and that it is highly probable that ever higher proportions will do so in the future as the drugs become more effective, this is worrying. For example, one obvious effect could be on the creativity of our artists and scientists, many of whom are depressive and whose creativity expresses the harsh Depressive Realism described in Chapter 2. Antidepressants could dull this fierce hunger for unsparing truths because they almost certainly foster the Positive Illusions found in undepressed people ('humankind cannot bear much reality') and whilst it might make our creative community happier if they took the drugs, it could cause a major depletion in the quality of their output.

Despite its large size, it is a simple matter to summarize the conclusions of the literature concerned with antidepressants. The thousands of scientific reports read like briefing papers for the drug companies' marketing departments rather than a disinterested search for truth and they leave a great many unanswered questions. In the absence of a scientific alternative, I shall do my best to address these through case histories and anecdote, drawing on my own interviews with users of antidepressants, interviews I have done with psychiatrists and published examples.

Similar problems are found with regard to the evidence regarding therapy, the subject of the next chapter. On the whole, the psycho-dynamic therapists (see Appendix III for definitions of the varieties of mental health professional), whose approach ultimately can be traced back to Freud, are far more interested in treating patients than in scientifically testing out the effectiveness of different therapies. This is not simply because they are scared of what such testing might reveal. Either such therapists tend to be escapees from empirical, medical approaches to emotional problems and are precisely not interested in traditionally scientific methods (e.g. psychiatrists who feel heartily disappointed thereby) or they have little training in scientific disciplines. For these reasons, there has been a regrettable lack of research testing the efficacy of dynamic therapies. The recently emerging cognitive therapies are more concerned with scientific evaluation. However, they can be criticized as being superficial both in terms of the therapies themselves and the way they measure success or failure. Their evidence is far from conclusive.

Thus, in my discussion of the merits of both pills and therapy for raising the individual reader's serotonin levels, I shall have to resort to case histories and anecdote to a large extent, or to put it bluntly, much of what comes in this chapter and the next is opinion. Wherever available, I cite relevant scientific studies but for many of the issues, there is little or none. I begin with an introduction to the kinds of antidepressant and then present a more detailed analysis of which ones seem to be most suitable for which low-serotonin problems.

AN INTRODUCTION TO ANTIDEPRESSANTS

There are four main modern antidepressants used in Britain, available from General Practitioners to anyone reporting the relevant symptoms, which raise serotonin levels and end the depression of two-thirds to three-quarters of sufferers, without any significant side-effects. Surely, it might be said, if it is as simple as that, need we look any further for the solution to the low-serotonin individual? But, of course, it is *not* as simple as that. For one thing, many people feel a distaste at the idea of taking pills for their emotional problems; for another, there are many reasons to question the widespread use of such drugs in a mature society.

If few people bring no prejudices to the issue of the use of pills to treat emotional problems, there is also a great deal of ignorance about the most basic facts. The most common confusion is between antidepressants (e.g. Prozac) and antianxiety drugs such as Valium. Most people realize that Valium is addictive and that it creates a glazed, dozy, worry-free and unreal existential state. But Valium or any of the barbiturates are not used to treat depression and with the exception of two antidepressants which are slightly addictive (called Paroxetine and Citalopram, although neither is nearly as addictive as Valium), modern antidepressants neither addict nor glaze.

I can exemplify their experiential effects from a television documentary that I produced for BBC2 in 1995 (entitled *Prozac Diary*). Five artists agreed to be filmed over a period of three months during which they took Prozac, to see how it affected their creative work. Two were unambiguously helped by it. Rock star Bernard Sumner (whose most famous bands were called Joy Division and New Order) had not written any lyrics for his new album after 15 months. The musical backing was complete but whenever he sat down to write words for the songs a hyper-critical voice began to trash his attempts as worthless. Likewise, poet Alan Jenkins (whose day job is deputy editor of *The Times Literary Supplement*) had been blocked for over a year. He also heard a 'belittling voice' running him down when he put pen to paper. He told me that 'when my last book won a prize the effect was to shut me up completely. I was terrified of doing something that wasn't nearly as good and have produced nothing more than the odd desultory scribble since.'

In both cases, the self-attacking stopped once the Prozac had kicked in, they became less moody and melancholic, allowing their muses to return. Sumner said, 'On the drug, I didn't put barriers in front of myself any more. There was still an element of self-criticism but it wasn't self-destructive. Prozac put things into focus. It helped me deal with small problems, which made my life feel more enjoyable.' He did not have the glazed, unreal or sedated feelings that are typical of Valium, feeling more, not less alert.

In Jenkins' case, after six weeks a poem emerged 'out of nowhere'. Although he agreed that taking the pills had made him less hard on himself, less self-belittling, he was careful to say that he could not be sure that it was the Prozac that had freed him up. He told a journalist that 'I can't discount several other possibilities. Maybe I just have a natural rhythm of not doing much, then having a burst. Maybe being involved in the TV project, I was curious about what turned some cogs. Getting things off my chest with Oliver certainly had a therapeutic effect' (we discussed his emotional life at some length during the filming; as we shall see, the combination of antidepressants with therapy can be the most effective approach of all). Jenkins also described himself as more vibrant and able to cope with everyday difficulties.

Interestingly, the drug seemed to change the content of their work. Sumner's lyrics are notorious for their darkness but on the drug, his usual themes of wrecked relationships and emptiness (his most famous song, 'Blue Monday', began with the words 'How does it feel to treat me like you do?') were given a rest. 'I'm less sad on the drug so my lyrics are less sad,' he said afterwards. Jenkins had hoped the drug might broaden out the subject matter of his poems from perennial concerns of the death of his father and problems in relationships and he was not disappointed. He wrote a poem about post-colonial Britain and the culture of greed in the City. 'I don't usually write poems in somebody else's voice. This was from the standpoint of an Essex Boy who gets obsessed with the trading floor and over-reaches himself. It's exciting and new. It's not about my trouble with girls any more.'

I shall return to the issue of what effect antidepressants may have on creativity but for now, the point is that Sumner's and Jenkins' psychic experiences were very typical of Prozac takers and yet very different from Valium, with which many people confuse them.

SOME BASIC FACTS ABOUT ANTIDEPRESSANTS

There are two main families of antidepressant, the Tricyclics and the SSRIs (Selective Serotonin Reuptake Inhibitors).

The antidepressant effect of the Tricyclics (so named because of their triadic molecular structure) was discovered by accident in the 1950s. Today there are several dozen available but the most commonly used is called Dothiapin (brand name Prothiadine), with Imipramine and Amitryptyline close behind. They are known as 'broad spectrum' drugs because they affect a great many brain chemicals. Their efficacy is thought to be mainly through acting on another brain chemical (noradrenaline) rather than serotonin. Because they are so scattergun in their action, they have a great many side-effects.

By contrast, the SSRIs were specifically developed to be cleaner and only to raise serotonin levels, first becoming available in the late 1980s. SSRIs have much fewer side-effects because they do not affect such a broad spectrum of brain chemicals. The four main SSRIs used in Britain are called Fluvoxamine (brand name Faverin), Fluoxetine (Prozac), Sertraline (Lustral) and Paroxetine (Seroxat), although there are several others (some of them supposedly a Third Generation because they affect noradrenaline as well as serotonin).

Numerous studies comparing the two families have shown they are equally effective in reducing depression but there are two major advantages to the SSRIs: their lesser side-effects mean patient are much less likely to discontinue taking the pills and they are not fatal when taken in overdose (whereas Tricyclics are one of the most commonly used drugs in suicides, a study of 87 Prozac overdoses found that half of the patients noticed no effects at all).[1] To this can be added the fact that, experientially, SSRIs are vastly superior.

The textbooks list side-effects of Tricyclics such as dry mouth, sweating, constipation, tiredness and drowsiness but they rarely make any mention of the most common experiential effect: a glazed, unreal, zombie-like deadness that seriously undermines the patient's well-being even further. Because drug companies have not explored the true subjective experiences associated with different drugs, there is no scientific evidence of this but it is a major reason why SSRIs are so superior to Tricyclics – most SSRI users report feeling more, not less alive.

Given the undeniable superiority of SSRIs in most cases of depression, it might seem surprising that of the 5.6 million prescriptions for antidepressants made in Britain in 1995 (three-quarters of them to women), 45% were for Tricyclics.[2] This is far more than can be justified on clinical grounds. Whilst it is true that there are patients who respond to Tricyclics and not to SSRIs and there are also some who find the side-effects of Tricyclics less problematic, between two-thirds and three-quarters of depressed patients younger than retirement age respond well to SSRIs. The main reason for such a widespread continued use of Tricyclics is probably cost. A month's treatment with Dothiapin is approximately £4 and Imipramine costs £1. Prozac costs about £20 a month so that every patient who is on Imipramine rather than Prozac is costing £228 a year less and those on Dothiapin represent a £192 saving. Precisely how these facts have been translated into prescribing behaviour is not clear, although doctors are made increasingly aware of their drugs bill and the Department of Health certainly does not pressurize doctors to use SSRIs rather than Tricyclics. But given the considerable disadvantages of Tricyclics, in most cases, it is hard to avoid the advice to anyone under 65 who has been prescribed a Tricyclic by their General Practitioner, to challenge the decision and check that it has been made on clinical rather than financial grounds (when I gave this advice in a newspaper article, several irate doctors wrote to complain, but their main argument seemed to be that it would cost the National Health Service an extra £100 million to prescribe SSRIs to those on Tricyclics – proving my point).

The crucial problem with Tricyclics is that the rates of discontinuation caused by side-effects are far greater than for SSRIs. All the studies find statistically significant differences in discontinuation, although on first sight the percentages do not seem all that dramatic: 15% discontinuation for SSRIs versus 20% for Tricyclics (averaged out from three large meta-analyses).[3] However, a large proportion (88%)[4] of Tricyclic prescriptions are for lower doses than those recommended by the manufacturers (to avoid side-effects) and the meta-analyses which produce the 15% versus 20% difference take no account of dosage – if the comparison was made between drop-outs given the full Tricyclic dose and SSRI takers, it would be much higher. Thus, the real rates of discontinuation of Tricyclics are much higher than this where the full dose is prescribed: as high as 60% according to one leading authority.[5]

On top of this, the lower-than-recommended doses often do not reduce depression, so the patient has less incentive to continue. A patient who discontinues prematurely is much more likely to develop a further bout of depression within four to six months.[5] Between 30% and 50% of discontinuers do so, whereas patients who continue are much less at risk.[5] Between 80 and 90% of people who suffer a bout of depression eventually suffer a subsequent one if they come off the drugs.[5] For this reason, the leading British authority in this field argues that the drugs should be taken indefinitely in most cases, to avoid recurrence.[5] The implications of this position are daunting: at least one fifth of the population would be on SSRIs for life if this advice were adopted by everyone who suffers from symptoms that are treated by SSRIs (depression, Obsessive Compulsive Disorder and eating disorders). Indeed, I think it is very possible, nay, probable, that at least this proportion of the population will be taking serotonin-enhancing drugs within 20 years (see Chapter 9).

WHICH SSRI?

Given that SSRIs are the best compound for most cases, which is best for which problem? Again, the scientific evidence is to say the least equivocal. As we saw in Chapter 1 (and Appendix II) there are a large number of emotional problems and behaviours which have been shown to correlate with low serotonin levels in humans, yet at present, SSRIs are only licensed for use to treat depression, OCD (Obsessive Compulsive Disorder) and eating disorders. A GP cannot legally prescribe them to treat aggression and violence, alcoholism, cocaine addiction, ecstasy use, gambling, chronic fatigue and ME, smoking or sexual addictions, despite the fact that every one of these has either been demonstrated to be helped by SSRIs or has been shown to correlate with low serotonin or depression and therefore is likely to benefit from such drugs. I suspect that for political and commercial reasons (discussed below and in Chapter 9), neither the drug companies nor the governments of the developed world have encouraged research proving that SSRIs would reduce these problems, even though the potential market for the manufacturers would be immense.

Another problem is the extremely shallow nature of the research that has been done. Although experienced clinicians tend to agree that there are some generalizations to be made about which drugs are better for which problems, the published research utterly fails to study the issue properly. A simple example is the evidence regarding sexual side effects, an acknowledged problem with all the SSRIs (as well as the Tricyclics). In the case of Prozac, its manufacturers claim that sexual dysfunction is found in about 3.5% of cases and this is the figure I have been cited by the company several times. However, there is a large body of evidence to suggest that the true figure is at least ten times greater, anywhere between 30% and 70% of all users (see footnote 6 for discussion of how the drug companies obfuscate this).

In the absence of adequate evidence I shall present the best advice I have been able to cull from clinicians with extensive experience of the various drugs, explaining the side-effects and the existential experiences commonly connected with them.

SIDE-EFFECTS OF THE SSRIS IN GENERAL

For reasons not yet known, it usually takes two weeks before the anti-depressant effect of SSRIs (and Tricyclics) begins. If no effect has occurred after four weeks it is rare that any occurs, although in some cases it can kick in after six weeks.[5] During the initial stages of treatment, for most people there may be some mild side-effects, although these are usually fleeting, and in many cases there are no side-effects at all for the whole of the treatment. Thus, in reading the following list of ailments, the reader should bear in mind that most people do not suffer them and that almost all drugs cause side-effects for a minority of users.

Approximately one quarter to one third of patients treated with SSRIs for depression either experience no improvement or suffer sufficiently severe side effects to discontinue taking the drugs. In other words, the drugs work for two-thirds to three-quarters of depressed patients.[7]

Between 25 and 30% of SSRI takers suffer some nausea during the early stages, 3–4% so severe that they discontinue.[7] Other gastrointestinal problems can include stomach cramps, diarrhoea, constipation, flatulence, dry mouth and vomiting.

The second most common problem is headaches, experienced by 16% of SSRI takers.[7] Insomnia is found with some of the drugs and with others, sleeping too much. Sexual problems may include lessened libido, delayed ejaculation, difficulties in obtaining a sufficiently stiff erection and for women, delayed or absent orgasm. Some of the drugs can increase anxiety.

Pros And Cons Of Specific SSRIs For Specific Problems: Depression

A psychiatrist (who could be any of 15 psychiatrists that I have interviewed, but am presenting in this way to protect their anonymity and that of their patients) summarized the different merits and problems associated with the four main SSRIs as follows:

'Fluvoxamine (Faverin): not very good as an antidepressant, works with OCD, makes everybody sick.

'Fluoxetine (Prozac): that stimulant, "better-than-good" effect. There can be sexual dysfunction, hypomania [i.e. hyperactive thought and behaviour], agitation in the early stages.

'Paroxetine (Seroxat): better effect on anxiety but at the cost of sedation. Also has sexual dysfunction and a definite withdrawal syndrome [i.e. is addictive].

'Sertraline (Lustral): sub-Prozac with a shorter half life [i.e. it remains in the body for a shorter time – Prozac stays in the body for six weeks, whereas Lustral is all gone two weeks after discontinuation]. Can be an advantage on sexual problems if stopped on a once-a-week basis – you can not take it on Friday and Saturday mornings, still feel OK and be all set for a Saturday Night Special. Less sedating, less antianxiety, wider dose range than the others.'

Broadly speaking, this was the view of all the psychiatrists I spoke to: Prozac and Lustral are the best SSRIs for depression, Faverin is not as effective in reducing depression and Seroxat has more side-effects, as well as being addictive. However, the evidence on the considerable sexual side-effects of Prozac[6] and my own impressions from cases I have encountered suggests that of the two, Lustral is the least problematic in most cases because it is widely acknowledged that Prozac is more likely than the others to cause severe anxiety in some patients. Since anxiety is found in a high proportion of depressed people, this is a considerable problem.

A psychiatrist gave me a typical example of a case of anxiety provoked by Prozac. 'I saw a young lad recently – nothing very dramatic. He had the standard adolescent family conflicts, had been a little bit stressed out and then his girlfriend dumped him and he got quite depressed and he went to see his GP who put him on Prozac (not as a first reflex, the GP waited a bit). Two weeks after starting on Prozac he was manic, with all the typical features of that – rapid thoughts, hyperactivity and so on. We withdrew the Prozac obviously and within a week he was very much back to his previous self. I've seen that more often with Prozac than with other drugs, although what literature there is suggests it's not more common with Prozac.'

More typical was another case. 'I saw a woman psychologist, who had had postnatal depression in about 1987, treated with Imipramine. She got well, stayed on it for nine months to a year, came off it. Two to three years later she had a further episode of depression, not baby-related. It was treated with Prozac and she got well in a very typical way for that drug. The differences between the two drugs, as reported by her, were: on the Imipramine she got well but she knew she was drugged; on the Prozac she got well but she felt her normal self. The only abnormality was that she popped a pill in her mouth every morning.

'She was a high achiever, rather perfectionist. She had a non-specific viral infection which required her to take several months off work, then she got a thyroid infection, and it was after that that she had the second episode, a clear-cut depressive illness. The first episode had to do with having given birth to a daughter and stopping work. She needed the ego boost of her career. She's been completely well for donkey's years since, still taking Prozac. She tries stopping it, but she finds herself going back to depression so she just remains on it and is well.'

Some further examples of the difference between Prozac and Tricyclics were provided to me in response to a newspaper article. Mrs Kathleen Finney, 66, of Stoke-on-Trent had spent 15 years suffering periodic bouts of depression treated with Tricyclics, but they only slightly reduced the gloom and had considerable side-effects. 'I sweated a lot, had a dry mouth and felt groggy. I wasn't really myself.' Before taking Prozac she 'couldn't face another day, it was agony to even get up', but within a few weeks of taking it she was no longer depressed. She also said her personality altered radically. 'My family noticed it. I used to be very snappy and criticized them all the time. Now they say, "It's a pleasure being with you, Mum."' A quiet, withdrawn woman throughout her life, she became far more sociable. 'Before, if I went out I tended to shy away from people, I didn't like them to ask me questions. Now I'm just the opposite. I start conversations, I've become really outgoing.'

A 26-year-old mother of three for whom Tricyclics had been 'like wading through thick dough', reported a similar experience. 'I was always tired, irritable and the kids couldn't do anything right. Now I'm calm and can cope.' Again, it was not only the depression that had been treated. 'Within a week I was completely different from how I've ever been. I've started going out and I talk to people about myself. I have joined Weightwatchers and for the first time in my life I feel really confident.'

This raises the interesting question of the alleged effect of Prozac on personality as well as mood. It was first identified by Peter Kramer in his best-selling book, *Listening to Prozac* (1992, London: Fourth Estate).

'Prozac represents a change in mankind's relationship with himself,' he told me during a telephone interview in 1992. '20–30% of people who take it aren't just returned to the state they were in before they became depressed. Their selves are completely transformed.'

In his book, Kramer presented the example of his patient Tess. After years of psychotherapy she was becoming progressively less energetic and more unhappy. First of all Kramer prescribed a Tricyclic and the depression partly lifted. But Kramer felt there were still signs that Tess was not functioning to her full capacity – although she considered herself no longer depressed – so he raised the dose. When that led to side-effects he switched her to the newly launched Prozac, since it was reported to have fewer side-effects.

His object, he wrote, in prescribing the new drug was merely 'to return her to her premorbid (undepressed) self, not to transform her' but the effects, within a few days, were 'astonishing'. Tess arrived at his surgery looking quite different. So was her manner, more playful – teasing even – compared to the old seriousness. Very soon her social life changed. A pattern of intense co-dependence on abusive men was replaced by lots of dating, with a new-found-ability to enjoy the attention of men and to carry out the experiments in courtship that her earnest, un-self-confident former self had been incapable of. The poisonous cocktail of low self-worth, lack of competitiveness, fear of jealousy, shyness and fear of intimacy evaporated.

As time went by, she changed her friends. Some left because they had only been able to relate a depressed Tess, new ones were attracted by her newly sanguine personality. A masochistic attraction towards screwed-up, depressing people disappeared. She was able to move away from the town where her (deeply depressed and depressing) mother lived and to maintain a better emotional distance. At work she became less conciliatory, firmer, less afraid of confrontation and negotiated a big pay rise.

Kramer was amazed by the extent of the difference between the effects of the Tricyclics and Prozac. After nine months, Kramer took her off the Prozac. To begin with the transformation continued but after eight months Tess felt she was slipping back. What Tess told Kramer then made him realize just how fundamentally different this drug was. 'I haven't felt myself since I stopped the Prozac,' she said. The un-medicated self was less truly 'her' than the drug-affected one. After much soul-searching Kramer prescribed Prozac again. In doing so he had to acknowledge that he was giving it not as a treatment for depression. Tess was a normal, mentally healthy woman. The pills were to enhance her performance at work and play and to enable her to be herself. Kramer suddenly registered the enormity of what was happening. He had begun to medically improve the normal and healthy, or as he called it, to engage in Cosmetic Pharmacology. 'Here was a patient whose usual method of functioning changed dramatically,' Kramer said of the Prozac'd Tess. 'She became socially capable, no longer a wallflower but a social butterfly. Where once she had focused on obligations to others, now she was vivacious and fun-loving. Before she had pined after men; now she dated them, enjoyed them, weighed their faults and virtues.'

Kramer maintains that a key factor in the effect of Prozac is the way people react to losses, rejections and being alone. We all react to disappointments: a date stands us up, a bad grade or critical review; the rejected business proposal, grant submission or application for promotion. Perhaps a friend announces he is moving away, a phone call is not returned, an expected invitation doesn't arrive. All of us feel a visceral response when let down, a feeling of weakness, confused thoughts, sadness and world-weariness. For most of us the leaden feelings pass; but not in a significant minority. They are more easily provoked into these feelings and they last longer when rejections happen. Such extreme reactions to loss and disappointment are not a mental illness, but they tend to profoundly affect the quality of life. Kramer reports that Prozac often transforms delicate flowers into robust plants.

His patient Lucy's mother was shot dead when she was aged ten. She grew into a woman terrified of rejection in relationships, always putting men first, and presenting a damaged self-image. In therapy she revealed that if her boyfriend merely looked away at the TV for a moment she felt distressed. She hated it if he said 'I' instead of 'we' when describing events they had shared to a third party. She would be listless for a week if she saw him talking to another girl. She set magical tests of whether he loved her: If I set my book down will he do the same? Will he notice the pin I'm wearing?

On Prozac these fears and irrationalities evaporated. Suddenly, whether alone or with her boyfriend, she no longer expected their relationship to collapse. Because she was one of the patients who suffered side-effects, she was unable to take Prozac for long but even this short period was enough to show her a different way. When some of the rejection fears returned, with the help of normal psychotherapy, she was able to get on top of them by comparing them to how she had been when on the drug.

Kramer believes her fears were caused directly by her mother's murder, an environmental rather than a genetically inherited cause. But the experience was encoded in her brain, had a physical expression in the lowered serotonin levels that made her chemically terrified of even the most fleeting separation or loss of attention from loved ones. Simply by taking Prozac, the chemical expression of the trauma was reversed and subsequently, the reversal could be sustained through the talking cure of psychotherapy without the need for more chemicals (Kramer is not against psychotherapy; he works as a psychotherapist and spent two years in psychoanalysis at the mecca of Freudianism, London's Anna Freud Centre).

Eli Lilley, the makers of Prozac, deny that it affects personality as well as mood, but since there have been no proper studies to test the 'Better-than-well' hypothesis, they are hardly in a position to do so. I have certainly encountered such reactions and so have many of the psychiatrists I have interviewed. One told me: 'I've been prescribing Prozac since 1988 – quite early in this country – so the numbers of patients I have prescribed it to is well into the hundreds, perhaps 300. One is aware of those people who run on Prozac 10% above normal.

'Doctors are often pretty bog simple. If you give someone Prozac and they're "better-than-better" you think you've done a "better-than-better" job. There are patients where there isn't a single symptom of hypomania, sleeping entirely normally, their thought-speed and generation is entirely normal, it's just that it's positive and they are happy and smiley. I think it is a phenomenon specific to Prozac, I don't see it with any of the other SSRIs. The wife of a colleague of mine is intermittently on Prozac and I always know when she's on it because she's great, she's wonderful, and then she comes off it and I never understand that wholly. There is no reason for her ever to stop taking the drug, I think. When she comes off it she's miserable, she resents her husband's work.'

The case for trying Prozac over Lustral is that it does seem to work 'better-than-well' for some people. If the patient does not have anxiety as well as depression, if they are fortunate enough not to suffer sexual or other side-effects and if they are one of the 'better-than-well' minority, then it is best. But the proportions fitting all these categories are probably small.

Some psychiatrists mentioned that it was possible to reverse the sexual side-effects with still other drugs. 'I tried Citahepridine, an antihistamine which also affects some of the serotonin receptors. The result is that it temporarily reverses the sexual dysfunction, it's short acting, for three or four hours. But like many antihistamines, it's quite sedating, so you either get lucky or you go to sleep. I've used that in a dozen patients and in three it's very clearly worked. I had a chap just the other day, an American who's on 80mgs of Prozac [the largest dose]. He's been on all the SSRIs and got partial sexual dysfunction with all of them. But he's noticed a marked difference using Citahepradine, and so has his wife. But he's also noticed that he gets knocked out by it.'

Most psychiatrists (and patients) would prefer not to have to give drugs to compensate for side-effects and Lustral seems less likely to require it. Although none of the psychiatrists said that Lustral ever made patients 'better-than-well', they agreed it was less side-effect-ridden, particularly with regard to sex and anxiety. An interesting example of a Lustral case was described by one psychiatrist: 'A woman who had a typical upper-middle-class upbringing had a rather fierce Lieutenant-Colonel kind of father. She was brought up with low self-esteem, the mother was a bit of a doormat, the boys went off and had careers, the girls – it was a case of 'find somebody nice to marry, darling, and how about a cooking course'. She had chronic low self-esteem and she found a husband who is a large rugby-playing, fundamentally perfectly nice, but rather rigid, authoritarian type – her father figure. She became depressed after she had had a couple of children. She was vegetating at home, her husband working harder than usual, with no sense of self or achievement once the children had grown up a bit. She had had a bit of therapy and had identified what some of the issues were but continued to feel depressed. She was very against the idea of chemicals but eventually took Lustral once a therapeutic relationship had been established with me. Within a predictable number of weeks she began to feel better, and was then able to make use of therapy instead of just having it done to her. She stayed on the Lustral for about nine months and was weaned off it over a further three. She remains well and has been off antidepressants now for two or three years. She had a mixture of straightforward cognitive therapy and more dynamic interpersonal therapy, looking at her relationship with her mother and what she projected on to her husband and so on. [Why did you give her Lustral rather than Prozac?] I gave her Lustral because she was very reluctant to take drugs in the first place having read scare stories about Prozac in the press and she didn't want to be on Prozac.'

The 'scare stories' arose as a result of reports that Prozac increased the danger of acting out in suicidal or homicidal patients. Over 100 cases have been brought against Eli Lilley in America by murderers claiming a Prozac Defence, none of them successfully. No cases have been brought to court in Britain. The research shows that Prozac does not increase suicidal or violent behaviour.[8] However, some psychiatrists admit that in a tiny minority of cases it is conceivable that Prozac could have this effect. One psychiatrist said, 'Everyone knows about that aspect of Prozac. It enhances anxiety in a significant percentage of patients. It's sometimes something quite different from anxiety. It's an inner psychic restlessness, a bit like the restless legs that some antipsychotic medication creates so you want to wander around, but psychically. A restlessness of the mind that is often not the same as anxiety. I suspect that it's that kind of feeling in the very rare patients who machine gun their granny or jump off the bridge whilst on Prozac.'

For this reason, many psychiatrists are reluctant to prescribe Prozac to anxious patients or ones who have persistent and specific thoughts about committing violence against themselves or others. Nonetheless, given that at least 10 million people have taken Prozac worldwide, if it does ever cause acting out that would not have otherwise happened, it must do so extremely rarely because even the drug companies would not be able to deceive us about that.

Regarding Seroxat, the studies suggest it has as good an antidepressant effect as Lustral and Prozac but the psychiatrists felt it was only suitable for a minority of patients.[1] 'The main problem is that quite a lot of people seem to find Seroxat is a sedative. A lot report tiredness and it's difficult to know whether to increase or decrease the dose. The manufacturers promoted themselves in their original licence as having dual-acting effects on depression and anxiety. The sedating effect reduces anxiety in some, although with many they end up taking it at night rather than in the morning because they feel so sleepy.

'Of all of them it has the highest incidence of withdrawal syndrome. It comes on pretty abruptly, not long after the last dose was skipped. It's terribly reminiscent of the Valium argument. People said, "Yes, you get a recrudescence of what was there before", and then they said, "Maybe it isn't", and it isn't – it happens to patients who have never had a day of anxiety in their life. The main features are nervousness, depressed mood, sometimes sweating, sleeplessness, nausea, anorexia, all clearly distressing and relieved within an hour by taking a Seroxat pill. I suspect the incidence is quite high. It can happen with all the SSRIs but way ahead of the field is Seroxat.'

In conclusion, Prozac may be worth trying first for older people less concerned about sexual problems who are not anxious or potentially violent. But for a great many cases, the more obvious SSRI in treating depression is Lustral.

SSRIs For OCD (Obsessive Compulsive Disorder)
All the SSRIs have been shown to work with OCD, although they usually require a dose that is three to four times the one recommended for depression.[9] The psychiatrists claimed that it often takes a lot longer to

have an effect on OCD than on depression – several months rather than two weeks. Of the SSRIs, Faverin was said to be the most effective but unfortunately, it also seems to have a high incidence of side-effects. 'Faverin came in quite early, before Prozac, and I think they got the dosage schedule wrong because it seemed like everybody who went on it felt sick and it's not such a good antidepressant. It has a particular use for OCD, the best of the SSRIs. That's certainly the opinion of the OCD experts in this country.'

The main alternative considered by clinicians is a Tricyclic which is the only one to raise serotonin levels significantly. Unfortunately, its side-effects seem to be at least as problematic as Faverin. A psychiatrist said, 'The general view is that the Tricyclic Clomipramine (brand name Anafranil) is the best drug for treating OCD, albeit it's got all sorts of side-effects – sweating is the worst. But it's the Tricyclic which hits the serotonin. I tend to use Faverin now because Anafranil tends to be so troublesome with side effects. If anything Faverin has less anti-depressant effect than Anafranil. I personally wouldn't hand Faverin out for depression at all, some people do probably because they got into the habit.'

One example of a successful treatment with Faverin was as follows. 'He was a nice American guy, 35, who presented with anxiety attacks and depression and in the course of the interview revealed a massive and longstanding OCD. Although he'd had treatment, the OCD had never been focused on. He had classic obsessions with numbers, the way things were arranged, and elaborate rituals to do things in particular ways. He came from an American-Italian Catholic family so there were issues around sex. It emerged he had been celibate since a drunken homosexual incident 15 years previously when he had gone off with some man he'd met in a bar, had oral sex and for 15 years been convinced that he had HIV, which formed the basis of many of the OCD compulsions – was he an evil person, rituals to ward off evil and so on. He was quite depressed too and we treated him in hospital initially with behavioural therapy and Faverin and over two or three months he got steadily better and then was able to start looking at the deeper-seated issues of sexual identity, etc. His sex life was always masturbatory, but he didn't have a problem with that except that his imagery was homo-erotic. I still see him occasionally from time to time. He gets the odd flicker of OCD but is able to handle it, knows what to do to handle the anxiety and is making slow progress on the sexual issues. He started on the maximum dose and is now down to the minimum and will probably come off it altogether.'

SSRIs FOR EATING DISORDERS

Both anorexia and bulimia have been successfully treated with large doses of SSRIs, especially Prozac.[9] However, because Prozac (and all SSRIs) reduce appetites of all kind, including for food, some studies show that it decreases eating in anorexics.

Several of the Prozac takers interviewed by me in connection with a newspaper article had been cured of eating disorders by Prozac. An ex-anorexic who had been close to death said that after six years of trying everything else, the drug has saved her life. 'It was as though I had spent the last six years seeing everything through a dark haze, now I see in colour. I do still have off days but I am much better with people and have become a much warmer person.'

Since eating disorders are similar to the compulsiveness of OCD and since between one and two-thirds of OCD sufferers are also depressed, it is sometimes hard to establish whether the Prozac is directly affecting the eating disorder or reducing OCD symptoms or depression.[10]

SSRIs FOR AGGRESSION AND VIOLENCE

Given the mass of evidence that aggressive and violent animals and humans are liable to have low serotonin levels (see Appendix II), it might be expected that SSRIs would help people with these problems. However, the use of drugs to contain violence is such a hot political potato that research has not progressed much in recent years.

Some of the leading researchers, like the American Emil Coccaro or the British Community Psychiatrist Dr Veronica O'Keane, believe that if impulsively violent men (who account for most violence) were treated with drugs, many would become better able to find constructive outlets for their aggression. You might imagine Tory Party Home Secretaries would have leapt at the idea, although they have not. It ought to be of more than passing interest to New Labour and Tony Blair as well. 'I feel that socialists should be in favour of testing this thesis out – it may be the best chance some young men will get,' says O'Keane. But so far the idea has not been taken up by any political party or by mainstream psychiatry. There are two main reasons.

The first concerns the fears about Prozac. In 1990 a scientific paper suggested that it could cause suicidal and homicidal behaviour.[11] Soon afterwards these claims were shown to be false[12] but the damage had been done. Solvay Duphar, a company which had begun a research programme to develop 'Serenic' drugs to treat violence, hastily abandoned it. It became impossible for researchers to get funding. 'I cannot think of a single drug company that has got a research programme in this area today, although it would be a big market. The drug companies were scared off by the publicity,' I was told by Ted Dinan, Professor of Psycho-pharmacological Medicine at London's St Bartholomew Hospital.

The second reason was a rash statement made by a top American researcher in 1992. Dr Frederick Goodwin was alleged to link violence among inner-city youths to the violent behaviour of monkeys in the wild. 'The same hyperaggressive monkeys who kill each other are also hyper-sexual, so they copulate more and therefore they reproduce more,' he said.[13] Few commentators doubted that he saw more than an analogy between the monkeys and those Blacks who are aggressive and promis-cuous who figure so disproportionately in America's violence statistics. These comments were linked to findings by researchers[14] who had received grants from Goodwin in his role as head of the US National Institutes of Mental Health. These studies claimed to be able to distin-guish recidivist from nonrecidivist violent boys with an 84% accuracy using tests of serotonin and glucose levels.[14] Given that Blacks are the group to whom his findings would most apply in America, this claim translated in that country as meaning 'We can distinguish the dangerous violent Blacks from the relatively harmless.' Referring to violent youths in an earlier paper the same author had written, 'In such persons experi-mental treatment with Serotonergic drugs should be initiated.'[15] The response to Goodwin's utterances stigmatized as racist any mention of research into the use of serotonin-enhancing drugs to treat violence and scared the living daylights out of the drug companies. The issue became highly politicized and Dr Ron Walters, a vocal Black critic of Goodwin who believes that treating the social and economic causes of violence as physiological is the politician's easy way out, stated that 'The politicians are supporting this medical strategy [SSRIs for violent boys and men] because for one thing, it really gets them off the hook. They don't have to spend as much on social strategies as they would if they accepted that violence is caused by poverty. To deal with it you have to spend signifi-cant sums of money to enrich the lives of people in inner city areas.'[16]

Thus, research into the use of SSRIs ground to a halt in 1992 and has not recovered. However, before then a good deal of evidence had already accrued. The first studies were done on rats and monkeys. Left to their own devices, rats are liable to launch unprovoked and sudden attacks on mice (known as muricide). Rats with low levels of serotonin are more likely than ones with high levels to be muricidal.[17] Muricidal rats with low serotonin levels were injected with Fluoxetine (Prozac) and became less so. When levels were raised using drugs with other species, the result was the same.[18]

Regarding humans, as long ago as the 1970s it was shown that prescribing the antidepressant drug Lithium reduced aggression, at least in part because of its effect on serotonin levels.[14] In the mid 1980s a drug named BuSpa was proven to reduce violence in mentally handicapped patients by raising serotonin levels and it is still commonly used for this purpose. Three studies of depressed patients showed that they were less prone to anger attacks (outbursts of rage and impulsive, explosive aggression) when given Prozac.[19] The only study currently being done is by Emil Coccaro in America. He has been following 40 impulsively aggressive men and women over the last four years. He told me, 'They are the sort of people who may fly off the handle for no apparent reason. They start screaming and shouting hysterically when in traffic. They get violent – women as much as men – towards their spouse and may throw things.' The results so far clearly show that taking Prozac makes this kind of behaviour much less common. Says Coccaro, 'One guy was a comedian but when hecklers got to him he would charge down off the stage and attack them. He was losing gigs and in danger of being banned from the circuit until he took the drug that raised his serotonin levels.'

A definitive study would be needed to prove Coccaro's case with regard to violence. A large group of impulsively violent men would be given SSRIs and the degree of their aggression compared with an equivalent group who believed they were also being given the drug (in fact, they would be given a 'placebo'). Ted Dinan predicts that 'Those on the drug would become less impulsive than those not on it – the only question is by how many more. If the results were as impressive as seems likely, the widespread introduction of such treatment could have a major effect on violence statistics. The Medical Research Council (the British government research body) should fund the study if the drug companies won't.' Based on treating violent men already, clinicians such as Dr O'Keane in Cambridge are confident the approach would work. She described one of her patients: 'A man came to me after he had seriously hurt his wife – given her a real beating. He felt terrible about it and desperately wanted to change. The antidepressant drugs helped him to drink less and his violence ceased.'

I could not find any leading psychiatrists who disagreed with the idea that SSRIs would be likely to reduce impulsive violence. However, some raised practical problems. Although Professor Malcolm Lader of London's Institute of Psychiatry agrees that the pills would reduce impulsive aggression, he sees major potential pitfalls. 'Would young men actually take the drugs or just pretend to, perhaps to satisfy probation officers or court orders? A lot of them might not be motivated to do so if they suffered side-effects. Sexual problems such as delayed ejaculation and even impotence are quite common; they would be completely unacceptable to most young men.' This could rule out as much as 30 to 70% of men taking Prozac but Lader admitted there are already alternative drugs (such as Lustral) available that have fewer side-effects and he is convinced that within 20 years there will be side-effect-free drugs available.

It is interesting, also, that there seems to be a closet sexism in public responses to the idea. It will be recalled that violence and depression are closely linked – three-quarters of convicted violent men are depressed, much more than nonviolent convicted criminals – yet men are much less likely to be prescribed antidepressants than women, preferring to self-medicate with alcohol and other 'drugs of solace'. In 1995, there were 4.1 million prescriptions for antidepressants made out to women, compared with only 1.5 million for men. Nearly one half of low-income mothers are prescribed psychoactive pills (tranquillizers and antidepressants) by their doctor at some point in their lives. Little is heard about this fact, yet public uproar greets talk of their husbands and sons also receiving drug treatment. Apparently it's alright for women to take these pills, but for some reason if young men do so it connotes Aldous Huxley's *Brave New World* or the Thought Police of George Orwell's *1984*.

Thus, for people who are suffering at the hands of violent intimates or who are themselves violent, there is already good reason to suppose that SSRIs will help. Obviously, Prozac is not the first candidate but Lustral could make a considerable difference to paranoid, impulsive spouse-beaters or young men who routinely get into scraps, alike. However, in order to persuade a GP to make the prescription it would be necessary to convince them that there are symptoms of depression – which in many cases will be true.

SSRIs For Other Problems

As noted above, there is evidence that low serotonin levels or depression are strongly associated with a great many other common problems of modern life and therefore, if SSRIs were prescribed, it is highly probable that they would alleviate them. Appendix II shows that alcohol abusers are liable to low levels and that treatment with both Prozac and Lustral can reduce alcohol use and help abstinence. There is persuasive evidence that ecstasy use reduces serotonin levels and good reason to suspect that many users are medicating depressed mood (see Appendix II). Five small studies where cocaine users have been prescribed SSRIs found it helped them to abstain.[20] Likewise, seven small clinical studies of people with personality disorders (such as impulsiveness and narcissism) found that SSRIs reduced anger.[21] Sexual obsessives were helped by the drugs.[22] There are a number of other problems which might also be helped: compulsive gamblers tend to be impulsive, smokers and sufferers from chronic fatigue are more likely to be depressive, all might benefit.

However, the drug companies are curiously reluctant to fund studies testing these (extremely plausible) applications of their products so that their licences could be extended to cover them, despite the fact that they could result in huge revenues. It is unlikely that the companies do not want to sell more of their products so there must be other, presumably political reasons why they are not pressing ahead with such research. One may be that they are extremely sensitive to the accusation that they are trying to extend the use of pills to treat problems of everyday life, rather than medical illnesses. The fuss over Prozac and violence undoubtedly scared them and they are well aware that the furore caused by the addictive nature of such drugs as Valium is still fresh in many memories. A second reason could be that the cost to the National Health Service would be considerable and they would face governmental opposition. But perhaps most fundamental of all is the huge resistance of the British public to the idea of the widespread use of pills.

PROS AND CONS OF SSRIS AS A TREATMENT FOR THE LOW-SEROTONIN INDIVIDUAL

The author and comedian Stephen Fry formulated the following paradox: 'The world is divided into two sorts of people: those who divide the world into two sorts of people and those who do not. I fall resolutely into the latter category.' Despite Fry's admonition, I would hazard that the world is divided into two sorts of people when it comes to treatments for emotional problems: a basic, gut inclination towards either pills or therapy.

People attracted to pills want a simple, mechanical solution, to treat chemicals with chemicals. They are also more likely to believe that problems have a physical cause, be they genetic or physiological. They are reluctant to 'blame' their parents and sceptical that a lot of pussyfooting psychobabble is going to help. By contrast, those attracted to therapy are liable to say that they want a 'natural' solution and that they 'do not like the idea of putting a chemical into my body'. They may not want a 'blame the parents' ethos either but they like the idea that their problems are not genetic and have a social or childhood origin and they may enjoy the feeling that they can gain control of problems through using their thoughts and words in therapy. Very few people start out with an open mind in this area and will countenance both therapy and pills. There is a profound antipathy towards the mindset and solutions of each group by the other (if you do not believe me, conduct a simple experiment: raise the subject of their desirability in the pub or at dinner; you can talk all you like about sex, politics or religion, but beware of lighting the 'Prozac-versus-Therapy' fuse).

Not that Britons are by and large enthusiastic about pills or therapy. Most would prefer to have nothing to do with either. You have to be mildly depressed to live in Britain – self-disparaging, falsely modest, undemonstrative, emotionally deadpan. We will take a lot of convincing that it would be better to become show-offs (as we refer to people who are open about their achievements), whether drug- or therapy-induced. We seem to rather like feeling bad. But if push comes to shove, forced to opt for one or other the reasons given for our position are rarely very rational.

In the case of people who dislike pills (I shall deal with the anti-therapy camp in the next chapter), they often believe that prescription drugs for physical illnesses are fine, but not pills for the mind. 'If it makes you feel good it must be morally bad' is their attitude. Most are happy to correct nutritional deficiencies with vitamins or to pursue a 'healthy' diet, yet they boggle and recoil at ingesting antidepressants. They want to believe in a 'natural me' yet medical artifices have been heavily influencing the course of their lives since before birth, have even caused their conception or offspring in cases of Artificial Insemination. 'I would never use artificial ways to change my personality,' says a friend across the dinner table, his normal reticence loosened by a long draught from his fourth glass of wine and the lighting of another cigarette. 'I'd rather be the real me than something a drug has made me.' But it is illogical to regard a drug with horror if it rids you of unwanted faults, makes you far better able to enjoy your life and is harmless, just because it was manufactured by Eli Lilley or Wellcome. To prefer the products of the British American Tobacco Company or Arthur Guinness – proven to be life-threatening – is downright perverse. American psychiatrist Gerald Klerman described these attitudes as Pharmacological Puritanism (initially he used the word Calvinism): 'If a drug makes you feel good, it not only represents a secondary form of salvation but somehow it is morally wrong and the user is likely to suffer retribution with either dependence, liver damage or chromosomal change, or some other form of medical-theological damnation. Implicit in this theory of therapeutic change is the philosophy of personal growth, basically a secular variant of the theological view of salvation through good works.'

Another fear is that pills could spell the end of Great Art. My BBC2 documentary about artists on Prozac partly bears this out and partly contradicts it. Observing what happened when artists were on or coming off Prozac seemed a good way of anecdotally exploring Freud's theory that artists are motivated by angst.[23] According to him, art is barely distinguishable from a neurotic symptom – such as a phobia about travelling. Within this theory, a childhood trauma can be equally expressed by writing a novel or by irrational fears. The only difference is that the artist uses a fiction – a story, a painting, a song – to express their emotional turmoil by inventing a more acceptable reality or one that distances them by putting it at one remove. Nonartists with the same trauma would simply be neurotic about travelling. Prescribing moody artists Prozac or seeing what happened if they stopped taking it seemed a good method for exploring this idea: chemically remove the angst by pills and would they still be creative?

Novelist Michael Bracewell had suffered from panic attacks ever since he was a teenager. Two years before I met him they had escalated to the point where he was virtually incapacitated. 'I remember sitting in a cafe drinking some hot chocolate thinking, I am a severed head. I was morbidly aware of the constraints of my skull. I actually considered trepanning because it seemed such a limited space inside my head.' He was desperate to get on with his fifth novel. 'I was due to go to Amsterdam but my doctor was very dubious that I was well enough. The idea of travelling across London – let alone going in an airplane – was not something I wanted to even think about.' The doctor prescribed Prozac and within a few weeks the words were flowing and his anxiety attacks had ended. He took the drug for 15 months and wrote a novel (*St Rachel*) about a man on Prozac.

When I first met him he had decided to come off the drug to see whether he could write without it. Removing angst by taking Prozac had helped, rather than hindered his writing, contrary to what Freud's theory would predict. Stopping the drug was also revealing. Five weeks after doing so, the anxiety attacks were returning. He had the feeling that he was not in his body, that he did not exist. As a way of countering this, he decided to write a novel in the first person about a man with a strong sense of identity. 'If nothing else it should be good displacement therapy,' he told me. Three weeks later he had written the opening paragraphs, including, poignantly: 'I was brought up to believe it's wrong to talk about yourself. How do you earn the right to tell your own story? Other lives have to describe your own.' Alas, that was about as far as he got. Soon after writing those words he suffered an horrific panic attack.

He put the novel to one side and accepted a contract for a nonfiction book about Englishness.

The problem was that the fictional first-person character was him. 'First-person narrative has to be distanced from the self otherwise it becomes autobiography. What I wrote was too close to being me,' he said afterwards. As he had put it in the fragment he had been able to write, 'other lives have to describe your own'. He wondered whether, instead of using his novel as a therapist, it would be better to visit a real one. He preferred this idea to going back on Prozac because he dislikes the idea of being beholden to a drug.

Bracewell's experiences with Prozac both contradict and support Freud's theory. On the one hand, if the theory was right he should have been less productive when on the drug – angst-free he should have lost his motivation – and more able to write off it because more fuelled by angst. On the other, as Freud suggested, Bracewell clearly did try to use his art as a way of relieving angst, albeit unsuccessfully.

As noted earlier, poet Alan Jenkins and rock lyricist Bernard Sumner seemed to have been helped to overcome mental blocks by taking Prozac, contradicting Freud. However, both bore Freud out in that they drew inspiration from difficult childhoods and troubled emotional lives. Unlike the other artists, the distinguished painter Michael Heindorff did not suffer from depression, but he was eager to see how the drug would affect his unusual feelings about painting. Off the drug, he felt the canvas told him what to paint next, that he was almost governed by the marks on the canvas and that he was not responsible for what happened. This dated back to an infancy afflicted by severe eczema (an itchy skin disease). He was strapped to Bakelite tubes to stop him scratching himself, and because he had to be passive he developed a heightened visual awareness. His home was full of paintings and he would spend happy hours imagining himself living in them, a place more comfortable than his itchy, scarred real life. This gave him his feeling that the paintings have volition and control as an adult artist. On the drug his relation to the canvas changed. He had a greater sense of being in charge. 'I feel more responsible for the work, that it is more willed. I am less doubting, less pondering and scratching my head waiting to see what comes next.' That Heindorff's artistic impulse dates so clearly back to his childhood is consistent with Freud's ideas. However, if they were totally right, the painter should have lost his will to paint on the drug.

A final, fascinating example was the novelist Alice Thomas Ellis. Considering that her husband Colin had only died three months before, she seemed remarkably cheerful when I first met her but it soon became apparent that she had not fully grasped that he was lost forever. 'It hasn't sunk in at all that Colin's really gone. I just don't have the feeling that he's gone very far. His presence in this house is just so real, it's just his house, every inch of it, every area, it's implicit with his presence. The fact that he's dead hasn't altered anything,' she told me.

Alice lost a son when he was 19. The experience of losing Colin and her reaction to it were very different from the experience of losing her son. 'My son had a fall and went into a coma for 11 months and then he died. I wanted to tear up the garden and rub earth in my hair and claw my face with my nails. But I haven't had that feeling with Colin. I think I'll be married to him to the end of my days.' Alice had tried Prozac once before Colin's death but not for long enough to have an effect. She wanted to try it again to help her deal with the chaos his death had caused and to get back to writing novels. 'I'd take any drug that would help me to be a bit tidier. The house is a mess, I haven't even begun to look at all Colin's bits and pieces, his papers and letters and photos. I think my mind would tidy up if I tidied those things up. I can't write in all this mess.' So she began taking the Prozac.

When I returned nine days later, her opening comment was that she was 'sadder and crosser' on the pills. She immediately took me up to Colin's study where she had begun the mournful task of going through his papers. Contrary to what one might have expected, the drug seemed to have sent her into mourning, although she did not like the feeling. 'I don't want to connect with his death, I preferred it before, when I could ignore it. I don't see the advantage in feeling this sad. If there was a pill that stopped you feeling anything, ever, I'd be keen. That was the whole point of drink but I don't fancy it any more, since that blithering pill.'

Her friend Janet Boud, who was nanny to two of her children and is now her full-time assistant, confirmed that Alice had become dramatically sadder since taking the pills and that she no longer imagined that Colin would suddenly reappear, as she had previously done. 'They spent a lot of time apart and it's really only sunk in now that he's gone, not going to suddenly ring her up.' Janet pointed up a further change, that 'she's more assertive', one that Alice also did not welcome. 'Normally I wouldn't get cross but the other day I came very close to telling someone to shut up and go away, which is not my mode. It might be good for me but it's not good for them, is it? I've never been a believer in "We've got to talk this out": if someone irritates me I let them go on and wait for them to leave, then I avoid seeing them for a while. I don't see any point in confrontation.' According to Janet, Alice usually gets others to keep the banished friends at bay. But this had changed too. 'Alice is telling the lies herself, which is much healthier.' However, none of this was helping Alice to get any writing done. 'The *Daily Mail* asked me to write 1,000 words on *Brookside* and I couldn't even do that – not that I can watch it at the moment because they're about to dig up Trevor from under the patio [a plotline in which a wife has murdered her husband].'

Alice felt that she puts her unexpressed feelings into her fictions. Her female characters 'do all the things that I don't actually do. They lose their temper and are frightfully rude to people. So it is an outlet. That's what novels are, they're lies. If I start telling frightful lies myself in my real life maybe I won't write another one. Is the drug going to stop me ever writing again? If I go roaring about the place expressing myself I might stop altogether.'

We next met at the memorial party she held for her husband at the Duckworth's bookshop in Golden Square. Beryl Bainbridge, her long-time friend and fellow novelist, agreed that she had become sadder since taking the pills. She also opined that art is a substitute for life. 'Anybody who does anything in the artistic way, if they had any sense, they wouldn't do it, they'd just be happy and live. They wouldn't muck about on their own.'

Two days later Alice stopped taking the pills. I went with her back to the churchyard in Mid-Wales where her husband now lies, her first visit there since his burial four months earlier. Off the drug she seemed more cheerful again. She compared taking it to stripping off the layers of an onion. 'T.S. Eliot was right, I don't think humankind can bear too much reality. The Prozac puts you in touch with what's really happened . . .' Like the sadness of her husband's death? 'I prefer not to feel that way, so one does take any escape that one can instead of being a brave little soldier.'

Drug-free, the temporary assertiveness had abated, as had the sadness, but the greater consciousness of Colin's actual demise had remained. Her feelings more battened down again, she felt a novel coming on. 'It's that experience of death which so many of my books are about, but coming at it from a new angle.' Her conclusion was that the drug had prevented her writing by making her too self-expressive in real life. She regards suppression of emotion as her central motivation. 'Being brought up not to express one's emotions plays a big part . . . I save up my feelings just to use in books. I think it's politer than throwing yourself about and weeping. The books, I've discovered, are actually a very good outlet in themselves.'

Her last word on Prozac was, 'It put me in touch with something I don't really care for – reality.'

*

My unscientific little experiment neither proved nor disproved Freud's ideas. What this very small sample did seem to suggest is that many melancholy artists – and numerous studies show that artists are more likely than the general population to suffer from some kind of emotional problems[24] – would probably be both more productive and happier if they took antidepressants.

The big question is, whilst such artists may be more sanguine and more prolific, would their art be as good? Personally, I find it inconceivable that Tolstoy would have written *War and Peace* or Charlotte Brontë written *Villette* on Prozac. I suspect that most great art has to be drawn up from a well of despair and that genius will become a thing of the past if too many artists start reaching for the pills, rather than the whisky bottle, which at present is their more usual solace.

The tragedy is that most people are extremely resistant to one or other of pills or therapy. I know of many individuals whose refusal to countenance pills is wrecking their life: after years of therapy they are still depressed and their resistance to taking them is one of their symptoms of depression and associated fear of loss of control. But I know of just as many others whose rejection of therapy is equally harmful: they will take pills but are terrified of addressing the causes of their problems, which might free them from the need to take anything. A psychiatrist described such a man: 'I had a man who said, "This is how I am on these pills and it's great, but I don't like it. It's like having a dirty table and putting a beautiful tablecloth on it and everything looks absolutely wonderful, the candelabra and so forth, but actually the dirty table is still there and unaddressed. What I want is just a normal kitchen table."' Yet when the psychiatrist suggested this person enter therapy because it could totally remove the need for pills if he understood the childhood origins of his problems and developed mental techniques to control symptoms he said, 'Oh no, that's not for me. How could I trust a stranger with my secrets? All that blabbing doesn't help, you might as well take up religion.' The patient's desperate longing for a normal kitchen table was outweighed by his fear of the best means of obtaining it – therapy.

Sadly, the professionals make matters worse by being at war in the background. The therapists tend to see pills as an existential menace and a dangerous threat to their livelihood. The psychiatrists see therapy as a challenge to their power and as something they neither understand nor trust. Extreme ignorance of what each side has to offer the other is rife.

My own view is neither pro-Prozac nor anti-therapy. It is that both treatments can be extremely effective ways, sometimes alone, sometimes in combination, to raise serotonin levels. This may sound like the worst kind of eclectic blurring of the real issues, but I hope that it will become apparent why I take this view over the course of the next two chapters. For the time being, I quote a comment made to me by Peter Kramer, with which I heartily concur. 'Diversity is important,' he said, 'the worst nightmare would be if we all became the same because we were taking drugs. There will always be some people who will say that the pleasure in life is to play the hand that you are dealt and they must be allowed to do so.

'But we are entering an era in which medication can be used to enhance the functioning of the normal mind. The capacity of modern medication to allow a person to experience, on a stable and continuous basis, the feelings of someone with a different temperament and history is among the most extraordinary accomplishments of modern science.'

Chapter 8

Therapy

Solutions For The Low-Serotonin Individual,
Part II

This is not a Self-Help book and it is not my intention to provide a comprehensive guide to how to Climb Out of the Cellar of Your Mind (as Thomas B. Harris' best-selling *I'm Okay, You're Okay* was subtitled). There are already innumerable books that do this, not all of them by 'think positive' American mystics (for example, Paul Gilbert's *Overcoming Depression*, London: Robinson; or Elizabeth McCormick's *Change for the Better*, London: Cassell, offer first-rate advice and guides to self-analysis using cognitive techniques). However, there are some practical applications of the argument of this book for the low-serotonin individual. For what it is worth, at the end of the chapter I shall offer my overall advice regarding pills and therapy (for brevity I shall be using 'therapy' to denote all forms of psychological treatment), pulling together the conclusions of this and the last chapter: be tough on junk thoughts using pills and cognitive-behavioural therapy; but also, be tough on the causes of junk thoughts through psychoanalytical therapies. I end with a statement of the basic implications of earlier chapters for the life and mind of the low-serotonin individual.

THERAPY: INTRODUCTORY

Although the studies of the effectiveness of therapy are as limited and flawed as those for antidepressants, they do at least prove that on the whole, people who have therapy are less depressed afterwards than equally depressed people who had no treatment during the same period.[1] This suggests that therapy can raise serotonin levels (although I am not aware of any research directly testing the idea). Thus, however much the reader may feel a distaste for the whole idea, if you are suffering the

269

symptoms of low serotonin you would be well advised not to dismiss therapy out of hand.

In fact, I do not know anyone who would not benefit from conducting an unsparing inventory of 'the causes of me' with a therapist. All of us would be well advised to attempt to identify the extent to which our particular pattern of traits has a genetic basis, to use the knowledge to moderate and direct our ambitions and work to our strengths and around our weaknesses. We need also to develop as clear and accurate a picture of what went on in our childhoods as possible. Our culture, our dutiful-ness and love for our parents and siblings, coupled with a common terror that we will go mad if we think about ourselves in this systematic way, often create a reluctance to make this inventory. Friends and intimates can be invaluable, but their biases make them unable to do the job fully. That is why I doubt there is anyone who would not be helped to do this by at least a few sessions with a good therapist. On top of the childhood and genetic causes of our problems come the trends that have led to an increase in low-serotonin individuals and therapy can be extremely help-ful in countering these (see the last section of this chapter). However, quite apart from the healthy British scepticism towards such things, I acknowledge that there are substantial, enduring and realistic reasons for being nervous about seeing a therapist.

The first problem is how to decide which sort of therapy is best for you. The term therapy is now so loosely applied that it is almost mean-ingless. There are at least 75 different training organizations for 'psycho-therapists', some of which treatments seem to me to be at best a harmless waste of money (see Appendix III for definitions of different kinds of mental health professionals). I find it extremely hard to believe that there will ever be any scientific reason to suppose that astrologically based treatments are worthwhile, for example. Whilst there may be people who have benefited from astrologer-therapists – just talking about one's life to a sympathetic person can be better than not talking at all – I would take a lot of persuading that the money would not have been better spent on therapists with a more conventional approach. I shall run through the therapies that I consider plausible below.

The second problem, a major one, is in finding a therapist who is any good. When seeking the services of a professional, whether it be a doctor, lawyer or accountant, some are a great deal better than others and the same is true of therapists. It might be thought that, having settled on the right therapy for you, you would be no more likely to end up with a poor practitioner of that particular approach than of landing up with a second-rate accountant to do your tax return. But there are probably far greater variations between therapists from the same training than those from other professions. Training therapists is an inexact science. Any qualified accountant employed to prepare your tax return can generally be relied upon to address all the basic legal requirements, so that the document you sign and return to the Inland Revenue is unlikely to be in breach of the law. Accountants may vary in their ability to give specialist advice (e.g. the most tax efficient arrangements) but they are nearly all capable of doing a legal return. The same is not true of the psychic equivalent. Whereas you could safely stick a pin in the Accountancy section of the Yellow Pages telephone directory, to do the same for the Therapy section would be much riskier. There would be a grave danger of picking one incapable of providing the full psychic audit required in your particular case. This is only one of a number of tricky problems in choosing a good therapist (see below).

What follows is very far from comprehensive. It is a highly selective, personal view. I shall answer the question 'Which therapist?' after considering 'Which therapy?' but first, another question:

WHAT HAPPENS IN THERAPY?

Put very crudely, therapies either start from the premise that emotions cause thoughts or that thoughts cause emotions. The emotion-based approach is the one that derives from Sigmund Freud and psychoanalysis (known as 'psychodynamic psychotherapy'). The thoughts-based ('behavioural-cognitive') approach derives from academic cognitive psychology and behaviourism. But whether the therapy attempts to change feelings through thoughts or vice versa, there are some features in common.

It may be presumed that talking has been a psychological treatment ever since language evolved but the history of formal psychotherapy (as opposed to such practices as Confession in the Catholic church) begins in the mid-nineteenth century when Anton Mesmer's (as in mesmer-ic) dabbling in hypnotism was separated from its mystical and superstitious foundations and considered as a potential medical practice by a Manchester doctor called James Braid. At that time there also existed a method of psychological treatment akin to psychotherapy, involving only rational argument with no hypnosis, known as 'persuasion'.

In 1886, Freud witnessed Charcot's demonstrations of hypnotism in Paris to treat hysterical patients, began using it himself and to evolve his emotion-based theory. Not a particularly skilled hypnotist, Freud soon decided he could achieve equally effective results by asking his patients to lie on a couch and give voice to whatever thoughts came into their minds. Called 'psychoanalysis', this technique has been the foundation of all psychodynamic psychotherapy, spawning a large number of variants. Below I present a separate section devoted to the effectiveness of psycho-analysis, illustrated with a variety of cases, since it is the Gold Standard for therapies in this tradition.

The behaviour-based tradition can be traced back to 1920s techniques of 're-education' allied to the development of theories of conditioning, based on rewarding and punishing animals. In the early years of the century, the Russian Ivan Pavlov conducted the famous experiments which demonstrated that dogs could be trained to salivate on presenta-tion of a previously neutral stimulus which had become associated in their mind with food – without any food actually being presented. The implication for humans was that, as a result of punishments or rewards, they might also develop associations. For example, if your father beat you with a slipper as a child, in later life you might be seized by a sudden nameless terror on passing a shoe shop with a particularly prominent dis-play of slippers.

It was not until the 1950s that much attempt was made to apply these theories to psychiatric problems but since then, a wide variety of tech-niques have been shown to modify behaviour. The thought-based cogni-tive therapy developed as a related approach. Whereas behaviourists sought to change cognitions through changing behaviour, cognitive therapists targeted cognitions first. Many approaches today combine both approaches in Cognitive Behaviour Therapy but the cognitive is increasingly paramount.

In very general terms, what happens in psychodynamic and cognitive-behavioural therapies is as follows. The patient is usually referred to the therapist by a GP or a psychiatrist. Many psychiatrists (i.e. doctors trained in the administration of chemicals or electricity for physically treating mental illnesses) have also had some training in therapy (plenty also engage in it without any training). However, it is of course both legal and quite common for patients to hear about private therapists by word of mouth and to refer themselves.

In all therapies, at the outset the patient outlines the problem as they see it and the therapist will generally discuss what aspects are to be treated. The aims of the work will be considered and the possible length of treatment specified. At this point the two types of therapy diverge.

In psychodynamic therapies, the patient is encouraged in subsequent sessions to describe the problem and to exemplify it, with the therapist prompting for details of how the patient felt, thought and behaved at the time. In general, the therapist says little to allow the patient to use the time to think aloud. Emotionally painful subjects that the patient might prefer to ignore may be raised by the therapist and their contribution to any difficulties considered. As themes emerge, the therapist is likely to return to them. To a greater or lesser extent, the patient may be asked about their childhood experiences and connections made with present-day problems. Patterns which may have made sense in the past but which are being inappropriately carried into the present may be pointed out. Alternative ways of thinking, feeling and acting are offered. The patient's ideas about the therapist may be a focus of attention supposedly demonstrating patterns of relationship carried over (or, 'transferred') from childhood. Thus, if the patient repeatedly accuses the therapist of making critical judgements, the therapist may draw the patient's attention to the fact that a parent behaved like this and that the patient now assumes that such criticism will occur in intimate relationships (known as 'transference'). The therapist may also pay close attention to how the patient makes them feel, regarding this as information about how **the patient** may be feeling now or in the past.

In cognitive-behavioural treatments there is a tighter focus on targeted patterns of thought and behaviour which are agreed as requiring change. The therapist is generally much more interventionist than in psychodynamic treatment, asking the patient to rehearse and adopt various practical behavioural and cognitive strategies for change. For example, some behaviourist therapists will treat a person with a phobia about spiders by very gradually familiarizing them with the animal, first through thoughts and finally through actual exposure to spiders. By contrast, psychodynamic therapists will rarely if ever attempt or suggest specific practical solutions.

What both approaches have in common is that they work through talking and listening, they attempt to build the patient's morale, they entail a release of emotion and they offer a rationale for what is wrong and how to put it right.

With these generalities in place, let us consider the different therapies and how to find the right therapist.

WHICH PSYCHODYNAMIC THERAPY?
Evidence as to whether psychodynamic as opposed to cognitive-behavioural methods are more effective is scant, nor is there a clear scientifically based indication as to which problems are best treated by each. Such research is costly and poses awesome methodological difficulties and as a result, although there have been numerous studies of the effectiveness of both approaches,[1] all of them are flawed. For example,

in many of the studies of the psychodynamic therapies the person rating whether the treatment has succeeded or not is often the therapist – hardly a very independent source – and the definitions of what is deemed success vary greatly. In the case of cognitive treatments, the outcomes measured are often very crude so that it is impossible to establish how profound has been any change. Studies comparing the two approaches are often not comparing like with like, so that the dynamic therapists may be concerned with intangible existential outcomes such as changes in the 'sense of self' or degrees of 'narcissism', whereas the cognitive therapists are measuring brute numbers of times an agoraphobic patient has left their house per week or the number of negative verbal statements per hour. Comparing these kinds of entities is a bit like trying to compare the validity of the concept God with the numbers of cans of Coca Cola sold per year in different nations – they are different logical types.

Overall, the studies suggest that therapy is broadly better than no therapy but to say that anything more than this has been definitively proven would be to overstate the value of the evidence. No studies have yet been conducted in a way that could produce results that can be relied upon as regards which therapy is best. Whilst it would be possible in what follows to cite research chapter and verse in support of my views, in practice all I would be doing would be wheeling out flawed studies that happen to suit my prejudices, so I shall not make any pretence that what follows is anything more than opinion based on my clinical experience, discussion with other clinicians and reading.

SOME GENERALIZATIONS ABOUT PSYCHODYNAMIC APPROACHES

The psychodynamic approaches can be divided up according to the amount of practical and emotional commitment demanded. In terms of commitment, there is a continuum:

HIGHEST . . . . . . COMMITMENT . . . . . . *LOWEST*

Psychoanalysis . . . Psychodynamic . . . Brief Dynamic . . . Counselling
Therapy   Therapy

Full **psychoanalysis** is the therapy which is most ambitious in its goals and it is also the one that costs the most time and money – at least £100 a week, requiring one session every weekday, on average for six years. It is also the only one in which the patient always lies on a couch.

Psychodynamic therapy demands a considerable commitment too (two to three times a week at £20-plus a session, usually for at least three years) and may employ a couch, although not necessarily. **Brief dynamic therapy** lasts 16–20 sessions and is much more focused, with therapist and patient usually seated opposite each other. **Counselling** is the least demanding in every sense, used in a wide variety of settings from the Samaritans to supporting victims of disasters.

The trainings vary in direct proportion to the intensity of the treatment, with psychoanalysis at one extreme and counselling at the other. Whereas you can become a counsellor within a year, it takes at least five to become a psychoanalyst. As might be expected, the more you put in, the more you expect to get out. Put very crudely, psychoanalysis generally aims to enable a fundamental change in your personality and emotional state (in terms of a visit to the garage, a new engine for your psychic car) and as you move along the continuum, the goal becomes limited to helping you to modify your existing self and circumstances (dynamic therapy – a full service), to being focused on particular problems (brief dynamic therapy – repairs to a dented wing), towards simply enabling you to survive in your present state (counselling – checking the tyres and filling up with petrol). In the case of a depressed, potentially suicidal person, for example, counselling by a Samaritan is concerned to support them through a crisis and no more, brief dynamic therapy might concentrate on the suicidal thoughts specifically, dynamic therapy would regard the suicidal and depressive symptoms as reflecting deeper problems related to childhood history and psychoanalysis would do the same, even more exhaustively.

Conventional psychodynamic wisdom is that the more severe the ailment, the more intensive the treatment required,[2] although there are limits to how disturbed the patient can be. Therapy cannot work if the patient is so deluded or distressed that they are not capable of attending sessions and forming a relationship, and very few therapists would be prepared to take someone in the midst of an episode of major depression or schizophrenia. It is the patients with serious but less extreme problems than these, such as Borderline Personality Disorders (e.g. antisocial, impulsive or narcissistic types), who are more likely to benefit from the intensity and longevity of psychoanalysis. At the opposite extreme, the more that the problem seems to have been provoked by a temporary misfortune, such as a bereavement; the more that it is specific (such as a phobia) and not part of a wider pathological picture; then the more likely it is that short-term treatments will work. Using full psychoanalysis to treat an isolated phobia would be like installing a new engine to achieve an oil change. Thus, apart from the practical questions of how much time and money can be afforded, the cause of the problem, its seriousness and its prognosis are all relevant in deciding which kind of psychodynamic treatment is appropriate.

All these treatments entail a one-to-one conversation, usually lasting 50 minutes. To them can be added a variety of group dynamic treatments including Group Analysis (eight patients and a therapist, twice a week for two to three years), Marital Therapy (specifically for couples) and Family Therapy (usually for families in which an adolescent's disturbance is believed to express a collective family pathology). Group treatment is generally recommended for patients whose problems are primarily in their relationships rather than specific ones like phobias. Marital treatments vary in intensity, often using a male and a female therapist simultaneously, and the same is true of Family Therapy.

The theories underpinning these many different methods are manifold. No single theory is shared by all kinds of therapist but there are four fundamental ones used to govern the therapist's interpretation and precise technique. Modern **Freudian** theory is increasingly eclectic in its sources but remains the closest to the original insights of the founder of psychoanalysis. Interpretation still focuses on the Nuclear Complex, the experience of being part of the triad of mother, father and child. The child's fears of retribution from its same-sexed parent for its desires towards its opposite-sexed parent during early childhood (three to six years) are held to be a fundamental cause of subsequent neuroses and depression. How parents actually behaved towards children is often considered secondary to what the patient made of what happened. In terms of technique, Freudian therapists tend to speak little and to offer an emotional blank screen upon which patients can project the movie of their personalities and histories. Some patients experience this disengagement as frosty and complain that the therapist 'never gives me any advice'. Freudians will use the transference of past experiences on to the therapist as a technique for enlightening the patient but compared with the next group, in moderation. Freudians are often prepared to help the patient address their current, everyday problems as well.

Kleinian theory was invented by Melanie Klein and sets the key determinants of adult problems in earliest infancy. According to Klein, the infant is born in a 'Paranoid-Schizoid' psychic position. That is, it is liable to feel persecuted by its uncontrollable bodily sensations and environment (paranoid); and it has a basic tendency to map its inner world on to the outer and to deal with the world in crude absolutes of good and bad (schizoid). For reasons that are not very clear within Klein's theory (although her descendants are starting to fill this vacuum), the infant may or may not progress to the Paranoid-Depressive position, in which it ceases to split the world (especially its feelings about its mother and her body) into good and bad and accepts the reality that these can coexist, that the world is not all good or all bad (the use of the word depressive to describe this accomplishment is somewhat confusing). Kleinians also strive to be a blank screen, in terms of the therapist's personality, although there is a great deal more intervention and challenging of the patient's perceptions compared with Freudians. Kleinianism is controversial within therapeutic circles partly because there is an abundant use of jargon often from the very first session, which some patients cannot understand (an adolescent girl of my acquaintance returned from her first session and asked her mother, 'Did the milk go bad in one of your breasts when I was a baby?': her therapist had told her that her mother had been a 'bad breast' for her), and partly because it relies heavily on interpretation of the transference. At their most extreme, Kleinians will interpret almost everything the patient says as a form of transference, at all times. Thus, if the patient arrives for a session in a flaming temper because they have just been sacked by an unreasonable boss, the extreme Kleinian might respond immediately that 'you are telling me that you feel angry with me and that you feel you have been emotionally sacked by me'. If the patient then replies, 'No, I am angry with my ex-boss, not you,' and becomes even more enraged, the therapist may further interpret this reaction as evidence of a resistance to the truth of the initial interpretation, and so on. At best, this entails a lack of diplomacy and at worst, it is simply incorrect and increases the patient's problems. However, despite its controversial nature, most therapists accept that Kleinian theory and practice (when used judiciously) can be courageous in its stringent pursuit of the deepest levels of psychic turmoil and can help patients to confront otherwise invisible and intolerable conflicts, with benign consequences.

Jungian theory (developed by Carl Jung in opposition to Freud) focuses more on the dreams and artistic creations of the patient than the others, although contemporary problems are by no means ignored. Jung claimed that there are unconscious archetypes found in all humans, evolved from our primeval past (many evolutionary psychologists have a soft spot for his ideas as a result, e.g. see Paul Gilbert's *Human Nature and Suffering*, 1989, Lawrence Erlbaum). As well as linking the patient's offerings to this schema, the Jungian may also interpret the patient's present as expressing their childhood past. In general, Jungian therapists are less disengaged from the patient, more prepared to reveal information about themselves and to be active in offering suggestions for solving problems – less of a blank slate. They are less concerned to interpret the transference than the others. Because Jung was particularly interested in old age and maturation, Jungians are often felt to have more to offer elderly patients than therapists with other theoretical backgrounds.

Finally, **Middle Group** therapists (so called because they stand between the Freudian and Kleinian views) may use theories from all the above, as well as from certain other key thinkers (the most prominent being Donald Winnicott). Middle Groupers tend to be more emotionally engaged with the patient, more prepared to show sympathy and support for present-day problems than Freudians or Kleinians. All the other theories tend to focus primarily on the patient's inner fantasy world, starting from the assumption that it does not matter whether a remembered experience really occurred or not, whereas Middle Groupers usually seek to identify actual trauma and neglect. Thus, a strict Kleinian would regard a patient's memories of being sexually abused as a child as 'Phantasy' like any other set of thoughts and feelings in the patient's mind and would not regard it as important to establish if the events had truly occurred. By contrast, a Middle Grouper would ask detailed questions seeking to verify what had actually happened, as well as analysing what the patient has made of it. Having established the patterns of childhood abuse and neglect, the Middle Grouper indicates to the patient how they are recreating or re-experiencing them in their daily lives and relationship to the therapist.

All these theories are foursquare in the psychoanalytic tradition but there are literally dozens more that can generally be characterized as psychodynamic which are part of an American tradition known as Third Force Psychology (the first force being psychoanalysis and the second being behaviourism). Third Force theories were a reaction against the perceived determinism of the other two. They include Transactional Analysis (see Thomas B. Harris' *I'm Okay, You're Okay*), Rogerian co-counselling (after its creator Carl Rogers), George Kelly's personal construct theory and Abraham Maslow's hierarchy of needs. Mostly, these theories inform the work of counsellors although there are some dynamic therapists who use them in more intensive work. They are strictly non-judgemental and often entail offering a warm, 'unconditional positive regard'.

TALES FROM THE COUCH
For most people, psychoanalysis is not an option because it is extremely expensive. Some patients receive free treatment or low-cost treatment

through schemes organized by the Institute of Psychoanalysis in London, but for the rest, it costs at least £100 a week. Nonetheless, because it was the first dynamic therapeutic treatment and the source from which all others flowed, I shall examine the effectiveness of psychoanalysis in some – albeit wholly anecdotal – detail, drawing on over 100 reports of cases from psychoanalysts and patients known to me. I shall attempt to provide a more intimate picture of the cases than is normally visible in published empirical studies.

Given that the psychoanalytic training is the most exhaustive (solely available in Britain at the Institute of Psychoanalysis in London) and that the treatment takes longer and entails the most patient-therapist contact, it can be argued that if psychoanalysis does not work then no analytic therapy does (although many dynamic therapists would hotly dispute this assertion). During training, every analyst undergoes analysis himself with a top exponent, attending five days a week for 50 minutes a session, for at least five years (usually longer). On qualification, patients are seen on the same basis, although many psychoanalysts also treat some of their patients less intensively (the majority now have posts in health and welfare institutions as well as their private practices).

Of course, I have no way of knowing if the patients who seemed to have benefited in my informal survey would have improved anyway without analysis, or of knowing whether the ones who seemed not to have benefited (or even got worse) might have been even more disturbed without. Nevertheless, when you get into the details of these people's lives, it is hard not to believe that, at least in some cases, it made a huge difference for the better, although in a few it was disastrous (perhaps fatal in one case).

I classify the cases according to the reasons they were seeking treatment, heeding Freud's criterion of success, namely, that a healthy person is able to function effectively in work and love. But I was also concerned to see if more subtle changes could be considered as well.

Analysis seemed to be most effective at helping those who had difficulties in working, or in finding work that fulfilled them. This makes it particularly valuable as a treatment for low-serotonin individuals who have been overwhelmed by guilt, depression and confusion about identity (often induced by the subordinating social comparison pressures and relative deprivation described in Chapters 2 and 3, as well as their childhood experiences) and are consequently unable to fulfil their working potential.

Although from a wealthy background, Emily (now aged 90) left school with no qualifications and her headmistress told her parents she lacked sufficient intelligence for anything more exacting than 'outdoor work' such as gardening. Her mother committed suicide when she was aged ten, her father was a remote man and although she was close to some of her siblings, their lives were also often shrouded in tragedy. Aged 18, she made a number of friends from the Bloomsbury Group and began to doubt her headmistress' assessment. Her new friends encouraged her to enter analysis and after three years of it and with the help of a crammer, she sailed through the necessary exams in record time, went to university and on to a successful professional career. She was also enabled to marry happily and successfully raise three children. Today she is convinced that without analysis she would have been a dead loss at work and love. I identified at least 20 similar stories, some of whom went from total paralysis to become leading figures in our society.

A number of other similar cases were extremely wealthy and able people who, despite years of analysis, still did no work. Should we assume that this is necessarily an unsuccessful outcome if the person can afford not to do paid work? All these cases made stable and happy marriages and concentrated on their children, perhaps trying to supply the care that they felt they missed out on themselves. I believe it unlikely that they would have found this domestic contentment without analysis.

There were also cases of highly talented people, with top degrees from top universities, who despite poor backgrounds settled for low-level, part-time work and domestic happiness instead of success. Should they be 'fulfilling their full work potential' for us to say that their analyses succeeded? In some cases I felt 'yes', because they seemed to be frustrated by their lack of achievement but in others I suspected they would have had serious nervous breakdowns if they had pushed themselves more – analysis had helped them to find a *modus vivendi*. Others still, as a direct effect of analysis, had resigned from promising careers for more self-expressive but less prestigious work, such as in the arts. I regarded these as successes. Emotionally deadened by the lack of creative opportunities in their old jobs, they had been enlivened by the career changes.

There were examples of all the most common psychiatric diagnoses among these various kinds of cases, including some who had suffered from major mental illnesses, yet they had happy endings. I am convinced that there is no other form of psychological treatment available that can be as effective in helping distressed individuals to find their *métier*. Whilst analysis is rarely a cure as such, it can enable people to play the hand they are dealt with much better results than might otherwise have been the case. In this sense it is an antidote to the failure of modern life to meet status needs and the pressures of social comparison: it helps distressed individuals to sort out what is best for them in a society that places enormous strain on identity. If they feel humiliated and depressed by social comparison processes as well as problems dating back to childhood, it can help them to discover what is uniquely important to them, rather than what the society or their parents say is important (see the end of the chapter).

Patients who suffered from serious mental illnesses, such as severe depression and schizoid (potentially schizophrenic) tendencies, as opposed to milder disturbances were sometimes the most dramatically improved, although there were several depressives who remained depressed. One was particularly unfortunate. Sarah's mother had derided and criticized her from birth, often with great cruelty. Depressed and withdrawn, in her late teens she attended a rigid Kleinian analyst. When Sarah's father died suddenly in a tragic accident, she was told her wish to miss a session in order to attend the funeral was an excuse to avoid the therapy. Sarah was not allowed to talk about her father's death in the therapy and whatever the subjects of her dreams or fantasies, the therapist always seemed to have the same answers.

At its worst, analysis imposes theories on patients regardless of whether they fit the material but luckily most analysts (including most Kleinians) are not like this and there were plenty of patients with major depression who had been helped. Sonia was driven by her domineering and ambitious mother, achieving highly at school and university only to be admitted to a mental hospital for a depressive breakdown soon afterwards. Six years of analysis transformed her from an-unself-confident, unassertive, subordinated wreck into a creative, lively woman who was able to become the effective mother of a large family with a conspicuously happy marriage. She was also able to pursue a part-time career, not the high-powered one of her mother's aspirations but one she enjoyed which served a hugely valuable social purpose. Crucially, there was a real affinity between Sonia and her therapist. They were of similar class and culture and shared a love of music which helped Sonia to feel understood and her analyst to understand. This issue of compatibility is, I believe, critical (see below). The pattern in this story was repeated almost exactly in several other women patients.

Among the schizoid – distant people with a weak grip on reality, prone to delusions – there was a tendency for the patients to drift in and out of treatment. Since these people are very likely to have miserable and lonely lives, it is particularly hard to tell how they would have turned out without help. A few cases were unambiguous, like the wife of an Oxford don who ended permanently incarcerated in a mental hospital, despite analysis. But some were enabled to form stable relationships (something schizoids find hard) and settle down. A university professor who was able to develop a real affection for his wife might be counted as a success story, except for the fact that his wife became a depressed alcoholic. A few of these cases found the strain of sharing a life was too great, concluding that their best bet was to live alone or, if they had lovers, not to try and unite their lives with them.

A related group of patients were unable to love. The reasons varied greatly, from sexual neurosis to diffidence, but on the whole they fared rather well. A doctor who had not formed any stable relationships at university was enabled to settle down and make a happy marriage; a rootless heir to millions did the same; a beautiful young woman who found sex repulsive ceased to do so. There were one or two who had not seemed to be helped at the end of the treatment but who eventually found some contentment. A high-achieving Oxbridge-trained lawyer somehow managed to drag herself to her 7a.m. sessions in Hampstead five mornings a week for eight years before going to her City firm. After all this she did not seem much more secure and able to feel love for others. However, I strongly suspect that this unfortunate woman's analyst is exceptionally useless and interestingly, the patient eventually did find a husband to whom she is passionately attached. For the most part, analysis helped people with this kind of problem. If they were suffering from severe attachment problems, perhaps devastated by divorce, the relationship with the therapist could act as a prototype for forming better attachments with lovers and offspring.

At least in the past and undoubtedly to some extent still today, dynamic therapy has been homophobic (it is still the case that the Institute of Psychoanalysis does not in practice accept homosexuals for training, although it claims there is no formal bar). A few patients with homosexual leanings seemed to be helped but not surprisingly, there were some tragic tales as well. James is arguably an example of someone who was actually killed by analysis. He was a talented ballet dancer as a child in the 1920s with a predilection for women's roles. He had a passionate affair with another boy at his public school and when he became a successful professional dancer in later life, had a series of affairs with prominent homosexuals. His parents were appalled by his proclivities and eventually, in his late twenties, he was dragooned into analysis. After a few years it persuaded him of his heterosexuality and he married but it was not long before he began to have episodes of delusion and schizophrenia. The birth of a son made no difference and in the end he took his own life. Would this have been the outcome if no one had interfered?

Another man of the same generation also had a predilection for women's clothing in childhood (a strong predictor of subsequent adult homosexuality), but his treatment was less disastrous. He had a catty, paranoid personality and was prone to idealizing women. His analysis made him much more pleasant company and swayed him away from homosexuality enough to marry an heiress. Sadly, she was unable to reproduce and perhaps because he felt thwarted, the nastier side of his personality returned. He was able partly to recompense himself by becoming a leading professor of English Literature and living the life of a country squire. Analysis had probably saved this man from much unhappiness.

The same was true to some extent of Sheila, also now in her late seventies. Her marked masculinity was not altered by years of analysis but she was able to find a healthy outlet for her sexual desires towards young girls by helping them professionally. Whilst she had some conspicuously lesbian friends, she did not practise as one herself. By channelling her sexual preferences through her work she was able to do a great deal of good without ever acting improperly, felt deeply satisfied by her professional life and was a happy, positive person. On the other hand, the fact that she had no active sex life of any kind could be regarded as a grim shortcoming of the treatment.

Gerald was another homosexual case with mixed results. As a boy he longed to be an instrumental musician and despite family pressures, spent several years training in Berlin in the 1930s, befriending the likes of the homosexual W.H. Auden and Christopher Isherwood. Analysis bent him back towards women and he returned to England and married an extremely dominating woman, much like his mother. Sadly, he never fulfilled his musical ambitions, devoting the rest of his life to a Jungian analysis of Beethoven which was never published. It is probable that analysis 'saved' him from homosexuality but it seems equally likely that had it not done so, he might have stood a better chance of living the homosexual, artistic life which has accompanied the creation of much fine art – would Auden or Isherwood have achieved what they did if 'cured' of their sexual preference?

One class of patient that was rarely helped at all were people with 'imposturous' tendencies. Analysed during the 1940s, Sam would be called a 'bullshitter' today. The son of a successful doctor, he qualified as one himself but only by cheating (he obtained advance warning of the questions for his final exams). He did not start a medical practice but instead set himself up as an important thinker on social affairs, using contacts to get two books of hot air published. A member of several gentlemen's clubs, he hobnobbed with the Great and Good, his finest hour being when he was pictured in *The Times* alongside the creator of the welfare state, Lord Beveridge. He married a wealthy wife and lived very grandly until her early death. He was a treacherous philanderer in his dealings with women and a neglectful, irresponsible father. Analysis made no impact on this antisocial personality.

Graham was more visibly in pain than Sam when he sought analysis. From a wealthy family, he made himself up as he went along, at work and play. He would last about two years in any social circle before the various deceptions caught up with him. At its peak he had three women, all of whom believed they were his one and only girlfriend. He had spells of about the same length in accountancy, estate agency and the City before being found out each time. He never actually broke the law but would always cut corners when it came to the truth, at its most extreme actually passing himself off as another person. Occasionally he suffered bouts of incoherence, feeling confused and disorientated by the multiplicity of personae. Emotional conmen have a constant battle to remember who they have told what to but the biggest problem is their lack of any integrity – they are always at risk of disintegrating. In temporary despair, he attended an analyst well known for dealing with this sort of delinquent. Despite being desperate to learn the truth about himself and to change, he could not resist giving the analyst fictional accounts of his dreams and life. He could see that to dupe the analyst (at £30 a session) was only to dupe himself but he was incapable of the trust that truth telling would have required. Although he evaded regular attendance, his analyst was so skilled that he managed to sustain a sporadic relationship with Graham which endures to this day. He remains as imposturous as ever.

There were six other similar stories. One of them, 'Prince' Masud Khan, was a famous analyst. I already knew of at least two affairs he had had with patients and of his charismatic and unreliable personality but I was surprised to learn from a biography published recently[3] that he was not, as was believed throughout his life, a Pakistani prince but actually of humble origins. The best that you could claim for his analysis was that it may have prevented him from full schizophrenia – claiming he was Jesus Christ.

Another imposturous analyst in my survey, Tim, trained back in the late 1950s. As part of the training he had to analyse a patient and attend weekly supervisions of the case with a distinguished analyst. He was supposed to be seeing his patient five times a week but he told a friend (who told this tale to me) that he did not really see the point of so many sessions and actually only saw the patient once a week. As a result he was very short of material – the dreams and childhood traumas that make up an analysis – to report to his supervisor, so he made them up! Although he was never caught out, the Institute must have realized that there was something fishy about Tim because he only qualified on condition that he worked outside Britain. Today he runs a psychological consultancy in one of our former colonies and it is said he makes a good job of it.

In general, I can think of very few cases in which the patient's basic character was significantly changed but there were many who became better adjusted to their nature and nurture. The depressive Sonia no longer has any depressive leanings, the workshy Emily lost all her inability to perform effectively. But much more common were the cases, such as some of the schizoids, who simply learnt to adjust more effectively to their emotional handicaps.

As regards the reasons for success or failure, the quality of the analyst was certainly important. I know of analysts I would not wish on my worst enemies but much depends also on the fit between analyst and patient, whether they hit it off. Even the best analyst in the world would probably be no use for some kinds of problem – they all have their blindspots.

Clearly some kinds of problem are more amenable to the analytic approach than others. Patients suffering full-scale depressive or schizophrenic episodes need drug treatment in the short term. For those (in my view, very few) cases which are almost wholly caused by genetics and remit only briefly, talk can do little to help.

Overall, despite its unendingly bad press in this country, psychoanalysis can be extremely valuable and the fact that this is so suggests that other dynamic therapies can be so as well. What, then, are the grounds for choosing one dynamic therapy over another?

WHICH PSYCHODYNAMIC THERAPY?
It may be seen that much depends on the nature of the problem and its causes but for most people, psychoanalysis will not be an option either because it is too expensive or because there are no analysts living nearby (nearly all live in London, mostly in Hampstead). In general, it is an extreme recourse that should not be attempted until other less committing methods have failed.

For people who have suffered a temporary setback but who have no history of previous emotional problems, counselling may be sufficient. Bereaved people suffering the normal agonies of mourning, for example, can benefit dramatically from a few visits from a bereavement counsellor.

The fact that counselling is less intensive and 'profound' does not mean it is not often remarkably helpful. However, for problems that are long-standing, where there is a pattern that keeps repeating itself, brief dynamic therapy or dynamic therapy are indicated. Some typical examples of longstanding problems might be:

- Always ending up with lovers who treat you badly or dissatisfy you
- An inability to find work that is satisfying or rewarding and which you feel is sufficiently demanding in relation to your training or capacities
- A tendency to melancholia and to negative feelings about the present, past or future
- Sexual problems, despite the fact that you love and desire your partner
- A constant sense that there is more to life – you wish you had a better lover, you feel there is an exciting world out there that is somehow passing you by
- Persistent eruptions of explosive anger or violence
- Phobias, obsessions or a tendency to hysterical overreaction in certain situations
- A pattern of problems with authority as shown by constant falling out with bosses (whose fault you always feel it is but deep down, you know it is your behaviour that is the real cause) or repeated breaches of minor laws (e.g. traffic violations, shoplifting)

Dynamic therapy can help reduce all these problems by enabling you to trace their childhood roots and to find less pathological ways of being, through the relationship with the therapist. All these problems may be symptomatic of infantile disturbances to the sense of self as well and be hard to change. Narcissistic 'Me, Me, Me' people who only feel comfortable if the conversation is revolving around them, for example, may have trouble in recognizing they have a problem in the first place and even if they do so, in seeking help. The same is true of imposturous, antisocial and grandiose-omnipotent people. For them, psychoanalysis or a long period of dynamic therapy are the best (and probably the only) hope. For persistently depressive people who are not so depressed that they are totally incapacitated and require hospitalization, psychoanalysis and dynamic therapy can also help, but I believe there are few such cases who should not be taking antidepressants as well (see below; alas, many therapists will try to dissuade such patients from doing so).

WHICH PSYCHODYNAMIC THERAPIST?

Having decided which kind of therapy is applicable, the next problem is to find a therapist who is right for you. The British are right to regard any treatment or belief system which claims to be able to transform you with a healthy scepticism. It is incredibly hard for people to change in any fundamental way. For all that, therapy often improves the quality of experience to a dramatic extent and if a low-serotonin individual wishes to change, they must be prepared to make the necessary act of faith to some extent.

However, it is not necessary to put aside all your rational faculties and make the same kind of mental leap that is required in religious belief. There are some guidelines which can reduce the likelihood of your ending up in the hands of an incompatible, incompetent or charlatanish therapist.

The first and most fundamental safeguard is the training that your therapist has undergone. There are at least six trainings (apart from the Institute of Psychoanalysis) for dynamic therapists which are direct descendants of the tradition started by Freud and whose graduates can generally be relied upon not to be utterly mad or bad because all have been analysed properly themselves and subjected to a reasonably rigorous vetting procedure. Most of these trainings are part of an umbrella body called the British Confederation of Psychotherapy (BCP) which has 11 bodies belonging to it (listed in footnote 4). The BCP will send members of the public a leaflet informing them how to approach these organizations, most of which offer reduced-fee treatment for those of little means (therapists anyway tend to run a 'pay according to means' approach, so that the rich patients may subsidize the poor ones). I can also vouch for several other organizations as reputable purveyors of dynamic therapy (all in London, listed in footnote 5).

The second fundamental safeguard is to find the therapist through someone whose opinion you trust. This can be easier said than done, but the closer to the following ideal scenario the better: you know two people well who have seen the same therapist, both of whom have benefited from the treatment, and you feel confident that their improved state is due to the therapy (not to winning the lottery or some other change in their circumstances); on top of this, the problems that they had are of a similar order of gravity as your own. Of course, this scenario is extremely rare. More likely is that you will know a friend who knows a friend. Given that it is likely to be a ramshackle, messy business, your best bet is to identify at least two, preferably three, therapists who you are reasonably sure have helped at least one person, and to see all three for a consultation, being careful not to make up your mind which is best for you until you have seen all of them. You will have to pay for these meetings, but the money will be well spent. If you do not know anyone at all who has been in therapy you will have to contact the British Confederation of Psychotherapy (whose literature will be sent out for free). When taking pot luck like this it is even more important to see more than one before you commit.

How are you to decide which therapist is best for you from one meeting? Probably it will be with difficulty. If, for example, one of your problems is that you find it hard to trust others you can hardly just go on gut instinct – you would end up finding fault with anyone. Yet gut instinct is all you will really have to go on because dynamic therapists are generally reluctant to reveal much about themselves.

Personally (and these are very much not the opinions of most experts in the field) there are several rules I would apply. I would not recommend going to see someone of a different gender, class, culture or sexual persuasion to yourself if you can avoid it. Most dynamic therapists would disagree, arguing that the transference of your feelings about your parents from your childhood will occur regardless of these 'superficial' (as they would describe them) factors. But I believe this reflects their failure to take sufficient account of the influence of past and present reality as opposed to fantasy on who we are. You are going to spend many hours with your therapist and if their tastes and proclivities are alien to you it will be harder for you and them to share and understand your deeper feelings. It is no coincidence that the vast majority of people marry others of similar class, opinions, tastes and so on, or that friends tend to be similar in these respects. A therapist is like a spouse, parent or friend and too much dissimilarity creates a barrier to empathy.

A further prejudice that I hold concerning the seeking of a therapist is in favour of those who regard what actually happened in childhood as more important than what you made of it, and likewise, present-day reality. The greatest weakness of dynamic therapy is its tendency to ignore these things in pursuit of theories. Unfortunately, it is extremely hard to find out in one consultation what a therapist's beliefs are – they emerge through the interpretations they offer of what you say. Nonetheless, I would advocate asking a potential therapist what their view about this is and even trying them out – tell them about a troubling incident from your childhood and see what they make of it.

This point relates to the next one, the preferred theoretical orientation of the therapist. Assuming you have not read the works of Freud, Klein, Jung and so on, I do not recommend embarking on them. Reading will tell you little about your potential therapist because they may have a very particular interpretation of their school's view. My own preference is for Middle Group, more reality-based theories (to some extent represented, if a little extremely, by Alice Miller's very readable book *Banished Knowledge*; despite the fact that Miller totally rejects all dynamic therapy, her account of the traumatic causes of emotional distress is impeccable). Jungian theory, although fascinating, seems to me to have little practical application other than as a more positive worldview, an antidote to the relentless pessimism of Freud and Klein. Kleinian theory is certainly remarkable and in the right hands, the interventionist techniques of transference interpretation can have impressive results, but many Kleinians are too inflexibly set on this one theory for my tastes (see Charles Rycroft's *Psychoanalysis Observed*). It is anyway often argued that the theories the therapist has are less important than whether they are a warm person and have basic common sense. I would agree with that, so long as the therapist is not too beholden to one approach.

On top of this, there is the question of finding the right fit with the therapist. This is more likely if you share a culture, class and so forth. However, it is also to do with the therapist's own personal history. As a therapist myself, for example, I found it much easier to treat patients whom I basically liked but on top of this, if their histories of trauma and neglect rang bells with my own, it was that much easier to empathize (doubtless some dynamic therapists will say that this tells us more about me than it does about how to select a therapist). Therapists will claim that one's training ought to make it possible to work professionally with all kinds of people, but I believe this is nonsense. In the end, however 'professional' the therapist, what counts is that there are two people meeting together regularly, one trying to help the other out of a psychic jam, and it is vital that the therapist has a feeling for the person and the problems.

Of course, you can follow all these precepts and still come unstuck but properly qualified dynamic therapists who actually behave immorally are few. I have worked with Mary Edwardes, co-founder of the Prevention of Professional Abuse Network and met some of the victims of the ghastly abuses of trust that unquestionably do occur. One aid to solving this problem would be if all therapists had to present their patients at the beginning of treatment with a list of their qualifications, a statement of their preferred method and the telephone number of an independent supervisory body to be rung if the patient feels that anything inappropriate or untoward is taking place. But overall, I do not believe that the main risk of dynamic therapy is that your therapist will try to have an affair with you; it is that they will either be not very good or that they will not fit with you and your problems.

COGNITIVE-BEHAVIOURAL THERAPY AND THERAPISTS

Although there are many differences of detail between different cognitive-behavioural therapists, they tend to have far more in common than different dynamic therapists. The fact that the level of financial and temporal commitment is generally not more than 20-odd sessions, combined with a greater consensus as to theory and practice, means that the questions 'Which therapy?' and 'Which therapist?' are less of a problem. Most properly qualified cognitive therapists can be relied upon to do a thorough job by the lights of their profession – in terms of psychic auditing, they are more like accountants in the predictability of what they do – although as with all professionals, some are obviously better than others.

Many cognitive therapists are either clinical psychologists (people with a psychology first degree who have done a further training to treat the mentally ill) or psychiatrists who have had extra training. The most influential modern theorist is the American Aaron Beck and his ideas are employed to some extent by almost all of them. Beck started out as a psychoanalyst in the 1950s but he became dissatisfied with this approach. His Damascene conversion occurred whilst listening to a patient describe some sexual material. She became markedly more anxious and at first Beck assumed this was due to the delicate nature of the material, but further questioning revealed that the anxiety concerned how she felt Beck was regarding her: she felt he did not like her, was bored with her and the more she had these thoughts, the more anxious she became. He went on to label these kinds of junk thoughts as 'automatic thoughts', a series of immediate, consciously available ideas, beliefs and interpretations, often negative, often evaluative of self and others. Sometimes they flash in and out of the mind, at others they may be intrusive and enduring. Paul Gilbert prefers the term 'automatic fantasies' to discriminate them from ordinary practical ideations, such as 'I must remember to set the video/feed the cat', which have no powerful emotional significance. He points out that they often flash into our minds as images or mini-films. For example, the lover who does not phone as expected may lead to the idea that they are having an affair or having a good time, laughing, getting drunk, being happy to be away from you. Further thoughts may follow, such as the angry accusations that will be made when the lover does phone or even acts of revenge.

Cognitive therapy aims to help the patient identify the immediate thoughts and chains of faulty inferences, and to challenge them. There is a tendency for the initial idea to generalize out to a broader set which are false, and for irrational ideas about the self and others to take root.

Gilbert gives the following example: 'If my friend ignores me then it means he/she does not like me. This is because I am a boring person. If I am a boring person then I am unlovable. If I am unlovable I will never find a loving relationship and will be alone and depressed forever.' There is a dangerous inflation from a single negative idea to a globally black worldview.

The first step in treatment is to identify these inferential chains. Unlike a dynamic practitioner, the cognitive therapist does not interpret hidden unconscious meanings or suchlike, but through active and direct questions prompts the patient to discover for both of them what the thought patterns are. Once identified, there are a number of techniques with which the therapist helps the patient to recolonize his mind. For example, the therapist may prompt the patient to take a 'fantasy journey'. Gilbert had a patient who was having difficulty describing their fears so he asked them to describe any fear-filled scenario, in this case, a train journey:

THERAPIST: OK, so here you are on the train and you feel it start to move. What is going through your mind?
PATIENT: I might get anxious.
T: Okay you get anxious. What would happen then?
P: I start to sweat.
T: And that bothers you because?
P: Other people might see this.
T: I see. So you are worried that you may become anxious and this might lead you to start sweating. If this happened other people might see it. Is that how it seems to you?
P: Yes.
T: Okay, can we explore the meaning of sweating and other people being able to see this? Let's just focus on that for a moment and see what is the most worrying thing about that.
P: Well, they may think there is something wrong with me, like I'm ill or something.
T: Like you are ill or something?
P: Yes, they may feel I'm contagious and be repelled by me.
T: Repelled by you?
P: Yes, repelled by the way I look. Later I think if I can't control this I will always be alone.

A similar technique is 'speaking in pictures' in which the patient is asked to describe a previously inchoate set of thoughts and feelings in a picture. One patient depicted his feelings of depression to Gilbert, as follows: 'It's like I can see this party going on and I'm standing in the garden or somewhere. It's very cold, maybe snowing and very dark. I know that no matter what I do I will not be allowed in, but must stay outside just looking in and being on my own.'

Role play is also often used, in which the patient is asked to enact their feelings and thoughts either as a rehearsal for behaving in a desired fashion or to re-enact a traumatic or aversive experience. Thus, a person who is unassertive may be asked to play the part of an assertive one in a pretend situation, or an experience of being humiliated or maltreated may be relived.

An important aid to the work is the use of 'recursive feedback' in which the therapist provides the patient with diagrams specifying sequences of adverse thoughts and possible escape routes from the vicious circles. At the heart of all this work is an attempt to enable the patient to challenge irrational beliefs and meanings. Just recognizing that a sequence of thoughts already identified as aberrant is in progress can lead to escape. The rehearsal of specific alternatives to the junk thoughts also provides a different and less distressing way of being.

In its most ambitious forms, cognitive treatment for depression explores much of the territory examined in some dynamic therapies. Negative thoughts and feelings are forced out of their murky corners into the bright glare of rationality, with a concerted attempt to precisely identify different styles. Self-bullying, including name-calling and self-criticism, is exposed for what it is. Likewise, the need for approval, fear of shame and the dangers of subordination are explored. Bullying others is often uncovered, as well as being bullied, as are anger, aggression and grudge-bearing. Learning to convert these into assertiveness and forgiveness and confronting disappointment and lost ideals is also encouraged. For Dominant Goal depressives, who endlessly torment themselves with demands for high achievement, the destructive effects of perfectionism and competitiveness are exposed. Whilst dynamic therapists might dress these various problems up in different jargon, there is considerable overlap.

PROS AND CONS OF COGNITIVE-BEHAVIOURAL THERAPY

A number of debates exist within cognitive therapy. Recent evidence suggesting that emotions may often exist independently of thoughts and are often automatic contradicts the central assumption of the theory that thought can be used to alter emotion: if much emotion is unaffected by thought then the techniques will not work.[6] Likewise, there are good

scientific grounds for supposing that much experience is truly unconscious and therefore, not available to be manipulated by conscious
thought.[6] Other research suggests that depressives vary considerably in
the degree to which their thoughts are unrealistic. As we saw in Chapter
2, there is good reason to suppose that it is the optimism of normal people
that is illusory and that some depressed people are suffering precisely
because they are so painfully realistic (however, I would argue that,
whilst this realism may be accurate, there is often an irrational overcon-
centration on it to the exclusion of equally realistic, positive prospects).
A further criticism has been that, like psychoanalysts, cognitive therapists remain an ultimately neutral presence rather than providing
warmth and support. For subordinated, low-self-esteem people, it is
argued, directly boosting their self-belief and making them feel truly
valued is important. This links to the criticism that vehemently cognitive
approaches see distressed humans as essentially logical beings who
require re-education and rationality to be instilled. No allowance is made
for their spiritual and emotional need for human contact, and there is a
tendency to ignore great swathes of the patient's being by concentrating
on just one small area of symptoms. As Gilbert has pointed out, many
depressed people are suffering from the subordinating effect of modern
life and are often trapped in a state of longing for approval. Coldly mental
approaches may actually exacerbate their diminished sense of status and
desire to feel appreciated and needed.[6]

The more behavioural the treatment the more it is open to these criticisms. In purely behavioural therapy, the relationship with the therapist
is ignored altogether in favour of a strictly functional programme.
Patients are taught how to increase the amount of positive rewards they
receive, by observing the precise circumstances which are rewarding and
learning to avoid the ones that are aversive. Situations which are anxiety-
provoking (e.g. as in a phobia about spiders) may be confronted directly
in a series of deconditioning experiences (e.g. gradual introduction into
the company of spiders, escalating contact to the point where the spider
can sit on the patient's hand). Social skills training may be done, in which
the patient is directly taught what to do and say in order to overcome a
problem such as shyness or aggressiveness. Little or no attention is paid
in these treatments to the childhood or other origins of the problems and
the social comparative system is also ignored.

DYNAMIC VERSUS COGNITIVE-BEHAVIOURAL THERAPY
I shall begin with a comparison of the two therapies and then offer a view
of what works best for what problems.

Strengths and Weaknesses Of The Two Approaches

When done well, the strengths of cognitive-behavioural therapy are:

- It offers solutions through direct questioning and does not leave the patient feeling high and dry
- It is low-risk in the sense that it takes up little time and money and does not involve an intense relationship with a therapist who may have alien (to the patient) theories about human development – it does not in any way resemble a religion, and hardly ever, I suspect, does more harm than good
- Its use of thought to control feeling can be highly effective
- It seeks to accentuate the positive and eliminate the negative, which is sometimes the best that a person can realistically hope to do

The weaknesses of the approach are:

- It can seem cold, rational and not meet the patient's emotional needs for warmth and support
- If applied beyond its capacities it can seem to the patient (especially highly intelligent or sophisticated ones) like a series of mental gimmicks which do not change how they feel fundamentally, or only do so very transiently – it is often criticized by dynamic therapists as being 'superficial' and sometimes, it is
- It ignores the opportunity for learning that is presented by the transference to the therapist
- The refusal to consider cause, especially childhood causes, with such a heavy concentration on just a few symptoms can mean that golden opportunities to free the patient from the grip of lifelong patterns are squandered

Done well, the strengths of dynamic therapy are:

- It can result in a fundamental change in the patient, beyond 'mere' symptoms, which creates a new, richer existence
- It addresses the true causes of the problems
- It makes full use of the therapeutic relationship

The weaknesses are:

- It offers no solutions: despite the claims of purists that it would interfere with the transference, there is no real reason why dynamic thera-

294

pists of all kinds could not offer cognitive techniques to reduce symptoms on top of the other work (indeed, as analysts become more confident later in their careers they often effectively do this, although they might not admit to it if challenged)
- It is relatively risky: full analysis or dynamic therapy are a large commitment which can exceed the rewards considerably and at worst, if the therapist is doctrinaire or subscribes to a marginal, batty theory, can do real harm
- Its fundamental belief system can conflict with the development of the positive illusions which are a cornerstone of contentment: Freud's dictum that 'neurosis is the rule not the exception' is not a very inspiring rallying cry for the unhappy person; psychoanalysts can be so concerned to uncover the 'true' feelings 'beneath' the psychic defences that anything a person feels or thinks conceals some ghastly, 'deeper' problem; analysts sometimes seem like a patriotic American in the 1950s hallucinating pathological reds under the psychic bed

WHAT WORKS: MY ADVICE WITH REGARD TO THERAPY

Unless you feel your problems are deep-seated, longstanding ones, a basic principle is to start out with some kind of brief treatment and only commit to more if that does not work. Very few problems would not benefit from a cognitive approach and I would heartily recommend that this is where you start. However, in many cases, it will not be sufficient and other treatment will be necessary as well.

Broadly speaking, most cognitive-behavioural therapists are offering a brief treatment akin to brief dynamic therapy. As described above, I suspect brief therapies are appropriate for specific and relatively minor ailments. For these, the cognitive approach can be extremely effective, perhaps more so than brief dynamic therapy. Some examples might be phobias, such as a fear of flying or of snakes, and mental blocks, such as being unable to complete a thesis or a specific sexual hang-up. For deeper problems, I believe cognitive treatments can also be useful in providing some relief from symptoms – much as drugs are. Few depressives would gain no benefit at all from learning some cognitive techniques to resist their negativity and people with enduring anxiety and hysteria will also be helped if they learn to identify the situations which are provocative. However, for these and other problems which are part of a wider psychological pattern that has enduring roots in genes or childhood, I believe dynamic therapy is needed as well.

The sadness is that it is often a case of either/or. Although there do exist attempts to take the best from both approaches, such as Cognitive

Analytic Therapy (which is often excellent and evolved in Britain) and Interpersonal Psychotherapy (a similar American approach), most therapists do not. If you are seeing a dynamic therapist, they might not object to your seeing a cognitive one briefly, as well, for specific symptoms, and I would strongly recommend this if there are obvious symptoms that might benefit.

For people with enduring depression and symptoms of borderline personality (e.g. impulsiveness, antisocial tendencies, grandiosity, narcissism, and, I would add, addictions) I would say that if the brief methods, whether cognitive or dynamic, do not help, then full dynamic therapy or psychoanalysis are still the best there is, imperfect though they may be – except that that is not all there is. It is time to return to the vexed question of antidepressants.

PROZAC VERSUS THERAPY: TOUGH ON JUNK THOUGHTS, TOUGH ON THE CAUSES OF JUNK THOUGHTS

In the end, I suspect that the best advice for most low-serotonin individuals is to use both kinds of therapy and to use pills. Pills and cognitive therapy are good for treating the symptoms (tough on junk thoughts), dynamic therapy for treating the causes (tough on the causes of junk thoughts).

Studies comparing outcomes of depressed patients treated with both drugs and therapy show that about 40% of cases do better with the combination than if they have only one or other treatment.[7] Whilst these studies are no less flawed than all the others, this is at least one scientific indication that the combination can be efficacious. However, all sorts of problems are raised to such an approach.

On the one hand, dynamic therapists (and some cognitive-behaviourists, although fewer) may strongly resist their patients taking pills, often actively discouraging them from doing so on the grounds that it interferes with therapy. On the other, the psychiatrists who prescribe the pills are often as irrationally biased against dynamic therapy, often sabotaging their patients' attempts to seek deeper insight into their problems. The loser, I believe, is the patient. All too often one is reminded of the battles that are said to occur in America after a major accident, with private ambulance services, litigation lawyers and television news reporters fighting to get their hands on potentially lucrative victims.

Let me now spell out what I believe. Depending on the nature of the problem and how it responds to treatments, there are a series of stages of commitment you can make to solving your problems. Almost all people will benefit from cognitive treatment directed at reducing particular symptoms but in most cases, dynamic approaches will be needed as well, as may drug treatment. In short, for many people my advice is: do them all but in the following order:

Stage 1: If you are feeling mildly depressed or anxious as a result of a recent misfortune such as a bereavement, a lost promotion or a broken love affair, and you feel it is all a bit too much to take, seek out a Cognitive Analytic Therapist (CAT) through your General Practitioner for a series of 16 sessions. If there are no CATs available locally, either go to a cognitive-behavioural or to a self-help counsellor such as those provided by Relate and Cruse, available locally across most of the country. Do not seek medication.

If this does not work, go to Stage 2.

Stage 2: If your problem is more longstanding (e.g. you are aware that this has been a problem for one to two years), such as minor depression, irrational fears, overeating so that you are fatter than you would like or general loss of appetite (without actual starvation), lack of friends or manic oversocializing because you fear being alone, persistent patterns of difficulties with sex and lovers, incapacity to achieve at work, chronic fatigue, excessive substance use (smoking or drinking or marijuana use) or general irritability, seek out a brief dynamic therapist for 16 to 20 sessions.

If this does not work . . .

Stage 3: If you dislike the idea of taking antidepressants, seek out a dynamic therapist and attend initially for two sessions a week. If you dislike the idea of therapy, go to your GP and get them to prescribe you a course of SSRIs (see Chapter 7 for advice on which one – do not be passive about this) and stick with them for at least six months, preferably a year – do not stop taking them as soon as you feel better or until well after this has happened. SSRIs are only supposed to be prescribed by a GP for symptoms of depression, OCD and eating disorders. All the list of problems in Stage 2 can be legitimately represented as symptoms of depression and as was shown in Chapter 7, there is good reason to believe that they correlate with low serotonin and therefore, will be helped by SSRIs. Ideally, take SSRIs and visit a dynamic therapist at the same time but in many cases, one or other of your doctor or therapist will try to sabotage the other's involvement.

If this does not work . . .

Stage 4: You may have deeper problems than you first thought. You may have a genetic tendency to be depressed or have had such a difficult childhood that depression is provoked by not much adversity in your life. You may also have borderline personality features – narcissism, grandiosity, antisocial tendencies, addictive tendencies. If you are like this, I believe it is essential that you try an SSRI and keep taking it for a long time, if it works. I would put this ahead of the other step I would recommend: full dynamic therapy or psychoanalysis.

SOME FURTHER 'TOP TIPS' FOR RAISING SEROTONIN

Over and above pills and therapy, there are a wide variety of other steps that many people claim have helped them. The important thing here is to keep an open mind and to try different approaches out to find ones that suit you.

In his invaluable book *Overcoming Depression* (London: Robinson), Paul Gilbert lists a number of 'initial steps' for reducing depression. Many of these may seem trivial and commonsensical but for depressed people, they are often critical. The first step is to get into the habit of breaking down seemingly large problems into smaller ones. By identifying and concentrating on each of the actions that a problem requires in order to be solved and not worrying about the outcome, generalized unproductive fear and rumination can be reduced. He also stresses the obvious but nonetheless important need to plan positive activities. Depressed people easily find themselves swamped by boring chores and end up never getting around to enjoyable ones. Boredom is a major problem for the depressed and the first solution is to actually recognize that you are bored. Plans can then be made to do something enjoyable. Another fundamental is creating time and space for yourself. Many depressed mothers feel their lives have been hijacked by their children. By finding others to take the strain, even if it is only for an hour a week, they can create gaps in which to give themselves treats. Finally, Gilbert stresses the importance of organizing sleep properly. For example, many people imagine that a drink or two helps with this, but in fact it leads to disturbed patterns – lurid dreams, nightwaking.

On a purely practical level, a number of other changes have been found useful:

Relaxation, anti-stress, physical methods: any of Yoga, Transcendental Meditation and The Alexander Technique (a way for improving posture) done for 10 to 20 minutes first thing every morning, often seems to raise mood (of these, Yoga may be the most effective for depression). Contrary to popular stereotypes, none of these activities entails adopting kinky, outlandish positions, nor do they require extreme sup-pleness or the fitness of an athlete. Regular vigorous exercise is, nonetheless, often helpful.

Low-serotonin people often do not look after their bodies well. Gilbert lists some basic techniques for improving your breathing and muscular relaxation. He also describes mental techniques, such as creative visualization – ways of bringing pleasant images into your mind – to reduce stress.

Rest: many people either spend too much or too little time relaxing in bed. People with chronic fatigue may need to discipline themselves into a programme of energy conservation, taking it very easy for most week-day evenings for example, or having an afternoon nap on Saturdays and Sundays. Pursued over a period of six months, combined with other Top Tips, rest can be critical. However, some people find that when they lie down they are filled with gloomy rumination. SSRIs may help a great deal with this, enabling previously manic people to have the odd lie-in or nap in the early evening, not because the drugs make the person dozy but because their mind is less troubled by negative junk thoughts. On top of this, there is abundant evidence that taking regular and proper holidays is beneficial to mental health – surprisingly many people do not take them.

Diet: people are often amazed at the improvement in mood that follows the adoption of a 'healthy' diet and having seen the results, wonder out loud what on earth is going into modern food that is so damaging (needless to say, there is virtually no good research in this area; it would hardly be funded by the food or agro-chemical industries, the government show minimal interest because the medical profession tend to dismiss the whole idea as hysterical, unscientific poppycock – so of course it remains untested and they can say 'there is no evidence' . . . because they will not allow the research to be done or do it themselves). One approach is to consume only the juice extracted from pears, sweet beet-root (from Marks and Spencer) and carrots, from a juice extractor for a period of three days every month, consuming as many apples as are required if hungry in the interim. Another approach (well described in Leslie Kenton's *Raw Energy*) is to restrict oneself to raw foods for spec-ified periods. I suspect that very few people would not benefit from cut-ting out all junk food, alcohol, dairy products, red meat, sugar (especially chocolate) and carbohydrate for short periods from time to time. Ideally, these approaches should be sustained fanatically for at least three months before slowly returning to more normal diets before mental benefits are obtained. A book already exists for those wishing to use diet to control serotonin levels: *The Serotonin Solution* by Judith

Wurtman (1996, published by Fawcett Columbine: New York).

A fundamental problem facing many low-serotonin people is that they are effectively addicted to drugs of solace, quick fixes for making them feel better in the very short term.

Sugary, milky foods such as chocolate provide a brief sense of well-being often shortly followed by sickly feelings and self-attacking thoughts that can turn into bulimia (making yourself sick).

Alcohol is far more of a problem than most of us realize. It raises serotonin in the short term but from around the third drink onwards, reduces it and in the morning, can lead to such low serotonin that . . . you have another drink to cheer yourself up. Most people regard a drink in the early evening as a reasonable way to relax, but for those with low serotonin it is liable to create melancholy or bad temper. Because alcohol is so endemic in our culture, knitted into its rituals, it is hard to avoid. The best way is to have periods when you abstain totally, removing your choice in the matter. This can be for weekdays or two particular days a week or one month on, one month off. The main thing is to have such periods because it will make you realize just how much harm it is doing. For those who are also concerned with weight problems, it is worth remembering that the average unit of alcohol contains a lot of calories and that half a bottle of wine is equivalent to a meal.

Finally, young people with low serotonin often are attracted by illegal drugs precisely because they provide a temporary solace from their daily despair. In many cases, these drugs distract from the true problem and conceal a depression. For those who take ecstasy, I would strongly recommend that they read the section on drugs in Appendix II: there is a very real likelihood that this drug actually destroys the receptors in the brain synapse which receive serotonin. Given this probability, anyone with low serotonin would be extremely unwise to take this drug.

BASIC IMPLICATIONS OF MY ANALYSIS FOR THE LIFE AND MIND OF THE LOW-SEROTONIN INDIVIDUAL

All of us suffered trauma and neglect as children to some extent and coupled with our genetic inheritance, this makes us more or less vulnerable to the new strains placed on our well-being by modern life since 1950. If we were wholly rational, which of course we are not, it would be a simple matter to counter these new strains but because we are not, therapy can help us to observe the following dicta, derived from the analysis of previous chapters:

COUNTERING THE EFFECTS OF MALADAPTIVE SOCIAL
COMPARISON

We compare ourselves with other people too much, too often and in self-
destructive ways:

1. **Individualism And Aspirations**: Your need to be 'different' has
been inflated as have your assumptions about how much 'better off' other
people are than you – getting more sex, money, friends, better marriages.
The inflation happens to suit the interests of that abstract entity called
'advanced capitalism'. There is no conspiracy but, for example, it is in the
commercial interests of everyone whose living derives from the manufacture, marketing and sale of drugs of solace (legal and illegal) for you to be
in need of solace – to have depressed mood, irritability, discontentment –
and therefore, little attempt is going to be made to protect you. Your discontent is exploited by purveyors of other goods and services as well,
because nearly all of us seek solace in material possessions and the purchase of services from others, encouraged to believe we can fill the inner
void with external solutions. It is also in the interests of advanced capitalism for your tastes to become ever more diverse – New, Improved, Better
versions of products that have only very marginal differences from their
predecessors or competitors can only sell if you are convinced that you are
defining yourself through the decision to buy this rather than that.

On the oracle in Delphi were written the words 'Nothing In Excess'
and 'Know Thyself' and the passage of 2,000 years makes that wisdom
no less relevant. Ask yourself these questions: How much do I define
myself through my consumer behaviour? How realistic are my aspirations for wealth, status, power, beauty, handsomeness, sex, a better marriage? Where do these come from – how much are they created by the
society I live in, my parents, my peers? Above all, what would my needs
be if I completely ignored what other people have got in these respects
and focused on what I want regardless of this?

The implication of these questions is not that you should become a
Trappist monk with no material, social or sexual needs. It is merely to
point out that many people are making themselves unhappy by having
unrealistic expectations and irrational urges for individualism. It is not
being suggested that there is anything wrong with wanting a compact
disc player or a better tennis racket, let alone a more exciting job or
improved marriage. It is simply to question the extent to which all these
changes derive from you, are realistic and serve your needs. If purchas-
ing something or if changing your love or work life really are expressing
your needs, then fine, but all too often they are the product of excessive,

undiscounted upward social comparisons generated by an overheated society.

Therapy can help to address these problems, not only through examining your parents' role in creating them in your particular case, but also through strengthening identity.

2. **Media**: advertising, television (factual and drama), feature films, newspapers and magazines encourage your Wannabee tendencies. They stimulate your interest in new possessions and identities and offer a bogus illusion that you can have or be something you have not or are not. The vast majority of women of all ages cannot possibly hope to resemble the tiny minority of spectacular beauties who decorate the media. Most men cannot attain the looks, status, power and wealth of the media roles and models offered to them. It is crucially important to challenge the tendency to make undiscounted comparisons with these media portraits and to reinstate the boundaries between fantasy and reality which the skill of the artists who create them erodes. The magical thinking at the heart of advertising, the suspension of disbelief necessary for fictions and the successful appeals to one's emotional lowest common denominators (sex, cruelty, greed) on television must all be enjoyed for what they are and not confused with the personal reality of your everyday life.

Therapy can help to do this. In the relationship with the therapist it is possible to identify the ways in which you falsely invent them, based not just on your childhood experiences but also on the media exposure, and to discover or rediscover the difference between reality and fantasy. Having done so, fantasy becomes more a fulfilling source for your own creativity rather than a means for commercial interests to stimulate desire for their products.

3. **The Happiest Days Of Your Life**: if school ever was the happiest time of the average person's life, it is very hard to believe that it still is. At ever earlier ages we are required to begin the agonizing process of failing. However well you did at school, it was not good enough. From around the age of seven to nine years old you compared yourself to others who for whatever reason – greater motivation, better parental tuition, higher genetic intelligence – came higher in class. If you were top of the class, there was always a school somewhere else where you would not have been. The relentless undiscounted upward comparison at school creates a permanent inferiority complex for large swathes of the population.

Therapy will, of course, examine how your parents reacted to your educational performance, but it can also reduce the lasting resentment and humiliation many people feel on recalling their schooldays and reclaim your abilities and their evaluation for yourself. Instead of that lurking sense of inadequacy, you can establish for yourself which talents are important and a potential source of fulfilment. The drive to educate all the population is an admirable one, but the use of social comparison and peer pressure to hothouse overachievement has been a major cause of depression and anger.

4. **Occupational Pressures**: again due to circumstances completely beyond your control, you probably blame yourself for feeling either that your career is not as successful as it 'should' be or that it is not as fulfilling as you would like. Yet your 'failure' or lack of an interesting job is not your fault but a feature of modern life. It is partly due to increased individualism and aspirations but also to the increasing tendency for people to define themselves and to be defined by their occupation. This is extremely damaging to self-esteem since, inevitably, the vast majority of people occupy low-status posts in unstimulating professions – there are always be a great many more indians than chiefs in advanced capitalist societies as currently organized.

Therapy can help to develop other criteria for success or failure than how much power, status or wealth is attached to your occupation (although it should never be denied that these will always be important for most of us). You may cease comparing yourself with people who are utterly irrelevant to your true ambitions, redefine the role of work in your life as more secondary, identify other occupations or leisure activities which are more important and above all, become less prone to evaluating yourself and others by what they 'do'.

COUNTERING THE TREND TOWARDS BROKEN ATTACHMENTS
The nub of this problem is divorce and separation and again, over-stimulated expectations and individualism play a significant role. Too many of us blame our problems or sense of dissatisfaction on our partners without realizing that our expectations of what personal relationships can deliver have often spiralled way beyond what is likely. Too many spend a substantial part of their life searching for 'the right person' only to find that the same patterns that occurred in their first marriage repeat. Leaving aside the damage that this odyssey does to partners and children, it often results in the traveller finishing up at a bitter and twisted psychic destination in middle and old age. Far too many depressive and angry people are using their relationships as a vehicle for their problems, rather

than seeking treatment. Anyone with children contemplating divorce who believes that 'the problem' lies primarily in their partner would benefit from a reality check with a therapist. Of course there are marriages that for all sorts of reasons are better off ending than continuing and the positive aspect of the increased divorce rate is that there is no longer any need to stay in these torture chambers. But if you are aggressive or depressive it is imperative that you receive treatment for these problems, however much they may be caused by your current partner.

A crucial area demanding insight and tolerance from both parties is employment. Neither emotionally nor financially can men afford to continue to be so put out by women's work. If the mother of their baby wants to work it is almost certainly better for the mental health of that baby that she does so, for if she stayed at home she would be at high risk of becoming depressed. So long as the substitute care is adequate, there need be no damage to the child or mother. Above all, if the man feels so strongly about it, he should consider being the mother himself.

However, women must let men into that role, which they often do not ,and they must not treat the women who substitute for them as dim-witted employees to be hired and fired at whim. They must also be much more tolerant and less threatened by the choices other women make. Full-time career women are very liable to look down their noses at full-time mothers (and the women they employ to care for their babies), and vice versa. Hopefully this is a temporary problem that will largely disappear in future generations.

The sexual shambles we are currently in will also hopefully become realigned to a happier consensus before too long. Again, the proclivities of both genders should be respected by each other rather than stigmatized. Somehow we have to reconcile the evidence that physical appearance is still extremely important to men and that ambition-industriousness is important to women with our sincere belief that it should not be so. If men are attracted to younger women it does not help if older women sneer at both for their 'shallowness'. Equally, the attraction of women to power, status and wealth in men does not have to cause both parties to become cynical about love and to see all sexual relationships as more or less approximating to prostitution.

For all these problems, therapy can help to distinguish what is real from what is modish flim-flam. Quite apart from being a rigorous customs checkpoint for the large quantity of baggage that we bring to our adult relationships from childhood, it can save marriages or encourage responsible and fruitful behaviour where separation is unavoidable.

Chapter 9

Treating The Low-Serotonin Society

Aligning Advanced Capitalism To Our Basic Instincts

'We were not put on this earth to enjoy ourselves'
(The aunt of a friend of mine)

It should be apparent by now that my central argument is that advanced capitalism as it is currently organized is not meeting our evolved needs for status and attachment. A *simple* solution to this problem would be to recreate the conditions for which our genes were evolved – a low-density population living in a technologically primitive world in which humans were nomadic. Of course, this is not a realistic option anyway. I do not believe that it is inevitable that advanced capitalism should create low-serotonin societies. Karl Marx maintained that capitalism always caused 'alienation' (the emptiness and despondency of which are similar to some of the psychological symptoms of people with low serotonin) but I do not accept this view. Some capitalist nations are making a much better fist of creating decent, satisfying societies than others. If there is a bland general statement arising from this book it is that, working within a capitalist framework, we must reorganize ourselves so that our technology and wealth operate in our emotional favour rather than against it, drawing on existing successful models and devising new ones where feasible.

The problem is that it is not in the interests of advanced capitalism for us to be more contented. 'Advanced capitalism' does not plan it that way, but just as 'selfish' genes evolve gradually in the direction that will most increase their likelihood of reproduction, so advanced capitalism blindly evolves in the direction of profit. If making people unhappy is more profitable then that is what advanced capitalism will favour. Encouraging dissatisfaction with one's current possessions and circumstances, by stimulating needs and dangling ever better alternatives, generates sales of goods and services. A discontent that is anything but divine has become a cornerstone of advanced capitalism. An unhappy person is more likely to consume, to 'shop till you drop' or to purchase drugs of solace (illegal ones, alcohol, cigarettes) or to spend money on modern compulsions (lotteries, consumer fetishism, overworking). This may help to explain the usefulness and popularity of the concept of an 'addictive personality', in which a propensity to interchangeable addictions to almost anything is posited. Although its adherents pathologize the individual and often believe that this personality type is genetically inherited, if the addictive personality exists it is probably a by-product of advanced capitalism. People from certain kinds of dysfunctional childhoods become compulsive when overstimulated to want, want, want, and their compulsions are indeed often easily switched between abuses of different activities (e.g. gambling, eating disorders), chemicals and aspects of relationships. So long as we continue to mistake for a reality the mirage that short-term material consumption can relieve our psychic problems, this will continue.

Even the grim statistics arising from broken attachments represent substantial economic activity. Consider the money that changes hands every time gender rancour and inflated expectations break up a family. There are the legal fees for the divorce. There is the need for the departing partner to buy or rent a new home (if they buy: estate agents' fees, chartered surveyor and legal fees, mortgage, decorating costs, furnishings) and to purchase a second set of 'essential' electrical goods (TV, video, stereo system). Finally, there are the medical costs resulting from the increased likelihood of mental and physical illnesses caused by the divorce.

Advanced capitalism also benefits from the massive costs of the crime wave which heightened material and professional aspirations and broken attachments have spawned. There are the insurance costs resulting from theft. There is the expense of sustaining a large police force, of the judicial system processing felons once they are apprehended, of incarcerating them and of supervising them once they are released (the probation service).

There are dozens of other examples, of which cigarette smoking is perhaps the most astonishingly blatant: the income and jobs that they represent so far outweigh the costs of treating the illnesses they cause that no government dares to stamp them out. So long as people feel depressed and powerless and cigarettes are available there will be plenty of smokers and plenty of profits.

In short, the low-serotonin society simply cannot afford for its citizens to be happier.

SHORT-TERM CHANGES: MORE ENCOURAGEMENT TO TAKE ANTIDEPRESSANTS?

A few months ago I had the opportunity to discuss some of the issues in this book with Jack Straw MP, before he became Home Secretary. I put it to him that he should see his future task as being to raise the serotonin levels of that large proportion of the population who are dispirited, disappointed and angry. He was mildly amused at such a mechanistic formulation, but I do believe this is a useful way of thinking about the problems he faces in his job.

The fact is that SSRIs counteract the effects of relative deprivation with extraordinary precision. The psychic changes they bring about are almost exactly the ones that are required to make most people more fulfilled – they create a more realistic perception of need. Contrary to popular mythology, they do not douse vitality, induce docility or create an unrealistically optimistic mental state. Rather, they *increase* realism. A dictator trying to keep the lid on a disaffected nation would be unwise to encourage the widespread use of SSRIs because they *increase* awareness of real problems and make it less likely that people will buy into false solutions. Thus, for the subordinated, they reduce the number of junk thoughts ('I'm stupid', 'I'm inadequate' when you are not or need not be) which are the real unreality of depression. People whose self-love and confidence have been destroyed by social comparison and broken attachments are much less likely to feel hopeless and helpless and will arrive at realistic solutions to their particular problems. SSRIs also increase assertiveness, which for many depressed people is a major problem, and they often replace aggression with assertion, which for violent men would be a considerable advance. There is less need to hit someone if you can make your point effectively with words. Many of these men are highly articulate within their own argot but have not learnt to use their wit and verbal dexterity to assert themselves because it did not work for them at home or in the playground at school. Such men often feel very badly about themselves and have very good reasons for doing so: their families, teachers and employers have been telling them, implicitly and explicitly, that they are worthless (literally in the case of employers – the monetary value placed on their labour is low) all their lives and they have come to believe it. On top of this, SSRIs reduce neediness and impulsiveness, both common in people who resort to violence and to drugs, alcohol and food for solace.

It is probably a happy accident that the drug companies have managed to develop drugs at this particular moment in history that are so well attuned to treating the psychic damage wrought by relative deprivation and broken attachments. Obviously, as an averagely liberal, expensively educated product of the privileged sector of British society, I would prefer that Mr Straw achieves the raising of serotonin by social change rather than through pills. However, I am realistic enough to know that the costs and practical difficulties of such social changes make them unlikely in the short term. Meanwhile, millions of us face the following psychological problems:

- Depressed, aggressive spouses who blame their relationships for their problems and obtain a divorce but who find that exactly the same problems recur in subsequent relationships
- Depressed, antisocial teenagers who are unable to benefit from educational opportunities because they lack confidence and concentration and who, as a result, become the largely unemployable . . .
- Depressed, aggressive men from low-income families who feel like 'losers' because of their childhood experiences and lack of career opportunities and who act violently or destructively to their intimates or to strangers
- Aggressive, bullying wealthy or powerful men who torment and humiliate their intimates and employees, thereby successfully transferring their unhappiness into others
- Depressed, irritable mothers who feel isolated and undervalued for their work who are hostile and destructive to their intimates
- Depressed, irritable working mothers who wish they could spend more time with their families
- Depressed, impulsive people who use drugs of solace and compulsions like gambling to make themselves feel better.

The scientific evidence presented in Appendix II and in Chapter 7 suggests that all these groups would be much better able to take advantage of the good things on offer (material and emotional) in their lives, and to create more thereof, were they to take SSRIs. In the case of people with low incomes and few qualifications, it is difficult to see what else is going to happen to help them to join the affluent society, even in the long term. Yet it is not only me who feels deeply uncomfortable with such a proposition.

SHOULD JACK STRAW AND HIS COLLEAGUES ENCOURAGE MORE
OF US TO TAKE ANTIDEPRESSANTS?
Let us be absolutely clear about the scale of the problem.

The proportion of adult Britons suffering from psychiatric morbidity at any one time is now almost one third if the survey by Glyn Lewis (see Appendix I) is correct. If the definitions were widened to include all low-serotonin problems, such as violence and impulsive aggression, it would be around one half – perhaps 20 million people. The majority of them receive no formal treatment (pills or therapy) to raise their serotonin levels.

Estimates vary as to the proportions of specifically depressed people who are receiving no treatment but it is at least one half and may be as high as two-thirds.[1] Although the Royal College of Psychiatrists mounted a campaign in 1992 to increase awareness of the problem and although the number of prescriptions for antidepressants has increased they are nowhere near enough to reach the many untreated depressed people. The proportion of violent or aggressive men who receive no treatment (apart from self-medicated alcohol) is even higher.

The costs of depression are staggering. In Britain, the annual expense of major depression alone in 1993 in terms of lost days at work, reduced productivity and so on is estimated to be £3 billion.[2] Against this, £420 million is spent on healthcare costs in treating depression, of which only £47 million is spent on drug treatment (three-quarters of it on women). In America the annual cost of major depression alone was estimated to be $53 billion.[3] If the costs of violence and impulsive aggression (to the judicial system, in healthcare, victims' days lost at work, motorcar accidents and so on) were added to these bills, they would be considerably higher.

Thus, on a purely mercenary cost-benefit analysis, the benefits far outweigh the costs of increasing the numbers taking SSRIs. Depending on the scale of the increase, it might add £100–300 million to the national drugs bill and as the figures cited above show, the savings would more than pay for this. But of course the issue is not purely mercenary. We are talking about the inner lives of human beings.

It is highly probable that the proportions taking these drugs will increase substantially within 20 years: perhaps then the majority of us will be routinely taking drugs to improve ourselves. Professor Malcolm Lader told me that 'Over the next 20 years, normal, healthy people will become able to manipulate their mood using drugs without side-effects, it's going to happen. The only question is how much normality we allow to be treated with drugs. The drugs won't be so precise that we can give someone a pill that will throw them into ecstasy on hearing Beethoven's Fifth Symphony, but not his Sixth, but there will be drugs to tweak the general sense of well-being, affability and *bonhomie*. Or if you're a bit manic or overly outgoing, there will be drugs that will make you more introverted and contemplative.' Lader is no marginal quack with a bee in his bonnet. He is the Professor of Psychopharmacology at Britain's foremost psychiatric research centre, the Maudsley Hospital's Institute of Psychiatry, and his view was confirmed by five other leading psychiatrists whom I polled.

However, running against this, most Britons are Pharmacological Calvinists, as noted in Chapter 7. Medical drugs for physical illnesses, fine, but psychodrugs? As I have suggested, you have to be mildly depressed to live in Britain – self-disparaging, falsely modest, undemonstrative, emotionally deadpan – it is part of our culture and many benefits ensue, such as our ironic humour, healthy scepticism and intellectual rigour. We rather like feeling bad and the Worst Case of the psychiatrists' pharmaceutical heaven sounds like a science-fiction dystopia . . .

Regular personality tests from early childhood (just like eye or dental checkups) . . . managers unhappy with the performance of employees enforcing a visit to the company pill doctor as a condition of employment . . . the end of exceptional achievement – artists, scientists and visionaries 'cured' of their genius . . . warring couples and families prescribed drugs to create a 'better' balance . . . chairmen of drug companies more powerful than elected leaders . . . systematic drugging of five-year-old boys identified as potentially violent.

The undrugged Briton reels in horror. But these ideas are fantasy. It is extremely unlikely that anyone will be coerced into taking the drugs. Perhaps we prefer to create these straw men than look coolly at the very real benefits that might accrue. We are already using medical drugs to change ourselves in all sorts of ways. Just as we correct nutritional deficiencies with vitamins today, very soon we may think nothing of supplementing the chemicals that make up our thoughts and feelings. At the moment we improve on our physical health when we are not technically ill, so why not our Selves? When we take drugs for baldness or Hormone Replacement we do not see it as treatment for a disease. That may be the way we will think of drugs for our personalities. What is called normal today may be regarded as pretty depressed in 20 years' time.

In theory the benign potential of psychodrugs is enormous but few of us see it that way. As we have seen, millions of hours are lost every year to emotional problems that do not qualify as mental illnesses. Cooperation and creativity are destroyed by the low serotonin of bullying bosses, and in low-serotonin employees, lack of confidence and stunted creativity are common. There would be no need for Big Brother to force us to take the drugs because the logic of becoming a more successful worker – and therefore better paid, with more power and status – would be overwhelming to all but the most intransigent. As a little experiment

I telephoned several successful managing directors to ask what they thought about the idea. Every one of them expressed deep abhorrence.

Charles Morgan, heir to the sports car company of that name and production manager at its Malvern factory, has 120 employees to look after. 'I see reason rather than drugs as the best solution to any human problems. The process is at least as important as the getting there.

'In every team you need variety. I'm an idealist and it would be disastrous if you drugged the pessimists who pour cold water on my wilder schemes.' He most definitely would not take drugs for his faults. 'I'm impetuous, that's my biggest one. But it's my role to be like that. Life is a series of complications and drugs are not the answer to them.'

Stephen Verral is managing director of Policymaster, a Midlands company producing computer software for the insurance industry. He is boss to 130 people. 'I think it's a bizarre idea. What happens when an employee comes in, Kalashnikov blazing, because he's been given the wrong pills? Surely we don't know enough about the brain. I'm highly sceptical, I bet this idea comes from America.' Verral believes in 'changing causes not symptoms. It's better not to paper over the cracks. I have some very talented people on my team. What might you lose if you gave them drugs?' Regarding himself, he was having none of it: 'I'm too abstract, not rigorous enough. But I prefer to change by working it out myself.'

Perhaps the profoundest fear is that the drugs will make us all the same and dope away high achievement. Studies of geniuses and high achievers show they suffered more than average amounts of childhood adversity, such as the death of a parent or gross maltreatment or neglect. Their outstanding ability was often a way of converting the emotional fallout from being a destructive bomb to an energy source. It is not that little bit more that made them great, it's that little bit less. Correct the chemical deficits that childhood traumas cause by putting back what is lacking and it could be the end of progress. Where would we be today if Winston Churchill's or Isaac Newton's Black Dogs of depression had been locked in a pharmaceutical kennel, if the conspicuous weirdness of the Prousts and Van Goghs had been chemically corralled into the fold of normality? Use drugs to remove the anger, self-hatred and lack of identity that many great men feel and they might not be great any more, just content. We begrudge them that. We like the idea that William Blake took hallucinogens and Sartre sought inspiration in amphetamines (knowing it would hasten his death) and we would hate them taking antidepressants to make them happier and more like the rest of us. Psychoanalyst Dr Anthony Storr has analysed the lives of dozens of geniuses. He told me, 'If you iron us all out with drugs you're going to diminish human achievement, as well as help-ing people. We don't want to end up with a lot of grey mediocrities. Where are the political leaders going to come from if we are all well balanced? Since it's an insane ambition, Parliament would be empty.'

But if high achievers are more emotionally disturbed than average, they could be even more successful if some of the problems were cor-rected. A study of 24 manic-depressive artists who were prescribed Lithium showed treatment can increase productivity.[4] Six of them reported no change and another six supported Storr's view in that although it made them happier it also reduced their output. But 12 became more productive as a result of the drug, as well as happier. It is not reported how aesthetically edible was the fruit of the increase, so it must be admitted that there is the possibility that a medicated poet or painter lacks the angst to really deliver the goods. Nonetheless, in the case of many great achievers it is possible that carefully targeted drugs could have improved output without loss of quality. Dostoyevsky and Nietzsche spent a great deal of their lives in a state that can only be described as delusional. They might have done even more important work had they been spared these periods.

But most of us are not potential Dostoyevskys. On the face of it, there are good economic and psychiatric reasons why the shy, the oversensitive and the un-self-confident, let alone the depressive and aggressive, should be taking SSRIs. Being a recent invention the drug is still expensive, costing 20 times as much as older preparations, so the Department of Health are unlikely to be in a rush to bring this about. Yet the overall sav-ings to the national economy would be huge if a significant number of previously impaired workers ceased taking days off, underperforming, bullying and so on.

Another criticism is that we do not yet know for sure that long-term use of the drugs is not harmful in some unforeseen way. SSRIs such as Prozac are still very new and it is conceivable that all sorts of undesired effects of taking them daily for decades could emerge. There are sound reasons for doubting this. Tricyclic antidepressants have been with us for more than 30 years and there are millions of people who have been tak-ing them continuously. Since Tricyclics do something very similar to SSRIs, and since no unforeseen, adverse long-term effects have resulted, there is no reason to suppose that SSRIs will be different. But for those who want to believe that cosmetic pharmacology will never come about there is plenty of ammunition and Ted Dinan, Professor of Psychological Medicine at St Bartholomew's Hospital, is eager to fire it. 'Psycho-pharmacology has grown so fast because of luck. Just because a few drugs have accidentally turned out to work doesn't mean we can complete the jigsaw. Our understanding of the brain is in the Stone Age compared with our knowledge of other organs. We are many many decades from being able to target specific traits like shyness or overseriousness.' Dinan points out that we do not know even the structure, let alone the function, of the vast majority of neurochemicals. 'The amines, like serotonin, that we have begun to understand – and only very partially at that – constitute just 0.01% of all the brain's chemicals. We know that there are at least 1,000 peptide brain transmitters, for instance, but we haven't even got a clue what their structure is, let alone what they're for.'

But Professor Dinan also admits that he is at heart a pharmacological Calvinist and that his values rather than science motivate many of his views. He regards the prospect of drugged normality with a mixture of disgust and fear. 'It's an appalling vista, a very, very frightening avenue to go down, you are painting a real nightmare scenario.' That is his feeling but he does not deny that it would only require us to maintain the rate of change of the last 30 years for Professor Lader and the other psychiatrists' predictions to be fulfilled regarding the next 20.

My conclusion is that the fact that pills are the short cut away from the low-serotonin society should not prevent us keeping an open mind about their potential benefits. There are too many groups of people for whom SSRIs may be the best short-term hope, in some cases, the only one. My challenge to Jack Straw or anyone else who disputes this is: what are you going to do that is as simple and effective a way of raising serotonin? Consider some examples from the groups listed earlier:

The archetypal 25-year-old man with a history of violence and delinquency who drinks heavily, paid for by participation in the black economy since he has no job and little prospect of obtaining one that he will feel is satisfying.

Perhaps he needs to scale down his material ambitions. Jack Straw will say he should take responsibility for himself and cut down on his drinking so that he is less violent. But in the real world, it will take time to help him to realize that some of his aspirations are unrealistic and in some parts of the country, his chances of obtaining even a menial job are small. What is the objection to offering him the opportunity, as a free and voluntary act, of choosing to take SSRIs for a year or two which might enable him to make use of the training courses available to him, to drink less and feel more confident about getting on with his life in a more productive fashion? Do the objections take account of the men and women he will assault in the meantime?

His 23-year-old ex-partner, a single mother with two small children by him and another man. Although she has a secretarial qualification she does not want a job, not because she is workshy but because she wants to look after her children. Overstretched and exhausted, of course she sometimes thumps them and is unable to meet their emotional needs to the extent that she would like. She feels swindled by life. Her mood is mostly bleak and despondent but she does not like visiting doctors.

There may be as many as one million women in this country in these circumstances with this mental state, many of whom have received no treatment. In her case, although I know of no scientific evidence to support this, I suspect that she would be more likely than a wealthy counterpart to be prescribed Tricyclics rather than SSRIs if she were to see her GP. The GP might not be a fundholder and therefore, more influenced by the extra cost of the newer drug.

I would far prefer that Jack Straw and his colleagues introduced welfare programmes such as those found in Denmark or in some parts of America (see below). They would provide her with the support she needs, plugging her into her community and giving specialist assistance to her children who even by now, will be headed towards the lowest reaches of the educational system. But it is highly unlikely that such a programme will be affordable for the foreseeable future. In the meantime, what should be done to help her, today? If taking SSRIs for a year (or several years) made her feel better about herself and her circumstances she might be more capable of taking control of her life ('responsibility for herself') and making the best of it, so what are the objections to this? Do they take account of the damage that is being done to her children, in the meantime?

Both these examples involve people of low income. In the last 20 years in several developed nations (Britain, America, Canada, Australia), the numbers of such people have grown because inequalities have hugely increased. Liberals (amongst whom I count myself) will feel a sharp pain in their guts at the thought of trying to use drugs to address problems with blatantly socio-economic causes. The only reason I can advance for doing so is that I do not know of a better way of immediately countering the ill-effects of modern inequalities and empowering those whose serotonin levels have been diminished by being made to feel like losers. For some people in seemingly hopeless predicaments, the drugs might better enable them to understand them, regain control over their lives and find constructive solutions. Given the triumph of Market Economics which forbids increased welfare spending, the challenge to liberals is to come up with a better alternative.

As for wealthy people with low serotonin, they should not rule out antidepressants either, although the last chapter presented an array of therapies that might also help, some of which are not available to low income people. In later sections I shall suggest a variety of changes that might help us all in the longer term but in the immediate present, pills and therapy are the best the individual has got.

Because I am not a politician or civil servant, I shall not even begin to suggest how the greater use of SSRIs might be legislated for but there are a few points worth considering. I am convinced that the Department of Health should make the funds available for the millions of prescriptions currently of Tricyclics to be replaced by SSRIs. Whilst there are a minority of low-serotonin patients who only respond to the older drugs, I believe that the vast majority of patients on them today are only so treated because their GP cannot afford the alternative or because of ignorance.

A further step would be for a research study to be mounted testing whether impulsively violent offenders commit less violence (compared with a control group) if prescribed SSRIs. When (rather than if) the study proved that this is so, the probation service and GPs should be encouraged to give such men the choice of taking the drugs.

On top of this, it would be possible for the Department of Health to encourage GPs to prescribe SSRIs much more readily than they do at present for the mass of low-serotonin symptoms that come before them every day. There is at present among many GPs a fear of making the mistake of their predecessors in doling out large quantities of barbiturates to which the patients became addicted. But it is already clear that, with the exception of Paroxetine, SSRIs are not addictive and there is no scientific reason for this fear. The Department of Health should therefore be re-educating GPs in this matter.

Of course, nothing that I have written so far is a solution. It is merely a temporary expedient that would help millions of people. I attach far less importance to it than the subject of the next section: encouraging therapy.

SHORT-TERM CHANGES: GOVERNMENT REGULATION AND SUPPORT FOR THERAPY

The organization of therapy in Britain is a shambles, an absolute disgrace. The blame falls foursquare on the shoulders of the government of the last 18 years. Despite numerous requests by the various therapy training bodies for legislation, the Department of Health has repeatedly refused to become involved on the grounds that it is a privatized industry that must be left to Market Forces. The result is an unregulated mishmash in which anybody can still set up as a therapist and fleece the public of their money, or even worse – and that is just the completely untrained therapists. There are over 70 bodies who train a huge variety of kinds of therapists, some of whom should not be allowed to so designate themselves. For example, if astrologers wish to practise astrology, then good luck to them, but it should be illegal to pass themselves off as therapists.

It is imperative that the new government sets up a body to define and to regulate therapists. In order to establish which activities can justifiably present themselves as psychotherapeutic it should apply the same standards as it does to psychotropic prescription drugs: only those therapies should be approved that have been proven through scientifically conducted research to be more effective than no treatment. Some therapies, such as many dynamic and cognitive therapies, have already been tested in this way. Others would need to be independently assessed. A committee of suitable experts could decide which therapies were based on theories and methods worth testing at all – it would be a waste of money to test the astrological varieties, for example.

On top of this, as already suggested in the last chapter, an independent body should be created to deal with potential breaches of ethics. No patient should begin treatment without knowing the telephone number and address of this body and without a detailed professional curriculum vitae of their therapist, complete with a leaflet agreed by the training body explaining the basic theory behind the treatment and its typical practices.

On top of all this, there is a great deal the Department of Health could be doing to ensure that well-trained therapists are available throughout the country. Having established which therapies are worthwhile, it should support and nurture them, not leave them to lead a hand-to-mouth existence which means that some trainings are a great deal more rigorous than others. Currently, most therapists must pay for their own training. Unless they have substantial private means, they must occupy a full-time job whilst training, a situation that is not conducive to creating the best possible therapists. Although posts for therapists are gradually becoming more common within the National Health Service, there are still far too few to meet the demand. For those who can afford private treatment this is no problem, but for the rest there is an urgent need for this kind of treatment to be made available.

At present, the mental health field is dominated by doctors. It will be seen from my earlier comments that I am far from being hostile to the prescription of drugs for mental illnesses. Furthermore, I fully recognize the nightmarish difficulties facing psychiatrists (some of my best friends . . .) who have to treat the severely mentally ill. They work extremely long hours, they are increasingly required to mop up effects of social problems that are not strictly speaking the province of specialists in mental illness – problems such as violence and the fallout from domestic and marital disputes. The 'care in the community' programme has made many psychiatrists' lives a bureaucratic hell. Faced with a woman who believes she is the Virgin Mary and who is convinced that God has given her a mission to save her children from an evil world by killing them, the psychiatrist must find a safe place for her, yet all too often, finding a bed in a mental hospital takes up much of the day. I make these points to emphasize that I am not against psychiatry in any way and that I believe psychiatrists often do a fine job in trying circumstances.

First and foremost, psychiatrists are doctors who have had a further training in the administration of chemicals (and electricity) in order to change the physical state of brains. Whilst many of them are wise and sensible, some know little about basic psychology and child development and some are actively hostile to it. It is such people, for the most part, who advise the Department of Health on how best to spend taxpayers' money in improving mental health and not surprisingly, their advice is driven by their training and professional loyalties. It is only an accident of history that has led to their dominance over the mental health field and it may be that the government should reconsider its extent. Such a development is exactly the kind of reallocation of resources within existing budgets that the present government is committed to.

Compared with therapists, psychiatrists are expensive and GPs are nearly always far too short of time to provide therapy, even if they are qualified. For many low-serotonin problems that arise in the community, a psychiatrist is not required. For example, we saw in Chapter 7 regarding minor depression that psychiatrists themselves state that there are only a few antidepressants to choose from which are best. Of course, a medically qualified person should be the one to evaluate which drugs are required but in most cases this is a GP, not a specialist. Perhaps some of the resources currently spent on psychiatry could be spent on creating properly qualified and regulated therapists and their training, but since the 8,000 psychiatrists are already stretched to the limit, it may be that extra money will have to be found.

Far more than any changes to the arrangements regarding the prescription of SSRIs, these innovations in the world of therapy would help to break what Keith Joseph labelled the 'cycle of deprivation'. Truly, those who forget the past are condemned to repeat it and although Joseph was concerned with the plight of the most disadvantaged, this dictum applies as much to the wealthy. All of us, probably without one single exception, need to carry out an inventory of our childhoods. Of course therapy is not a panacea and unfortunately, not enough therapists (of all kinds) are sufficiently focused on helping the child in their patient to identify what actually happened in their childhood family. All of us suffered as children and we spend the rest of our lives making what we will of it. Taking responsibility for ourselves can only carry us so far. There is a limit to what we can achieve alone or with friends and if the government were to throw its weight behind creating properly organized and scientifically based therapy, it would be a great investment in our futures.

When John Major won the 1992 election he spoke of a property-owning democracy in which wealth would be 'cascading down the generations'. Tony Blair has the opportunity to create a more mentally healthy society in which the wealth that cascades down the generations is psychological insight, not the fees of estate agents.

LONG-TERM CHANGES: TACKLING THE RISE IN ASPIRATIONS AND INDIVIDUALISM

Chapters 2 and 3 identified four main causes of our increased tendency to subordinate ourselves by excessive and maladjusted social comparisons: the rise in individualism and aspirations; the media; the education system; and the job market. Of these I shall devote most attention to the first.

COMMUNITARIANISM ON THE COUCH

It will be recalled that Juliet, the 25-year-old woman described in the Introduction, is considerably more individualist and aspirational than her equivalent would have been 40 years ago and it seemed that these impulses caused her to suffer from relative deprivation which, in turn, contributed (along with her other problems, such as her parents' divorce) to her suffering from low serotonin. Jim, the young man with whose emotional crisis the book began, suffered from very similar problems. Does this mean that they need to scale down their personal and professional ambitions to something more realistic and better suited to their particular case? If so, what can be done in the long term to help the millions of Juliets and Jims to achieve such an adjustment?

Two interrelated solutions are currently in fashion. The first is best exemplified by the highly influential work of Amitai Etzioni. If Baroness Thatcher's guru was the economist Milton Friedman, Prime Minister Blair's is Etzioni, an ethical philosopher with a sociological training, also imported from America. Any discussion of solutions must begin with the work of Etzioni since his thinking dominates our present leaders. New Labour use his key words ('rights' and 'obligations') repeatedly and many of their policies are similar in detail to proposals that he has made.

In his 1992 book *The Spirit of Community*, Etzioni makes a heartfelt plea for a 'moral revival'. As well as proposing numerous specific measures, he offers some general moral principles of which by far the most important (almost a mantra for New Labour) is that all rights carry with them responsibilities. According to him, we have forgotten that when we assert our rights, they carry obligations which must be fulfilled. For example, American surveys of young people show that they regard it as a right that they should be tried by a jury if accused of a crime, yet when asked if they are prepared to do jury service, they are reluctant. Most American parents were in favour of the 1992 Gulf War, but few wanted their offspring to have to fight in it.

Etzioni begins his book with a rousing 'Declaration' headed 'We hold these truths.' There follows a list of moral changes that 'we hold', almost all of them carefully tempered by a disclaimer that it is not his intention to curb freedoms. For example, the first paragraph of the Declaration is as follows: 'We hold that a moral revival in these United States is possible without Puritanism; that is, without busybodies meddling into our personal affairs, without thought police controlling our intellectual life. We *can* attain a recommitment to moral values – without puritanical excesses.' Etzioni claims that the critique of 1950s values which occurred in the 1960s was necessary and desirable but that along the way we have lost something. He claims that 'a return to the language of social virtues, interests and above all social responsibilities will reduce contentiousness and enhance social cooperation . . .'. He argues that the political Right have stolen the word 'moral' from the Left but believes that law and order, the virtues of the family, disciplined education and commitment to the community are the true preserve of liberals. Entitling his view 'communitarianism' and citing historical precedents, he argues that fundamental change will come not from government intervention but from the creation of a 'social movement'. He writes that 'what America needs now is a major social movement dedicated to enhanced social responsibility, public and private morality and the public interest'.

There are several novel (although few original) aspects of Etzioni's analysis, not the least of which is its lack of cynicism and refreshing optimism. It is a brave attempt to regain control over our fate using morality as the tool. But it is not a view that should be accepted uncritically.

As we shall see, placing immorality at the heart of his explanation runs counter to almost all the major theories and most of the empirical evidence of social science. Whether it be Marx (economic infrastructure causes social and cultural superstructure), Durkheim (science replaces religion as the division of labour in society multiplies) or Weber (the spirit of capitalism neatly dovetailed with the Protestant Ethic), or if you review the empirical evidence, there are strong reasons to doubt that morality is a cause rather than an effect of social and economic structures. Cross-national and historical studies suggest that our beliefs about right and wrong and the cosmological ideas underpinning them arise in response to our material conditions and our position within society. To maintain, as Etzioni does, that our problems derive from the collapse of morality is to scratch the surface. Whilst he may (or may not) be right that if more of us subscribed to his morality we should be happier, his account does not properly explain why so many of us have ceased to do so, compared with 1950.

Another problem with his analysis is that, despite the repeated protestations to the contrary, he *is* proposing to curb our freedoms. I have no objection to this in itself whatsoever (indeed, I shall be proposing curbs myself and agree with some of his), but it creates an uncomfortable tension in his book between proposals that sound remarkably like a return to the discipline, obedience and respect for authority that existed in the 1950s, and effectively, that we can carry on enjoying the same freedoms. For example, he proposes that families should reinstate the habit of eating meals together rather than in front of the television or that random testing of drivers for drink and drugs should be applauded. Both ideas seem eminently sensible, my point is merely that he cannot maintain in the same breath that there will be no restrictions of the individual resulting. Children who do not want to sit at meals with their (perhaps abusive and cruel, at least in some cases) parents will have to be forced to do so if his plan is implemented, likewise, those who drink or take drugs regularly will have to reduce their intake. He does not wish to be a killjoy, he says he will not interfere with our enjoyment of the hedonistic party that started in 1960, but when we read the smallprint, it rather looks as if it will be a lacklustre, teetotal event, with no loud music, ending well before the pubs close. He often sounds like a host inviting us to a party in which the instincts for sex and drugs and rock'n'roll will be kept under close control, or like an officious neighbour, complaining about the noise.

But the greatest problem is his all-pervasive emphasis on morality. In essence, what he has done is to take relative deprivation theory and substitute the word 'rights' for the words 'aspiration' and 'entitlement'. Instead of a proper analysis of why our expectations have spiralled out of control, he starts from the fact that they have – we are convinced that we are entitled to too many rights without having any obligations. The solution is for us to just accept that in this we are quite simply wrong, morally. Repeated utterance of the mantra 'no rights without obligations' has served New Labour well, not just in getting them elected but in reinstating a greater realism. This is fine. But the core problem is not just our sense of entitlement, it is our feeling that there are all sorts of commodities – material things, relationships, psychological states – that we are being deprived of, the feeling of relative deprivation. As we shall see, moral decay is more of an effect than a cause. The analysis in Chapters 2 and 3 suggests that the problem is caused by the demand for advanced capitalism to generate dissatisfaction in us, to multiply our individual needs and wants, to encourage us to believe that consuming can fill the void and that, in the words of the National Lottery publicity, It Could Be You who magically becomes rich enough to afford the advertised goods.

Etzioni cannot have his cake and eat it too. Either we can curb our excessive aspirations and individualism (preferably by addressing their true causes) or we can carry on as before. Both things cannot be true and relocating the whole problem to a moral framework does not solve it.

COMMUNITARIANISM AND INDIVIDUALISM-COLLECTIVISM

The second fashionable solution to the problem of the increased aspirations and individualism of the Juliets and Jims derives from the substantial body of theory and evidence concerning the differences between individualist and collectivist cultures. Indeed, Etzioni could have named his new social movement collectivism, so close are the parallels between it and communitarianism (perhaps collectivism would have had too oppressive a feel to it – communitarianism sounds more cuddly and voluntary). In general, a large body of evidence has consistently found that the English-speaking nations and much of Northern and Western Europe tend to be individualist, whilst some parts of Southern Europe (e.g. Greece, Southern Italy) and most of Africa, Asia and Latin America are collectivist.[5]

In individualist societies, identity is 'achieved' by educational, occupational and economic activity, through open competition in a supposedly meritocratic system regardless of gender, class and race.[5] In such societies, the self is defined by reference to inner feelings and thoughts rather than to externally preordained roles, such as kinship ties like 'mother' and 'husband'. The goal of the individualist is to express oneself, whether through hedonism, achievement or consumerism. In order to realize the achieved self, it must break away from ascribed kinship ties

321

to parents and families and become an individuated, separate person. The adolescent must seek out new ties and become part of a network of many groups – school, university, occupational – to whom they have divided loyalties. Families are small and parents see their job as being to foster self-reliance, independence and creativity in their children. Relations between citizens are regulated by laws and law enforcers rather than by moral pressure from kin and community. Crimes break laws and are punished for this reason, not because of group feeling that something 'wrong' has occurred that must be avenged. Interactions are based on principles of social equity, competition, noninterference in the business of others and social justice. Economic and personal exchange is regulated by legal contract.

By contrast, in collectivist societies identity is ascribed on the basis of kinship ties preordained by birth.[5] The goal of the ascribed self is to put other people's and the group's interests before one's own through a 'willingness and ability to feel and think what others are thinking and feeling, to absorb this information without being told and to help others satisfy their wishes and realize their goals'.[6] The erasing of hedonistic and selfish desires is valued as part of the successful execution of social roles and obligations, the cardinal virtue is sensitivity to the potential impact of one's individual actions upon the common fate. Unlike in the individualist culture, an adolescent is not encouraged to cut loose from parents and family. On the contrary, collectivist cultures tend to have large families at risk of descending into chaos and the goal of parents is to inculcate obedience, reliability and proper behaviour. The collectivist does not belong to many social groups with the result that loyalty to just a few is intense. Relations between citizens are based on trust and not losing face, rather than legal contracts, and are between occupants of social roles rather than Woody Allen-like individuals in search of their true self. Institutions are seen as an extension of the family, with paternalism and moralism reigning supreme.

In general, a growth in individualism coincides with urbanization.[7] Studies of change in attitudes and behaviour when people raised in traditional, collectivist societies become urbanized typically show a shift towards the following: positive attitudes to achievement; freedom from blood ties and parental authority and membership of achieved groups; openness to innovation; self-reliance and a belief in personal efficacy; belief in science rather than religion; and positive attitudes to education and higher aspirations therein.

The rise of liberal individualism in English-speaking nations represented a significant break with the medieval worldview and contrasts sharply with the collectivist Confucianism which dominates the moral-political philosophy of much of Asia. Whereas the liberal view insists upon the individual's right to choose and to engage freely in a search for personal gratification, the Confucian model promotes collective welfare and harmony.

Of course, as many authors have pointed out,[7] there are individualist and collectivist elements in all societies and individuals vary in the extent to which they 'sample' these different aspects, which are found to some degree in everyone. Studies within cultures (e.g. Illinois in America[8] or Puerto Rico[9]) show that the more individualist a person, the more achievement orientated, but also the lonelier and more alienated (which probably means low serotonin). A key factor seems to be the amount of social support the person receives – whether they have supportive intimate relationships. Thus, even in collectivist communities within India,[10] the amount of actual support a person receives is directly related to their degree of alienation, regardless of how much they sample collectivist rather than individualist elements in their society. Studies of social support among mothers with low incomes in developed nations suggest the same.

There are also variations within different sections of societies. Within developed nations, women are more collectivist than men, low-income classes more collectivist than affluent ones and people may be collectivist in some contexts (e.g. at home) and individualist in others (e.g. at work). It used to be assumed (in 'modernization theory') that individualist nations were more economically successful than collectivist ones but this is clearly no longer true: the success of Japan and the Asian Tiger economies demonstrates that both modes can create affluence under capitalism.[7]

This body of evidence provides strong grounds for supposing that in a wide variety of societies morality is largely an effect, not a cause, of socio-economic factors. Religion and superstition are replaced by scientific thinking when urbanization brings education and affluence. Cosmological beliefs cease to be the foundation of social cohesion as much as legal statutes and a great diversity of individual ethical systems emerge with an advanced Division of Labour. In low-technology, collectivist, rural societies, morality is the glue that binds, cooked by kinship ties. In individualist, high-technology, urban societies, individuals are encouraged to develop their own custom-built ethos, and the judicial system – rather than notions of right and wrong – protects each from the other. Whilst a society-wide code may exist, it is based more on rational arguments, such as social justice, rather than cosmological belief. Etzioni's communitarianism is an unmistakable call for a return to the collectivist mode. The list of 'truths' in his 'Declaration' is remarkably similar to it: a 'return' to moral values, reinstatement of law and order through community pressure, reconstruction of the family to boost ascribed rather than achieved identity and above all, putting a moral obligation to the common weal ahead of the selfish pursuit of rights.

TACKLING INDIVIDUALISM AND INCREASED ASPIRATIONS: THE PSYCHOLOGY OF ADVANCED CAPITALISM, A LESS MORALISTIC, MORE SCIENTIFIC MODEL OF THE PROBLEM

In May 1997 a Labour government was elected with a huge majority. Whilst much of the rejoicing that this event prompted may have been joy at the ejection of a loathed administration rather than true optimism at what New Labour have to offer, in terms of the evidence presented in this book, I believe there are two aspects of the election which provide grounds, albeit tenuous and speculative, for genuine good cheer.

Firstly, Mick Jagger of the Rolling Stones rock group once famously intoned that 'my heart says Labour, my head says Conservative' and historically, the electorate have tended to put his dictum into practice. In this election, almost no one disputed that the outgoing Conservative government had left the economy in good shape. Yet despite this and the fact that the Conservatives were offering most of their potential constituency yet further financial incentives to stick with them, the voters elected Labour. The causes of the victory were manifold but one may have been that the electorate had intuitively realized the significance of the research presented in Chapter 2: becoming richer as a nation makes no difference to the well-being of developed nations. Bearing this out were the polls showing that the majority of voters would actually prefer a government which increased taxes if the purpose was to invest in educational and health services.

The second cause for hope was that although he won, the Labour leader Tony Blair went to great lengths to douse expectations about how much he could achieve. In contrast to previous contenders for government, he did not claim to have a panacea. He emphasized that he would deliver certain very specific promised changes but no more than that. In terms of relative deprivation theory, the fact that voters were attracted by such rhetoric could be taken to suggest that they have become more realistic, reducing their aspirations and placing less emphasis on material advancement.

Prime Minister Blair's emphasis on reinstating obligations and personal responsibility has been successful, politically. But from a scientific stand-point, neither his nor Etzioni's reliance on a cosmologically based moral-ity as the foundation for their argument is necessary. In fact, rather than using moral imperatives at all as their justification they could have drawn on evolutionary theory. Since our genes were evolved primarily within societies which were much more collectivist than individualist developed nations, we evolved to be collectivists, not individualists. In status terms, collectivist societies have rigid roles and demand strict adherence to authority – operate through ascribed identities. By this argument, we evolved to create rankings and to obey them and the modern Wannabee individualist who competes fiercely to rise up the rankings ahead of his or her 'natural' position is flouting instinct. Likewise, it is 'unnatural' for us to have so many intense attachments and loyalties beyond our ascribed tribal ones and to keep breaking them by 'achieving' new ones. Intellectually, this is a perfectly tenable argument that has the advantage of not resorting to unscientific assumptions for its basis. The further advantage is that it puts into sharp focus what has gone wrong: a discrep-ancy between who we were evolved to be and our current circumstances. But is the solution to the problem Etzioni's 'return' to collectivism?

According to him, it was right that the individualist 1960s challenged the values of the more collectivist 1950s. However, in effect, with a few modifications, the 'return' he calls for is to these latter. The bog-standard liberal critique of a 1950s (relatively collectivist) society is that it is oppressive, stifling the individual's opportunities for self-realization. Hence, the project of the 1960s was to liberate the oppressed (particularly women and low-income people) from poverty, ignorance and entrap-ment in repressive family and occupational hierarchies. Etzioni pays lip service to this project but, despite his protestations, it is hard to see how his proposals for a return to collectivism would not result in a return to the oppression as well. As posed, the problem seems insoluble: we need to be more oppressed in order to be better aligned to our genes, yet our liberal values and selfishness recoil from such a statement. However, I do not believe the true conflict is as between individualism and collectivism. The real one is between an advanced capitalism that works for us, rather than against.

My starting point is the statement by Hofstede in 1980 that a 'capital-ist market economy fosters individualism and in turn depends on it'. Hofstede's survey of 117,000 employees in a multinational business, from 66 different nations, was the impetus for much of the research establishing the enduring distinction between individualist and collec-tivist societies.

If a return to collectivism was the solution, the evidence would clearly demonstrate that this mode is the one in which human beings are least likely to suffer low serotonin. This is far from being the case because the evidence is equivocal. On the one hand, there are some gung-ho summaries (mostly by red-in-tooth-and-claw American academics) of the literature which suggest that individualism, social equality and higher income – i.e., for the purposes of this argument, the ethos of the 1960s – correlate strongly with each other and with well-being.[11] On the other, there is the abundant evidence already cited that key aspects of collectivism – i.e. 1950s values – such as social support are critical to well-being. It would appear that there is something else operating which can explain serotonin levels in both individualist (e.g. America) and collectivist (e.g. Japan) modes. I believe it is the way advanced capitalism, as currently organized, clashes with our evolved instincts.

Paul Gilbert has spelt this out and I shall quote his view in detail.[12] Contrasting our inherited tendencies to compete with and to care for each other he writes that where capitalism is unconstrained 'our psychology becomes focused on winners-losers, superior-inferior, social comparison, shame and humiliation avoidance, envy and possessiveness of physical resources as status symbols . . . our instinct for superior-subordinate ranking goes out of control: people simply go for more and more so that accumulations (of power, status and wealth) build up and those with power are able to exert greater (subordinating) control over those without. All kinds of tactics are used to maintain disparity: deception, cheating, secret deals, monopolies, old-boy and family networks, special education for the privileged. The rich are very rich and the poor are very poor. Our competitive minds worry not a bit about that, over and above policing our accumulations.' He goes on to discuss how unfettered market capitalism affects our psychology. 'In our modern day, nothing can protect us from the globalization of markets, the need to change quickly or the renewed downward pressure on wages. The owners and controllers of capital and finance are now able to cruise the world searching out low-wage labour forces and shift investment accordingly. Apart from drugs and pornography, or those things that are outright illegal, the major financial markets and services of the world care little for where profits come from. Nor do they care from "what" the returns on investment accrue. They care only for the returns to shareholders and the salaries on their own deals. Thus, many industries, like textiles, shoes and toys, freed from international labour laws, have migrated to low-wage economies where exploitation is easier. Such forces, which are way beyond the individual to control, leave many high and dry in a world of uncertainty, insecurity, unemployment and/or poverty. To the receivers of this international investment are the benefits of new industrial ghettos, with their pollution, overcrowding and bleak two-dimensional lifestyles – work and consumption. Undoubtedly this will bring some benefits especially if education improves. But what we have seen is that the social irresponsibility of the market culture of competing individuals may be good for business but can become uninhabitable for many . . . our competitive psychology is failing to come to terms with the realities of the modern world.'

Gilbert lists a number of myths and contradictions which are propagated to underpin this status quo. Individuals are held responsible for their behaviour yet all too often, their volition has played no part in their predicament. For example, the workers at a factory which has been closed down so that the industry can be transferred to a lower-wage economy in another region or country are encouraged to believe that it is their abilities which are in question, to blame themselves. Schools are ranked in league tables and deemed failures without any attempt to adjust for the fact that the social class of their catchment areas are critical – like is not compared with like, encouraging rampant undiscounted comparison and unfairly placing blame on the individual teachers and schools. Doubtless some are better than others and it may be that more rigorous evaluations are required, but if all schools are compared as if they are operating on the same level playing field, the comparison will merely induce anger and depression.

Similarly, those working at the top, we are told, must be motivated by high rewards yet the same principle is not applied to the bottom: they must accept relatively low pay with no increases even adjusting for inflation. Apparently they have a different motivational system. The result is growing inequalities in many societies, for, argues Gilbert, 'the magic of monetarism and trickle down economics does not work – it is all trickle up'.

Rather than morality, Gilbert places the problem of consumerism at the heart of his analysis. He describes how this evolves in developing nations: 'People trade the social wealth of their communities for physical wealth – comforts. Once hooked on physical comforts and exciting things, and enthused with the status desires to become "modern", especially in the young, it is difficult to get back to what it was. From here it is mostly downhill into competitiveness and the belief that since a little made things better, more will make things even better still. More is the route to happiness and less, the route to unhappiness and depression. Many writers have noted that the pursuit of happiness, as a goal and ideal and written into the American constitution, is illusory. It is illusory because it is so tied to consumption of things not tied to the quality of life . . . advertising worries not at all about stimulating desires that can be fulfilled only by the few. In this it is cruel – as cruel in a way as showing a child a new toy and marvelling at it then saying "Ah, but you are not good enough to have it."

'So consumerism is a practice that depends on creating, activating and stimulating desires, wants and envy . . . we are hooked on the appeal for immediate gratification, the over-valuation of objects and the inability to deal with frustration. The problem is that we have a hunter-gatherer psychology and tend to believe that these things grow on trees (or in the back of the shop).

'Consumerism is more than just a fulfilment of material need, it fulfils many psychological ones. It can be used to provide pleasures and offset boredoms of modern life, to travel and play. It can be used to maintain one's social status or raise it. In my son's school, to have the right football strip is a sign of prestige, no less than having a certain type of car or going to certain types of restaurants or joining the right golf club . . . for many, consumerism is a skilful education in narcissism . . . one must have "it" whatever it is. We find it difficult to tolerate frustration and if we lose resources, this can bring abject misery.

'The problem with consumerist ideals is that we tend to see consumers and producers as separate people. But to be a consumer we have to work . . . the quality of our inner lives and our happiness depends as much, if not more, on the quality of our lives as producers. For the majority, participation in the consumer society requires considerable sacrifice of time in (often meaningless) activity. From the day we first go to school to the day of our retirement our free time is highly structured. We exist in a socially segregated and limited world of nine-to-five, or longer. We are brought up knowing that much of our lives will be spent in factories, offices and other places of work which, were we to win the lottery, we certainly would not choose. We may have to associate with strangers and people we may not like; bosses who bully and threaten, men who sexually or racially harass and people whose personalities simply grate on us. We battle against bureaucrats and worry that if we do not keep going all that we have built around us will turn to dust. Increasingly, we recognize that our jobs are unstable and easily lost. To compensate for the long hours spent in these factories or offices, and the stress of it, more material things are needed to feel better, to reward us. This is captured in the dictum "I worked hard for it so I deserve it". And our expectations of what we deserve are built day-by-day by advertising, social comparison and envy. So we work to satisfy the addictions we have been infected with, to protect from insecurity and until the recent instability of the job market, to contextualize us in society by taking personal identities from our occupations.

'There is general agreement that our lives as producers (at work) have become more harsh and unpleasant in the last decade or so. We have concentrated so much on efficiency and competition (to produce the most at the least cost) that we seem to have forgotten that the quality of our lives comes from our relationships and sense of security . . . a patient of mine has told of how a new private security firm has come in to run his division. They cut the hourly rate from £7 to £4.50, saying they never pay more, and asked for increased working hours (twelve-hour shifts). One person who cannot afford his mortgage has become depressed and my patient took a serious turn for the worse . . . if the workers do not like it, they are told they are free to leave. And these environments do brutalize people, make no mistake, and advantage those ruthless enough to "get results" . . . I believe there is a hidden rage in us from finding ourselves contextualized in these worlds of work or poverty, that eat up so much of our time. We have to put up with this because not to do so threatens us with being dumped outside a "productive" life. By middle age many are looking to retire, provided they have the means to create reasonable lives. Our rage spills out in consumerism and lack of care for what we consume and how we produce it.'

I leave it to the politicians to decide whether or not to dress the solution in the garb of morality but one thing is clear from this analysis: we shall not reverse the epidemic of social comparison and relative deprivation without doing something about advanced capitalism's need to make individualist, consumption-obsessed wannabees of us all. The solution to Juliet's or Jim's overstimulated search for an achieved identity is not to replace it with ascriptions based on their family backgrounds. Nor is it to tell them they are bad people who are wrong to be as they are. If we blame them for their current predicament by endlessly reiterating their individual responsibility for themselves, it will only serve to make them feel worse. Juliet already feels unattractive enough, lacks self-confidence and is utterly confused about her goals in life. Jim has been equally self-doubting and confused. Only by encouraging them to reassess the way they compare themselves with others and the falsehoods of their professional aspirations (as a way of bolstering their fragile self-esteem) can they be helped.

The solution is to create a system of competition within and between commercial companies which does not wreck our emotional lives. There is no escaping the fact that this will entail curbing the way they promote their products and the basis of competition between their employees: if they have the right to sell us their products they must also meet their obligations to do so in an undamaging way.

This is not a return to Socialism. It was concerned primarily with redistribution of wealth, whereas realigning capitalism to suit our basic instincts is something else. There are already many proposals by economists as to how this can be achieved. Will Hutton's best-selling book, *The State We're In*, advocating stakeholding by employees, is one example. The Americans Robert Frank and Philip Cook are another, arguing that we must reverse the trend towards a Winner-Takes-All system of remuneration, in which a few highly talented individuals receive unprecedentedly huge rewards, leaving little to be divided between the remainder. There are many others, but the higher reaches of economic theory are where I encounter the limits of my competence and qualification.

There are also many sociologically based proposals that could help, like some of Etzioni's ideas. He attacks the way in which the American legislature has been bought by special interests and argues on moral grounds that this must be stopped. Whatever the intellectual justification, there is little doubt that these changes would put the mental and physical health of America ahead of the profits of specific industries. Likewise, reinvigorating the family unit and local communities could not be anything but worthwhile (although it may prove difficult to achieve without some of the social and economic changes proposed below for addressing our maladjusted, excessive social comparison). If people felt more valued through personal ties there might be less resort to grandiose and international social comparisons that subordinate, less hunger for the identities being flogged in magazines and advertisements.

Broadly speaking, the least-worst capitalist systems today incorporate some of these ideas already: the Scandinavian countries, especially Denmark, where communities are strikingly cohesive, there is greater stakeholding in businesses and fewer Winner-Takes-All disparities in pay. The more we model ourselves on them and the less we use America as our ideal, the better it will be for us. In Denmark is to be found the concern of the Japanese business for the welfare of its employees without the paternalism. There is the encouragement of individualism and creativity of the American system, without the Dog-Eat-Dog, savage competition and inequality. There are problems with the Danish system (e.g. its divorce rate, see below) but in terms of social comparison and relative deprivation, they are far closer to a society that works for rather than against us. Not only is Denmark one of the most successful economies in the world, despite its unfashionably high taxes, it is usually among the top three developed nations in surveys of well-being. When they do mention them, it is fashionable for newspaper commentators to lump all the Scandinavian nations together, citing Sweden's economic problems as if they applied to all of Scandinavia and exaggerating Sweden's plight. But for the most part the American and British intelligentsia prefer to ignore Scandinavia altogether, even though it is in many respects the model we should be looking to – not the largely grotesque example of the United States of America.

Although it may seem fanciful, I do seriously believe that the American system has become so corrupt and so confused that it is in some respects like Russia in 1905. There is a vast swathe of people at the bottom of the system with virtually no hope at all of ever achieving the education and wealth required for membership of the wider society. Yet these people are constantly being told that any of them can be President, that they live in the Land of the Free, and daily they spend four to six hours having the lifestyles of the rich dangled in front of their eyes on television. Much as the serfs of Russia in 1905 were pressing against the shop window of relative affluence and opportunity, so with the American Black community today. One difference is that it would be far easier for the Blacks and disenchanted Whites to lay their hands on a means of violent insurrection: automatic, high-velocity rifles and even more advanced weapons. If only a tiny minority of the 25 million or so Blacks were to become as well organized as the IRA is in Northern Ireland, they could wreak havoc in such an enormous landmass. These ideas may be dismissed as wild fantasy but how many people predicted the fall of the USSR or the war in the former Yugoslavia – so rapid is the rate of change in the modern world that hardly a year passes without extraordinary and completely unforeseen international events occurring. I believe there is a significant likelihood that the American union will disintegrate unless it becomes a more cohesive, just society.

It is for economists and politicians to decide how best to bring about the broad changes I have discussed but one thing seems unavoidable: somehow Juliet and Jim must be encouraged to be more realistic in their aspirations and less bothered about whether they stand out from the crowd. The commercial businesses in whose interest it is to make them like this must also be discouraged by government from doing so. Many millions of people, especially women and people from low-income families, have benefited from increased equality of opportunity since 1950. Although recreating oppressive communities, such as those of the 1950s or before, which ascribe these people roles regardless of ability and personal disposition might align us more closely to our evolved natures, even if that were the only way to achieve our goal, the genie is already out of the bottle and only a totalitarian regime could get it back in and insert the stopper. Instead, we should continue to strive to offer equal opportunities for self-fulfilment to all but we must explode the myths that obscure what is realistically achievable by individuals and reemploy the myth-makers in less destructive roles in a less damaging system.

LONG-TERM CHANGES: THE MEDIA, EDUCATION AND THE JOB MARKET
REDUCING DESTRUCTIVE MEDIA SOCIAL COMPARISON

Media images profoundly affect concepts of attractiveness. As we saw in Chapter 3, the repetitive diet of pictures of beautiful women can be depressing for the 99.9% of women who do not look like the models and actresses, encouraging men to compare them adversely with their lovers. TV dramas present a lopsidedly affluent world, a taunt to unsuccessful people and a spur to already self-destructively overambitious others. Advertisements deliberately mislead us about the potential benefits of products and encourage magical thinking. Crimes of larceny have been increased by the introduction of television and permission to act violently has also been given by this medium. Taken together, the media as a whole and television in particular play a critical role in encouraging maladjusted and excessive social comparison.

For what it is worth, if a politician were to follow through the logic of the argument of this book, they might consider the following (often quite extreme) measures:

Much stricter rules regarding advertising. All advertisements would be viewed by a body whose job would be to prevent exaggerated and misleading claims. Of course there is already an advertising standards authority, but it is largely reactive to public complaints rather than pro-active. My body would prohibit any attempts by advertisers to create magical connections between products and outcomes. The misuse of 'beautiful people' would be restricted, the precise use of words would be insisted upon and attempts to encourage maladjusted social comparisons would be rejected. The advertisements would undoubtedly become a great deal more dull, but it is a small price to pay. The regulatory body would inevitably be making arbitrary value judgements but there would be no court of appeal. Advertisers would suddenly become a great deal more careful and responsible in their work. In the jargon of New Labour, advertisers must have a right to draw the public's attention to their products but they must also be forced to recognize their obligation not to spread misery and crime in the way they go about it.

Television channels of all kinds would be brought under the authority of one body and the same criteria that are applied to the BBC in terms of quality and taste would be applied to all. Satellite transmissions and other methods that were delivering unapproved programming would be rigorously resisted by jamming the relevant airways. Only 5% of TV programmes would be permitted to be American-made – including films. Some exceptions would have to made, but these would be very specific: for example, sports events (such as the soccer World Cup or the Grand Prix) that were owned and sold by American companies might be excluded. European Union companies wishing to sell television products in Britain would be required to prove that they were not benefiting American shareholders. There would be government incentives to make and broadcast programmes made by British companies in Britain by Britons. Such draconian measures would decrease the amount of American-inspired maladjusted social comparison. The government would actively campaign for these measures to be introduced throughout the EU.

We may laugh at the French laws against the use of Anglo-Americanized abbreviations for shop signs and advertisements, but perhaps these are not so foolish. The French have used quotas successfully to limit the number of American films on television and in cinemas and as a result, they have a thriving indigenous film industry.

Strict quotas would be introduced to prevent the ownership of cinemas by American companies and to severely restrict the numbers of American-originated films. Their content would be subject to the approval of a body which would apply similar criteria to the television authority regarding the potential for fostering maladjusted social comparison. At the same time, greater encouragement would be given to the British film industry to produce more indigenous products, in collaboration with European partners.

Newspaper ownership would be only by British-owned companies. As with the other media, advertisements would be subject to strict social-comparison censorship.

Of course, for all sorts of reasons, it is not probable that any of these changes will be introduced. But if we were serious about treating the low-serotonin society, the various objections to such extreme measures (e.g. censorship, loss of jobs and revenues, breaking of Free Trade agreements) would evaporate. There is little doubt that American film and television are hugely destructive to our well-being, as well as providing a great deal of amusement and some enlightenment. It might be worth the sacrifice to do without them. Likewise, foreign owners of our newspaper press stimulate it and provide investment but in the end, they care principally about their profits and sometimes appear little concerned with the health of our culture – the *Sun* may sell well, but has Rupert Murdoch ever asked himself if it is a 'good thing' for Britain? If they can make money from stoking and exploiting discontent, they will do so – unless the government prevents them. They are far more exercised by their obligations to their shareholders than to us, and there is little questioning of their right to make money out of us. Whether there are other fields in which businesses should have that right removed, I do not know – it is debatable, for example, whether cigarette manufacturers should have the right to sell them at all, but given that they do, surely they should also meet their obligation to the customers who they make ill – but the media is far too influential of our Being to be the preserve of the whims of foreign magnates.

EDUCATION, EDUCATION, EDUCATION

It is a painful fact of human existence that our childhood is a gradual process of realization that the external world operates largely independently of our wishes and fantasies. We start life as solipsists and through a million personal experiments, discover that Not-Me has an independent existence. In exchange for self-repression, discipline and some acceptance of the power of 'Not-Me' over 'Me', we are enabled to feel more in control and we may derive much pleasure in a process of which education is a part.

Social comparison plays a key role in helping us establish where we stand in relation to others. It can be benign and necessary but if it is misused by a society to hothouse small children, it is subordinating and destroys playfulness and vivacity. If seven- to nine-year-olds are over-pressurized to compare their performances to each other, then emotional death is a real risk. Applied to many British schools today, this account is not hyperbole. Parents and politicians must ask themselves for whose benefit they are stealing their children's childhoods.

An Education Secretary who had fully accepted the findings of this book might do the following:

Visit Denmark and analyse how it can be that in one of the most successful economies in the world, children do not begin formal education until the age of seven. They might then introduce this practice in Britain, taking care to introduce other measures that made it possible for parents to do as the Danes do: teach their children to read and write.

They would reverse the trend towards earlier and earlier examination and selection. Whatever the rationale, in practice it is a method for identifying the minority of high-achieving, mostly affluent children, who will achieve good results (almost whatever the system), and for subordinating the majority at a young age. The saying 'First in school, last in life' is often true. Many of our finest scientists, politicians, artists and industrialists were disastrous pupils and late developers. Such people have increasingly little chance of making good and there is a large waste of talent. Furthermore, obtaining a First Class Degree is the last time too many able people achieve anything of note. There is too much pressure to succeed, in social comparison terms, too young. Thus, we have the right to educate our children as we see fit but we have an obligation to them not to wreck their lives with our misconceived notions of how to squeeze the most achievement out of them.

Etzioni makes a case for moral education in schools. I do not share the fears of those who say that in the wrong hands, this could become similar to the brainwashing that occurred in Communist nations. But I feel there is a far more important aspect of education, which thankfully is already being introduced: emotional literacy. The more that children can be taught to understand their own, their families' and their peers' emotions and relationships, the better it will be. There is a substantial overlap between moral and emotional education: helping children to understand how their behaviour makes others feel is as important as helping them to understand how others affect them. We have a right to force children to conform to the educational system but we also have an obligation to help them emerge from school emotionally aware and feeling good about themselves.

Having said all this, when Tony Blair stated that his main imperative was 'education, education, education' he was right if he meant to make better education available to the great majority who attend state schools. There is no doubt that societies which invest in the education of the less-advantaged sectors benefit overall, not just economically but in terms of social cohesion and law and order.

From a social-comparison standpoint, the key issue is whose interests are best served by the present system, which starts formal teaching too young and is too intensive and exam-orientated. From a clinical psychological standpoint, it is difficult to see many benefits to the children and a great many destructive consequences. The traditional liberal educationists' view (e.g. A.S. Neil, Bertrand Russell) is that hothousing is principally about creating an obedient workforce who are trained to be of use to employers, not about stimulating creativity (a very 1960s word rarely heard today). In an advanced capitalist society it is to the good of all if its members are taught to be disciplined and given useful skills. But these goals have become so all-consuming that they exclude other, equally important functions: schools can play a role in enabling young people to emerge into the workplace feeling good about themselves – even if they have not particularly shone academically – rather than creating a sense of being a lifelong loser, which is too often the case today at the top, as well as the bottom. Both Juliet and Jim are highly intelligent and were near the peaks of achievement in their educational performances. Yet neither feel particularly good about themselves because they make disastrously self-destructive upward comparisons with other high achievers and benefit very little from downward comparison because they discount their own successes. The schooling system is a major reason for this and it need not be so, without any lowering of standards.

THE WORLD OF WORK

Developing nations are gradually acquiring the technology to process the raw materials which were once shipped to us and they can manufacture the end products at low cost because they are still low-wage economies. This trend will continue until they are as affluent as us. In the meantime, since we are used to a relatively high standard of living, we cannot compete by offering lower wages. Instead, we shall have to be more highly skilled and create ever more complex industries and services which only we can offer. The implications for our psychology could be positive but so far, they have not been.

Increased competition for jobs has led to ever more elaborate attempts by employers to select the right candidates. This creates a preoccupation with self-definition through others, an alterated mentality in which building your curriculum vitae and sucking up to potentially useful contacts become all-consuming. It breeds destructive social comparison and encourages an obsession with what 'they' want rather than what 'I' have to offer – let alone any thought about what I would actually like to do that would be fulfilling.

For low-income, little-qualified people, the obvious imperative is money. This is probably inevitable and certainly understandable. However, even an unqualified, unemployed 20-year-old man might be able to progress more fruitfully if he asked himself what really interests him. If it is a sport, for example, perhaps he could head in that direction in looking for his low-wage job. When people are genuinely fascinated by a field, it is remarkable what they can achieve.

As for the more privileged, such as the Juliets and Jims, they have barely caught their breath before they are rushed to the next hurdle, oblivious of whether the status, wealth and power on offer are what will satisfy them. Is it just starry-eyed idealism to wonder whether such people – for whom almost any career is an option – should also seek out work that interests them, rather than a job that will impress their friends or please their parents?

Government *can* play a significant part in changing attitudes: look at the success that Prime Minister Thatcher had in stimulating an entre-preneurial, winner-loser work ethic. Her legacy is a divided nation in which one section works ludicrously long hours to the detriment of its physical and mental health and another sector can find no work at all, or only very low-paid work.

Among the professional occupations there is minimal job flexibility yet there are many cases where three jobs could be shared between four employees, allowing one extra day a week off. For example, print and broadcast news journalists are often worked off their feet and many would perform better if they worked shorter hours. Of course, such arrangements involve lower pay and in the present atavistic work culture, there would be a fear that participating would signal lack of ambition to bosses. But what amazes me is the number of people who for one reason or another do not need financially to work so hard but who would reject any such suggestion.

Given that our economic fate will largely depend on our inventiveness and technological innovation in the next century, it is anyway greatly in our interest to encourage Juliet and Jim to discover the work that truly excites them. That this argument may carry more weight than the suffering which their low serotonin has wrought sums up where our priorities lie.

LONG-TERM CHANGES: MENDING AND PREVENTING BROKEN BONDS

A return to a more collectivist society would certainly be more in accord with our evolved instincts to make stable attachments – small-scale social groups are where we came from. On a practical level there could be many boons. Creating more stable, cohesive communities might reduce the iso-lation of many groups, such as mothers of small children and the elderly, and it would provide a more secure network for the raising of children. It would reduce crime and create cooperation that would help to mitigate ill-effects of the job market, such as unemployment. Put like this, rather than as a moral manifesto, there is little doubt that many of Etzioni's pro-posals are desirable.

However, these changes alone will not be enough – the social-comparison problems would persist – and above all, it very much remains to be seen how possible they are. While whole towns can still be thrown into disarray by decisions taken 3,000 miles away at a corporate head-quarters, it will be difficult for governments to protect communities. In a Global Market economy, Norman Tebbit's famous advice in the early 1980s to the unemployed to imitate the example of his father during the recession of the 1920s and to 'get on your bike' will continue to apply. Of course, every time a breadwinner does so and finds a job in another part of the country, they leave a community and contribute to its fragmenta-tion. Furthermore, in those nations which have become dramatically more unequal, no amount of declarations of community spirit will douse the feeling that communities serve some a great deal better than others.

Whether or not New Labour will succeed in its admirable ambition of rebuilding communities, in the meantime there are many practical steps which might reduce and prevent the breaking of emotional ties.

CHILDCARE

On this subject I have little to add to Penelope Leach's two books about creating a more child-friendly society. The first, in 1979 (called *Who Cares?*, London: Penguin), advocated a long list of practical changes which would succeed in this goal. Sadly, the second, in 1994 (called *Children First*, London: Michael Joseph) had to repeat many of the earlier proposals because depressingly little had changed from the time of the earlier book.

In both books she implores us to make the care of small children a far higher priority in every way and to offer parents – and especially mothers – a much higher status than they currently enjoy. In both she calls for a family centre or 'child-place' to be set up in every community as a place to meet with other parents. She also argues that there should be 24-hour drop-in services available and that town planners and other administra-tors should be forced to consider the impact of their plans on childcare.

In the second book she refines her earlier suggestions. Of group day-care, in 1979 she wrote: 'I believe that for children under three there should be no form of socially approved *group* daycare. My ideal society has no day nurseries, residential centres or crèches in it. None at all. Babies and very small children each need a "special" and continuous per-son or people and they need to have their daily lives based on somewhere they know as home.' By 1994, Leach is not much more impressed by group care, preferring the use of fellow mothers as a substitute, with childminders next on the list. However, she offers some positive sugges-tions for easing the lot of mothers. Rather than creating work crèches, employers should encourage working from home wherever possible.

Where this is impossible, more flexible hours that fit with the task of parenting and more job sharing are proposed. On top of this, she makes a powerful case for Paid Parental Leave – paying working parents to take time off to care for their babies. A more recent feasibility study of this idea has suggested it could have many benefits for the mental health of the children concerned[13] as well as being economically practical.

As regards low-income parents, she cites the substantial body of research showing that American programmes, such as Headstart, in which parents are offered a multidisciplinary support team, can produce dramatic results. She describes a Yale University project which offered low-income mothers a comprehensive package, including a paediatrician. Followed up five and ten years later, only 28% of the children whose mothers had been supported were suffering 'school adjustment problems' compared with 67% of a control group of similar families who had no support. Another scheme in Washington and New York had equally successful results. In this one, almost unlimited help was on offer, with each case worker assigned only three families. They were prepared to offer any kind of assistance, up to and including housework, and not only did the hard-pressed, poorly educated parents benefit, their children did dramatically better as well. Of course, these kinds of Headstart projects to aid the disadvantaged are extremely costly in the short term, but in the longer term they save a fortune. It has been estimated that for every one dollar spent, six were saved 20 years later in terms of the mental and physical healthcare, judicial expenses resulting from crime and so on, which were prevented. Unlike their predecessors, Prime Minister Blair and Home Secretary Straw are well aware that such interventions hold the key to reversing the crime epidemic and creating a more equitable society, but I do not envy them the task of finding ways to pay for them in the short term.

That it is possible for developed nations to put a higher priority on helping parents and children is shown by numerous European examples. In Denmark and Sweden, paid parental leave has been the norm for several decades and France has long been in the vanguard of child-friendly policy-making, as has Holland. By comparison, America and Britain are in the Stone Age.

As we saw in Chapter 4, the fact is that the majority (60%) of mothers of under-three-year-olds in Britain do not work at all, and only a small minority (13%) work full-time. It is very hard to predict whether we shall move more towards the American pattern (where half of mothers of small children work full-time with minimal state support) or towards the Scandinavians. If Catherine Hakim is right, mothers are voting with their feet by continuing to care for their small children rather than work and attempts, for example, to encourage single mothers to work more, will come up against their preference for childcare. Alternatively, it could be that the practical difficulties of finding a decently paid job and adequate substitute care are putting many mothers off, although Hakim's research suggests this is not often the case. It is difficult for the government to achieve the right balance between providing real opportunities to those mothers who want to work (and would be at high risk of becoming depressed if they did not), and pressurizing mothers who are quite happy to care for children full-time to work (where they would also be at risk of depression).

Finally, the most radical long-term change of all would be if men became more inclined to take on the role of mother and if women were to encourage them to do so more. Wander down any street during the daytime in Denmark and you will see a remarkable sight: at least as many men as women pushing baby buggies and ushering toddlers around the shops. Evolutionary psychologists argue that such behaviour runs counter to male instincts but this is highly debatable. Whilst it may be that women have a genetic disposition, caused by the hormonal changes during pregnancy, to care for small infants, it is possible that after that, the disposition is not related to gender. If this is so, we should expect a great many more nations to resemble Denmark in the medium future. Such a change would go a long way to reducing the present burden that is placed largely on women.

GENDER RANCOUR

There is one important respect in which Denmark is a less than exemplary model for us: it has an even higher divorce rate (50%) and that is just the couples who marry. Half of parents do not and this is the general pattern throughout Scandinavia. Given that cohabiting parents are even more likely to separate than the married (about three times more so in Sweden), this suggests something is very rotten indeed in the state of Danish relationships. If we have already caught a nasty dose of American crime statistics from becoming more like them structurally and culturally, the Danish divorce and separation rates are one virus we would like to avoid if we were to take them as our model.

It is not clear why the Scandinavians are like this. Our stereotype of them is as depressive, suicidal, alcoholic and sex-crazed. In fact, their depression, suicide and alcohol rates are better than some Southern and Eastern European countries. It is true that they start sex younger and have more partners at younger ages, especially the women, but I am not aware of any evidence that this is the root of the problem.

Evolutionary psychologists would doubtless be tempted to speculate that the cause is their long-term commitment to equalizing opportunities for women, a supposedly unnatural practice. Because of their childcare policies, women expect and are able to have careers and only briefly to interrupt them for motherhood. As we saw in Chapter 5, this often upsets fathers. Whether the New Men of Scandinavia have overcome such rancorous feelings I do not know but it is possible that they play a part. It is also important to recall that mothers with their own means are more likely to leave a relationship.

Philip Blumstein's study of American couples is interesting in this regard.[14] 12,000 couples filled in a questionnaire about how money, work and sex affected the relationship and he interviewed 120 of the couples (78 of them married, 42 cohabiting) in depth and followed them up 18 months later.

Regarding money, the couples who did not pool their incomes were more at risk of divorce or separation – Blumstein argued that they had not fully given up their independence. As in other studies (see Chapter 5), wives who said they liked to be financially self-sufficient were more likely to leave. Wives who had little money were less likely to do so – perhaps because they lacked the cash.

If the couples argued a lot about the intrusive effect of one of their jobs it was a bad sign, especially if newlywed wives were unhappy with the time the husband was giving to it. Ambitious men and women were more at risk and related to this, if the couples spent a lot of time apart it was a problem. Men who felt their wives did not do as much housework as them were more likely to leave.

Arguing about sex was a predictor but strangely enough, the amount that the couples actually had was not. Men who regarded physical desirability in a wife as particularly important were a worse bet, as were couples who accepted that affairs were inevitable.

Whether these findings would be replicated in Scandinavia is debatable but if they were, it would certainly make sense. Their mixture of sexual liberation, sexual equality and female affluence could be expected to increase the rate of fissure. On top of this comes the evidence presented in Chapter 6 regarding differences between the sexes as regards attraction and desire. If the evolutionist interpretation of this evidence is correct, then an instinctive attraction to ambitious-industrious men by women and to youthful, beauteous women by men would play havoc in a genuinely egalitarian system.

My own suspicion is that there is a process of adjustment going on between the genders and today is somewhere near the centre of the most turbulent, stormy period. It is extremely hard to see what practical steps government can take to still the tempest.

The fundamental problem is that we expect too much from our relationships. We expect too much sex, we expect too much intimacy and we expect the personal to override the practical job of raising children, if we become parents. This new emphasis has occurred at the worst possible moment in history, a moment when social mobility (e.g. moving house, jobs that keep partners apart) and fragmented communities are unprecedentedly great and the old gender values continue to be very dominant in most developed nations. Even if a government were to take a strong view regarding what is natural, for example, committing itself to policies which assumed men and women are essentially the same, or to the opposite (sociological) view, it would take a long time before they altered attitudes, if at all. This is one area in which Etzioni's claim that social movements rather than the state are often most influential may be correct. As a set of beliefs and new behaviours, feminism evolved of its own accord, usually in direct contradiction of the prevailing status quo. It would be a brave man or woman who felt they could confidently predict what will evolve next in the realm of sexual politics.

All sorts of proposals have been made to enable the nuclear family unit to recover from the battering it has suffered since 1950. Etzioni has proposed an end to no-fault divorce and the reintroduction of a moral framework for marriage. He also suggests waiting periods prior to divorce, cooling-off periods and counselling. Ideas like these have already been introduced in Britain and we shall see what effect they have. Although cohabitation by parents has increased substantially in recent years, in many cases this is followed by marriage and there is little sign of a fundamental antipathy to the institution itself.

These ideas could help to weed out the relationships where one or both partners are suffering from low-serotonin problems and blaming it on their compatibility. If such cases could be identified and appropriately treated more often, it might go some way to reducing the number of broken families.

How much will be achieved by these and other similar measures I am not qualified to judge, but I suspect that unless our overheated aspirations and individualism cool, it may be little. In essence, we are asking too much of our relationships and until we cease doing so, we will continue to believe that there is something better out there, just waiting to happen.

CONCLUSION

Those readers who have found this book a somewhat depressing read should remind themselves that we live in a time of hope. The spectre of nuclear holocaust has faded with the ending of the Cold War. For all the problems, parents are probably showing more affection to their children than ever before. We are getting better and better as a society at identifying and prioritizing our problems and developing solutions to them. My mother, who is not known for rampant optimism, actually told me the other day that she felt as inspired by the election of Tony Blair as she had in 1945 when the Labour government ousted Winston Churchill.

If only we can tackle the joint evils of maladjusted social comparison and of broken attachments, we can begin to enjoy our affluence instead of being angered and depressed by the processes whereby it is created. Thus far, advanced capitalism has mercilessly exploited our instinct to rank ourselves against each other. But there are other instincts which could also be favoured by our system which are currently subdued. Of these our instinct for cooperation is the most important.

Appendix I

A Brief Review Of The Scientific Evidence That Rates Of Depression Have Increased Since 1950

The most comprehensive study, by Gerald Klerman,[1] examined the like-lihood of suffering from a 'major depression' during their lifetime in a total of 39,000 people from nine surveys of the general community in eight different countries and of 4,000 people from three studies of depression running across the generations within families with high rates. Major depression means a severe mental illness (see footnote 1 for detailed definition), not just a case of feeling a bit down: things like having a depressed mood most of the day nearly every day for at least two weeks for no good reason; feelings of worthlessness or excessive guilt; and recurrent suicidal ideas. The studies were all done in the 1980s.

Klerman found that older generations were significantly less likely than younger generations to have suffered depression when young. Thus, in the general community, 25-year-olds born before the Second World War were much less likely to have suffered than 25-year-olds born after it – from three to ten times more likely. The same was true in the families with high risk of depression – the older generations suffered less than the younger ones. There were variations between countries in how much the risk of depression had varied, but in all of them it was substan-tially greater. A reanalysis of the largest sample in Klerman's survey, the Epidemiological Catchment Area (ECA) study of over 18,000 Americans, found that people born after 1945–55 were ten times more likely to suffer from depression by age 34 than people born 1905–14.[2] A subsequent study of 8,000 Americans, the National Comorbidity Survey, has confirmed the basic pattern of increased risks of depression since the ECA study.[3]

Klerman's approach has been criticized because it relied on people's recollections of whether they had suffered[4] – these might not be accurate – but most authorities in this field tend to agree with his conclusions.[5] A detailed analysis of the problem of recollection still found a significant and substantial increased risk of depression in recent cohorts, even after allowance had been made for recall effects.[5]

A further reason for supposing that Klerman's work is correct is that most studies which test the theory prospectively, by measuring rates at different times, also find increasing rates.

A study of 2,550 Swedes showed that rates of mild and mild-to-severe depression there had doubled between the 1950s and the 1970s, although major depression did not increase.[6] The sample were examined by psychiatrists in 1947, 1957 and 1972 with most of the increase occurring after 1957, including a ten-fold increase among young men. An American study showed a similar pattern.[7] Although there is one prospective American study which did not show an increase,[8] this contained major flaws.[9] Along with the retrospective evidence, the scientific case that depression has increased in America is a strong one.

That it applies to Britain is supported by Glyn Lewis' more recent study.[10] He compared the results of a 1977 survey of 'psychiatric morbidity' in a representative sample of 5,684 people with those from a study conducted in 1985 of 6,437 people using the same methods. 'Psychiatric morbidity' included neurotic symptoms like panic attacks and phobias as well as depression. Whereas 22% of the 1977 sample reported psychiatric morbidity, this had risen to almost one third of the population (31%) by 1986.

Appendix II

Psychological And Psychiatric Correlates Of Low Levels Of Serotonin

SEROTONIN AND DEPRESSION

About 3% of the population suffer from a major depression in any one year, and about 5% will develop the illness during their lifetime.[1] Milder, but nonetheless severely debilitating, depression is much more common, rising to 30% in some groups – this is the proportion of women who either qualify for a full diagnosis or are on the borders thereof.[2] Perhaps not altogether surprisingly, 100% of women with three or more children, who lost a parent before they were 14, who have a low income and who have little social support were depressed in one study.[2] Women are twice as likely as men to report feeling depressed,[3] although this gap may be closing slightly, with men becoming more depressive (because, perhaps, they are more prepared to admit to it) and women more aggressive (because, perhaps, they are more prepared to direct their aggression outwards rather than against themselves).[4]

There is now little doubt that people who suffer from most kinds of depression are significantly more likely to have lower levels of serotonin than undepressed people. The evidence comes from several sources.

Numerous studies of animals show that mammals such as monkeys and rats who display withdrawn, fearful and depression-like symptoms after negative experiences have lower levels of serotonin than normal mammals. In humans, all the various methods for measuring serotonin levels used over the last two decades have shown lower levels in depressed compared with nondepressed.[5][6] These include direct observation of the brain using imaging techniques and indirect measures, where

346

levels of by-products of serotonin or chemicals essential in its manufacture are measured in spinal fluid, blood or urine. Levels of these are seen as 'markers' of levels of serotonin in the synapse. Low serotonin levels have also been shown in people who attempt or complete suicides, most of whom are depressed[7][8] (suicidal ideas are one of the defining features of depressive illness).

Compelling evidence is also supplied by experiments in which humans have been given drugs that increase levels of serotonin – antidepressants, such as Prozac.[5][6] After taking the drugs (usually not until several weeks have passed), the serotonin levels rise and the depression tends to decrease. Because the two go together it is inferred that the rise in serotonin causes the decrease in depression and that low serotonin levels and depression are linked.

Although there is no research directly addressing the issue and it is purely a speculation, it seems highly probable that many of the 50% of adults who suffer from anxious attachment – who are more prone to depression and disharmonious marriages – will turn out to have low levels of serotonin. Because they suffer repeated feelings of rejection and abandonment, such people are likely to feel negative in ways that people with low serotonin levels often report. That several studies have shown that various species of mammals have lower levels as a result of being separated from their mothers in childhood strongly suggests that the same will be true in humans.

Of course, large numbers of other chemicals – individually and in complex interactions – are involved in the neurochemistry of depression and not all people who are depressed have low serotonin levels. But there is no doubt now that the levels of depressed people are statistically significantly likely to be lower than those of the undepressed and that these low levels often are what is making the difference. If rates of depression have increased since 1950, there must be a higher proportion of the population with low serotonin levels.

AGGRESSION AND DEPRESSION SINCE 1950

The levels of aggression in general, and of antisocial behaviour in particular, in a community are, at least partly, an index of the amount of angst. With the exceptions of Switzerland and Japan, since 1950 there has been a steady increase in antisocial and aggressive behaviour throughout the developed world.[4] In 1950 in England and Wales, for example, there were 6,249 crimes of violence against the person recorded by the police. In 1996, there were 239,100. Whilst increased population, changes in recording practices and so on may account for a proportion of this rise, it is clear that it represents a real and sustained change in behaviour, and especially in the last decade: the number of crimes nearly doubled from 1986 to 1996 (from 125,944 to 239,100). There can be no doubt that a much greater proportion of today's population perform acts of criminal violence than in 1950 and that the unprecedented, threefold increase in the rate at which violence has risen since 1987 is a sign that more of our young men are acting violently.[4]

Strictly defined, only a small proportion of the population can be said to be actually suffering from a full-blown 'Antisocial Personality Disorder' (see footnote 9 for psychiatric criteria) – impulsive, aggressive, prone to criminality. In all, about 1% in any one year and 4% over the course of their lifetime meet the psychiatric criteria, with men outnumbering women by a factor of five.[9] But it is clear that a much higher proportion than this have many of the defining features. One highly respected study, which followed 412 boys from the age of eight, found that 42% of those from the lowest-income families had become seriously violent at some point by age 32.[10] There are also signs that British citizens have become less civil and more impulsively aggressive. Surveys of British shop, health and welfare workers and of teachers and General Practitioners[11] show that violence towards them by their clienteles increased during the 1980s. British driving organizations and the police report increases in the amount of 'road rage'.[12]

Obviously, the increase in violent aggression is linked to a rise in frustration but does it really prove there has been a rise in unhappiness and low serotonin?

To the lay person it may not seem intuitive but aggression and depression are closely linked.[4] A man smashing his fist into another man's face does not immediately bring to mind the image of a person sitting haggard and bowed in a curtained room, sobbing with melancholy. The two appear poles apart yet, psychologically, they are close blood relatives. The depressive is paralysed by a self-loathing which is distinguishable in its hatred and anger from the violent person's only by its target – the self. If he takes a razor blade to his wrist he is launching an assault whose motive may be identical to his brother's, as he wields one taken from the same packet but put to a different use, at a football match. That he is slashing another person, whereas the depressive attacks himself, should not distract from the identity of psychological purpose in the two acts: destructiveness. Someone who feels frustration and anger can direct these feelings outwards or inwards. The cause of the unpleasantness can be taken to be external, and having attributed blame, an attack launched. Alternatively, the frustrating stimulus may be taken to be oneself and the anger directed inwards in self-attacking thoughts and actions.

The closeness of the two is shown by the numerous studies proving that violent men and boys are also more likely to be depressed and paranoid as well.[4] Conversely, depressed people are more hostile and aggressive to their close intimates.[4] The two go hand in hand, whichever side you come at it from. Convicted homicides and violent men in general are more likely to commit suicide than nonviolent criminals (in one British study, one third of convicted homicidal men subsequently killed themselves).[13] John Bowlby, one of the most influential psychologists in the second half of this century, theorized that 'It is my belief that the (violent) affectionless character is intimately associated with depression and may perhaps be fruitfully looked upon as chronic depression of a very early origin.'[14] Studies since then have confirmed that aggressive behaviour in boys is likely to mask underlying depression. As well as violence, the delinquent behaviour may take the form of disobedience, temper tantrums, truancy and running away.

The interchangeability of depression and violence is shown by analysis of the differences between the sexes: worldwide, on average, females are twice as likely to say they are depressed than men,[15] men are seven times as likely to commit violent crimes.[16] One study[17] of a large (4,204) sample of 14- to 18-year-olds and their parents found that there was significantly more depression in the girls compared with the boys and the boys were more delinquent – as nearly all studies find. To explain this, the researchers proposed the idea that 'antisocial behaviour is the equivalent among boys of depressive mood among girls', a 'substitution of behaviours or masked depression'. The simple method was to add together the numbers of boys who were depressed or delinquent and to see if they equalled the number of depressed or delinquent girls. If delinquency and depression could be regarded as interchangeable ways of expressing the same emotional needs, and if these needs are generated in children of both sexes in equal amounts, then the amounts would be similar. And so they were, almost identical: there were as many more delinquent boys than girls as there were more depressed girls than boys; overall the sum totals matched. The result perfectly fits the theory that in any group of adolescents there is a proportion of both sexes who are frustrated and angry (mostly as a result of such experiences as physical abuse and emotional neglect), but the genders express these feelings in different ways. If the study had substituted 'violence' for 'delinquency' as a measure (delinquency includes a good deal of nonviolent behaviour), the result might have been even more decisively supportive of the hypothesis.

There is also a third alternative to directing frustration and anger inwards or outwards: projection of the emotions onto others, or paranoia (thinking you are being got at when you are not). Experimental and observational studies have demonstrated that aggressive boys[18] and violent men[19] as well as depressed people[20] are significantly more likely than normal people to be paranoid – to attribute malign intentions to neutral actions of others. One study[21] measured the depression and aggression of 220 boys and girls (108 boys, 112 girls) but in addition, their patterns of thought were also tested by asking them to make inferences about motives in six stories which they were read by the experimenter. As with other studies, depression was significantly more common in girls, aggression more common in boys. But most interestingly of all, both aggressive and depressive children showed a significant bias generally towards attributing negative intentions (paranoia) and to focusing on negative aspects of the stories. The aggressive were more likely to identify others as the cause of negative events, whereas the depressive attributed negative situations to internal or global causes. Children who were both depressive and aggressive had the attributional patterns of both types. This is potent evidence that paranoid, depressive and aggressive ideation are close relatives and that all three can coexist in one person.

Given the close links between depression, aggression and paranoia, it would not be surprising if sufferers from the latter two problems also have the low serotonin levels of the depressed, and they do.

AGGRESSION AND SEROTONIN
American Army scientists in the late 1970s first discovered the connection between low serotonin and violence whilst studying servicemen. Subsequent studies showed serotonin levels predicted the likelihood of violent behaviour in future: low levels in violent prisoners successfully predicted the ones most likely to reoffend on release.[22] In another study, depressed patients with low levels were found to have had significantly more contacts with police and arguments with relatives, spouses, colleagues and friends than depressed patients with normal levels.[23] Many studies have found that people who are impulsive have low levels too.[24] For example, arsonists who are impulsive have lower levels than those who plan their fire-setting and are nonimpulsive.[25] Antisocial people – who are often both violent and impulsive – have also been shown to have low levels.[26-29]

The relationship between impulsive aggression and low serotonin extends to nonviolent people. When levels in a sample of ordinary people were lowered using a drug, they became more likely to administer electric shocks to strangers (who were in fact actors pretending to be shocked).[30] Other studies suggest that normal people who are nonetheless prone to irritability have lower levels of serotonin than calm people.[31]

The low levels may go back to childhood. They have been found in children who torture animals;[32] who are very hostile towards their mothers;[33] and who score high on aggression tests.[34] Low levels in childhood predicted which of 29 disruptive 8- to 10-year-old boys (who all were impulsive, hyperactive and aggressive) would be the most physically aggressive two years later.[35] Other well-established predictors of aggression, such as previous aggressivity or degree of antisocialness, intelligence, parental mental health and low parental income, did also predict the outcome, but none of them was as powerful, either individually or collectively, in predicting which boys would be violent as serotonin levels (which explained 52% of the variance).

Paranoid people have low levels of serotonin too. Since depressive and violent people are prone to paranoia, this is what we would expect. Studies of paranoid, psychopathic and antisocial convicts show that their levels are lower than normal ones.[26-29]

Thus, as with depression, there is substantial evidence that paranoia and violent aggression are associated with low serotonin levels. Given that violence has increased substantially, it stands to reason that a correspondingly higher proportion of the population have low serotonin levels than in 1950.

SEROTONIN AND SUBSTANCE ABUSE

There have been large increases in alcoholism, heroin addiction and other substance abuses since 1950. One way of regarding this increase is as an attempt by a significant portion of the general population to medicate away their low serotonin levels – depression, aggression and paranoia – with self-prescribed treatments. Dr Donald Cameron, a prominent British community physician, has described tobacco as one of the 'drugs of solace', along with alcohol and illegal drugs like marijuana.

He depicts them as[36] 'folk remedies, self-cures for a group of diseases for which medicine can offer little help. People use these drugs of solace to treat a number of dis-eases, including loneliness, shyness, sexual incompetence, social incompetence, ignorance, boredom, anxiety and depression.' The corrollary of this argument is that if a group of people – such as young women – are suffering more from these dis-eases, they will resort more frequently to drugs of solace. A fine example is the increase in cigarette smoking by young women. Although smoking has decreased overall since 1950, rates among young women have rocketed. Rates of lung cancer among women doubled between 1971 and 1991 and fell by 30% among men. 29% of pregnant women still smoke, threatening the intelligence and physical health of their foetuses.[37]

As already noted, depression, eating disorders, alcoholism and a host of other problems are far more common in the younger generations of women, for reasons explained in Chapters 2 to 6. Although their circumstances can be said to have improved in many ways compared with 1950, young women who are vulnerable to emotional distress are a group particularly at increased risk of suffering. This is illustrated by their increased use of drugs of solace, especially cigarettes. Smokers are significantly more likely than nonsmokers to suffer from depression and other emotional problems. In one study,[38] 44,000 Americans were asked how often in the previous two weeks they had felt depressed, lonely, restless or upset. Once the effects of age, income and so forth were removed from the equation (these have a big effect on how depressed, etc. you are likely to be) the smokers were significantly more likely to suffer from these problems than the nonsmokers. Other studies have shown that depressed people are less likely to give up than the undepressed.[39] Still others show that people with serious mental illnesses, such as major depression and anxiety disorders, are significantly more likely to smoke.[40] Three different studies have found that a staggering 90% of schizophrenics smoke.[41]

In fact, whilst they provide temporary relief, drugs of solace often only succeed in making matters worse. Many of the substances involved temporarily raise serotonin levels, alleviating depression or aggression. But in the longer term the substances actually result in serotonin decreasing to below the levels before substance use – creating more misery and an impulse to take further substances.[42–35]

Substance abuse is closely connected with both depression and violence. The majority of violent assailants have been using stimulants at the time of the assault.[4] About 50% of alcoholics are also depressive and use alcohol as an attempt to cheer themselves up.[46] The American psychologist Myrna Weissman, one of the foremost authorities on depression, described the role of alcohol as follows:[3] 'Depression and alcoholism are different but equivalent disorders. Women get depressed. Men are reluctant to admit being depressed and accept treatment. Instead, they tend to drink alcohol. Thus, men self-prescribe alcohol as a psychopharmacological treatment for depression.' Given that substance abuse, depression and aggression all tend to go together, it is not surprising to find that abusers are also more likely to have low serotonin levels.

Studies of rats have shown that ones who have been trained to prefer alcohol to water have lower levels than ones who only drink water.[42 47] In one study[42] of humans, levels were compared in alcoholics 48 hours after admission to hospital for detoxification and again after four weeks' abstinence. The levels were lower after the abstinence and compared with a comparison group. The researchers concluded that alcohol transiently raises serotonin levels but that they subsequently drop lower and that the alcoholics keep returning to the bottle in order to raise them again. Other studies have shown that the lowest levels are found in depressive alcoholics whose families who have a history of alcoholism[48] and in violent compared with nonviolent alcoholics.[49] [50] Postmortem studies of alcoholics who subsequently commit suicide suggest they may have lower levels than some categories of nonalcoholic suicides.[45] Several studies in which alcoholics have been administered serotonin-raising antidepressants have shown that they can reduce rates of recidivism and reduce drinking.[51] This suggests that alcoholics suffer from low serotonin.

Overall, it seems highly probable that many alcoholics are using the temporary lift they get from a drink to treat low serotonin levels. Given the fact that alcohol consumption has hugely increased since 1950, it suggests that more people are finding themselves in need of a stimulant because more are suffering low levels.

The same argument applies to the epidemic of abuse of substances other than alcohol, especially among the young. There is abundant evidence that those who abuse illegal drugs are suffering from depression and anger, and therefore, are likely to have low serotonin levels. A recent British study of 86 people found that those who had taken ecstasy (MDMA) more than 20 times were more likely to be impulsive and to have depressive features in their personalities than those who had never taken drugs, and numerous studies of animals show that the main impact of MDMA is to raise serotonin levels sharply but that subsequently there is an equally severe depletion.[52] Another study showed that ecstasy users were more angry.[53] As a recent *British Medical Journal* research note pointed out, numerous studies of animals have already proven that the drug causes irreversible harm to serotonin axons and receptors[54] and most workers in this field expect the same will turn out to be true of the estimated 500,000 Britons who take the drug every week.

Following American work showing damage to human mood, mental processes and anxiety levels[55] Michael Morgan's recent British work has shown damage to higher mental functions, including memory.[56] When complex and swift performance was required, the ecstasy users had problems. Many young ecstasy users will not realize the drug is damaging their mind. But as we get older, the number of serotonin receptors in our brains drops and the destruction caused by ecstasy could increase many kinds of psychiatric and neurological problems in old age.[57]

Media focus has largely been on ecstasy fatalities. But the total number of Britons who have actually been killed by ecstasy is thought to be 50. The main concern of scientists is not whether it kills but how the drug affects mental abilities and mood in the long term.

A recent British study suggests the effect on mood may be profound.[58] Dr Valerie Curran of University College, London, measured the mood of ecstasy users on a Saturday night after they had taken the drug. She measured it again on the Sunday morning and again in the middle of the next week. The ecstasy users were significantly more depressed midweek than they had been on the Sunday. They were also more depressed compared with a sample of people who had taken no drugs at the weekend, who showed no change in midweek mood compared with the weekend.

The most probable explanation is that the ecstasy caused a lowering of serotonin levels, resulting in depressed mood. According to Dr Curran, 'midweek, some of the ecstasy users actually qualified for a psychiatric diagnosis of mild depression, whereas none were depressed on the Sunday'.

On the current evidence, Dr Morgan's 'best-case' scenario regarding the consequences of the ecstasy epidemic is that 'Ecstasy users will react less well to stress than if they had never taken the drug.' His 'worst-case' scenario is that 'my findings turn out to be the tip of a neuropsychological iceberg of severe mental problems. As the users age they could lose serotonin function and be more likely to develop a mass of problems, including memory deficits, depression, impulsive aggression and even, be more vulnerable to Parkinson's disease.'

Professor Richard Green of Loughborough University, who wrote the research note in the *British Medical Journal*, says: 'A crucial factor will be how much ecstasy it takes to cause damage: will one large dose be enough? Will many small ones taken over a number of months or years be sufficient? It will be some time yet before we know.'

Numerous studies have shown that substance abuse of all kinds is more common in people who are prone to antisocial behaviour.[59][60] There is also a mass of evidence that substance abusers are much more liable than normal to have depressed mood.[61] Although cocaine and heroin primarily seem to affect other neurotransmitters (dopamine) than serotonin, the fact that their use has increased so much suggests there is more angst. There are also studies showing that treatment with serotonin-increasing antidepressants can reduce cocaine use, suggesting that low serotonin is involved.[62] Cocaine and amphetamine users are often seeking to boost their confidence, cheerfulness and ability to cope in social situations.

Heroin users are often trying to blot out unhappy feelings and traumatic memories, often dating back to childhood. There are five small clinical studies showing that administration of Prozac helps cocaine abusers to abstain (footnote 20, Chapter 7).

Taken as a whole, the fact that there has been such an explosion in substance abuse since 1950 and that abusers are liable to have low serotonin levels strongly suggests that there are more of us turning to drink and drugs to compensate for the negative psychological effects of low serotonin levels.

SEROTONIN AND OTHER COMPULSIVE DISORDERS

Substance abuse is only one of many compulsions that have increased since 1950 which are associated with low serotonin levels.

It is estimated reliably that 3% of the adult populations in developed nations are problem gamblers.[63] In Britain there are about 500,000 gamblers who are described as 'pathologically compulsive' and a further one million for whom gambling is a serious problem, causing significant damage to their family or professional lives. Gamblers are sensation-seeking risk-takers who have been shown to have different neurochemistry in a variety of ways from nongamblers.[64][65] They mostly have impulsive personalities[61] which is a predictor of low serotonin levels. They are also more likely to suffer from depressed mood and to be antisocial, and about 20% of those who receive psychiatric help have attempted suicide[61] – all problems linked to low levels.

Eating disorders – bulimia (binge eating) and anorexia (self-starvation) – are yet another compulsive behaviour that is linked to low serotonin levels and that has risen substantially since 1950.[66]

About 70% of bulimics also suffer from a major depression at some point in their lives and as we know, depression and low serotonin levels go together. Not surprisingly therefore, numerous studies have shown that bulimics are more likely to have low levels than nonbulimics.[67] When they are treated with serotonin-raising drugs, their bulimia often disappears.

Fasting reduces serotonin levels. Studies of both normal and anorexic samples who have fasted show that their levels drop during the starvation and return to higher levels when food is eaten again.[68] Thus, anorexics during their illness are liable to have low levels. However, compared with bulimics, when they are treated with serotonin-enhancing drugs they are less likely to recover their appetites[69] – not surprisingly, since such drugs tend to reduce appetites of all kinds, including that for sex.[70]

Interestingly, there are reasons to suppose that some kinds of sex addicts may also suffer from abnormal serotonin levels. Treatment of men with a variety of sexual pathologies with serotonin-raising drugs in seven small clinical samples was found to reduce them (see footnote 22, Chapter 7). In one study, the drugs made no difference to compulsive masturbators, paedophiles or sado-masochists, apart from to delay ejaculation or decrease libido in some cases. However, men with Obsessive Compulsive Disorder (OCD) did report relief from such compulsions as staring at crotches and obsessive thoughts about how semen is contaminated and sex is sinful.[71]

This may have been due to the effect of the drugs on the obsessionalism *per se* rather than the libido. There is abundant evidence that the symptoms of OCD respond well to drugs[72 73] such as Prozac and that people with the disorder have abnormal levels of serotonin.[72 73] The most common symptoms are obsessions about dirt or contamination accompanied by ritualistic washing. Many sufferers compulsively worry about irrational matters, such as that they have left the light on at home or the door unlocked or that their car is illegally parked, and have to constantly check. They may be compelled to position their possessions in special configurations, such as in straight lines.[61] About 3% of the population suffer from this problem.[74] But interestingly, unlike all the other emotional problems discussed so far, the role of serotonin seems to be complicated in this syndrome and in the associated one of Generalized Anxiety (from which about 4% of people suffer).[74] In many studies, serotonin levels are actually **too high** in people with these problems and after drug treatment, the levels go down to normal.[72 73] This suggests that serotonin levels can cause problems if they are too high as well as too low and that drugs such as Prozac enable the central nervous system to adjust them either way, back to a healthier level. It also provides a clue to why Prozac sometimes heightens anxiety – perhaps it raises the levels too high.

SEROTONIN AND OTHER PROBLEMS

It is clear that rates of depression,[75 76] delinquency[77] and substance abuse[78] among children and adolescents have risen substantially since 1950, with the rate of increase accelerating in Britain since the mid-1980s. Serious depression is now found in about 3% of children[79] but at least 10 to 12% are described by their teachers as being miserable for much of the time.[71] Thieving and violence are now extremely common among young boys. Between one quarter and one third of boys in inner cities are declared delinquent by officers of the state (teachers, police, social workers) at some point, of whom half go on to be convicted of a crime in adolescence; half of them get an adult criminal record.[77] Surveys of children and adolescents also reveal huge increases in drinking, drug use, smoking (especially among girls) and gambling.[80] On top of this, there is good reason to suppose that rates of anxious attachment – irrational fears of rejection and abandonment in relationships – have increased from the 40% of all children generally found to have this problem in studies in the early 1980s and before.

None of this is surprising when it is recalled that the adults who are their parents are increasingly likely to suffer from the problems listed above, that there has been a fourfold increase in the divorce rate since 1950 (divorce promotes anxious attachment and delinquency), that for many years children were raised in the shadow of a potential nuclear holocaust, that youth unemployment and job prospects have declined and that pressures to succeed at school have increased dramatically.

As noted above,[81–84] there is evidence that antisocial and aggressive children suffer from low levels of serotonin. Whilst there are few studies of serotonin levels of depressed children, there are reasons for supposing that serotonin may function differently in them compared with adults. However, there has already been one study showing that rates of depression in 96 8- to 17-year-olds were reduced by treatment with Prozac.[85] If so, the increases in childhood depression could be linked to an increase in the numbers of children with low levels and it seems probable that the huge rise in childhood delinquency reflects an increase in the numbers with low serotonin.

At least five studies have shown that some symptoms of personality disorders can be reduced by taking Prozac (see footnote 21, Chapter 7). Impulsiveness is reduced and so is anger.

A final problem which may be linked to low levels of serotonin is chronic fatigue. Full-blown Chronic Fatigue Syndrome (often described as ME – for Myalgic Encephalomyelitis – or Yuppy Flu) is rare, with most studies showing that less than 1% of the population have the illness at any one time.[86] However, large numbers of people suffer from chronic fatigue – complain of feeling constantly weary, tired, exhausted or weak. In most surveys of the community or of symptoms complained of by patients visiting General Practitioners, fully 20 to 30% report this symptom.[86] Since nearly all such people are liable to also suffer from minor depression, it is likely that they have low serotonin levels.

Rates of chronic fatigue have increased substantially since 1950. One American study found that 9% of a sample of 1,170 outpatients in 1960 complained of the problem.[87] When the study was repeated in 1990, nearly one third of the patients complained of the problem.[88] It would seem that modern life is a good deal more fatiguing than in the past, and it is likely that part of this weariness is due to the fact that more of us have low levels of serotonin.

Appendix III

Varieties Of Mental Health Professionals And Treatments

Some years ago Ernest Gellner, the distinguished philosopher and anthropologist, published a book (*The Psychoanalytic Movement*, Paladin) arguing that the rise of therapy had occurred as a substitute for religion. The differences between therapies are as diverse and complex as the differences between religions.

I believe it should be mandatory for anyone offering therapeutic services to provide their patients with a pamphlet (agreed by the training body) at the outset stating their qualifications, what the basic theories behind the approach are and the typical methods.

There should also be the telephone number of an independent regulatory body which could be called if the patient feels anything untoward or unethical is going on.

In the meantime, here is a brief guide to the different kinds of expert in the mental health field:

Psychoanalytic treatment was the first therapy, invented by Sigmund Freud. It works through interpreting the 'transferences' the patient makes from his childhood past on to the behaviour and mind of the therapist. Perhaps you think your therapist is criticizing you (when they are not) because you had critical parents or you feel they are not supportive enough – like your parents were. There is only one rule: that the patient must say whatever comes into their head. Dreams, fantasies and childhood memories are thrown up for analysis by this process.

A psychoanalytic (or psychodynamic/dynamic) psychotherapist works in the Freudian tradition and has been psychoanalysed three times a week for 50 minutes for at least three years whilst attending lectures. Most are not medical doctors.

There are at least 70 training bodies that provide 'therapy', but only 12 of these offer psychoanalytic therapy. The British Confederation of Psychotherapy (0181-830-5173, 37a Mapesbury Rd, London, NW2 4HJ) has a nationwide register of all bodies which will enable you to find a therapist living near you.

A psychoanalyst is a therapist with knobs on. He or she has had more psychoanalysis himself (five times a week for at least four years) and offers the same to patients, although some also work less intensively. They aspire to go deeper into the patient's past than therapists, hoping to achieve the nearest thing to a total refit of personality that is on offer. Analysts can only be trained at one place, the Institute of Psychoanalysis in London. At least half are medical doctors.

A counsellor is someone nice to talk to who won't make a lot of value judgements. Their training could be anything from three weeks to three years. The two most rigorous training bodies are Regent's College and the Westminster Pastoral Foundation, in London. They usually do not attempt to guide the patient to talk about their childhood, dreams and fantasies as much as psychoanalytic therapists or psychoanalysts. They can be very supportive during a crisis. The Samaritans, Relate and Cruse (for bereaved people) all provide free and reliable services and are in the phone book.

Counselling was originally a reaction to the 'determinism' of psychoanalysis and behaviourism. It was created in the 1950s and 1960s by American psychologists such as Carl Rogers (inventor of Co-Counselling), George Kelley and Abraham Maslow. Treatment is once a week and much briefer than psychoanalytic therapies. Transactional Analysis is generally a form of counselling.

A psychiatrist is a medical doctor who has done a further training in the use of chemistry and electricity to alter the brain (e.g. Anthony Clare, who is not a therapist). Most also receive primitive training in therapy but should not be regarded as therapists just because of that.

A clinical psychologist has a psychology degree and a further training, usually in the use of reward and punishments to change behaviour and techniques for thinking constructively. Most do 'Cognitive Therapy', which concentrates on changing the way you think about how you feel using structured methods, often including homework. Not all cognitive therapists have also trained as clinical psychologists and this is not essential. It takes less time than psychoanalytic psychotherapy.

A group, family or marital therapist usually applies basic psychoanalytic or cognitive-behavioural principles to group settings. The way patients react to being in the group is often regarded as emblematic of how they felt in their original family. The peer pressure exerted by the group may be used to help change behaviour.

Art, drama and music therapists use self-expression through painting, acting and music to identify emotional problems and as a basis for interpreting them. If creativity has not been developed or has been stamped upon, these arts are seen as a useful outlet for repressed emotions.

Footnotes

CHAPTER 1

1. Diekstra, 1995
2. James, 1995
3. Automobile Association, 1997
4. Health and Safety Executive, 1986; National Association of School Masters, 1986; Brown, 1986; Wilkie, 1992; Hobbs, 1994
5. Silbereisen, 1995
6. Hughes, 1995
7. Fisher, 1996
8. Rozenweig, 1987; Fombonne, 1995
9. Office of Population Censuses and Surveys, 1995
10. Robins, 1992
11. Burvill, 1995
12. Eaton, 1992
13. Coccaro and Murphy, 1990
14. Klerman, 1992. *Diagnostic and Statistical Manual of Mental Disorders*, Fourth Edition, American Psychiatric Association, p 327. 'Criteria for Major Depressive Episode:
A. Five (or more) of the following symptoms have been present during the same two-week period and represent a change from previous functioning: at least one of the symptoms is either (1) depressed mood or (2) loss of interest or pleasure. Note: Do not include symptoms that are clearly due to a general medical condition or mood-incongruent delusions or hallucinations.
1. depressed mood most of the day, nearly every day, as indicated by either subjective report (e.g. feels sad or empty) or observation made by others (e.g. feels tearful)
2. markedly diminished interest or pleasure in all, or almost all, activities most of the day, nearly every day (as indicated by either subjective accounts or observation made by others)
3. significant weight loss when not dieting or weight gain or decrease or increase in appetite nearly every day
4. insomnia or hypersomnia nearly every day
5. psychomotor agitation or retardation nearly every day
6. fatigue or loss of energy nearly every day
7. feelings of worthlessness or excessive or inappropriate guilt
8. diminished ability to think or concentrate or indecisiveness nearly every day
9. recurrent thoughts of death
B. The symptoms do not meet the criteria for mixed episode (p 335)
C. The symptoms cause clinically significant distress or impairment in social, occupational, or other important areas of functioning
D. The symptoms are not due to the direct physiological effects of a substance or general medical condition
E. The symptoms are not better accounted for by bereavement.'
15. A single gene has been identified as playing a crucial role in the manufacture of the protein on which serotonin relies. A recent study (Ogilvie, 1996) discovered that people with a special variation in the alleles on the serotonin gene were more likely to suffer from unipolar (but not manic) depression. However, the difference this variation made was small. It was thought to play a critical role in only 10% of the unipolar depressives. Thus, direct evidence of a large effect of genes on serotonin levels in major depression remains to be seen, although the twin studies would suggest it will turn out to be more than 10%.
In the case of minor depression, another recent study identified an even smaller role for genes (Murphy, 1996). This is not surprising since studies of identical twins suggest that genes play a small role. At most they explain about 20% of the difference between minor depressed and undepressed and it may be a good deal less. At the

moment, there is no direct evidence that the genes of people with minor depression differ from the undepressed and it is unlikely that a big role for genes will be found in the future, given the large effect of social status and income on this problem. As regards violence, twin and adoption studies suggest that genes play a minimal role. Whilst no direct studies of genetic differences in the serotonin gene of violent men have been done, we should not expect much influence (Burvill, 1995).

As regards compulsions, there is almost certainly a role played by genes but again, it is probably a small one. Compulsive drinking, for example, clearly has a genetic component but it is not great and there is no evidence for a direct effect on serotonin levels in alcoholics.

16. Fairbanks, 1988
17. Fairbanks, 1989
18. Raleigh, 1991
19. McGuire, 1993
20, Miczek, 1989
21. Motcuk, 1997
22. McGuire, personal communication
23. Madsen, 1984a
24. Madsen, 1984b
25. Madsen, 1986
26. Becker, 1964
27. Dohrenwend and Dohrenwend, 1974
28. Rutter, 1977; Warheit, 1976; Comstock, 1976
29. Brown, 1978
30. Burvill, 1995
31. Murphy, 1991
32. Kaplan, 1987
33. Stansfield, 1992
34. Weissman, 1977
35. Wolfgang, 1982
36. Farrington, 1989
37. Adler, 1992
38. Wilkinson, 1996
39. Plomin, 1987 and 1990

CHAPTER 2

1. Stouffer, 1949
2. Lawler, 1963
3. Olson, 1986
4. Crosby, 1986
5. Gurr, 1970
6. Martin, 1986
7. Easterlin, 1995
8. Diener, 1995
9. Diener, 1985

10. Studies of well-being are considerably more superficial than psychiatric evaluations of depression.

The well-being surveys entail a brief interview in which respondents are asked broad questions such as 'How satisfied are you with your life as a whole: very, fairly, not very, not at all, don't know.' Cultures differ in the extent to which it is permissible to express unhappiness and dissatisfaction with one's life. The distinctive historical experience of different nations seems to shape the degree to which the world is generally seen as hostile or benign. Within the societies, there are large differences in how much the citizens regard their government as trustworthy and supportive. Consequently, different societies may have different cultural baselines for the normal response to questions about how well one is doing.

11. Stevens and Price, 1996

12. The history of thought is littered with attempts to reduce human society and psychology to a few instinctual motivations. With hindsight they are often analysed as attempts by the individual theorist to make sense of his personal problems and their acceptance or rejection by the wider society – regardless of how scientifically valid the theory may be – analysed in terms of how the theory suited or challenged the ideological foundations of the ruling élite of that time. It has been suggested that Galileo Galilei (1564–1642), for example, the author of the radical astronomical theory, developed it because his father was also a radical theorist in this field and because Galileo was effectively an only child (Sulloway, 1996). Very few (if any) of the main thinkers in the history of the world have not been the object of similar psychological theorizing. Equally, their theories have been placed in ideological context. As every schoolchild knows, Galileo's ideas so threatened the worldview, and therefore power base, of the Papacy in 17th-century Rome that they led to his death. Another obvious example, this time a propagator of a theory of human need, is Charles Darwin (1809–1882) whose psychology has been extensively explored (including a biography by the eminent psychologist John Bowlby) and the reception of whose theories was famously hostile (it was only in November 1996 that the Vatican

finally accepted that his theories were correct). Freud is another example. In 1898 he announced to an astonished Viennese Psychiatric Society that there was an epidemic of child sexual abuse. Whilst some authors have tried to suggest that his subsequent reformulation – that the 16 female patients on whom he based his theory were fantasizing, expressing an unconscious wish rather than actually having sex with their fathers – was craven, it is more likely that in postulating a Nuclear Complex (in which we all have always shared these patients' incestuous wishes) Freud was merely coming up with yet another 'archetypal' human tendency which fitted better with his sexually repressed times. A more recent example, and very germane to this discussion, is Richard Dawkins' book *The Selfish Gene* which argued that the instinct to reproduce can explain almost any human behaviour and that this selfish ambition underpins all human life. First published in Britain in 1976, it was not until the 1980s that it achieved large sales and international renown, perhaps because it provided the perfect theoretical justification for the Free Market government economic policies that were then sweeping the developed world (it was the intellectual equivalent of the exhortation that 'Greed is good' by the character Gordon Gekko in the 1980s Oliver Stone film *Wall Street*). It is only now – as the adverse consequences for social cohesion and economic growth of Free Market policies are becoming apparent (Hutton, 1995) – that the grave shortcomings of Dawkins' work are all too obvious. As the evolutionary psychologist Paul Gilbert (1989) points out, 'to call genes selfish, as Dawkins does, is to play fast and loose with language and to convey an impression that genes have motives which they obviously cannot. It has clouded the whole area with emotive terms that are meaningless.'

This discussion should alert us to the dangers of declaring human characteristics archetypal or instinctual. For every hierarchy of fundamental needs, there will always be another being proposed and if their proponents are honest, such theorizing is always precarious. About the only thing that is certain is that in 10 or 20 or 50 or 100 years' time, a new consensus will emerge as to what is 'really' fundamental. Whatever the truth of the matter, we can be sure that other societies in other times will see the world differently and subscribe to other beliefs. This can be said of any scientific theory but perhaps the reduction of social and psychological processes to instincts is an especially vulnerable kind of theorizing. Not only is it very liable to be influenced by contemporary ideologies but it is also often unscientific. The problem is if this kind of ('functionalist') theory works backwards from a given human behaviour, seeking out a purpose for it. At its least scientific, it takes a behaviour such as violence, child abuse or sexual promiscuity and scratches around for a way in which it might have served the propagation of the species. Whilst some of the resulting theories may square with the known scientific facts better than others, the danger is in the assumption that everything without exception must in some way serve the species, however destructive and unhelpful it seems to be, otherwise it would have been naturally selected out of our genes. The possibility that there could be enduring features of human beings which serve no evolutionary purpose whatever and which evolved for reasons other than natural selection is simply not considered. Extremely inconvenient facts are swept aside or made the subject of mind-bogglingly complicated rationalizations. Speculation dressed up as science, ironically, these advanced theories are often as unscientific as those offered by Freud and his descendants, a brush with which the likes of Richard Dawkins would particularly loathe to be tarred. For example, a fact that is highly uncomfortable for 'The Selfish Gene' theory is that the more successful a person is in a developed society, the fewer children he is likely to have. Indeed, many career women today (such as the actress Emma Thompson) are opting not to reproduce themselves at all. Whilst it is possible to advance evolutionary theories to account for this (Vining, 1986, makes a brave stab at fitting the lack of reproduction by the very successful into a long-term natural selection model), they make many psychoanalytic theories seem scientifically watertight by comparison. These issues are discussed further in Chapter 6.

13. Nietzel, 1990
14. Darwin, 1859
15. Gilbert, 1992
16. Sulloway, 1996
17. Bion, 1961
18. Seligman, 1991
19. Festiger, 1954
20. Feldman, 1987
21. Buss, 1989; Feingold, 1990
22. Graziano, 1993
23. Swallow, 1988
24. Cash, 1983
25. Wills, 1981
26. Wood, 1989
27. Tesser, 1980; Tesser, 1986
28. Hakmiller, 1966
29. Wood, 1985
30. Goethals, 1986
31. Martin, 1986
32. Lemaine, 1974
33. Taylor, 1988; Weinstein, 1993
34. Taylor, 1992
35. Taylor, 1994
36. Colvin, 1994
37. Pietromonaco, 1985
38. Carver, 1983
39. Pyszczynski, 1985
40. Diener, 1979
41. Trope, 1983; Trope, 1986
42. Dance, 1987
43. Brickman, 1977
44. Schacter, 1959
45. Kuiper, 1986
46. Hoberman, 1985
47. Coyne, 1976
48. Coyne, 1987
49. Miller, 1983
50. Swallow, 1987
51. Gibbons, 1986
52. Friend, 1973; Wilson, 1971
53. Collins, 1989
54. Bauemeister, 1989
55. James, 1995
56. Listed on p 7, McCraine, 1984
57. Bergner, 1988
58. Alnaes, 1988 and 1990
59. Gotlib, 1988
60. Arieti, 1974
61. Coopersmith, 1967; Rohner, 1986; Schore, 1994
62. McCraine, 1984
63. Gilbert, 1996
64. McConville, 1985
65. Parker, 1962
66. Eaton, 1955

CHAPTER 3
1. All the statistics for the changes since 1950 are listed in Smith, 1995
2. Hewitt, 1993
3. Watson, 1993
4. Campbell, 1980
5. Inglehart, 1990
6. Veroff, 1981
7. Zanna, 1987
8. Walmesley, 1987
9. Nagata, 1991
10. Pettigrew, 1971
11. Wilkinson, 1995
12. Witherspoon, 1992; Giorgi, 1990
13. Flanagan, 1982
14. Angeli, 1991
15. Halpern, 1995
16. Wood, 1989
17. Bandura, 1982
18. Suls, 1986
19. Major, 1991
20. Testa, 1990
21. Gilbert, 1992
22. Diener, 1979
23. Salovey, 1991
24. Schmitt, 1988
25. Roberts cited in Bush, 1977
26. Schoek, 1969; Davis, 1963
27. Swallow, 1988
28. Bellah, 1996
29. For statistics on inequality see James, 1995
30. Gerbner, 1976
31. Comstock, 1978
32. Kenrick, 1980
33. Kenrick, 1989
34. Kenrick, 1993
35. Kenrick, 1994
36. Buss, 1989; Feingold, 1990
37. For examples see Barocas, 1974; Cash, 1985; Farina, 1986; O'Grady, 1989
38. Wartella, 1995
39. Hennigan, 1982
40. Young, 1990
41. Linn, 1982
42. Phillips, 1996
43. Leach, 1995
44. Statistics supplied by the Bursar's office, Eton College, Windsor, Berks
45. Ruble, 1991
46. Ruble, 1987
47. e.g. five studies are listed on p 93, Ruble, 1991
48. Frey, 1987
49. e.g. four studies are cited on p 94 of

Ruble, 1991
50. Ruble, 1983
51. e.g. five studies are cited on p 93 of
Ruble, 1991
52. e.g. five studies are cited on p 103 of
Ruble, 1991
53. Parsons, 1977; Stipek, 1989
54. Harter, 1981
55. Diener, 1979
56. Dweck, 1983; Stipek, 1989; Higgins,
1983; four more studies are cited on p 93 of
Ruble, 1991
57. Carver, 1985
58. Frey, 1985
59. Trope, 1983; Trope, 1985
60. e.g. three studies are cited on p 100 of
Ruble, 1991
61. Diener, 1978
62. Parsons, 1982
63. Frey, 1987
64. e.g. the literature review of this field by
Drury, 1980
65. Marsh, 1984
66. Pettigrew, 1967
67. Stevens, 1996
68. Hutton, 1996
69. Blinkhorn, 1994
70. Ross, 1971
71. Olson, 1986
72. Walkerdine, 1997
73. *Sunday Times*, 1997

CHAPTER 4
1. Nietzel, 1990
2. Baumeister, 1995
3. Barnett, 1988
4. De Zuluetta, 1995
5. Armstrong, 1989
6. Carnelley, 1994; Brennen, 1991
7. Wolkind, 1985; Richman, 1982
8. Higley, 1991
9. Barry, 1959
10. Lanatser, 1990
11. Gurr, 1989
12. Wolfgang, 1981
13. De Mause, 1974
14. James, 1979
15. Whitten, 1974
16. Durkheim, 1933
17. Arieli, 1964; Swart, 1962; Macfarlane,
1978
18. Leach, 1982
19. Abbs, 1986
20. e.g. see Hindess, 1975
21. Bowlby, 1969, 1973, 1980; Ainsworth
1978
22. Violato, 1995

23. Clarke-Stewart, 1989
24. Violato, 1995; Belsky, 1990
25. Hofferth, 1987
26. United States Bureau of Census, 1987
27. 45% (of under-one-year-olds receiving
paid care or care from mother at work – the
assumption is that these are high risk for
anxious attachment) of 75% (proportion of
mothers of under-ones working full-time)
of 50% (of under-one-year-olds with a
working mother).
28. Leach, 1995
29. General Household Survey, 1993
30. Social Focus on Children, 1994
31. Hakim, 1996
32. Brown, 1990
33. Kessler, 1994
34. Brown, 1978
35. Pound, 1988
36. Joseph Rowntree Foundation, 1995
37. See Chapters 1 and 2, James, 1996
38. Klerman, 1989
39. See pp 50–3, James, 1995
40. Richardson, 1989
41. Vandell, 1991
42. Steinberg, 1986
43. Estimates by Office of Population and
Census, London
44. Smith, 1995
45. Murray Parkes, 1972
46. *Chronicle of the Second World War*, 1990,
Longman
47. Figures supplied by Office of Population
and Census, London
48. Kiernan, 1990
49. Kiernan, 1993
50. For a meta-analysis see Amato, 1991; see
also Wallerstein, 1988 and 1991; Kiernan,
1986; Elliott, 1991; Hetherington, 1988
51. Hess, 1996
52. Popenhoe, 1987
53. Buck, 1995a; Buck, 1995b
54. Haskey, 1992
55. See Hakim, 1996, pp 125–7
56. Wellings, 1994
57. Phillips, 1988
58. Easterlin, 1980
59. Haskey, 1983, 1992
60. Kiernan, 1986; Kuh, 1990; Elliott,
1991
61. Halpern, 1995
62. Stone, 1990; Social Trends, 1997
63. Kuh, 1990
64. Grundy, 1996
65. Bowlby, 1969, 1973, 1980; Alnswerter,
1978
65. Pollack, 1983

CHAPTER 5
1. See Appendix I, James, 1995
2. Weissman, 1974
3. See Gotlib, 1988, for a review
4. Gotlib, 1989
5. Merikangas, 1984
6. Beach, 1983
7. Gottman, 1991
8. Gotlib, 1990
9. Terman, 1935
10. The seven studies are listed in Kelly, 1987
11. Kelly, 1987
12. Kiernan, 1986
13. Wickramratne, 1989
14. Weissman, 1993
15. Weissman and Klerman's 1977 cross-national review of the studies showed that women were more commonly depressed than men in rates of treated depressives and of depression in random samples from the general community. By 1987 several more studies of representative samples had been done and Nolan-Hoeksma's (1987) review reported a ratio of 1.8 women depressives for every 1 man within the USA and of 2 to 1 in surveys outside the USA. Weissman's (1993) analysis of four surveys in the USA, Canada, Germany and New Zealand concluded that rates of increase had stabilized in women born after 1945 but were still rising in men in that age cohort. However, Kessler's reports (1993, 1994) of the 8,089 subjects in the American National Comorbidity Survey concluded (1994) that there had been 'no major change in the sex ratio over the 40-year period retrospectively covered in the survey'. Wickramratne's (1989) reanalysis of the Epidemiologic Catchment Area study of 18,000 Americans finds female depression stabilized for cohorts born between 1945 and 1960. For males, it continued rising until 1955, stabilized until 1960 and then rates 'continued to increase between the years 1960-1980 among both men and women of all ages studied'.
16. Nolen-Hoeksma, 1987
17. James, 1995
18. Schwartz, 1991
19. Block, 1991; Kandel, 1980; Quiggle, 1992
20. Merikangas, 1985
21. Higley, 1991
22. Harris, 1991
23. Gove, 1979
24. Kessler, 1983
25. In his National Comorbidity Survey of 8,089 Americans (1993, 1994), Kessler found that the sex difference in ratios emerged in early adolescence, before adult sex roles had been acquired. This led him to doubt the validity of a sex role position (1993): 'Our results point to a difficulty with currently popular sex role theories of depression which argue that adult sex role stresses are important determinants of sex differences in depression. This is an inadequate explanation because sex differences in onset risk first emerge among early adolescents, prior to full adult sex role differentiation.'
It might be countered that although the living out of the adult sex role does not occur before puberty, the socialization of it does. What is interesting is that Kessler has clearly changed his tune to a remarkable extent, having been a chief advocate (along with Gove) of a sex role explanation for over 20 years.
26. Weissman, 1977
27. Srole, 1980
28. Kessler (1983) states: 'There is a serious bias in this study. As noted previously (Kessler, 1981), in the 1954 survey of 1,600 respondents, there was no age-standardized sex difference in GMH [General Mental Health]. But among the 695 respondents successfully reinterviewed in 1974, there is a marked sex difference in 1954 GMH scores, women having significantly higher scores than men. This finding indicates that there is a systematic attrition bias in the longitudinal sample that distorts the relationship between sex and mental health found in the original sample. Considering this bias, it is difficult to place much emphasis on trend data about a changing relationship between sex and mental illness.'
29. Wilhelm, 1989
30. Egeland, 1983
31. Loewenthal, 1993; Loewenthal, 1995
32. Schwartz, 1991
33. Horney,1967; Miller, 1976; Scarf, 1980
34. Frieze, 1978
35. Mirowsky, 1989
36. See footnotes 9-18 in Schwartz, 1991
37. See footnotes 1 and 19–27 in Schwartz, 1991
38. Brown, 1978
39. Brown, 1990

40. Brown (1990) stated: 'Given that almost all nonworkers [unemployed mothers in the sample], but few in part-time work, had a child under five, it is impossible therefore to rule out that it is negative circumstances surrounding the care of young children that explains the greater insecurity of the marriages of nonworkers and hence their greater risk.'
41. Owen, 1988
42. Hock, 1988
43. Kessler, 1982
44. Stanley, 1986; Hakim, 1996
45. Houseknecht, 1984
46. Weiner, 1979; Clayton, 1980
47. Atkinson, 1984
48. Stanley, 1986
49. Staines, 1986
50. For example, see Campbell, 1993
51. Hakim, 1995
52. Ginn, 1996
53. Hakim, 1996
54. Shaw, 1987
55. p 133, Hakim, 1996,
56. p 63, Hakim, 1996
57. p 101, Hakim, 1996
58. Hofstede, 1980, 1994
59. Human Development Report, 1995
60. p 86, Hakim, 1996
61. pp 87–8, Hakim, 1996
62. p 104, Hakim, 1996
63. p 93, Hakim, 1996
64. p 97, Hakim, 1996
65. p 70, Hakim, 1996
66. pp 61–5, Hakim, 1996
67. p 79, Hakim, 1996
68. p 91, Hakim, 1996
69. 'The 11' accept that there has been no increase in full-time working women, that part-timers may show more commitment to their families and express greater satisfaction about their jobs and that women's employment is less stable than that of men. However, they disagree profoundly on the interpretation and explanation of these facts, arguing that the lack of an increase in full-time work is not as significant as Hakim maintains, that both part-timers' commitment to work and their less stable employment patterns are explained by such factors as the kind of occupations entailed, rather than gender, and they argue that women's expressed 'satisfaction' with their low-paid, low-status jobs is a form of false consciousness.
70. p 201, Hakim, 1996
71. Hoyenga, 1993
72. Brannen, 1994
73. Rubery, 1994
74. Elias, 1994
75. There are still very dramatic differences in social conditioning, especially in early life, the ways parents and teachers react to children of different sexes which may have nothing to do with genes and everything to do with endemic sexism. Long before adult men and women are exposed to radically different pressures, with different rates of pay, expected roles and all the other major discrepancies of which feminism has made us aware, as children they receive very different treatment. Here is a brief summary of the most significant findings: (James, 1995)
1. At all ages in childhood, parents react differently to different-sexed offspring, encouraging sex-typical behaviour and discouraging behaviour expected of the opposite sex.
2. From infancy, boys get more reactions from both parents, both positive and negative.
3. Boys are given toys that require active problem-solving and parental involvement. Girls' toys give less opportunity for innovation, adult involvement and initiative.
4. Boys are encouraged to explore and play more and to do so alone. Girls are kept within mothers' eyesight, making them more used to having to conform to adult expectations.
5. Fathers play rougher with boy infants than girl infants and insist on higher, achievement-orientated standards from their sons. They encourage dependent, passive behaviour in daughters by comparison.
6. Mothers respond to requests for help with problems from sons but with criticism of daughters making the same requests.
7. Fathers encourage assertiveness and directness in sons and react, like mothers, with criticism to daughters by comparison.
8. Both parents interrupt and talk across daughters when they are talking more than sons, who get listened to.
9. Studies of teachers show they are liable to presuppose aggressiveness in boys and social cooperation in girls even if they do

the opposite.

10. From as soon as they are mobile, children form groups according to gender and are encouraged to do so. This limits their experience of opposite-sexed behaviour and peer pressure to behave other than as their sex is meant to.

One author summed these differences up: (hops, 1990) 'Girls, compared to boys, receive encouragement to display dependency, affectionate behaviour and express tender affectionate emotions'. This evidence (and there is a lot more of the same, for both sides of the debate) (Hoyenga, 1993) shows it is too early to accept a central role for biology in determining female patterns of employment.

76. Hops, 1990
77. Wilkinson, 1995; Veroff, 1969; Campbell, 1981; Hakim, 1996
78. Silverstein, 1986a
79. Silverstein, 1986b
80. Silverstein, 1988
81. Bruch, 1978
82. Fombonne, 1995
83. Mann, 1983
84. Dornbusch, 1984
85. Silverstein, 1990
86. Silverstein, 1991
87. Kitson, 1982
88. Levine, 1988; Barry, 1959; Berry, 1976

CHAPTER 6
1. Townsend, 1987a
2. Hite, 1976
3. Hill, 1979
4. Dion, 1973
5. Biggar, 1989
6. Johnson, 1994
7. Lewin, 1982
8. Clement, 1984
9. Delamater, 1987
10. Carrol, 1985
11. Whitley, 1988
12. Leigh, 1988
13. Buss, 1989
14. Caporael, 1989
15. Wallen, 1989
16. Glenn, 1989
17. Borgia, 1989
18. Dickeman, 1989
19. Vining, 1986
20. Herrnstein, 1994
21. Naomi Wolff's widely reviewed book

The Beauty Myth – How Images of Beauty Are Used Against Women (1991, Vintage) makes no reference to Buss' work and fails altogether to address why men might so invariably prefer youth and looks in women – and this a book about female beauty. Likewise, Susan Faludi's *Backlash* (1992, Vintage), which claims there has been an 'undeclared war against women' as a backlash to feminism, makes no reference to Buss' work and no attempt to address his findings.
22. Townsend, 1987b
23. Buss, 1996
24. Clark, 1989
25. Kinsey, 1948; Kinsey, 1953
26. Blumstein, 1983
27. Ellis, 1990
28. Mussel, 1984
29. Kenrick, 1990
30. Graziano, 1993
31. Buunk, 1996
32. Popper, 1963
33. Kenrick, 1992
34. Schoen, 1992
35. Russel, 1992
36. Five studies are listed on p 243 in Townsend, 1987b
37. Elder, 1969
38. Goldthorpe, 1987
39. Udry, 1984
40. Taylor, 1976
41. Sigall, 1973
42. Bar-Tal, 1967
43. Walster, 1973
44. Broude, 1992
45. Van Den Bergh, 1992
46. Three studies are reported in Alley, 1992; the most definitive study is by Cunningham, 1986
47. Townsend, 1992
48. Harpending, 1992
49. Sadaella, 1987
50. Seven studies are listed in Cicone, 1978
51. David, 1976
52. Three studies are listed in Costrich, 1975

CHAPTER 7
1. Boyer, 1992
2. Donoghue, 1997
3. The three meta-analyses were Montgomery, 1994; Song, 1993; Feighner Research Institute, 1994
4. Donoghue, 1996
5. Montgomery, 1996

6. In the case of Prozac, a paper by Baier (1994) lists a total of 17 separate studies reporting significant sexual side-effects: any of difficulties with erection and ejaculation, lowered libido and anorgasmia in women. He concluded that many studies 'may grossly understate the association between sexual adverse events and antidepressant medication'. The rates for the other SSRIs are almost certainly higher than those claimed by their manufacturers.

The reasons for the discrepancy are several, but they boil down to a deliberate attempt by the drug companies to conduct their studies in such a way that the true rate of problems is not revealed.

Patients are reluctant to raise the issue of sexual problems. Often they only emerge as a result of precise and direct interrogation but not in response to printed questionnaires or open-ended questions. If these latter methods are used by the drug companies they know they will get lower rates.

The official 'Adverse Events' reporting system only asks for very gross and obvious dysfunctions, so unless patients are having a big problem, they may put their lack of libido or other problems down to general apathy or lethargy.

Most important of all, depressed people are anyway more likely to have lowered libidos and to have less sex and old people in general and depressed old people in particular are far less sexual – less masturbation, intercourse and fantasy. My suspicion is that the drug companies use the age factor in their favour. Many of the published studies do not provide information about the ages of the subjects and it is sometimes impossible to obtain this. In 1995, when the new SSRI Nefazodone (brand name Dutonin) was licensed in this country, I contacted its manufacturer Bristol–Myers Squibb for details of the trials. Despite a seeming desire to accommodate me, they never provided me with a detailed breakdown by age, gender and sexual side-effects of their sample. They sent me details of two studies showing the age breakdown but requests for further detail came to nothing. It is therefore impossible to evaluate the significance of their claim that there was virtually no difference in rates of sexual dysfunction between those taking the drug and those on a placebo.

If the drug companies were to do a study comparing a large sample of young (20- to 40-year-old), sexually active patients on SSRIs with an equivalent control group on no medication, I suspect it would reveal much, much higher rates than they claim. There is no excuse for the lack of such studies and this situation could not exist without the active connivance of the Department of Health. Having said all this, it is a fair point (one often made by the drug company representatives) that it is not in the interests of patients who are anyway reluctant to take antidepressants to discourage them with alarming evidence of sexual dysfunction. My suspicion, however, is that some of the drugs are much less of a problem than others – anecodotally, for example, many clinicians say that Sertraline (Lustral) is less likely to cause sexual side-effects.

7. Boyer, 1996a
8. On violence, see Heiligenstein, 1992; on suicide see Beasley, 1991
9. Boyer, 1996b
10. Boland, 1996
11. Teicher, 1990
12. Heiligenstein, 1992
13. Wright, 1995
14. Linnoila, 1990
15. Linnoila, 1983
16. BBC Television, 1992
17. Coccaro, 1989
18. *Archives of General Psychiatry*, 1992
19. Fava, 1991; Fava, 1993; Coccaro, 1990
20. For references see p 275, Boyer, 1996b
21. See pp 276–7, Boyer, 1996b
22. See p 277, Boyer, 1996b
23. Freud, 1963
24. Jamison, 1993

CHAPTER 8
1. Scott, 1995; Lazar, 1997
2. Lazar, 1997
3. Cooper, 1993
4. The members of the British Confederation of Psychotherapy are: British Association of Psychotherapy, the Lincoln Centre for Psychotherapy, the Tavistock Institute Society of Psychotherapists, the Society of Analytical Psychology (Jungian) and their Scottish branch, the Anna Freud Centre, the Association of Psychoanalytic Psychotherapists in the National Health Service and its Scottish branch, the

Association of Child Psychotherapists and the Northern Ireland Association for the Study of Psychoanalysis.
5. Examples of other worthwhile organizations (all in London) include the London Centre of Psychotherapy, the Women's Therapy Centre, the Institute of Group Analysis, the Family Therapy Institute and the Institute of Marital Therapy (at the Tavistock Institute).
6. p 405, Gilbert, 1992
7. Manning, 1990

CHAPTER 9
1. Pitt, 1992
2. Kind, 1993
3. Greenberg, 1996
4. Schoun, 1979
5. Kim, 1994
6. Kim, 1994
7. Kagiticbasi, 1994
8. Leung, 1987
9. Triandis, 1988
10. Mishra, 1994
11. Diener, 1995
12. Gilbert, 1997
13. Sainsbury, 1997
14. Blumstein, 1983

APPENDIX I
1. Klerman, 1992. *Diagnostic and Statistical Manual of Mental Disorders*, Fourth Edition, American Psychiatric Association, p 327.
'Criteria for Major Depressive Episode:
A. Five (or more) of the following symptoms have been present during the same two-week period and represent a change from previous functioning: at least one of the symptoms is either (1) depressed mood or (2) loss of interest or pleasure.
Note: Do not include symptoms that are clearly due to a general medical condition or mood-incongruent delusions or hallucinations.
1. depressed mood most of the day, nearly every day, as indicated by either subjective report (e.g. feels sad or empty) or observation made by others (e.g. feels tearful)
2. markedly diminished interest or pleasure in all, or almost all, activities most of the day, nearly every day (as indicated by either subjective accounts or observation made by others)
3. significant weight loss when not dieting

or weight gain or decrease or increase in appetite nearly every day
4. insomnia or hypersomnia nearly every day
5. psychomotor agitation or retardation nearly every day
6. fatigue or loss of energy nearly every day
7. feelings of worthlessness or excessive or inappropriate guilt
8. diminished ability to think or concentrate or indecisiveness nearly every day
9. recurrent thoughts of death
B. The symptoms do not meet the criteria for mixed episode (p 335)
C. The symptoms cause clinically significant distress or impairment in social, occupational, or other important areas of functioning
D. The symptoms are not due to the direct physiological effects of a substance or general medical condition
E. The symptoms are not better accounted for by bereavement.'
2. Wickramratne, 1989
3. Kessler, 1994
4. Giuffra, 1994; Simon, 1995; Klerman, 1989
5. Fombonne, 1995
6. Hagnell, 1982
7. Murphy, 1986
8. Srole, 1980
9. See footnote 28 in Chapter 5 for full quotation of the critique of the Midtown Manhattan study by Ronald Kessler
10. Lewis, 1992

APPENDIX II
1. Burvill, 1995
2. Brown, 1978
3. Weissman, pp 99-101, 1997
4. James, 1995
5. Coccaro, 1990
6. Brown, 1991
7. Roy, 1990
8. Apter, 1991
9. *Diagnostic and Statistical Manual of Mental Disorders*, Fourth Edition, American Psychiatric Association, p 649.
'Diagnostic Criteria for Antisocial Personality Disorder:
A. There is a pervasive pattern of disregard for and violation of the rights of others occurring since age 15 years, as indicated by three or more of the following:
1. failure to conform to social norms with

respect to lawful behaviours as indicated by repeatedly performing acts that are grounds for arrest

2. deceitfulness, as indicated by repeated lying, use of aliases, or conning others for personal pleasure or profit

3. impulsivity or failure to plan ahead

4. reckless disregard for the safety of self or others

5. consistent irresponsibility as indicated by repeated failure to sustain consistent work behaviour or honour financial obligations

6. lack of remorse as indicated by being indifferent to or rationalizing having hurt, mistreated or stolen from another

B. The individual is at least age 18 years of age

C. There is evidence of conduct disorder with onset before age 15 years

D. The occurrence of antisocial behaviour is not exclusively during the course of schizophrenia or a manic episode.'

10. Farrington, 1989
11. Health and Safety Executive, 1986; National Association of School Masters/Union of Women Teachers, 1986; Brown, 1986; Wilkie, 1992; Hobbs, 1994; Hobbs, 1994
12. Automobile Association, 1997
13. West, 1966
14. Bowlby, 1944
15. Simon, 1979
16. see Chapter 5, James, 1995
17. Kandel, 1982
18. Dodge, 1980
19. Blackburn, 1985; Blackburn, 1986
20. Weissman, 1974
21. Quiggle, 1992
22. Virkunnen, 1989
23. Van Praag, 1986
24. Roy, 1986
25. Linnoila, 1983
26. O'Keane, 1992
27. Linnoila, 1990
28. Von Knorring, 1987
29. Schukit, 1986
30. Benton, 1982
31. Roy, 1988
32. Kruesi, 1989; Brown, 1986; Kruesi, 1985; Plisza, 1988
33. Kruesi, 1990; Stoff, 1987
34. Markus, 1992
35. Coccaro, 1989
36. Cameron, 1986
37. Giovino, 1995

38. Schoenborn, 1993
39. Anda, 1990
40. See references 147-154 in Giovino, 1995
41. See references 142, 155, 156 in Giovino, 1995
42. Ballenger, 1979
43. Myers, 1978
44. Naranjo, 1987
45. Roy, 1987
46. Silbereisen, 1995
47. Le Marquand, 1994; Roy, 1989
48. Rosenthal, 1980
49. Linnoila, 1990
50. Branchey, 1984
51. See p 274, Boyer, 1991
52. Steele, 1987; Johnson, 1986; Callow, 1996
53. Davies, 1996
54. Green, 1996
55. Steele, 1994
56. Morgan, 1996
57. McEntee, 1991
58. Curran, 1996
59. Robins, 1992
60. Berman, 1993
61. *Diagnostic and Statistical Manual of Mental Disorders*, Fourth Edition, 1994
62. See pp 275-6, Boyer, 1991
63. Fisher, 1996
64. Coccaro, p 192, 1990
65. Zuckerman, 1984
66. Rozenweig, 1987; Fombonne, 1995
67. Brewerton, pp 166-72, 1990
68. Kaye, 1984; see pp 157-6, Brewerton, 1990
69. Brewerton, 1990
70. Baier, 1994
71. Stein, 1992
72. Zohar, 1990
73. Zohar, 1990
74. Eaton, 1995
75. Ryan, 1992
76. Klerman, 1988
77. Rutter, 1983
78. Hughes, 1995
79. Goodyear, 1990
80. Rutter, 1995
81. Brown, 1986
82. Plisza, 1988
83. Stoff, 1987
84. Markus, 1992
85. Emlie, 1996
86. Turnberg, 1996
87. Ffrench, 1960
88. Kroenke, 1990; Bates, 1993

Bibliography

(NB To save space, where there is more than one author only the first name is given, followed by 'et al')

Abbs, P., 1986, *The Development of Autobiography in Western Culture*, University of Sussex

Ainsworth, M.D.A. et al, 1978, *Patterns of Attachment*, New Jersey: Lawrence Erlbaum.

Alley, T.R., 1992, 'Perceived age, physical attractiveness and sex differences in preferred age mates' ages', *Behavioural and Brain Sciences*, 15, 92

Alnaes, R. et al, 1988, 'Major depression, anxiety disorders and mixed conditions', *Acta Psychiatrica Scandinavia*, 78, 632–8

Alnaes, R. et al, 1990, 'Parental representation in patients with major depression, anxiety disorder and mixed conditions', *Acta Psychiatrica Scandinavia*, 81, 518–22

Amato, P.R. et al, 1991, 'Parental divorce and the well-being of children: a meta-analysis', *Psychological Bulletin*, 110, 26–46

Anda, R.F. et al, 1990, 'Depression and the dynamics of smoking: a national perspective', *JAMA*, 264, 1541–5

Angeli, F., 1991, *Social Europe: In search of a common culture*, Rome: Centro Studi Investimenti Sociali

Apter, A. et al, 1991, 'Serotenergic parameters of aggression and suicide', in Brown, S-L., *The Role of Serotonin in Psychiatric Disorders*, New York: Brunner/Mazel

Archives of General Psychiatry, 1992, Special Supplement, 49:6

Arieli, Y., 1964, *Individualism and Nationalism in American Ideology*, Cambridge, Mass: Harvard University Press

Aries, P., 1975, 'De l'enfant roi a l'enfant martyr', *Revue Psychologie*, 68:6;

Arieti, S. et al, 1974, 'The psychological organization of depression', *American Journal of Psychiatry*, 137:11, 1360–5

Armstrong, J.G. et al, 1989, 'Attachment and separation in eating disorders', *International Journal of Eating Disorders*, 8, 141–55

Atkinson, M.P. et al, 1984, 'WASP (Wives as senior partners)', *Journal of Marriage and the Family*, November, 861–70

Automobile Association, 1997, London

Baier, D. et al, 1994, 'Effects of antidepressants on sexual function', *Fortschritte der Neurologie Psychiatrie*, 62, 14–21

Ballenger, J. et al, 1979, 'Alcohol and central serotonin metabolism in man', *Archives General Psychiatry*, 36, 224–7

Bandura, A. et al, 1982, 'Microanalysis of action and fear arousal as a function of differential levels of self-efficacy', *Journal of Personality and Social Psychology*, 43, 5–21

Barnett, P.A. et al, 1988, 'Psychosocial functioning and depresson: distinguishing among antecedents, concomitants and consequences', *Psychological Bulletin*, 104, 97–126

Barocas, R. et al, 1974, 'Physical appearance and personal adjustment counselling', *Journal of Counselling Psychotherapy*, 21, 96–100

Barry, H. et al, 1959, 'Relations of child training to subsistence economy', *American Anthropologist*, 61, 51–63

Bar-Tal, D. et al, 1967, 'Perceptions of similarity and dissimilarity in attractive couples and individuals', *Journal of Personality and Social Psychology*, 33, 772–81

Bates, D.W. et al, 1993, 'Prevalence of chronic fatigue syndrome and fatigue in a primary care setting', *Arch. Intern. Med.*, 153, 2759–65

Baumeister, R.F. et al, 1989, 'Self-presentation motivations and personality differences in self-esteem', *Journal of Personality*, 57, 547–79

Baumeister, R.F. et al, 1995, 'The need to belong: Desire for interpersonal attachments as a fundamental human motivation', *Psychological Bulletin*, 117, 497–529

Baumeister, R.F., 1991, *Meanings of Life*, New York: Guildford Press

BBC Television, 1992, 'Wot U Lookin' At?', *Horizon*

Beach, S.H. et al, 1983, 'The link between marital distress and depression: a prospective study', Presented at the Association for the Advancement of Behaviour Therapy, Washington DC

Beasley, C.M. et al, 1991, 'Fluoxetine and suicide: a meta-analysis of controlled trials of treatment of depression', *British Medical Journal*, 303, 685–92

Becker, E., 1964, *The Revolution in Psychiatry*, New York, Free Press

Beckman, L.J., 1981, 'Effects of social interaction and children's relative inputs on older women's psychological well-being', 41, 1075–86

Bellah, R.N. et al, 1996, *Habits of the Heart: Individualism and Commitment in American Life*, University of California Press

Belsky, J. and Rovine, M., 1987, 'Temperament and security in the strange situation', *Child Development*, 58, 787–795

Belsky, J., 1990, 'Parental and nonparental child care and children's socioemotional development: a decade in review', *Journal of Marriage and the Family*, 52, 885–903

Belsky, J., 1993, 'Etiology of child maltreatment: a developmental–ecological analysis', *Psychological Bulletin*, 114, 413–34

Benton, D. et al, 1982, 'Mild hypoglycemia and questionnaire measures of aggression', *Biological Psychology*, 14, 129–35

Bentovin, A. et al, 1988, *Child Sexual Abuse within the Family*, London: Butterworth

Bergner, R.M., 1988, 'Status dynamic psychotherapy with depressed patients', *Psychotherapy*, 25, 266–72

Berman, S.M. et al, 1993, 'Childhood antecedents of substance misuse', *Current Opinions in Psychiatry*, 6, 382–7

Berry, J.W., 1976, *Human Ecology and Cognitive Style: Comparative Studies in Cultural and Psychological Adaptation*, New York: Halstead

Biggar, R.J. et al, 1989, 'Trends in the number of sexual partners among American women', *Journal of Acquired Immune Deficiency Syndromes*, 2, 497–502

Bion, W., 1961, *Experiences in Groups*, London: Tavistock

Blackburn, R. et al, 1985, 'Reactions of primary and secondary psychopaths to anger-evoking situations', *British Journal of Clinical Psychology*, 24, 93–100

Blackburn, R., 1986, 'Patterns of personality deviation among violent offenders', *British Journal of Criminology*, 26, 254–269

Blaus, J. et al, 1982, 'The cost of inequality: metropolitan structure and violent crime', *American Sociological Review*, 47, 121

Blinkhorn, S. et al, 1994, 'The use of personality tests', *The Psychologist*

Block, J.H. et al, 1986, 'The personality of children prior to divorce', *Child Development*, 57, 827–840

Block, J.H. et al, 1991, 'Personality antecedents of depressive tendencies in 18-year-olds: a prospective study', *Journal of Personality and Social Psychology*, 60, 726–38

Bloom, B.L. et al, 1979, 'Marital disruption as a stressful life event', in Levinger, G. et al, *Divorce and Separation*, New York: Basic Books

Blumstein, P. et al, 1983, *American Couples*, New York: William Morrow

Boland, R.J. et al, 1996, 'Depression and comorbidity', in Feighner, J.P. et al, *Selective Serotonin Re-uptake Inhibitors*, London: Wiley

Borgia, G., 1989, 'Typology and human mating preferences', *Behavioural and Brain Sciences*, 12, 16–17

Bowlby, J., 1944, 'Forty-four juvenile thieves: their characters and their home lives',

International Journal of Psychoanalysis, 25, 19–52 and 107–127

Bowlby, J., 1969, *Attachment and Loss* Vol 1: *Attachment*; 1973, Vol 2: *Separation*; 1980, Vol 3: *Loss*; all New York: Basic Books

Boyer, W.F. et al, 1992, 'The safety profile of Paroxetine', *Journal of Clinical Psychiatry*, 53, supp. 6, 1–6

Boyer, W.F. et al, 1996, 'Other uses of selective serotonin reuptake inhibitors in psychiatry', in Feighner, J.P. et al, *Selective Serotonin Re-uptake Inhibitors*, London: Wiley

Boyer, W.F. et al, 1996a, 'Safety and tolerability selective serotonin reuptake inhibitors', in Feighner, J.P. et al, *Selective Serotonin Re-uptake Inhibitors*, London: Wiley

Branchey, L. et al, 1984, 'Depression, suicide and aggression in alcoholics and their relationship to pasma amino acids', *Psychiatry Research*, 12, 219–226

Brannen, J. et al, 1994, *Employment and family life: a review of research in the UK*, London: Department of Employment

Brennan, K.A. et al, 1991, 'Attachment styles, gender and parental problem drinking', *Journal of Social and Personal Relationships*, 8, 451–66

Brewerton, M.D. et al, 1986, 'Psychiatric aspects of the relationship between eating and mood', *Nutritional. Review*, 44, 78–88

Brewerton, M.D. et al, 1990, 'Serotonin in eating disorders', in Coccaro, E.F. et al, *Serotonin in Major Psychiatric Disorders*, London: American Psychiatric Press

Brickman, P. et al, 1977, 'Pleasure and pain in social comparison', in Suls, J.M. and Miller, R.L., *Social Comparison Processes: Theoretical and Experimental Processes*, Washington DC: Hemisphere

Broude, G.J., 1987, 'The relationship of marital intimacy and aloofness to social environment: a hologeistic study', *Behaviour Science Research*, 21, 50–69

Broude, G.J., 1992, 'The May-September algorithm meets the 20th-century actuarial table', *Behavioural and Brain Sciences*, 15, 94–5

Brown, G. and Harris, T., 1978, *Social Origins of Depression*, London: Tavistock Publications

Brown, G.L. et al, 1986, 'Relationship of childhood characteristics to cerebrospinal fluid 5-hydroxyindoleacetic acid in aggressive adults', in *Biological Psychiatry*, New York: Elsevier

Brown, G.W. et al, 1990, 'Motherhood, employment and the development of depression: a replication of a finding?', *British Journal of Psychiatry*, 156, 169–79

Brown, R. et al, 1986, *Social Workers at Risk*, London: Macmillan

Brown, S-L., 1991, 'The monoamine hypothesis of depression', in Brown, S-L., *The Role of Serotonin in Psychiatric Disorders*, New York: Brunner/Mazel

Bruch, H., 1978, *The Golden Cage*, Harvard University Press

Buck, N. et al, 1995a, 'Cohabitation in Britain', *Changing Britain*, Newsletter for the ESRC Population and Household Change Research Programme, 3, 3–5

Buck, N. et al, 1995b, 'New evidence on cohabitation spells from the British Household Panel Survey', *Working Papers of the ESRC Centre on Microsocial Change*, Colchester, University of Essex

Burvill, P.W., 1995, 'Recent progress in the epidemiology of major depression', *Epidemiologic Reviews*, 17, 1

Buss, D.M, 1989, 'Sex differences in human mate preferences: evolutionary hypotheses tested in 37 cultures', *Behavioural and Brain Sciences*, 12, 1–49

Buss, D.M., 1996, 'Vital attraction', *Demos Quarterly*, 10, 12–17

Buunk, B.P. et al, 1996, 'Sex differences in jealousy in evolutionary and cultural perspective: tests from the Netherlands, Germany, and the United States', *Psychological Science*, 7, 359–63

Callow, N., 1996, 'Use of snowballing techniques to investigate subjective mood and personality traits associated with ecstasy', Annual student conference, University of Glamorgan, September

Cameron, D. et al, 1985, 'An epidemiological and sociological analysis of the use of alcohol, tobacco and other drugs of solace', *Community Medicine*, 7, 18–29

Campbell, A., 1980, *The Sense of Well-Being in America*, San Francisco: McGraw-Hill

Caporael, L.R., 1989, 'Mechanisms matter: the difference between sociobiology and evolutionary psychology', *Behavioural and Brain Sciences*, 12, 17–18

Carnelley, K. et al, 1994, 'Depression, working models of others and relationship functioning', *Journal of Personality and Social Psychology*, 66, 127–40

Carrol, J.L. et al, 1985, 'Differences between males and females in motives for engaging in sexual intercourse', *Archives of Sexual Behaviour*, 14, 131–9

Carver, C.S. et al, 1983, 'Depression and components of self-punitiveness: High self-standards, self-criticisms and overgeneralization', *Journal of Consulting and Clinical Psychology*, 92, 330–7

Carver, C.S. et al, 1985, 'A control systems approach to the self-regulation of action' in Kuhl, J. et al, *Action Control*, Berlin: Springer

Cash, T.F. et al, 1983, 'Mirror mirror on the wall...? Contrast effects and self-evaluations of physical attractiveness', *Personality and Social Psychology Bulletin*, 9, 351–8

Cash, T.F., 1985, 'Physical appearance and mental health', in Graham, J.A. et al, *The Psychology of Cosmetic Treatments*, New York: Praeger

Chick, D. et al, 1987–8, 'A review of influences on sexual fantasy: attitudes, experience, guilt and gender', *Imagination, Cognition and Personality*, 7, 61–76

Cicone, M.V. et al, 1978, 'Beliefs about males', *Journal of Social Issues*, 34, 5–16

Clark, R. et al, 1989, 'Gender differences in receptivity to sexual offers', *Journal of Psychology and Human Sexuality*, 2, 39–55

Clarke-Stewart, K.A., 1989, 'Infant day care – Maligned or malignant', *American Psychologist*, 44, 266–73

Clayton, P.J., 1980, 'Mood disorders in professional women', *Journal of Affective Disorders*, 2, 37–46

Clement, U. et al, 1984, 'Changes in sexual behaviour: a replication of a study on West German students (1966–1981)', *Archives of Sexual Behaviour*, 13, 99–120

Coccaro, E. and Murphy, D.L., 1990, *Serotonin in Major Psychiatric Disorders*, Washington: American Psychiatric Press

Coccaro, E.F. et al, 1990, 'Fluoxetine treatment of impulsive aggression in DSM-III-R personality disordered patients', *Journal of Clinical Psychopharmacology*, 19:5, 373–5

Coccaro, E.F. et al, 1990, 'Serotonin in mood and personality disorders', in Coccaro, E.F. et al, *Serotonin in Major Psychiatric Disorders*, London: American Psychiatric Press

Coccaro, E.F., 1989, 'Central serotonin and impulsive aggression', *British Journal of Psychiatry*, 155:8, 52–62

Collins, R.L. et al, 1989, 'The affective consequences of social comparison: either direction has its ups and downs', unpublished manuscript

Colvin, C. et al, 1994, 'Do positive illusions foster mental health? An examination of the Taylor and Brown formulation', *Psychological Bulletin*, 116, 3–20

Comstock, G. et al, 1978, *Television and Human Behaviour*, New York: Columbia University Press

Comstock, G.W. and Helsing K.J., 1976, 'Symptoms of depression in two communities', *Psychological Medicine*, 6, 551–563

Cooper, J., 1993, *Speak Of Me As I Am – The Life and Work of Masud Khan*, London: Karnac Books

Coopersmith, S., 1967, *The Antecedents of Self-Esteem*, San Francisco: W.H. Freeman

Costrich, N. et al, 1975, 'When stereotypes hurt: three studies of personality for sex role reversals', *Journal of Experimental Social Psychology*, 11, 520–30

Coyne, J.C. et al, 1976, 'Going beyond social support: the role of social relationships in adaptation', *Journal of Consulting and Clinical Psychology*, 54, 454–60

Coyne, J.C. et al, 1987, 'Depression' in Jacobs, T., *Family Interaction and Psychopathology*, New York: Plenum

Coyne, J.C., 1976, 'Depression and the response of others', *Journal of Abnormal Psychology*, 85, 186–93

Criminal Statistics, 1994, London: HMSO

Crosby, F. et al, 1986, 'Relative deprivation and explanation: models and concepts' in Olson,

J.M. et al, *Relative Deprivation and Social Comparison, The Ontario Symposium*, Vol 4, New Jersey: Lawrence Erlbaum

Cummings, E.M. et al, 1985, 'Influence of conflict between adults on the emotions and aggression of young children', *Developmental Psychology*, 21, 495–507

Cunningham, M.R., 1986, 'Measuring the physical in physical attractiveness: quasi-experiments on the sociobiology of female facial beauty', *Journal of Personality and Social Psychology*, 50, 925–35

Curran, V., 1996, University College, London, personal communication, manuscript in preparation

Dance, K.A. et al, 1987, 'Self schemata content and consolidation: the impact of depression level and cognitive vulnerability in depression' (manuscript submitted for publication)

Darwin, C., 1859, *On the Origin of Species by Means of Natural Selection*, London: John Murray

David, D. et al, 1976, 'The male sex role: our culture's blueprint for manhood and what it's done for us lately', in David, D. et al, *The Forty-nine percent majority: the male sex role*, Reading MA: Addison-Wesley

Davies, G., 1996, 'Investigation of subjective mood and personality traits associated with recreational use of ecstasy', Annual student conference, University of Glamorgan, September

Davis, J.A., 1963, 'Structural balance, mechanical solidarity and interpersonal relations', *American Journal of Sociology*, 68, 444–62

De Mause, L., 1988, 'On writing the history of childhood', *Journal of Psychohistory*, 16:2, 135–71

De Mause, L., 1974, *The History of Childhood*, New York: Condor

De Zueletta, F., 1993, *From Pain to Violence*, London: Whurr

DeLamater, J., 1987, 'Gender differences in sexual scenarios', in Kelley, K., *Females, Males and Sexuality*, Albany: SUNY Press

Delongis, A. et al, 1988, 'The impact of daily stress on health and mood', *Journal of Personality and Social Psychology*, 54, 486–95

Diagnostic and Statistical Manual of Mental Disorders, 1994, Fourth Edition, American Psychiatric Association

Dickeman, M., 1989, 'Aggregates, averages and behavioural plasticity', *Behavioural and Brain Sciences*, 12, 18–19

Diekstra, R.F.W. et al, 1995, 'Suicide and suicidal behaviour among adolescents', in Rutter, M. and Smith, D.J., *Psychosocial Disorders in Young People*, New York: Wiley

Diener, E. et al, 1978, 'An analysis of Learned Helplessness: continuous change in performance, strategy and achievement cognitions after failure', *Journal of Personality and Social Psychology*, 36, 451–62

Diener, E. et al, 1979, 'Self-awareness, psychological perspective and self-reinforcement in relation to personal and social standards', *Journal of Personality and Social Psychology*, 37, 413–23

Diener, E. et al, 1985, 'Happiness of the very wealthy', *Social Indicators Research*, 16, 263–74

Diener, E. et al, 1995, 'Factors predicting the subjective well-being of nations', *Journal of Personality and Social Psychology*, 69, 851–64

Dion, K.L et al, 1973, 'Correlates of romantic love', *Journal of Consulting and Clinical Psychology*, 41, 51–6

Dodge, K.A., 1980, 'Social cognition and children's aggressive behaviour', *Child Development*, 51, 162–170.

Dohrenwend, B.P. and Dohrenwend, B.S., 1974, *Stressful Life Events: Their Nature and Effect*, New York: John Wiley

Donoghue, J.M. et al, 1996, 'The treatment of depression: prescribing patterns in primary care in the UK', *British Journal of Psychiatry*, 168, 164–8

Donoghue, J.M. et al, 1997, 'Cross-sectional database analysis of prescribing patterns of antidepressant medications', *British Medical Journal*, 313, 861–2

Dornbusch, S.M. et al, 1984, 'Sexual maturation, social class and the desire to be thin among adolescent females', *Developmental Pediatrics*, 5, 308–14

Drury, D., 1980, 'Black self-esteem in desegregated schools', *Sociology of Education*, 53, 88–103

Durkheim, E., 1933, *The Division of Labour*, London: Macmillan

Dweck, C.S. et al, 1983, 'Achievement motivation', in Mussen, P.J., *Carmichael's Manual of Child Psychology*, Vol III, New York: Wiley

Easterlin, R.A., 1980, *Birth and Fortune: the Impact of Numbers on Personal Welfare*, New York

Easterlin, R.A., 1995, 'Will raising the incomes of all increase the happiness of all?', *Journal of Economic Behaviour and Organization*, 27, 35–47

Eaton, K.W. et al, 1955, *Culture and Mental Disorder*, Glencoe, Illinois: Free Press

Eaton, W.W. et al, 1992, 'Panic and Phobia' in Robins, L.N. et al, 1992, *Psychiatric Disorders in America*, New York: Free Press

Eaton, W.W., 1995, 'Progress in the epidemiology of anxiety disorders', in *Epidemiologic Reviews*, 17, 1

Egeland, J.A. et al, 1983, 'Amish study I: affective disorders among the Amish', *American Journal of Psychiatry*, 140, 56–61

Elder, G., 1969, 'Appearance and education in marriage mobility', *American Sociological Review*, 34, 519–33

Elias, P., 1994, 'Job-related training, union membership and labour mobility: a longitudinal study', *Oxford Economic Papers*, 46, 563–78

Elliott, B.J. et al, 1991, 'Children and divorce: educational performance and behaviour before and after separation', *International Journal of Law and the Family*, 5, 258–276

Ellis, B.J. et al, 1990, 'Sex differences in sexual fantasy: an evolutionary psychological approach', *Journal of Sex Research*, 27, 527–55

Emslie, G., 1996, 'Treating Depression in Adolescent Patients' in Feighner, J.P. et al, *Selective Serotonin Re-Uptake Inhibitors*, New York: John Wiley

Engels, F., 1884, *The Origins of the Family, Private Property and the State*, Hottingen

Fairbanks, L.A. et al, 1988, 'Long-term effects of early mothering behaviour on responsiveness to the environment in vervet monkeys', *Developmental Psychobiology*, 21, 711–24

Fairbanks, L.A., 1989, 'Early experiences and cross-generational continuity of mother-infant contact in vervet monkeys', *Developmental Psychobiology*, 22, 669–81

Farina, A. et al, 1986, 'The role of physical attractiveness in the readjustment of discharged psychiatric patients', *Journal of Abnormal Psychology*, 86, 510–17

Farrington, D.P., 1989, 'Childhood aggression and adult violence: early precursors and later life outcomes', in Rubin, K.H. and Pepler, D., *The Development and Treatment of Childhood Aggression*, New Jersey: Lawrence Erlbaum.

Farrington, D.P., 1989, 'Early predictors of adolescent aggression and adult violence', *Violence and Victims*, 4, 79–99

Fava, M.D. et al, 1991, 'Anger attacks in depressed outpatients and their response to fluoxetine', *Psychopharmacology Bulletin*, 27:3, 275–9

Fava, M.D. et al, 1993, 'Anger attacks in unipolar depression Part 1', *American Journal of Psychiatry*, 150:8, 1158–63

Feighner Research Institute, 1994, Data on file

Feingold, A., 1990, 'Gender differences in physical attractiveness on romantic attraction: a comparison across five research domains', *Journal of Personality and Social Psychology*, 59, 981–93

Feldman, P., 1987, *Sex and Sexuality*, London: Longman

Festiger, L., 1954, 'A theory of social comparison processes', *Human Relations*, 7, 117–40

Ffrench, G., 1960, 'The clinical significance of tiredness', *Canadian Medical Association Journal*, 82, 665–71

Fisher, S. et al, 1996, *Gambling*, Home Office, HMSO

Flanagan, S.C., 1982, 'Measuring value change in advanced industrial societies: a rejoinder to Inglehart', *Comparative Political Studies*, 15, 99–128

Fombonne, E., 1995, 'Depressive disorders' in *Psychosocial Disorders in Young People*,

Rutter, M. and Smith, D.J., New York: Wiley

Fombonne, E., 1995, 'Eating disorders', in Rutter, M. and Smith, D.J., *Psychosocial Trends in Young People*, New York: John Wiley

Freud, S., 1963, 'The paths to the formation of symptoms', Lecture 23, Standard Edition, Vol XVI

Frey, K.S. et al, 1987, 'What children say about classroom performance: sex and grade differences in perceived competence', *Child Development*, 58, 1066–78

Frey, K.S. et al, 1985, 'What children say when the teacher is not around: conflicting goals in social comparison performance assessment in the classroom', *Journal of Personality and Social Psychology*, 48, 18–30

Frey, K.S., 1987, 'Coping responses of parents of disabled children', unpublished data

Friend, R.M. et al, 1973, 'Threat and fear of negative evaluation as determinants of locus of social comparisons', *Journal of Personality*, 41, 328–40

Frieze, I.H. et al, 1978, *Women and Sex Roles: A Social Psychological Perspective*, New York: Norton

General Household Survey, 1993, London: HMSO

Gerbner, G. et al, 1976, 'The scary world of TV's heavy viewer', *Psychology Today*, April

Gibbons, F.X., 1986, 'Social comparison and depression: company's effect on misery', *Journal of Personality and Social Psychology*, 51, 140–8

Gilbert, P., 1992, *Depression: the Evolution of Powerlessness*, New Jersey: Lawrence Erlbaum

Gilbert, P. et al, 1996, 'Parental representations, shame, interpersonal problems and vulnerability to psychopathology', *Clinical Psychology and Psychotherapy*, 3, 23–34

Gilbert, P., 1997, *Challenging the Myths of Competitive Modern Life*, Chapter 11 (book in preparation)

Ginn, J. et al, 1996, 'Feminist fallacies: a reply to Hakim on women's employment', *British Journal of Sociology*, 47, 167–73

Giorgi, L. et al, 1990, 'The protestant work ethic as a cultural phenomenon', *European Journal of Social Psychology*, 20, 499–517

Giovino, G.A. et al, 1995, 'Epidemiology of tobacco use and dependence', in *Epidemiologic Reviews*, 17, 1

Giuffra, L.A. et al, 1994, 'Diminished recall and the cohort effect of major depression: a simulation study', *Psychological Medicine*, 24, 375–83

Glenn, N.D., 1989, 'Intersocietal variation in the mate preferences of males and females', *Behavioural and Brain Sciences*, 12, 21–3

Goethals, G.R., 1986, 'Fabricating and ignoring societal reality: self-serving estimates of consensus', in Olson, J.M. et al, *Relative Deprivation and Social Comparison, The Ontario Symposium*, Vol 4, New Jersey: Lawrence Erlbaum

Goldthorpe, J.H., 1987, *Social Mobility and Class Structure in Modern Britain*, Oxford: Clarendon Press

Goodyear, I.M., 1990, *Life Experiences, Development and Childhood Psychopathology*, Chichester: Wiley

Gotlib, I.H et al, 1989, 'Depression and marital functioning: an examination of specificity and gender differences', *Journal of Abnormal Psychology*, 98, 23–30

Gotlib, I.H. et al, 1988, 'Depression and marital distress: current status and future directions', in Duck, S., *Handbook of Personal Relationships*, London: Wiley

Gotlib, I.H. et al, 1988, 'Depression and perceptions of early parenting: a longitudinal study', *British Journal of Psychiatry*, 152, 24–7

Gotlib, I.H. et al, 1990, 'The interpersonal context of depression: implications for theory and research', in Perlman, D. et al, *Advances in Personal Relationships*, Greenwich: JAI Press

Gottman, J., 1991, 'Predicting the longitudinal course of marriages', *Journal of Marital and Family Therapy*, 17, 3–7

Gove, W.R. et al, 1973, 'Adult sex roles and mental health', *American Journal of Sociology*, 78, 812–35

Gove, W.R., 1979, 'Sex differences in the epidemiology of mental disorder: evidence and explanations', in Gomberg, E.S. et al, *Gender and Disordered Behaviour*, New York: Brounner/Mazel

Graziano, W.G. et al, 1993, 'Social influences, sex differences, and judgements of beauty: putting the interpersonal back into interpersonal attraction', *Journal of Personality and Social Psychology*, 65, 525–31

Green, A.R. et al, 1996, 'Ecstasy and neurodegeneration', *British Medical Journal*, 312, 15 June

Greenberg, P.E. et al, 1996, 'Depression in the workplace: an economic perspective', in Feighner, J.P. et al, *Selective Serotonin Re-Uptake Inhibitors*, New York: Wiley

Grundy, E., 1996, 'Population review: (5) the population aged 60 and over', *Population Trends*, 84, 14–20

Gurr, T.R., 1970, *Why Men Rebel*, Princeton: Princeton University Press

Gurr, T.B. et al, 1977, *The Politics of Crime and Conflict: a Comparative History of Four Cities*, London: Sage

Gurr, T.B., 1989, 'Historical trends in violent crime: Europe and the United States', in Gurr, T.B., *Violence in America: Vol. 1 The History of Crime*, London: Sage.

Hagnell, O. et al, 1982, 'Are we entering an age of melancholia?', *Psychological Medicine*, 12, 279–89

Hakim, C., 1995, 'Five feminist myths about women's employment', *British Journal of Sociology*, 46, 429–55

Hakim, C., 1996, *Key Issues in Women's Work*, London: Athlone Press

Hakmiller, K.L., 1966, 'Threat as a determinant of downward comparison', *Journal of Experimental Social Psychology*, Supplement 1, 49–54

Halpern, D., 1995, 'Values, morals and modernity', in Rutter, M. et al, *Psychosocial Disorders in Young People*, London: John Wiley

Harpending, H., 1992, 'Age differences between mates in southern African pastoralists', *Behavioural and Brain Sciences*, 15, 102–3

Harris, T. et al, 1991, 'Is sex necessarily a risk factor for depression', *British Journal of Psychiatry*, 158, 708–12

Harrison, A.A. et al, 1984, 'Groups in exotic environments', in Berkowitz, L., *Advances in Experimental Psychology*, Vol 18, New York: Academic Press

Harter, S., 1981, 'A model of mastery motivation in children: individual differences and developmental change' in Collins, A., *Minnesota Symposium on Child Psychology*, Vol 14, New Jersey: Lawrence Erlbaum

Haskey, J., 1983, 'Social class patterns of marriage', *Population Trends*, 34, 12–19

Haskey, J., 1992, 'Pre-marital cohabitation and the probability of subsequent divorce: analsyes using new data from the General Houshold Survey', *Population Trends*, 68, 110–19

Hazan, C. et al, 1994, 'Attachment as an organizational framework for research on close relationships', *Psychological Inquiry*, 5, 68–79

Health and Safety Executive, 1986, *Violence to Staff*, London: HMSO

Heiligenstein, M.D. et al, 1992, 'Fluoxetine not associated with increased violence or aggression in controlled clinical trials', *Archives of General Psychiatry*, 4, 285–95

Hennigan, K.M. et al, 1982, 'Impact of the introduction of television on crime in the United States: empirical findings and theoretical implications', *Journal of Personality and Social Psychology*, 42, 461–77

Herrnstein, R.J. et al, 1994, *The Bell Curve*, New York: Free Press

Hess, L.E., 1995, 'Changing family patterns in Western Europe', in Rutter, M. et al, *Psychosocial Disorders in Young People*, London: John Wiley

Hetherington, E.M., 1988, 'Parents, children and siblings: Six years after divorce', in Hinde, R.A. and Stevenson-Hinde, J., *Relationships within Families*, Oxford: Clarendon Press

Hewitt, P. et al, 1993, *Social Justice, Children and Families*, London: Institute for Public Policy Research

Higgins, E.T. et al, 1983, 'Stages as subcultures: Social-cognitive development and the social life of the child', in Higgins, E.T. et al, *Social Cognition and Social Behaviour*, New York: Cambridge University Press

Higley, J.D. et al, 1991, 'CSF monamine metabolite concentrations vary according to age, rearing and sex and are influenced by the stressor of social separation in rhesus monkeys', *Psychopharmacology*, 103, 551–6

Hill, C.T. et al, 1979, 'Breakups before marriage: the end of 103 affairs', in Levinger, G. et al, *Divorce and Separation*, New York: Basic Books

Hindess, B. et al, 1975, *Pre-Capitalist Modes of Production*, London: Routledge

Hite, S., 1976, *The Hite Report*, London: HarperCollins

Hobbs, F.D.R., 1994, 'Fear of aggression at work among general practitioners who have suffered a previous episode of aggression', *British Journal of General Practice*, 44

Hobbs, F.D.R., 1994, 'General Practitioners' changes to practice due to aggression at work', *Family Practice*, 11, 1, 75–9

Hoberman, H.M. et al, 1985, 'The behavioural treatment of depression', in Beckman, E.E. et al, *Handbook of Depression*, Homewood, Illinois: Dorsey

Hock, E. et al, 1988, 'Maternal separation anxiety: its role in the balance of employment and motherhood in mothers of infants', in Gottfried, A.E. et al, *Maternal Employment and Children's Development*, New York: Plenum Press

Hofferth, S. et al, 1987, 'Child care in the United States, 1975 to 1995', *Journal of Marriage and the Family*, 49, 559–71

Hofstede, G., 1980, 1994, *Culture's Consequences: International Differences in Work-Related Values*, Beverley Hills: Sage

Hops, H. et al, 1990, 'Maternal depression, marital discord and children's behaviour: a developmental perspective', in Patterson, G.R., *Aggression and depression in family interaction*, New Jersey: Lawrence Erlbaum

Horney, K., 1967, *Feminine Psychology*, New York: Norton

Houseknecht, S.K. et al, 1984, 'Marital disruption among professional women: the timing of career and family events', *Social Problems*, 31, 273–84

Hoyenga, K.B. et al, 1993, *Gender-Related Differences: Origins and Outcomes*, London: Allyn

Hughes, P.H., 1995, 'Heroin epidemics revisited', *Epidemiologic Reviews*, 17:1

Human Development Report, 1995, New York: United Nations

Hutton, W., 1996, *The State We're In*, London: Vintage 65

Inglehart, R., 1990, *Culture Shift in Advanced Industrial Society*, Princeton: Princeton University Press

Jaffee, P. et al, 1986, 'Similarities in behavioural and social maladjustment among child victims and witnesses to family violence', *American Journal of Orthopsychiatry*, 56, 142–146

James, O.W., 1979, 'Anthropomorphization of infant behaviours in North West Ecuador', Thesis submitted for Masters degree, Child Development Unit, Nottingham University

James, O.W., 1995, *Juvenile Violence in a Winner-Loser Culture*, London: Free Association Books

Jamison, K.R., 1993, *Touched with Fire*, New York: Macmillan

Johnson, A.M. et al, 1994, *Sexual Attitudes and Lifestyle*, Oxford: Blackwell Scientific

Johnson, M.P. et al, 1986, 'Effects of enantiometers of MDA, MDMA and related analogues on {3H}-serotonin and {3H}-dopamine release from superfused rat brain slices', *European Journal of Pharmacology*, 132, 269–76

Jones, W.H., 1981, 'Loneliness and social contact', *Journal of Social Psychology*, 113, 295–6

Joseph Rowntree Foundation, 1995, *Income and Inequality*

Kagiticbasi, C., 1994, 'A critical appraisal of individualism and collectivism : towards a new formulation', in Kim, U. et al, *Individualism and Collectivism*, London: Sage

Kandel, D.B. et al, 1980, 'Epidemiology of depressive mood in adolescents', *Archives of General Psychiatry*, 39, 1205–1212

Kaplan, G.A. et al, 1987, 'Psychosocial predictors of depression', *American Journal of Clinical Epidemiology*, 125, 206–20

Kaufman, S.R., 1986, *The Ageless Self: Sources of Meaning in Late Life*, New York: Meridian

Kaye, W.H. et al, 1984, 'Differences in brain metabolism between nonbulimic and bulimic patients with anorexia nervosa', *American Journal of Psychiatry*, 141, 1598–1601

Kelly, E.L. et al, 1987, 'Personality and compatibility: a prospective analysis of marital stability and marital satisfaction', *Journal of Personality and Social Psychology*, 52, 27-40

Kenrick, D.T. et al, 1980, 'Contrast effects and judgements of physical attractiveness: when beauty becomes a social problem', *Journal of Personality and Social Psychology*, 38, 131-40

Kenrick, D.T. et al, 1989, 'Influence of popular erotica on judgements of strangers and mates', *Journal of Experimental Social Psychology*, 25, 159-67

Kenrick, D.T. et al, 1990, 'Evolution, traits and the stages of human courtship: qualifying the parental investment model', *Journal of Personality*, 58, 97-116

Kenrick, D.T. et al, 1992, 'Age preferences in mates reflect sex differences in human reproductive strategies', *Behavioural and Brain Sciences*, 15, 75-133

Kenrick, D.T. et al, 1993, 'Effects of physical attractiveness on affect and perceptual judgements: when social comparison overrides social reinforcement', *Personality and Social Psychology Bulletin*, 19, 195-9

Kenrick, D.T. et al, 1994, 'Evolution and social cognition: contrast effects as a function of sex, dominance and physical attractiveness', *Personality and Social Psychology Bulletin*, 20, 210-17

Kessler, R.C. et al, 1981, 'Trends in the relationship between sex and depression: 1957-76', *American Sociological Review*, 46, 443-52

Kessler, R.C. et al, 1982, 'The effect of wives' employment on the mental health of married men and women', *American Sociological Review*, 47, 216-27

Kessler, R.C. et al, 1983, 'Trends in the relationship between sex and attempted suicide', *Journal of Health and Social Behaviour*, 24, 98-110

Kessler, R.C. et al, 1993, 'Sex and depression in the National Comorbidity Survey I: lifetime prevalence, chronicity and recurrence', *Journal of Affective Disorders*, 29, 85-96

Kessler, R.C. et al, 1994, 'Sex and depression in the national comorbidity study', *Journal of Affective Disorders*, 30, 15-26

Kiecolt-Glaser, J.K. et al, 1987, 'Marital quality, marital disruption and immune function', *Psychosomatic Medicine*, 49, 13-34

Kiernan, K. et al, 1990, *Family Change and Future Policy*, London: Family Policy Studies Centre

Kiernan, K. et al, 1993, *Cohabitation: Extra-Marital Childbearing and Social Policy*, London: Family Policy Studies Centre

Kim, U. et al, 1994, *Individualism and Collectivism*, London: Sage

Kim, U., 1994, 'Individualism and collectivism: conceptual clarification and elaboration', in Kim, U. et al, *Individualism and Collectivism*, London: Sage

Kind, P. et al, 1993, 'The costs of depression', *International Clinical Psychopharmacology*, 7, 191-5

Kinsey, A. et al, 1948, *Sexual Behaviour in the Human Male*, Philadelphia: Saunders

Kinsey, A. et al, 1953, *Sexual Behaviour in the Human Female*, Philadelphia: Saunders

Kitson, G.C. et al, 1982, 'Marital complaints, demographic characteristics and symptoms of mental distress in divorce', *Journal of Marriage and the Family*, 44, 87-101

Klerman, G.L. et al, 1989, 'Increasing rates of depression', *JAMA*, 261, 2229-35

Klerman, G.L., 1988, 'The current age of youthful melanholia', *British Journal of Psychiatry*, 152, 4-14

Klerman, G.L., 1992, 'The changing rate of major depression', *JAMA*, 268:21, 3098-3105

Kroenke, K. et al, 1990, 'The prevalence of symptoms in medical outpatients and the adequacy of therapy', *Archives of International Medicine*, 250, 1685-9

Kruesi, M.J.P. et al, 1985, 'Carbohydrate craving, conduct disorder and low 5-HIAA', *Psychiatry Research*, 16, 83-6

Kruesi, M.J.P. et al, 1990, 'CSF monoamine metabolites, aggression and impulsivity in disruptive behaviour disorders of children and adolescents', *Archives of General Psychiatry*, 47, 419-26

Kruesi, M.J.P., 1989, 'Cruelty to animals and CSF5-HIAA', *Psychiatry Research*, 28, 115-6

Kuh, D. and Maclean, M., 1990, 'Women's childhood experience of parental separation and their subsequent health and socioeconomic status in adulthood', *Journal of Biosocial Science*, 22, 121–35

Kuiper, N.A. et al, 1986, 'Dysfunctional attitudes and a self-worth contingency', in Kendall, P.C., *Advances in Cognitive-Behavioural Research and Therapy*, Vol 5, New York: Academic Press

Lancaster, H.O., 1990, *Expectations of Life: a Study in the Demography, Statistics and History of World Mortality*, Berlin: Springer

Lawler, E.E. et al, 1963, 'Perceptions regarding management compensation', *Industrial Relations*, 3, 41–9

Lazar, S.G., 1997, 'Extended dynamic therapy – making the case in an era of managed care', *Psychoanalytic Inquiry*, 1997 Supplement

Leach, E., 1982, *Social Anthropology*, London: Penguin

Leach, P., 1994 , *Children First*, London: Michael Joseph

Leary, M.R., 1990, 'Responses to social exclusion: social anxiety, jealousy, loneliness, depression and low self-esteem', *Journal of Social and Clinical Psychology*, 9, 221–9

Leigh, B.C., 1989, 'Reasons for having and avoiding sex: gender, sexual orientation, and relationship to sexual behaviour', *Journal of Sex Research*, 26, 199–209

Lemaine, G., 1974, 'Social differentiation and social originality', *European Journal of Social Psychology*, 4, 17–52

LeMarquand, D. et al, 1994, 'Serotonin and alcohol intake, abuse and dependence: findings of animal studies', *Biological Psychiatry*, 36, 395–421

Leung, K., 1987, 'Some determinants of reactions to procedural models for conflict resolution: a cross-national study', *Journal of Personality and Social Psychology*, 53, 898–908

Levi Strauss, C., 1971, 'The principles of kinship', in Goody, J., *Kinship*, London: Penguin Education

LeVine, R. et al, 1988, *Parental Behaviour in Diverse Societies*, San Francisco: Jossey Bass

Lewin, B., 1982, 'The adolescent boy and girl: first and other early experiences with intercourse from a representative sample of Swedish school adolescents', *Archives of Sexual Behaviour*, 11, 417–428

Lewinsohn, P.M. et al, 1993, 'Age-cohort changes in the lifetime occurrence of depression and other mental disorders', *Journal of Abnormal Psychology*, 102, 110–20

Lewis, G. et al, 1993, 'Another British disease? A recent increase in the prevalence of psychiatric morbidity', *Journal of Epidemiology and Community Health*, 47, 358–61

Liederman, P.H. et al, 1977, *Culture and Infancy*, New York: Academic Press

Linn, M.C. et al, 1982, 'Adolescent reasoning about advertisements: preliminary investigations', *Child Development*, 53, 1599–1613

Linnoila, M. et al, 1983, in *Life Sciences*, 33, 2609–14

Linnoila, M. et al, 1990, 'Monoamines, glucose metabolism and impulse control', in Linnoila, M. et al, *Serotonin*, New York: John Wiley

Loewenthal, K.M., 1993, 'Levels of well-being and distress in orthodox Jewish men and women', *Journal of Psychology and Judaism*, 16, 225–33

Loewenthal, K.M. et al, 1995, 'Gender and depression in Anglo-Jewry', *Psychological Medicine*, 25, 1051–63

Lynch, J.J., 1979, *The Broken Heart: the Medical Consequences of Loneliness*, New York: Basic Books

Macdonald, J.S., 1978, 'The black family in the Americas: a literature review', *Sage Race Relations Abstracts*, 3

Macfarlane, A., 1978, *The Origins of English Individualism*, Oxford: Blackwell

Madsen, D. et al, 1984a, 'Whole blood serotonin and the Type A behaviour pattern', *Psychosomatic Medicine*, 46:6, 546–8

Madsen, D., 1984b, 'A biochemical property relating to power seeking in humans', *American Political Science Review*, 79, 448–57

Madsen, D., 1986, 'Power seekers are different: further biochemical evidence', *American Political Science Review*, 80, 261–9

Major, B. et al, 1991, 'Responses to upward and downward social comparison: the impact of esteem relevance and perceived control', in Suls, J. et al, *Social Comparison: Contemporary Theory and Research*, New Jersey: Lawrence Erlbaum

Mann, A.H. et al, 1983, 'Screening for abnormal eating attitudes and psychiatric morbidity in an unselected population of 15-year-old schoolgirls', *Psychological Medicine*, 13, 573–80

Mann, L., 1980, 'Cross-cultural studies of small groups', in Triandis, H. et al, *Handbook of Cross-Cultural Psychology: Social Psychology*, Vol 5, Boston: Allyn and Bacon

Manning, D.W. et al, 1990, *Combined Pharmacotherapy and Psychotherapy for Depression*, London: American Psychiatric Press

Markus, J.P. et al, 1992, 'A 2-year prospective follow-up study of children and adolescents with Disruptive Behaviour Disorders', *Archives of General Psychiatry*, 49, 6, 429–35

Marsden, C.A., 1996, 'The neuropharmacology of serotonin in the central nervous system', in Feighner, J.P. et al, *Selective Serotonin Re-Uptake Inhibitors*, London: Wiley

Marsh, H.W. et al, 1984, 'Determinants of students' self concept: is it better to be a relatively large fish in a small pond even if you don't learn to swim as well?', *Journal of Personality and Social Psychology*, 47, 213–31

Martin, J., 1986, 'The tolerance of injustice', in Olson, J.M. et al, *Relative Deprivation and Social Comparison, The Ontario Symposium*, Vol 4, New Jersey: Lawrence Erlbaum

Marx, K., 1964, *Pre Capitalist Economic Formations*, London: Lawrence and Wishart

Mawson, A.R., 1980, 'Aggression, attachment behaviour and crimes of violence', in Hirschi, T. et al, *Understanding Crime*, California: Sage

McConville, B., 1985, *Sisters*, New York: Pan Books

McCraine, E.W. et al, 1984, 'Childhood family antecedents of dependency and self-criticism', *Journal of Abnormal Psychology*, 93, 3–8

McEntee, W.J. et al, 1991, 'Serotonin, memory and the aging brain', *Psychopharmacology*, 103, 143–9

McGuire, M.T. et al, 1993, 'Life-history strategies, adaptive variations, and behaviour-physiologic interactions: the sociophysiology of vervet monkeys', in Barchas, P., *Sociophysiology*, New York: Oxford University Press

McRae, S., 1993, *Cohabiting Mothers: Changing Marriage and Motherhood?*, London: Policy Studies Institute

Merikangas, K.R., 1984, 'Divorce and assortative mating among depressed patients', *American Journal of Psychiatry*, 141, 74–6

Merikangas, K.R. et al, 1985, 'Genetic factors in the sex ratio of major depression', *Psychological Medicine*, 15, 63–9

Miczek, K.A. et al, 1989, 'Brain 5-HT systems and inhibition of aggressive behaviour' in Archer, T. et al, *5-HT in Behavioural Pharmacology*, New Jersey: Erlbaum

Miller, D., 1983, 'Counterfactual thought and social comparison processes', *Fourth Ontario Symposium on Personality and Social Psychology*, London, Ontario

Miller, J., 1976, *Towards a New Psychology of Women*, New York: Beacon Press

Miller, N.B. et al, 1993, 'Externalizing in preschoolers and early adolescents: a cross-study replication of a family model', *Developmental Psychology*, 29, 3–18

Mishra, R.C., 1994, 'Individualist and collectivist orientations across generations', in Kim, U. et al, *Individualism and Collectivism*, London: Sage

Montgomery, S.A. et al, 1994, 'SSRIs: meta-analysis of discontinuation rates', *International Clinical Psychopharmacology*, 9, 47–53

Montgomery, S.A., 1996, 'SSRIs in long-term treatment of depression', in Feighner, J.P. et al, *Selective Serotonin Re-Uptake Inhibitors*, London: Wiley

Morgan, M. et al, 1996, 'Lasting neuropsychological sequelae of recreational use of MDMA (Ecstasy): A controlled study in humans', in press

Motcuk, A., 1997, 'Losers get an attack of the nerves', *New Scientist*, 1 February, p 15

Murphy, D. et al, 1996, *Nature*, in press

Murphy, J.M. et al, 1991, 'Depression and anxiety in relation to social status', *Archives of General Psychiatry*, 48, 223–9

Murphy, J.M., 1986, 'Trends in depression and anxiety: men and women', *Acta Psychiatrica Scandinavia*, 73, 113–27

Murray Parkes, C., 1972, *Bereavement: Studies of Grief in Adult Life*, London: Penguin
Mussel, K., 1984, *Fantasy and Reconciliation: Contemporary Formulas of Women's Romantic Fiction*, Westport CA: Greenwood Press
Myers, R.D. et al, 1978, 'Alcohol and alcoholism: role of serotonin', in Essman, W.B. et al, *Health and Disease*, Vol 2, New York: Spectrum
Nagata, D. et al, 1991, 'Comparison, justice and the internment of Japanese-Americans', in Suls, J. et al, *Social Comparison: Contemporary Theory and Research*, New Jersey: Lawrence Erlbaum
Naranjo, C.A. et al, 1987, 'The serotonin uptake inhibitor citalopram attentuates ethanol intake', *Clinical Pharmacological Therapy*, 41, 266–74
National Association of School Masters/Union of Women Teachers, 1986, *Pupil Violence and Serious Disorder in Schools*, Birmingham: NASUWT
Nesse, R.M., 1990, 'Evolutionary explanation of human nature', *Human Nature*, 1, 261–89
Nietzel, M.T. et al, 1990, 'Relationship of dependency and achievement/autonomy to depression', *Clinical Psychology Review*, 10, 279-97
Nolen-Hoeksma, S., 1987, 'Sex differences in unipolar depression: evidence and theory', *Psychological Bulletin*, 101, 259-82
O'Grady, K.E., 1989, 'Physical attractiveness, need for approval, social self-esteem and maladjustment', *Journal of Social and Clinical Psychology*, 8, 62–9
O'Keane, V. et al, 1992, 'Blunted prolactin responses to d-Fenfluramine in sociopathy', *British Journal of Psychiatry*, 160, 643–6
Office of Population Censuses and Surveys, 1995, *Marriage and Divorce Statistics*, London: HMSO
Ogilvie, A.D. et al, 1996, 'Polymorphism in serotonin transporter gene associated with susceptibility to major depression', *The Lancet*, 347, 731–3
Olson, J.M. et al, 1986, 'Relative deprivation and social comparison: an integrative perspective', in Olson, J.M. et al, *Relative Deprivation and Social Comparison, The Ontario Symposium*, Vol 4, New Jersey: Lawrence Erlbaum
Olson, J.M., 1986, 'Resentment about deprivation: entitlement and hopefulness as mediators of the effects of qualifications', in Olson, J.M. et al, *Relative Deprivation and Social Comparison, The Ontario Symposium*, Vol 4, New Jersey, Lawrence Erlbaum
Owen, M.T. et al, 1988, 'Maternal employment and the transition to parenthood', in Gottfried, A.E. et al, *Maternal Employment and Children's Development*, New York: Plenum Press
Parker, S., 1962, 'Eskimo psychopathology in the context of eskimo personality and culture', *American Anthropologist*, 64, 76–96
Parsons, J.E. et al, 1977, 'The development of achievement-related expectancies', *Child Development*, 48, 1075–9
Parsons, J.E. et al, 1982, 'Socialization of achievement attitudes and beliefs: Parental influences', *Child Development*, 53, 310–21
Pettigrew, T.F., 1967, 'Social evaluation theory: convergences and applications' in Levine, D., *Nebraska Symposium on Motivation*, Vol 15, Lincoln: University of Nebraska Press
Pettigrew, T.F., 1971, *Racially Separate or Together?*, New York: McGraw-Hill
Phillips, M., 1996, *All Must Have Prizes*, London: Little Brown
Phillips, R., 1988, *Putting Asunder – A History of Divorce in Western Society*, Cambridge: Cambridge University Press
Pietromonaco, P.R., 1985, 'The influence of affect on self-perception in depression', *Social Cognition*, 3, 121-34
Pitt, B., 1992, *Depression*, London: Royal College of Psychiatrists
Plisza, S.R. et al, 1988, 'Plasma neurochemistry in juvenile offenders', *Journal of American Academy of Child and Adolescent Psychiatry*, 27, 588–94
Plomin, R. et al, 1987, 'Why are children in the same family so different from one another?', *Behavioural and Brain Sciences*, 10, 1-60
Plomin, R., 1990, *Nature and Nurture*, California: Brooks/Cole
Pollock, L.A., 1983, *Forgotten Children: Parent-Child Relationships from 1500-1900*, Cambridge University Press

Popenhoe, D., 1987, 'Beyond the nuclear family: a statistical portrait of the changing family in Sweden', *Journal of Marriage and the Family*, 49, 173–83

Popper, K., 1963, *Conjectures and Refutations: the Growth of Scientific Knowledge*, London: Routledge

Pound, A. et al, 1988, 'The impact of maternal depression on young children', *British Journal of Psychotherapy*, 4, 240–52

Poyner, B., 1980, 'A study of street crime', Tavistock Institute, London

Price, S.J. et al, 1988, *Divorce*, Beverley Hills: Sage

Pyszczynski, T. et al, 1985, 'Depression and preference for self-focusing stimuli after success and failure', *Journal of Personality and Social Psychology*, 49, 1066–75

Quiggle, N.L. et al, 1992, 'Social information process in aggressive and depressed children', *Child Development*, 63, 1305–1320

Raleigh, M.J. et al, 1991, 'Serotenergic mechanisms promote dominance acquisition in adult male vervet monkeys', *Brain Research*, 559, 181–90

Reis, H.T., 1990, 'The role of intimacy in interpersonal relations', *Journal of Social and Clinical Psychology*, 9, 15–30

Richardson, J.L. et al, 1989, 'Substance use among eighth-grade students who take care of themselves after school', *Pediatrics*, 84, 556–66

Richman, N. et al, 1982, *Pre-School to School: A Behavioural Study*, London: Academic Press

Roberts cited in Bush, S., 1977, 'The evil eye – a stare of envy', *Psychology Today*, 11, 154–5

Robins, L.N. et al, 1992, *Psychiatric Disorders in America*, New York: Free Press

Rofe, Y., 1984, 'Stress and affiliation: a utility theory', *Psychological Review*, 91, 235–50

Rohner, R.P., 1986, *The Warmth Dimension*, Beverley Hills: Sage

Rosenthal, N. et al, 1980, 'Monamine metabolits in cerebrospinal fluid of depressive subgroups', *Psychiatry Research*, 2, 113–9

Ross, M. et al, 1971, 'Some determinants of the intensity of social protests', *Journal of Experimental Social Psychology*, 7, 401–18

Roy, A. et al, 1986, 'Suicide and Alcoholism', in Maris, R., *Biology of Suicide*, New York: Guildford

Roy, A. et al, 1987, 'Reduced central serotonin turnover in a subgroup of alcoholics?', *Programme of Neuropsychopharmacologic Biological Psychiatry*, 11, 173–7

Roy, A. et al, 1988, 'Acting out hostility in normal volunteers', *Psychiatry Research*, 24, 187–94

Roy, A. et al, 1989, 'Studies on alcoholism and related behaviours', *Programme of Neuropsychopharmacologic Biological Psychiatry*, 13, 505–11

Roy, A. et al, 1990, 'Serotonin in suicide, violence and alcholism', in Coccaro, E.F. et al, *Serotonin in Major Psychiatric Disorders*, London: American Psychiatric Press

Rozenweig, M., 1987, 'Twenty years after Twiggy', *Journal of Eating Disorders*, 6, 59–65

Rubery, J. et al, 1994, 'Part-time work and gender inequality in the labour market' in MacEwen, A., *Gender Segregation and Social Change*, Oxford University Press

Ruble, D.N., 1983, 'The development of social comparison processes and their role in achievement-related self-socialization', in Ruble, D.N. et al, *Social Cognition and Social Development: A Sociocultural Perspective*, New York: Cambridge University Press

Ruble, D.N. et al, 1987, 'Social comparison and self-evaluation in the classroom: developmental changes in knowledge and function', in Masters, J.C. et al, *Social Comparison, Social Justice and Relative Deprivation*, New Jersey: Lawrence Erlbaum

Ruble, D.N. et al, 1991, 'Changing patterns of comparative behaviour as skills are acquired: a functional model of self-evaluation', in Suls, J. et al, *Social Comparison: Contemporary Theory and Research*, New Jersey: Lawrence Erlbaum

Russel, P.A., 1992, 'The evolutionary model is synthetic not heuristic', *Behavioural and Brain Sciences*, 15, 108–9

Rutter, M. and Quinton, D., 1977, 'Psychiatric disorder', in McGurk, H., *Ecological Factors in Human Development*, Amsterdam: North Holland

Rutter, M., 1983, in Mussen, P., *Handbook of Child Psychology*, 4, New York: John Wiley

Rutter, M. et al, 1995, *Psychosocial Trends in Young People*, New York: John Wiley

Ryan, N.D. et al, 1992, 'A secular increase in child and adolescent onset of affective disorder', *Journal of the American Academy of Child and Adolescent Psychiatry*, 31, 600–605

Sadaella, E.K. et al, 1987, 'Dominance and heterosexual attraction', *Journal of Personality and Social Psychology*, 52, 730–38

Sahlins, M., 1974, *Stone Age Economics*, London: Tavistock

Sainsbury, J., 1997, 'The benefits to children of paid parental leave', in Wilkinson, H. et al, *Time Off: The Costs and Benefits of the Introduction of Paid Parental Leave in the UK*, London: Demos

Salovey, P., 1991, 'Social comparison processes in envy and jealousy', in Suls, J. et al, *Social Comparison: Contemporary Theory and Research*, New Jersey: Lawrence Erlbaum

Scarf, M., 1980, *Unfinished Business: Pressure Points in the Lives of Women*, New York: Ballantine

Schacter, S., 1959, *The Psychology of Affiliation*, Stanford: Stanford University Press

Schmitt, B.H., 1988, 'Social comparison in romantic jealousy', *Personality and Social Psychological Bulletin*, 14, 374–87

Schoek, H., 1969, *Envy: A Theory of Social Behaviour*, New York: Harcourt Brace

Schoen, R., 1992, 'Marital choice and reproductive strategies', *Behavioural and Brain Sciences*, 15, 109

Schoenborn, C.A. et al, 1993, 'Negative moods as correlates of smoking and heavier drinking: Implications for health promotion', Hyattsville, MD: US Dept of Health and Human Services, National Center for Health Statistics, Publication no 236

Schore, A.N., 1994, *Affect Regulation and the Origin of the Self*, New Jersey: Lawrence Erlbaum

Schoun, I., 1979, 'Artistic productivity and lithium prophylaxis in manic-depressive illness', *British Journal of Psychiatry*, 135, 97–103

Schukit, M., 1986, 'Primary men alcoholics with histories of suicide attempts', *Journal for the Study of Alcoholism*, 47, 78–81

Schwartz, S., 1991, 'Women and depression: a Durkheimian perspective', *Social Science and Medicine*, 32, 127–40

Scott, J., 1995, 'Psychological treatments for depression', *British Journal of Psychiatry*

Seligman, M.E.P., 1991, *Learned Optimism*, New York: Knopf

Shaw, L.B. et al, 1987, 'Women's work plans: contrasting expectations and actual work experience', *Monthly Labour Review*, 110/11, 7–13

Sigall, H. et al, 1973, 'Radiating beauty: the effects of having a physically attractive partner on person perception', *Journal of Personality and Social Psychology*, 28, 218–24

Silbereisen, R.K. et al, 1995, 'Secular trends in substance abuse', in *Psychosocial Disorders in Young People*, Rutter, M. and Smith, D.J., New York: Wiley

Silverstein, B. et al, 1986a, 'Possible causes of the thin standard of bodily attractiveness for women', *International Journal of Eating Disorders*, 5, 907–16

Silverstein, B. et al, 1986b, 'Social correlates of the thin standard of bodily attractiveness in women', *International Journal of Eating Disorders*, 5, 145–59

Silverstein, B. et al, 1988, 'Bingeing, purging and estimates of personal attitudes regarding female achievement', *Sex Roles*, 19, 723–33

Silverstein, B. et al, 1990, 'Nontraditional sex role aspirations, gender identity conflict and disordered eating among college women', *Sex Roles*, 23, 687–95

Silverstein, B. et al, 1991, 'Gender differences in depression: historical change', *Acta Psychiatrica Scandinavica*, 84, 327–31

Simon, G.E. et al, 1995, 'Recall of psychiatric history in cross-sectional surveys: implications for epidemiologic research', *Epidemiological Review*, 17, 221–7

Smith, D.J., 1995, 'Living conditions in the twentieth century', in Rutter, M. et al, *Psychosocial Disorders in Young People*, London: John Wiley

Social Focus on Children, 1994, London: HMSO

Social Trends, 1997, HMSO

Song, F. et al, 1993, 'SSRIs: meta-analysis of efficacy and acceptability', *British Medical Journal*, 306, 683–7

Sours, J.A., 1974, 'The anorexia nervosa syndrome', *International Journal of Psychoanalysis*, 55, 567–76

Srole, L. et al, 1980, 'The Midtown Manhattan longitudinal study vs the "Mental Paradise Lost" doctrine', *Archives of General Psychiatry*, 37, 209–21

Staines, G.L. et al, 1986, 'Wives' employment and husbands' attitudes toward work and life', *Journal of Applied Psychology*, 71, 118–28

Stanley, S.C. et al, 1986, 'The relative deprivation of husbands in dual-earner households', *Journal of Family Issues*, 7, 3–20

Stansfield, S.A. et al, 1992, 'Social class and minor psychiatric disorders in British civil servants', *Psychological Medicine*, 22, 739–49

Steele, T.D. et al, 1987, 'Stereochemical effects of 3,4-methylenedioxymethamphetamine (MDMA) and related amphetamine derivatives on inhibition of {3H}-monoamines into synaptosomes from different regions of rat brain', *Biological Pharmacology*, 89, 539–551

Steele, T.D. et al, 1994, '3,4-methylenedioxymethampthetamine (MDMA, 'Ecstasy'): pharmacology and toxicology in animals and humans', *Addiction*, 89, 539–51

Stein, D.J., 1992, 'Serotonergic medications for sexual obsessions, sexual addictions and paraphilias', *Journal of Clinical Psychiatry*, 53, 267–71

Steinberg, L., 1986, 'Latchkey children and susceptibility to peer pressure: an ecological analysis', *Developmental Psychology*, 22, 433–9

Stevens, A. et al, 1996, *Evolutionary Psychiatry*, London: Routledge

Stipek, D. et al, 1989, 'Developmental changes in children's assessments of intellectual competence', *Child Development*, 60, 51–38

Stoff, D.M. et al, 1987, 'Reduction of {3H}-imipramine binding sites on platelets of conduct-disordered children', *Neuropsychopharmacology*, 1, 55–62

Stone, L., 1982, *The Past and the Present*, Boston: Routledge

Stone, L., 1990, *Road to Divorce: England, 1530–1987*, Oxford: Oxford University Press

Storr, A., 1972, *The Dynamics of Creation*, London: Penguin

Storr, A., 1989, *Solitude*, London: Flamingo

Stouffer, S.A. et al, 1949, *The American Soldier: Adjustment During Army Life*, Vol 1, Princeton: Princeton University Press

Sulloway, F.J., 1996, *Born to Rebel: Birth Order, Family Dynamics and Creative Lives*, London: Little Brown

Suls, J., 1986, 'Comparison processes in relative deprivation: a life-span analysis', in Olson, J.M. et al, *Relative Deprivation and Social Comparison, The Ontario Symposium*, Vol 4, New Jersey: Lawrence Erlbaum

Sunday Times, 1997, 'Clever girls racked by "imposter syndrome"', 30 March

Swallow, S.R et al, 1987, 'The effects of depression and cognitive vulnerability to depression on similarity judgements between self and others', *Motivation and Emotion*, 11, 157–67

Swallow, S.R. et al, 1988, 'Social comparison and negative self-evaluation: an application to depression', *Clinical Psychology Review*, 8, 55–76

Swart, K.W., 1962, 'Individualism in the mid-nineteenth century', *Journal of the History of Ideas*, 23, 77–90

Tambor, E.S. et al, 1993, 'Perceived exclusion as a common factor in social anxiety, loneliness, jealousy, depression and low self-esteem', in press

Taylor, P.A. et al, 1976, 'The utility of education and attractiveness for females' status attainment through marriage', *American Sociological Review*, 41, 484–98

Taylor, S.E. et al, 1988, 'Illusion and well-being: A social psychological perspective on mental health', *Psychological Bulletin*, 103, 193–210; Weinstein, N.D., 1993, References on perceived invulnerability and optimistic biases about risk for future life events, unpublished listing

Taylor, S.E. et al, 1992, 'Optimism, coping, psychological distress and high-risk sexual behaviour among men at risk for acquired immunodefieiency disease', *Journal of Personality and Social Psychology*, 63, 460–73

Taylor, S.E. et al, 1994, 'Positive illusions and well-being revisited: separating fact from fiction', *Psychological Bulletin*, 116, 21–7

Teicher, M.H., et al., 1990, 'Emergence of intense suicidal preoccupation during fluoxetine treatment', *American Journal of Psychiatry*, 147, 207–10

Terman, L.M. et al, 1935, 'Personality factors in marital compatibility', *Journal of Social Psychology*, 6, 143–71

Tesser, A., 1980, 'Self-esteem maintenance in family dynamics', *Journal of Personality and Social Psychology*, 39, 77–91;

Tesser, A., 1986, Some effects of self-evaluation maintenance on social cognitions and action', in Sorrentino, R.M. et al, *Handbook of Motivation and Cognition: Foundations of Social Behaviour*, New York: Guildford

Testa, M. et al, 1990, 'The impact of social comparison after failure: the moderating effects of perceived control', *Basic and Applied Social Psychology*, 11, 205–18

Townsend, J.M., 1987a, 'Sex differences in sexuality among medical students: effects of increasing socioeconomic status', *Archives of Sexual Behaviour*, 16, 425–44

Townsend, J.M., 1987b, 'Mate selection criteria: a pilot study', *Ethology and Sociobiology*, 10, 241–53

Townsend, J.M., 1992, 'Measuring the magnitude of sex differences', *Behavioural and Brain Sciences*, 15, 115–16

Triandis, H. et al, 1988, 'Individualism and collectivism: cross-cultural perspectives on self-ingroup relations', *Journal of Personality and Social Psychology*, 54, 323–8

Trope, Y., 1983, 'Self-assessment in achievement behaviour', in Suls, J. et al, *Psychological Perspectives on the Self*, Vol 2, New Jersey: Lawrence Erlbaum;

Trope, Y., 1986, 'Self-enhancement and self-assessment in achievement behavior', in Sorrentino, R.M. et al, *Handbook of Motivation and Cognition: Foundations of Social Behaviour*, New York: Guildford

Turnberg, L. et al, 1996, *Chronic Fatigue Syndrome*, London: Royal College of Physicians

Udry, J.R. et al, 1984, 'Benefits of being attractive: differential payoffs for men and women', *Psychological Reports*, 54, 47–56

United States Bureau of Census, 1987, *Current Population Reports*, Series P-70, 9, Washington DC

Van Den Bergh, P.L., 1992, 'Wanting and getting ain't the same', *Behavioural and Brain Sciences*, 15, 116–17

Van Praag, H., 1986, 'Affective disorders and aggression disorders', *Suicide and Life-Threatening Behaviour*, 16, 21–50

Vandell, D.L. et al, 1991, 'Children of the national longitudinal survey of youth: choices in after-school care and child development', *Developmental Psychology*, 27, 637–43

Veroff, J. et al, 1981, *The Inner American – a Self-Portrait from 1957–76*, New York: Basic Books

Vining, D.R., 1986, 'Social versus reproductive success: the central theoretical problem of human sociobiology', *Behavioural and Brain Sciences*, 9, 167–216

Violato, C. et al, 1995, 'Effects of nonmaternal care on infants: a meta-analysis of published research', Paper presented at the 55th annual convention of the Canadian Psychological Association, Penticon, British Columbia

Virkunnen, M. et al, 1989, 'Psychobiological concomitants of history of suicide attempts among violent offenders and impulsive fire setters', *Archives of Genral Psychiatry*, 46, 604–6

Von Knorring, I. et al, 1987, 'Personality traits in subtypes of alcoholics', *Journal for the Study of Alcohol*, 48, 523–7

Walkerdine, V., study in preparation for publication, Dept Psychology, Goldsmith's College, London University

Wallen, K., 1989, 'Mate selection: economics and affection', *Behavioural and Brain Sciences*, 12, 37–8

Wallerstein, J.S. et al, 1988, 'Children of divorce: a 10-year study', in Hetherington, E.M. and Arasteh, J.D., *Impact of Divorce, Single Parenting and Stepparenting on Children*, New Jersey: Lawrence Erlbaum.

Wallerstein, J.S., 1991, 'The long-term effects of divorce on children: A review', *Journal of the American Academy of Child and Adolescent Psychiatry*, 30, 349–60

Walmesley, J. et al, 1987, *Hothouse People – Can We Create Super Human Beings?*, London: Pan

Walster, E. et al, 1973, 'New directions in equity research', *Journal of Personality and Social Psychology*, 25, 151–76

Warheit, G. et al, 1976, 'An analysis of social class and racial differences in depressive symptom-aetiology: a community study', *Journal of Health and Social Behaviour*, 4, 921–999

Wartella, E., 1995, 'Media and problem behaviours in young people', in Rutter, M. et al, *Psychosocial Disorders in Young People*, London: John Wiley

Watson, G., 1993, 'Working time and holidays in the EC: how the UK compares', *Employment Gazette*, September, 385–403

Weiner, A. et al, 1979, 'Psychiatric disorders among professional women', *Archives of General Psychiatry*, 36, 169–73

Weintraub, S. et al, 1986, Competence and vulnerability in children with an affectively disordered parent', in Rutter, M. et al, *Depression in Young People*, London: Guildford Press

Weissman, M.M. et al, 1974, *The Depressed Woman*, Chicago: Chicago University. Press.

Weissman, M.M. et al, 1977, 'Sex differences and the epidemiology of depression', *Archives of General Psychiatry*, 34, 98–111.

Weissman, M.M. et al, 1993, 'Sex differences in rates of depression: cross-national perspectives', *Journal of Affective Disorders*, 29, 77–84

Wellings, K. et al, 1994, *Sexual Behaviour in Britain*, London: Penguin

West, D.J., 1966, *Murder Followed by Suicide*, Cambridge, Mass: Harvard University Press

Whiting, B.B. et al, 1988, *Children of Different Worlds*, Cambridge, Mass: Harvard University Press

Whitley, B.E., 1988, 'College students' reasons for sexual intercourse: a sex role perspective', 96th annual meeting of the American Psychological Association, Atlanta

Whitten, N., 1974, *Black Frontiersmen: a South American Case*, London: John Wiley

Wickramratne, P.J. et al, 1989, 'Age, period and cohort effects on the risk of major depression: results from five United States communities', *Journal of Clinical Epidemiology*, 42, 333–343

Wilhelm, K. et al, 1989, 'Is sex necessarily a risk for depression?', *Psychological Medicine*, 19, 401–13

Wilkie, C.P., 1992, *Violence and Aggression in the Workplace*, University of Leicester Centre for the Study of Public Order

Wilkinson, H., 1995, *Freedom's Children*, London: Demos

Wilkinson, R., 1996, *Unhealthy Societies*, London: Routledge

Wills, T.A., 1981, 'Downward comparison principles in social psychology', *Psychological Bulletin*, 90, 245–71

Wilson, S.R. et al, 1971, 'The effect of social esteem and situation on comparison choices during evaluation', *Sociometry*, 34, 381–97

Witherspoon, S. et al, 1992, 'Inglehart's Culture Shift (book review)', *European Sociological Review*, 8, 95–8

Wolfgang, M.E. et al, 1982, *Delinquency in a Birth Cohort*, Chicago: Chicago University Press

Wolfgang, M.E., 1981, 'Surveying violence across nations: a review of the literature, with research and policy recommendations', *International Review of Criminal Policy*, 37, 62–95

Wolkind, S., 1985, 'The first years: preschool children and their families in the inner city', in Stevenson, J.E., *Recent Research in Developmental Psychology*, Oxford: Pergamon

Wood, J.V, 1989, 'Theory and research concerning social comparison attributes', *Psychological Bulletin*, 106, 231–48

Wood, J.V. et al, 1985, 'Social comparison in adjustment to breast cancer', *Journal of Personality and Social Psychology*, 49, 1169–83

Wood, J.V., 1989, 'Theory and research concerning social comparisons of personal attributes', *Psychological Bulletin*, 106, 231–48

Wright, R., 1995, 'The biology of violence', *New Yorker Magazine*, 13 March

Young, B.M., 1990, *Television, Advertising and Children*, Oxford: Clarendon Press

Zanna, M.P. et al, 1987, 'Male reference groups and job satisfaction among female professionals', in Gutek, B.A. et al, *Pathways to Women's Career Development*, Beverley Hills: Sage

Zeanah, C.H. et al, 1992, 'Attachment disorders in infancy and childhood', in Mussen, P.H., *Handbook of Child Psychiatry*, London: John Wiley

Zohar, J. et al, 1990, 'Is there a specific role for serotonin in obsessive compulsive disorders?', in Brown, S-L., *The Role of Serotonin in Psychiatric Disorders*, New York: Brunner/Mazel

Zohar, J. et al, 1990, 'Serotonin in Obsessive Compulsive Disorders', in Coccaro, E.F. et al, *Serotonin in Major Psychiatric Disorders*, London: American Psychiatric Press

Zuckerman, M., 1984, 'Sensation-seeking: a comparative approach to a human trait', *Behavioural Brain Science*, 7, 413–71

Subject Index

Index of First Author Citations